Belize

THE BRADT TRAVEL GUIDE

The Bradt Story

The first Bradt travel guide was written by Hilary and George Bradt in 1974 on a river barge floating down a tributary of the Amazon in Bolivia. From their base in Boston, Massachusetts, they went on to write and publish four other backpacking guides to the Americas and one to Africa.

In the 1980s Hilary continued to develop the Bradt list in England, and also established herself as a travel writer and tour leader. The company's publishing emphasis evolved towards broader-based guides to new destinations – usually the first to be published on those countries – complemented by hiking, rail and wildlife guides.

Since winning *The Sunday Times* Small Publisher of the Year Award in 1997, we have continued to fill the demand for detailed, well-written guides to unusual destinations, while maintaining the company's original ethos of low-impact travel.

Travel guides are by their nature continuously evolving. If you experience anything which you would like to share with us, or if you have any amendments to make to this guide, please write; all your letters are read and passed on to the author. Most importantly, do remember to travel with an open mind and to respect the customs of your hosts – it will add immeasurably to your enjoyment.

Happy travelling!

Hilary Bradt

19 High Street, Chalfont St Peter, Bucks SL9 9QE, England
Tel: 01753 893444 Fax: 01753 892333
Email: info@bradt-travelguides.com Web: www.bradt-travelguides.com

Belize

THE BRADT TRAVEL GUIDE
Third Edition

Alex Bradbury
Updated by Peter Hutchison

Bradt Publications, UK
The Globe Pequot Press Inc, USA

First published in 1995 by Bradt Publications
This third edition published in 2000 by Bradt Publications
19 High Street, Chalfont St Peter, Bucks SL9 9QE, England
web: www.bradt-travelguides.com
Published in the USA by The Globe Pequot Press Inc, 246 Goose Lane,
PO Box 480, Guilford, Connecticut 06437-0480

The author and publishers have made every effort to ensure the accuracy of the
information in this book at the time of going to press. However, they cannot accept any
responsibility for any loss, injury or inconvenience resulting from the use of information
contained in this guide.

British Library Cataloguing in Publication Data
A catalogue record for this book is available from the British Library
ISBN 1 84162 008 4

Library of Congress Cataloging-in-Publication Data

Bradbury, Alex.
  Belize : the bradt travel guide / Alex Bradbury ; updated by Peter
Hutchison — 3rd ed.
      p.cm.
  Includes bibliographical references (p -) and index.
  ISBN 1-84162-008-4
      1. Belize—Guidebooks. 2. Belize—Description and travel. 3.
  Natural areas—Belize—Guidebooks. 4. Ecotourism—Belize—
  Guidebooks. I. Hutchison, Peter, 1966- II. Title.
  F1443.5.B73 2000
  917.28204'5—dc21
                                                              00-039319

Photographs
Cover Lawson Wood/Woodfall Wild Images
Text Jayne Bradbury (JB), Steve Brown (SB), Tim Cothren (TC),
Alan Godwin (AG), John Noble (JN),
Illustrations Alex Bradbury
Maps Steve Munns

Typeset from the author's disc by Wakewing, High Wycombe
Printed and bound in Great Britain by Guernsey Press Ltd

Authors

Alex Bradbury has been travelling throughout South and Central America since the early 1980s. His first book for Bradt was *Backcountry Brazil* followed by *Guide to Brazil* and two previous editions of *Guide to Belize*. His book research has taken him to Belize four times, accompanied by his wife Jayne, who first came to the country in the 1970s while it was still under British rule. Alex works as a marine biologist/diver, and his Caribbean diving itinerary includes Belize, Honduras, Mexico, the Cayman Islands and Martinique.

Peter Hutchison first travelled through Central and South America in 1993. After two years working as a journalist in Bolivia on the *Bolivian Times* he returned to the UK. Attempts to settle in the UK have now reached an enjoyable state of equilibrium. Living in London, he works as a freelance writer, specialising in Latin America. In addition to co-writing and editing *The Amazon: The Bradt Travel Guide* (1998), he has written for *The Independent, Geographical Magazine, Global Adventure* and several other travel magazines.

Contents

LIST OF MAPS

Acknowledgements/Dedication

I owe heartfelt thanks to Steve Brown, who accompanied us on our last trip, gathered valuable information, caught fish, took gorgeous photos, and kept us laughing. Rita Jordan supplied valuable updates, especially on Victoria Peak. Melinda Fyke and Amy Donovan contributed new information and insights on Caye Caulker, Placencia, and Toledo District. Hal Beattie and Bekah Ross helped with the sections on Guatemalan border crossings. Dwight Herren helped considerably with the maps and generously provided me with a computer. Robin Aiello graciously supplied underwater photos. Brian and Leslie Maule helped considerably with their update on the Placencia area, as did Eric and Heather on the San Pedro area. Special thanks are due the South American Explorers Club and *Great Expeditions* magazine, where a portion of this book first appeared in a different format. It would be impossible to list all the Belizeans who've helped this project along, but special mention goes to Geno and Janice Leslie, Joy Grant of Programme for Belize, William 'Chet' Schmidt, Tom Rackowski and Tom Ellis. Rich and Karen Childers provided a valuable update on San Pedro and Cayo for the third edition. And as usual, not a sentence would have been typed without the constant encouragement of publisher Hilary Bradt and my wife, Jayne Bradbury.

From Peter Many of the people who helped Alex in the first two editions were still at hand to help out with my hectic whizz round Belize in November and December of 1999. To them many thanks for your help and support. Also thanks to Alex for providing such a comprehensive guide to the country. With an update you have the chance to ask people in the country their thoughts on a guide and to develop the guide further. Everyone who took the time to read sections of the second edition complimented Alex on the comprehensive and detailed coverage achieved. I hope I have managed to build, in some small way, on the book first produced by Alex.

For Yossi – don't let the bugs get you down.

Introduction

Alone among Central American nations, Belize can boast that 45% of its land is still cloaked in rainforest, and less than 20% is cultivated. Offshore, the western hemisphere's longest barrier reef stretches in a nearly unbroken string of coral cayes, atolls, and mangrove islands. Hidden in the rainforests lie over a dozen major Maya ruins, one of which rivalled mighty Tikal. Belizeans like to point out that the tallest structure in the country is a Maya pyramid at Caracol. Belize's ethnic mosaic is unmatched anywhere in Central America; where else could you find Maya Indians, Creoles, *mestizos*, Mennonites, Chinese, East Indians and Afro-Caribs sharing the same postage stamp of a country?

Once the secret of scuba divers and anglers, Belize has of late been discovered by eco-tourists. Toucans, jaguars, Maya ruins, and rainforest herbs now rival the coral reef as tourist attractions.

If all this makes you wish you came to Belize ten years ago, before its 'discovery', consider the following: most of the country's nature reserves never existed ten years ago; in some cases, logging was going on where jungle again flourishes. In Maya and Afro-Carib villages, a cultural revival is now taking place that simply didn't exist until recently; visits to these villages are being carefully limited to avoid turning them into pathetic human zoos. And if you're concerned about crowds, here's a bit of good news from archaeologists: Belize's total population, travellers included, is estimated to be only a tenth of what it was during the Classic Period of Maya civilisation.

This book covers travel throughout Belize, from the rainforest of the Maya Mountains to the depths of Cousteau's Blue Hole on Lighthouse Reef. The slant is decidedly eco-touristic – jungle walks, dives on the reef, archaeological ramblings – but you'll also find tips on where to hear the latest punta rock, rent a sailboard, or get a cold Belikin beer. You'll find that the hotel, restaurant, transportation, and guide listings lean toward the budget, independent traveller. At the same time, I've attempted to include information on upscale alternatives and package tours where they exist.

Third edition

In this third edition of *Belize: The Bradt Travel Guide*, we have updated the hotel, restaurant and service listings completely. And once again have been able to include details of new national parks and expansions to those that already exist. These changes reflect Belize's sensible approach to attracting travellers, preserving at the same time those things that attract us as travellers in the first place.

Baird's tapir

Part One

General Information

Paca (gibnut)

Black howler monkey

FACTS AND FIGURES

Location

Belize (pronounced bay-LEES) was known as British Honduras until 1973. It lies wedged between Mexico's Yucatan Peninsula to the north, Guatemala to the west and south, and the Caribbean Sea to the east. It is the only country in Central America without a Pacific coastline.

Size

Including the offshore islands (known as cayes and pronounced 'keez'), the country encompasses 22,696km², an area slightly larger than the state of Massachusetts. The greatest length from north to south is 280km; at its widest, Belize measures 109km. It is Central America's second smallest nation (after El Salvador). The country is divided into six administrative districts.

Topography

The northern half of Belize is an area of low-lying hills, plains and swamps. A dissected plateau with several large ridge systems makes up the southern half. The Maya Mountains fringe the eastern portion of this plateau; the Cockscomb Range continues as an eastern spur, and boasts the dramatic 1,120m Victoria Peak which has recently been declared a national monument. A low coastal plain, much of it mangrove swamp, runs the length of the country. About 25km offshore, the largest coral barrier reef in the Western Hemisphere extends nearly 306km from north to south. Beyond the reef lie three large coral atolls. Much of Belize is covered with rainforest, with scattered savannas in the northeast. The Mountain Pine ridge in western Belize is a southern pine forest with a grassy ground cover. Cloud forests exist on the windward side of the higher peaks. Red and black mangroves fringe most of the coast.

History

The Maya civilisation grew and flourished in the area between 1500BC and AD1000. A number of important archaeological sites remain. English woodcutters first settled the area in 1638, and it soon became a centre of logging and piracy. Spain had claimed the land since Columbus, however, and attacks by both Spanish neighbours and rebellious Maya plagued the settlers for over a century. Britain first sent official representatives to the area in the late 18th century, but it was 1862 before British Honduras was established as a colony. In 1884 it became a separate Crown Colony, remaining one until 1964 when it was granted internal self-government. The name changed in 1973 and Belize gained full independence in 1981.

Government

Belize is a parliamentary democracy and a member of the Commonwealth. Like Costa Rica, it is an island of stability and peace in Central America. The National

Assembly consists of a Senate and House of Representatives. The Queen is titular head of state, a mere formality. From 1955 to 1984, George C Price dominated Belizean politics, becoming Premier in 1964 and Prime Minister in 1981. Opposition leader Manuel Esquivel won the 1984 elections, Price returned to power in 1989 after a narrow victory at the polls with Esquivel taking the premiership again in 1993. In August 1998 Said Wilbert Musa of the People's United Party won the elections.

Population
With an estimated population of 238,500 residents in 1998, Belize is the least populated country in Central America. Just under one quarter of the population live in Belize City, with another 25% living in six other major towns. Just under half of the population lives in a rural environment. Creoles, of mixed African and European descent, comprise 30% of the population. *Mestizos* (Spanish-Maya), many of them recent immigrants, now make up about 44%. About 7% are Garifuna, descendants of black slaves and Carib Indians. Maya Indians (Mopan, Yucatec, and Kekchi) represent 15%. The rest of the population is comprised of East Indians, Mennonites, Chinese, Lebanese, British and Americans. Nearly 55% of Belizeans are under the age of 19. The next census is in 2001.

Language
Belize is the only Central American nation where English is the official language. Most Belizeans speak English as well as Creole, an English patois. In the north, Spanish is the first language of a majority of the people, and it is now – due to recent immigration – the mother tongue of over a third of all Belizeans. Other commonly-heard languages include Garifuna, the three Maya Indian tongues, and Mennonite German.

Religion
Catholics make up 58% of the population, owing to immigration from Mexico and the Central American republics. About 28% are Protestants, mostly Anglicans, Methodists, Seventh Day Adventists, Mennonites, Mormons and Jehovah's Witnesses. Small groups of Muslims and Bahais also exist. Many Garifunas, though nominally Catholic, practice a Carib-African ancestor worship.

Economy
Agricultural exports (mostly sugar, citrus and bananas), provide 59% of the nation's foreign exchange. Seafood and cacao are also important, and Belize is one of the leading exporters of marijuana to the US. The Government's manifesto asserts that tourism is one of the twin pillars of the economy, along with agriculture. Indeed tourism may soon supply more foreign exchange than agriculture, and is already responsible for almost 20% of the gross domestic product, more than either industry or agriculture. Logging, traditionally the country's breadwinner, now accounts for only 1.5% of its export income. Oil was discovered in 1981, but not in commercial quantities. Because of its continued heavy reliance on imported food and other goods, Belize has a foreign debt of about US$159 million, the smallest in Central America. Annual growth rate is 3%, with inflation at 2% annually. Unemployment is 15%.

Currency
The Belize dollar has for many years been tied to the US dollar at a fixed rate of BZ$2 to US$1.

Climate

The climate is sub-tropical, with temperatures along the coast ranging from about 10°C (50°F) to about 36°C (96°F). The range is greater inland. Along the coast, trade winds temper the heat. Rainfall varies considerably from the north – where the annual average is 1,295mm – to the south, where it is 4,445mm. The main dry season runs from February through to May with the summer rains falling from June through to August. The *mauger* – a mini dry season – is in August and September with the winter rains starting in September and decreasing steadily until January.

Flora and fauna

Some 45% of Belize remains forested, and the rainforests, savannas, swamps and cayes continue to provide habitat for a vast array of terrestrial wildlife. There are over 500 species of birds, and healthy, protected populations of threatened species such as jaguars, black howler monkeys and manatees. Along the coral barrier reef and atolls, the diversity and abundance of marine life is equally stunning. A rapidly expanding system of government- and privately-operated nature reserves guarantees protection for the nation's natural heritage.

HISTORY
The Maya

(Author's note: Most archaeologists now use the word Maya as both noun and adjective; Mayan refers only to the languages spoken by the Maya. I have followed this convention throughout the book.)

The first Europeans to set foot in Belize found only the remnants of a remarkable civilisation, the greatest in the pre-Columbian Western Hemisphere. Some seven centuries earlier, the Maya world had collapsed, for reasons still only dimly understood. During their most productive 650 years – archaeologists now call it the Classic Period – the Maya built over 200 cities in Central America, lofty pyramids which rivalled those of Egypt, and a trade network which linked the highlands of Guatemala, the Belizean barrier reef, and the mountains of central Mexico. While Europe languished in the Dark Ages, the Maya created a complex writing system, something which neither the Aztecs nor Incas accomplished. They also devised a calendar, mathematics that included the concept of zero, a sophisticated political machine, a network of reservoirs and aqueducts, and environmentally sound, high-yield agricultural techniques. Their astronomers predicted solar eclipses and calculated the lunar month to within four decimal places of that accepted by modern scientists. Before receding back into the jungle, their dazzling world managed to survive six times as long as the Roman Empire.

The Maya emerged from the rainforests of Central America some 3,000 years ago. Their ancestors had crossed the Bering Strait roughly 20,000 years earlier, migrating south in search of game. Primitive agriculture eventually replaced the nomadic hunter-gatherer way of life, and soon a new type of society was born. This was the Maya civilisation, which dominated the modern Mexican states of Chiapas, Campeche, Yucatan, and Quintana Roo, as well as Guatemala, Honduras, and Belize.

Many archaeologists begin dating the Maya from about 2000BC, using the following divisions (a convention which I've used throughout this book):

Early Preclassic (2000BC – 800BC): Primitive fishing and farming villages form. Olmec culture flourishes in Mexico's Gulf Coast. Lamanai in northern Belize is first occupied.

Middle Preclassic (800BC – 300BC): The earliest writings and calendars appear. In northern Belize, the ceremonial site of Cuello is sanctified with a mass human sacrifice.

Late Preclassic (300BC – AD250): Temples, pyramids, and distinctive art forms are commonplace. Maya kings (ahauob) emerge as a social institution in cities like Cerros, a major trading port in northern Belize.

Early Classic (AD250 – AD600): Dynasties rule city-states, erecting elaborate stelae, temples, and ball courts. The Long Count calendar is developed. Caracol in western Belize conquers the mighty city of Tikal and assumes supreme position in the Maya heartland.

Late Classic (AD600 – AD900): Metal is first used in Mesoamerica. Maya culture reaches its artistic pinnacle. Maya populations shift from the southern highlands to the northern lowlands of the Petén, Belize, and Yucatan. In western Belize, Xunantunich is abandoned following an earthquake. Lubaantun is founded in southern Belize. Altun Ha flourishes in northern Belize.

Early Postclassic (AD900 – AD1200): Population declines, mass migrations and the end of most building all signal a general collapse of Maya civilisation. Altun Ha in northern Belize is abandoned.

Late Postclassic (AD1200 – AD1530): Columbus reaches the New World. Spaniards undertake the conquest of Mexico's Yucatan, and Chichén Itzá falls. Cortés marches through the southern portion of Belize on his way to put down rebellion in Honduras.

Colonial Period (AD1530 – AD1872): English woodcutters arrive in Belize. The Maya of Tipu and Lamanai in western and northern Belize revolt, expelling the Spanish for nearly 60 years until almost 1700. Yucatan's Maya rebel during the War of Castes in the mid-1800s, and *mestizo* refugees flee to Belize. 1872 marks the last armed Maya resistance in Belize, when the Maya general Canul is killed in battle near Orange Walk.

War, slavery and disease killed 90% of the Maya during the Colonial Period. Most of the few remaining links with the Classic Period were severed. Only in the mid-1800s was this vanished ancient culture rediscovered, when an American lawyer named John Lloyd Stephens and an English artist, Frederick Catherwood, hacked their way into the jungles of Central America. Ironically, although their expedition began in Belize City, Stephens and Catherwood pushed north and west, unaware that they were bypassing vast archaeological riches within Belize. Catherwood's eerily evocative drawings of abandoned temples swallowed by the jungle ignited interest worldwide in the lost Maya world. Stephens' books, still highly readable, became instant best sellers and archaeologists flocked to the Central American rainforest.

Some insights came easily. The Maya calendar, their number system, and glyphs representing certain animals and gods were quickly deciphered. The extensive glyphic texts, however, baffled scholars. Yet this didn't stop most archaeologists in their eager quest to explain the Maya civilisation. The calendar, the numerous references to astronomy, and the absence of obvious defensive structures led experts like Sylvanus Morley and J Eric S Thompson to conclude that the Maya were a peaceful, otherworldly people who spent their time contemplating the endless progress of time. In this view, the Maya became the Greeks of the New World, devoted to philosophy, while the Aztecs were equated with the crass, warring Romans. Most scholars concluded that the great ruins were religious centres rather than cities. And numerous experts pointed a finger at slash-and-burn agriculture – practised by modern Maya – as the prelude to soil depletion, famine, and the eventual collapse of the Classic Maya.

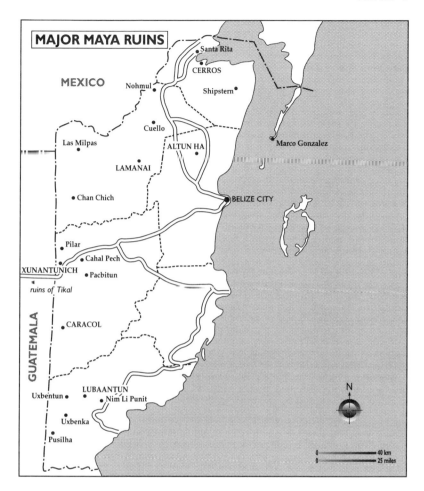

Most of us grew up hearing these theories, all of which turn out to be dead wrong. The great breakthrough in understanding the Maya began only in the 1960s, as scholars known as epigraphers learned to decipher the glyphic texts. And soon a new, less tidy picture of the Maya emerged. In 1960, Tatiana Proskouriakoff broke new ground with a brilliant re-interpretation of stelae from a Guatemalan site. She suggested that they recorded worldly events rather than arcane musings on the heavens. And in one of the grandest gestures of modern scholarship, the renowned Mayanist J Eric S Thompson publicly acknowledged her discovery, even though it turned the archaeological world on its head and contradicted much of his own life's work.

Most scholars now agree that the ancient Maya were not the peaceful, time-worshipping philosophers once imagined. They waged war on a regular basis, prompting archaeologist Linda Schele's comment that 'blood was the mortar' of Maya society. Their glyphs reveal an obsession with kings, politics, and worldly feats. Modern ruins were, for the most part, feudal cities rather than religious retreats. And recent evidence suggests that innovative and environmentally sound farming techniques managed to support vast populations.

Still, the all-consuming question remains: What caused the collapse?

Thompson's simple and long-accepted theory of a peasant revolt may still hold some water, but archaeologists now offer a host of other possible causes, none of them necessarily exclusive. Deforestation, famine, epidemics, a destructive new style of warfare, and gradual disenchantment with the ruling classes have all been suggested. The debate will undoubtedly continue for many years, with scholars splintered into different camps. Some argue that even though the glyphic texts are now decipherable, they present a gross distortion of Maya history. Some archaeologists even question the very notion of 'The Maya', a term they believe masks the existence of many independent groups. Despite all the controversy, we are probably edging closer to some kind of messy truth.

The map on page 7 shows the major Maya sites in Belize, all of which are discussed in more detail in the area chapters. *Appendix 2, Further Reading* gives some suggestions for further reading, but keep in mind that new insights are made constantly, and old theories discarded. Perhaps the best single introduction is Ronald Wright's *Time Among the Maya*, a masterful blend of travelogue, history and political commentary. Schele and Friedel's *A Forest of Kings* is more scholarly, but manages to put flesh and bones on the ancient Maya in a thoroughly exciting way.

And finally, don't forget that modern Maya culture is very much alive in Belize. See *Chapter 12* for suggestions on visiting some of the Maya villages in Toledo District.

The colonists

Columbus' closest brush with the area now called Belize came during his fourth visit to the west. He ventured into the Gulf of Honduras in 1502, but then turned south toward Panama. A second Spanish expedition a few years later also bypassed the coast of Belize. The first European of any note actually to set foot in Belize was probably Cortés, who passed through a corner of the Toledo District in 1525 on his way to put down a revolt in Honduras.

Various missionaries and *conquistadores* passed through the area, but shipwrecked English seamen get credit for the first real settlement, near present-day Belize City, in 1638. They stayed to cut mahogany and logwood, valuable in Europe as a dye, and perhaps to practise a bit of piracy under the direction of their Scottish leader, Peter Wallace. One story has it that Belize is a Spanish corruption of the name Wallace (although there is no real proof that Wallace ever set foot in Belize). Others claim that it derives directly from the Yucatec Maya word for muddy river, *beliz*. Belikin ('toward the east' in Mayan) also gets credit from some quarters.

English and Scottish pirates – including Edward 'Blackbeard' Teach – were soon haunting the cayes, coastline and atolls. Some turned their attentions to logwood cutting, shipping the product from the mouth of the Belize River, where Belize City now stands. They called themselves Baymen – after the Bay of Honduras – and by all accounts they were a motley bunch of drunken brigands.

In a half-hearted effort to maintain its claim of sovereignty over the area, Spain made occasional attempts to rout the British settlers. Several 18th century treaties between Spain and England left the Baymen in a sort of limbo: unable to colonise the area, Spain allowed the British to cut logwood, but claimed Belize for itself, forbidding them to build fortifications or farm the land. This murky arrangement suited no one, and Spain continued to attack the settlers. England, in turn, dispatched a 'Superintendent of His Majesty's Financial Affairs' to Belize, the first official representative.

The showdown came on September 10 1798, at St George's Caye, not quite 15km northeast of Belize City. In a battle lasting only two and a half hours, the settlers and a single British sloop managed to drive the Spanish fleet from shore. It was the last Spanish attempt to expel the Baymen.

Slaves played an integral part in Belizean history from the days of the Baymen. By 1790, slaves made up 75% of the population. But unlike in the West Indies, where slavery developed on the sugar plantations, Belizean slaves laboured cutting logwood and mahogany deep in the rainforest camps. Surrounded by marauding Spaniards, the last thing the Baymen needed was a slave revolt, and they tended to treat their African charges with a lighter hand than the plantation owners. And there were other incentives for leniency: life in the jungle camps often required slaves to carry machetes, and sometimes even guns for hunting game, so that the Baymen were constantly outnumbered by armed servants. The Spanish offered asylum and even freedom to slaves who fled the British, still another reason for masters to spare the whip. Yet leniency is a relative thing, and slavery was hardly the benevolent institution in Belize that some early historians claimed. Violent slave revolts and frequent desertions give the lie to those claims. Slavery was abolished in 1834, but British law conspired to keep a cheap labour force on hand by prohibiting land grants to ex-slaves. This deliberate attempt to discourage independent farming only made it more difficult for Belize to feed itself – a problem that continues to dog the country even today.

The road to independence

Even as Great Britain tightened its grip on Belize – now known informally as British Honduras – Guatemala was casting an envious eye on the new 'colony'. With Guatemala as its nucleus, the newly-independent Central American Federation had abolished slavery eleven years before Belize, a move the English suspected was merely a call for Belizean slaves to defect across the border; after all, the Central American republics had no slaves. Hostilities increased, and Guatemala officially called the Baymen 'trespassers' on land it had inherited from Spain. Just three years prior to British Honduras officially becoming a colony, Great Britain and Guatemala finally signed an accord recognising British sovereignty. The catch, however, was Britain's agreement to help build a road from Guatemala to the Belizean coast – a road that was never built.

British Honduras became a Crown Colony under the Governor of Jamaica in 1871. *Mestizos* were still fleeing Mexico's Yucatan, scene of the bloody War of Castes which began in 1848, and northern Belize was taking on the Latin flavour that still distinguishes it today. In 1884, all Jamaican ties were severed, and British Honduras got its own Governor. But problems besieged the colony. Mahogany workers rioted in 1894, as did Belizean soldiers returning from World War I to find their only reward was 'a kick and a smile'. Many credit the so-called Ex-Servicemen's Ríot of 1919 as the beginning of national politics in Belize. Even the weather conspired to destabilise the colony; a violent hurricane struck Belize City in 1931, killing almost 15% of the entire population.

Nationalist fervour grew throughout the 1950s, especially following the devaluation of the British Honduras dollar. Out of the confrontation grew the People's United Party (PUP), one of whose leaders, a former divinity student named George C Price, would come to dominate Belizean politics for the next 34 years. In 1954, the colonial government conceded a new, more liberal constitution that guaranteed Belizeans an elected majority in council, although ultimate power still rested with the Governor. The PUP swept election after election, and by 1961 George Price had been voted in as British Honduras' first Minister. That same year, Hurricane Hattie levelled Belize City, and prompted the building of a new capital in Belmopan.

George Price, appointed Premier in 1964, lost no time in designing a new national flag, an anthem, even a national prayer. Yet as the colony inched toward independence, Guatemala became increasingly strident in its claims to 'Belice'. Following British promises of full internal self-rule for Belize, Guatemala broke off diplomatic relations and threatened war. Mediation fell through, followed by a massing of Guatemalan troops along the border in 1972. Britain responded with her own troops and a naval fleet; three years later, British Harrier jets arrived to protect the newly christened nation of Belize. Led by Panama, a number of Central American republics gradually came to support Belizean independence, as did the United Nations in an historic 1980 resolution; Guatemala abstained.

Belize became fully independent in 1981. British presence remained – at the request of Belizeans – in the form of troops and Harrier jets, until 1994, when all 1,200 troops returned home.

In 1984, after decades of political power, Manuel Esquivel of the United Democratic Party (UDP) upset George Price's political dominance in a landslide election victory. Despite achieving nearly five years of economic growth, Esquivel and the UDP lost by a slim margin in the 1989 elections. George Price, still popular and energetic at 70, resumed power on a 'Belizeans First' campaign which made much of the UDP's pro-foreign investment stance. In 1993 Esquivel and the UDP returned to office for one term. The most recent elections took place in August 1998, with the PUP winning 26 of the 29 seats in the House of Representatives with the remaining three won by the UDP. The PUP and UDP continue as feisty, openly combative competitors, much to the frustrations of many Belizeans who would rather the country's politicians focused on running the country and solving its problems than picking squabbles with the political opposition. In 1991, Belize was granted a long-delayed membership of the Organisation of American States (OAS). Guatemala officially recognised Belize as a sovereign state in September 1991, and a British troop withdrawal was announced in May 1993. A failed Guatemalan coup and unrest since then, however, have returned a degree of uncertainty to Belize–Guatemalan relations. The Queen visited Belize in early 1994 to reassure the tiny nation that Britain has not abandoned its responsibility as protector. Guatemala has opened an embassy in Belize City, but, despite such gestures, the arrest of several members of the Belizean Defence Force in April 2000 by the Guatemalan army demonstratred how quickly the border situation can change.

CLIMATE

Belize has a sub-tropical climate divided into rainy and dry seasons. In general, the dry season runs from roughly December through May, with the driest months being February, March, April and May. During this four-month period, Belize City experiences on average only five rainy days per month. The wettest months are June, July and August. During the rainy season, there is generally a short dry spell in August and September lasting around six weeks called the *mauger*, when the winds die and insects abound. Rainfall varies considerably from north to south, however, even within this tiny country. Average rainfall ranges from 1,295mm in the north to 4,445mm in the south. In the north, the dry season beginning in December may last for three or four months, while the far south may get only a month of dry weather.

Travellers should keep in mind, however, that even during the wet season, much of the day's rain may come in buckets during a very short spell – sometimes at night – followed by sunshine for the rest of the day. Probably the biggest disadvantage is not these brief, violent downpours themselves but the effect they have on Belize's many dirt roads. Bus and even 4WD travel sometimes comes to a halt during intensely rainy periods, particularly along backcountry routes in the south and in Cayo District.

Temperature is less a factor for travellers in Belize than rainfall, ranging along the coast from about 10°C (50°F) during the coldest winter days – quite rare – to about 36°C (96°F) during the hottest summer days. The range is somewhat greater inland. Average year-round temperature is 26°C (79°F). Average minimum daily temperatures in Belize City range from a low of 19°C (66°F) in January to a high of 24°C (75°F) from May through August. Average maximum daily temperature is also lowest in January (27°C or 81°F) and highest from May through August (31°C or 88°F).

Humidity along the coast averages about 87% throughout the year, with November, December and January the stickiest months. It is greatest along the coast, but here the trade winds usually make it less of a problem. Humidity is usually greatest during the morning, before the wind picks up.

Easterly trade winds blow most of the year, making even the hottest days pleasant along the coast. The steady 10–15 knot trades from January through April subside to a light breeze in May and June, followed by stronger, more erratic winds August through December. Particularly during November and December, strong northerlies – 'northers' as they're called in Belize – occasionally sweep down over the Gulf of Mexico bringing squalls and low temperatures.

Belize lies west of the normal Caribbean hurricane track. The country has experienced only four hurricanes in the last 30 years, but the most likely months are August through October; hurricanes almost never form earlier than June. In October 1998, Hurricane Mitch literally 'walked round Belize'; an unsettling reminder to the country and its leaders that the next devastating hurricane will arrive one day – it is just a question of when.

Read *Chapter 6, Activities* for suggestions on the best time to visit for particular activities such as sailing, birdwatching, kayaking and scuba diving.

Blue-crowned motmot

The People and Culture

ETHNIC GROUPS

Belize ranks as the most ethnically and culturally diverse nation in Central America. Creoles, Maya Indians, Garifunas, *Mestizos*, Mennonites, Chinese, Lebanese and East Indians all share this tiny speck of land. Sometimes they even share the same room – I've stood in a Punta Gorda dry goods store and heard simultaneous conversations in Spanish, Garifuna, Kekchi Maya, English, and Hindi. So varied is this ethnic medley that no single group can claim a majority. Even the *Mestizos*, the most numerous group, make up only 44% of the country's population.

Many of these ethnic groups – including the Garifunas, Maya, Chinese, and Mennonites – originally landed on Belizean turf fleeing from persecution. You'll frequently hear it said that every Belizean is an immigrant or the descendant of an immigrant. Perhaps it's this feeling that has helped mould a cohesive society from such remarkable diversity. Even so, here as in other 'melting pots', you'll find some disharmony the closer you look. Light skin remains an advantage in many aspects of life. Antagonism, not always latent, exists between Creoles, Garifunas, and *Mestizos*. Resentment runs high against Salvadorean and Guatemalan refugees. And, as elsewhere, indigenous people still seem to occupy the lowest rung on the ladder.

The following section briefly highlights the most important ethnic groups in Belize. But recognise that these divisions are becoming increasingly blurred. Even the most determined demographer, for example, would have difficulty drawing the line between Maya and *Mestizos* in many parts of northern Belize.

Maya Indians

Once the original inhabitants of Belize, Maya Indians now represent only about 15% of the country's population. Few of the modern-day Belizean Maya are descendants of the Indians which were living in the region when the Spanish arrived; most of those settlements disintegrated after centuries of Spanish and English presence. The Maya living in Belize today are largely descended from Guatemalan and Mexican Maya immigrants. The first of such groups to arrive were the Yucatec Maya, who fled Mexico along with thousands of *mestizos* during the Caste War which began in 1848. Today, the Yucatec Maya of northern Belize have merged almost seamlessly with *mestizo* culture; they have discarded their Mayan dialect in favour of Spanish and English, and virtually all semblance of their traditions has disappeared.

The two other Maya groups living in Belize arrived during the 1870s and 1880s. Mopan Maya fled their homeland in Guatemala's southern Petén to avoid forced labour and taxation, establishing themselves in the Toledo and Cayo Districts. At about the same time in the Alta Verapaz highlands of Guatemala, Kekchi Maya escaped virtual slavery on German-owned coffee plantations; they too settled in Belize's Toledo District, regrouping in small, isolated villages. Today you'll find some forty Maya villages in the Toledo District, including a few mixed communities with both Mopan and Kekchi members. These two Mayan dialects, however, are mutually unintelligible, and some Indians have become proficient in Kekchi, Mopan, Spanish and English. Guatemalan Maya still trickle across the border in small numbers, mostly headed for established villages in the Toledo District.

While several of the more accessible villages have seen their cultural traditions diluted – evangelical missionaries and television being the biggest threats – you'll find others where life goes on much as it must have centuries ago. Language, farming methods, and the traditional *alcalde* system of local government still hold sway. A new spirit of cultural revival has taken hold in Toledo District, and travellers can now visit several Maya villages without threatening the dignity or traditions of those who live there (see *Chapter 12, Village Guest House Ecotrail Programme*).

Creoles

Descendants of African slaves and early white settlers, Creoles today make up about 30% of Belize's population. That will undoubtedly seem an underestimate if your first stop in the country is Belize City; about two-thirds of Belizean Creoles live in the former capital, with scattered settlements in other parts of the country. Although Garifunas dominate much of Stann Creek District, many coastal towns in this area remain Creole settlements, including Placencia, Gales Point, Monkey River and Mango Creek/Independence.

Creole also refers to the English patois spoken throughout Belize. Lilting, musical – and for many English-speaking visitors, utterly unrecognisable on first hearing – Belizean Creole is closely related to that spoken in other parts of the Caribbean colonised by the British. Creoles speak both standard English and Creole, often making the switch in mid-conversation. And, in keeping with the Belizean melting-pot tradition, there are now Spanish versions of the Creole dialect. Bookstores in Belize usually offer a volume or two of Creole proverbs 'translated' into English. If you're interested in learning Creole in the 'classroom', simply hang out at places like the Belize City market or the Placencia post office.

Mestizos

Spanish-speaking descendants of Amerindians and early Spanish settlers, or *Mestizos*, now make up roughly a third of Belize's population. You'll more often hear them referred to in Belize as simply 'Spanish'. The first *Mestizo* immigrants fled to British Honduras from Mexico's Yucatan during the bloody Caste War (1848-1858), when the Maya revolted against their Spanish conquerors. These Mexican immigrants settled mostly in the northern part of the country, in places like Corozal, Orange Walk, Sarteneja, Caye Caulker, and Ambergris Caye. Belize's *Mestizos* still concentrate in the north, but more recent Spanish-speaking immigrants have also settled in the Cayo District and many other parts of Belize.

Fleeing persecution, war, and stagnant economies, these recent *Mestizo* immigrants stream across the border from El Salvador, Guatemala, and, to a lesser extent, Honduras. Since 1979, the government has tried to accommodate the refugees, allowing them to homestead and farm in areas such as the 'Valley of Peace' near Belmopan. But illegal immigrants continue to cross the borders, and the 'alien issue' has become a sore point for the normally tolerant people of Belize. Government figures state that just under 9,000 registered refugees have settled in

Belize, but other sources estimate around 15,000 to 20,000 Salvadoreans and Guatemalans entered Belize between 1985 and 1990 alone. According to a report by the US Committee for Refugees, this influx from other Latin American countries 'poses serious economic and social problems for this tiny nation'. Even many Spanish-speaking Belizeans have come to resent the new immigrants, fearing that their jobs and quality of life will be threatened. Environmental concerns have also been raised, since many of the refugees practise slash-and-burn farming within Belizean forests.

Garifunas

The Garifuna (guh-RIHF-uhnuh) people constitute roughly 7% of Belize's population. Known also as Garinagu, 'Black Caribs', or simply 'Caribs' – the latter two terms now considered somewhat offensive – Garifunas are descendants of African slaves and Carib Indians. The two groups intermingled quite accidentally, following a shipwreck on the island of St Vincent in the eastern Caribbean during the 17th century. Persecuted for centuries, these independent, seafaring people migrated throughout the Caribbean. Modern-day Garifuna settlements exist along the coasts of Honduras, Guatemala, Nicaragua, and Belize. The focal point of the Belizean Garifuna population is Dangriga, with smaller settlements in Punta Gorda, Hopkins, Georgetown, Seine Bight Village, and Barranco. With their own distinct language, religion, music, dance, and food, the Garifuna are one of Belize's most fascinating ethnic groups. You'll find a more detailed description of their rich culture in *Chapter 11, Dangriga*.

Chinese

Chinese immigrants first arrived in British Honduras in 1865, but most of this original group soon moved to Mexico's Quintana Roo to live among the Santa Cruz Indians. Just before World War II, Chinese began fleeing the Japanese occupation of their homeland, and a small group of Cantonese farmers from Kwang-tung Province found their way to Belize City. Although still a tiny ethnic minority, Chinese-Belizeans are a visible presence in most towns, since they run many of the nation's groceries, shops and restaurants. Quite a few have Spanish surnames, adopted by immigrants who lived in Guatemala or Mexico prior to entering Belize. The name Quinto, for example, ('fifth' in Spanish) was taken by Chinese with the surname Eng ('five' in Hong Kong). Likewise, Kwan has become Quan. Belizeans of Chinese extraction are rapidly integrating into the mainstream culture, losing their ancestral languages and religion. Since 1989, Belize has granted as many as 10,000 Taiwanese residency or citizenship.

East Indians

East Indians came originally to British Honduras as the servants of colonial administrators or as deportees following the bloody Sepoy Rebellion. The present-day town of Calcutta (just south of Corozal) bears witness to those East Indians who worked as indentured servants on the sugar plantations during the 1880s. Recent immigrants from India concentrate in small settlements near Punta Gorda, Belize City and Orange Walk Town. It's estimated that East Indians comprise about 2% of the country's population.

Mennonites

Mennonite farmers first immigrated to British Honduras in the late 1950s. Members of an Anabaptist religious sect which originated in Switzerland during the 16th century, most Mennonites still speak a low German dialect called

Plattdeutsch, dress plainly, and live a simple agrarian life. They quickly became Belize's most productive farmers, and you're likely to see the men – blond, sunburnt, dressed in denim overalls and straw hats – at marketplaces throughout Belize. Church members have split into liberal, moderate and conservative groups. Nowadays you're just as likely to see Mennonites boarding a jet plane as a horse-drawn buggy. Mennonites, who now make up about 3% of the country's population, live in their own largely self-contained communities, with major settlements in the Orange Walk and Cayo Districts. You'll find a fuller description in *Chapter 10, Mennonites*, page 158.

Other groups

Lebanese immigrants and their descendants, many of them shopkeepers, make up another small portion of Belize's population.

Following the Civil War in the US, a group of Confederate refugees fled to Belize and opened sugar plantations in the Toledo District. This colony soon dissipated, but a new wave of Americans – many of them retirees – has hit Belize in recent years.

Finally, British troops became a permanent fixture in Belize until 1994, when the last of the 1,200 troops returned home. Only a handful of jungle warfare instructors remain, although some soldiers have stayed on, married Belizeans and become citizens of the country whose borders they once protected.

CUSTOMS AND ETIQUETTE

'No big ting, mon!' serves as a sort of unofficial national motto, and fairly sums up the relaxed Belizean attitude toward just about everything. Belize prides itself on its informality, its exuberant good humour, its openness. Consequently, its citizens don't take offence easily. Treat the people you meet with that same brand of informal courtesy and you'll do fine.

A few reminders, however. Maya Indians aren't as gregarious as Creoles or Garifunas. Visiting them in their quiet villages requires just a little more reserve on your part. Especially in the more remote villages, you should ask to meet the *alcalde* before making arrangements with villagers for lodging.

In Belize, as elsewhere, always ask permission before taking someone's photograph. This is particularly true in the case of the reserved Maya and Mennonite communities. Personally, I recommend leaving your camera in its case when visiting Maya Indians, even though they are usually too polite to refuse your requests for a photo. Garifunas, gracious and outgoing in virtually all other respects, seem particularly averse to cameras invading their private lives. A story circulates about a reporter in Hopkins who snapped pictures without asking, and was chased away by a group of locals throwing stones. My advice in Garifuna communities, again, is to leave the camera behind – if you want a depiction of Garifuna daily life that you can carry home, you'll find a number of paintings for sale by talented Garifuna artists in Dangriga.

Finally, don't get in the habit of giving candy, toys or other gifts to village children. One afternoon hiking near Blue Creek we were approached by a young Maya girl eager to show us her new toy: a tiny propeller fashioned of tree bark and mounted on a stick the size of a pencil. She scampered around us as we rested, clearly delighted with her simple toy and her audience. Don't spoil such moments – or children – by playing village Santa Claus. What most rural Belizeans really want from you is an insight into your strange way of life. Sit down and talk with them, show them pictures of your family and friends, play a song or teach them a dance – but leave the gifts at home.

MUSIC

Much of the music you'll hear in Belize won't be Belizean music at all. But this nation of immigrants has no qualms about embracing the music of its neighbours. As in the rest of the Caribbean, Jamaican reggae dominates the musical scene. Bob Marley's legacy still casts a long shadow here, but the airwaves also reverberate with more recent reggae offshoots like rockers, dj and dub. Not surprisingly, Belize is now producing its own reggae bands. *Soca* and calypso superstars from Trinidad, including David Rudder, Arrow and the Mighty Sparrow, also command plenty of radio time. Ride enough buses in Belize – two competing 'boom boxes' seems to be the norm on most buses – and you'll even hear American country-western music.

However, the music most thoroughly identified with Belize these days is *punta* rock. Like *soca*, *punta* rock is electrified Caribbean dance music with the emphasis on rhythm and good times rather than weighty lyrics. Yet *punta* rock is distinctly Belizean, growing out of a traditional Garifuna beat called, simply, *punta*. *Punta* relied strictly on the sounds of homemade drums, and *punta* dancing was – and still is – a part of the exuberant Garifuna 'wakes' known as *dugu*. Garifuna musician and painter Pen Cayetano usually gets credit for adding turtle shells to *punta* and putting it in the national spotlight. Cayetano's Turtle Shell Band, as well as the Waribagabaga Drum and Dance Troupe still perform this seminal brand of *punta* rock in Dangriga at irregular intervals.

Before long, Dangriga-based groups like Sounds Incorporated had added electric guitar, bass and keyboards to Cayetano's version of *punta*. But it was a former radio DJ from the Garifuna village of Barranco, Andy Palacio, who galvanized the country with his own energized *punta* interpretations. Ever since his late 1980s hit single 'Bikini Panty', Palacio has reigned as the 'King of Punta Rock'. Other popular *punta* groups include Babylon Warriors, Chatuye, Sopa de Caracol, the Smith Brothers, DJ Morgan, Michael Wagner, Chico Ramos, Dady Tracey and Super Furia (well-known for their hit 'De Donkey Want Watta'). Brother David, another musician hailing from Dangriga, has invented his own *soca*-like style called *cungo* music; with his band the Tribal Vibes, Bro' David puts on frequent shows in Belize.

Ironically, the easiest place to find *punta* rock on a consistent basis is in the US! Los Angeles' large Belizean emigré colony and the presence of top-notch recording studios keep at least a dozen of the nation's best-known bands in semi-exile. Belize Caye Fest, held during Memorial Day weekend in Los Angeles (ask Caye Records on belizemusic@themall.net or phone 213 291 2720), showcases authentic music, dance and food. In Belize itself – and particularly outside of Belize City – you can't always be guaranteed of finding live music even on the weekends. Besides Belize City, Dangriga, San Ignacio and San Pedro are the best bets on the weekend. But keep your eyes and ears open in other locales for news of local dances. Even in small communities like Seine Bight Village you may stumble across a live-music weekend dance, usually advertised via handmade posters.

Holidays and festivals almost always feature live music. Best bets are Independence Day (September 21) and St. George's Caye Day (September 10), both celebrated in Belize City, as well as Garifuna Settlement Day (November 19 in Dangriga). The *mestizo* towns of the north and west often feature live music – frequently *marimba* groups – during weekends and holidays. Traditional Maya music, played on handcrafted violins, guitars, and harps, is enjoying a revival thanks to the Maya Village Guest House Ecotrail Programme (see *Chapter 12* for details). Participating in the same programme is the village of Barranco, where Garifuna music can be heard.

Venus Records in Belize City (33 Corner of Albert and Bishop Streets) offers the best selection of Belizean music on cassette tapes. They'll gladly make suggestions and let you listen first. Caye Records, PO Box 431248, Los Angeles, CA 90043 USA (tel: 213 291 2720) specialises in Belizean music and is the best source outside Belize. Write or call for a catalogue.

In New York City, radio station WNWK, 105.9FM, occasionally plays Belizean music on Sunday afternoons.

RELIGION

The first Belizeans worshipped a panoply of Maya gods, from Mam the mountain god to rain spirits known as Chacs. Later, British settlers brought the Anglican faith and built the first Protestant church in Central America. But the majority of Belizeans today (62%) are Roman Catholics, mostly owing to immigration from Mexico since 1848 and the outreach work done by Jesuits. Roughly 28% of the population remain Protestants, with Anglicans the most numerous.

During the last two decades, however, US-based evangelical churches have claimed members from both the Catholic and Protestant camps. It's virtually impossible to spend a week in Belize and not run into missionaries or their converts. The most active evangelical and fundamentalist church groups include the Assemblies of God, Seventh Day Adventists, Jehovah's Witnesses, Church of Jesus Christ of Latter Day Saints (Mormons) and Baptists. Though well-meaning, fundamentalist missionaries have undermined many traditional Maya communities with their teachings and cultural impositions (although Catholicism must share the blame, having supplanted the ancestral Maya religion years ago). Mennonites, members of one of the oldest Protestant sects, have become an integral thread in Belize's social fabric ever since they began arriving in the late 1950s; you'll find more information in *Chapter 10, Mennonites*, page 158.

The Garifuna, although nominally Catholic, still practise an elaborate blend of African and Carib Indian ancestor worship (see *Chapter 11, Garifuna*, page 194). Small groups of Muslims, Hindus, Jews and Bahai's also practise their faiths in Belize.

MYTH AND FOLKLORE

Here as elsewhere, the belief in mythic creatures fades with each generation. But even the youngest and most urbanised Belizeans have grown up on stories of Brer Anansi, *duendes*, and their equally fabulous cohorts. Perhaps the richest repository of living folklore – and least documented – resides in the Kekchi Maya villages of Toledo District, where many residents know folk tales which originated more than 2,000 years ago during the Classic Period.

Easily the most popular of the country's mythic characters, Brer Anansi is a rascally creature, half-spider and half-man. Sporting a top hat, he rides tigers and leaves a trail of mischief and mayhem wherever he goes. The Sisemito is a forest monster of a far more sinister stripe. Something of a Belizean yeti, the Sisemito steals village women and sometimes attacks lone woodsmen, tearing them to pieces. Anyone familiar with South and Central American folklore will have heard of *duendes*, the elfin forest creatures with but four fingers on each hand. You may hear them referred to also as *ta-da-duendes*. Belizean woodsmen frequently report encounters with *duendes*, and rural children learn to greet them with a four-fingered salute (supposedly because the *duendes* are envious of anyone with thumbs). Angry *duendes* may either rip off the offending thumb or lead the person deep into the bush; a friendly *duende* pacified by the salute, however, often confers on the traveller the instant ability to play any one musical instrument he desires. *La Sirena* ('mermaid' in Spanish), half-snake and half-woman, spends her time along forest streams. A man who happens upon her will often be tricked into thinking she's his sweetheart, and follow her down a mazy jungle path from which he'll never return. Xtabi lures men in much the same way, hypnotising them along moonlit forest paths and leading them to certain death. Hashishi Pampi is a tiny beast the colour of ashes who likes to play in the burned remains of houses, hearths, or even burnt *milpas*. Other popular characters include Old Hega and the Warrie Massa.

For further information, pick up a copy of *Characters and Caricatures of Belizean Folklore*, published by the Belize UNESCO Commission and available at most Belize City bookshops and many gift shops.

HOLIDAYS AND FESTIVALS

The following are all public and banking holidays in Belize. Some are celebrated with more gusto than others. Where holidays are associated with a particular town, see the appropriate chapter for more details.

New Year's Day (January 1)
Baron Bliss Day (March 9). A sailing regatta off Belize City is the highlight of this holiday, which celebrates the English yachtsman who anchored offshore in 1926 and later willed over two million dollars to the tiny nation. The same will provides for the yearly regatta.
Good Friday (date varies)
Holy Saturday (date varies)
Easter Sunday and **Easter Monday** (date varies). Easter is most joyously celebrated in the Spanish-speaking northern towns like Corozal and Sarteneja. In Sarteneja, the festivities include a regatta for the local fleet of working sailboats, all crafted by townspeople. The resort town of Placencia also overflows with merrymakers.
Labour Day (May 1)
Commonwealth Day (May 24)
St George's Caye Day (September 10). Also known as National Day, this is a grand excuse for Belize City to party. Festivities start several days in advance, culminating in a parade on the 10th. But the momentum continues right on through to Independence Day.
Independence Day (September 21). Ostensibly honouring Belize's independence from Great Britain, this holiday is little more than a carnivalesque carryover from St. George's Caye Day, with parades, music, food and drink. Celebrations often begin as early as September 15.
Columbus Day (October 12). Also referred to as Pan American Day, this is a major event in the Spanish-speaking northern towns like Corozal and Orange Walk, with parades, music and merrymaking.
Garifuna Settlement Day (November 19). Honours the first major landing of Garifunas on Belizean shores. Dangriga erupts yearly on this date in what is surely the nation's wildest celebration. You'll be very lucky to find lodging for this blow-out with less than a year's advance booking.
Christmas Day (December 25)
Boxing Day (December 26)

In addition to these public holidays, you'll run across scores of local festivals, some of them far more interesting than the officially sanctioned national holidays. Many of the Maya villages in Toledo District and Cayo District celebrate the feast days of their patron saints. If you keep a low profile and leave your camera in its case, your presence as an onlooker is usually tolerated. Popular fiestas of this sort include the Feast of San José in San José Succotz, Cayo District (March). Be forewarned – a good deal of drinking goes on during these bashes, and they can get quite unruly.

Trade-oriented or informal festivals such as the National Agricultural Show (in Belmopan around April/May) offer music, food and a variety of other activities. Crooked Tree Village holds a Cashew Festival on May 7-8, and Caye Caulker celebrates the Coconut Festival in February.

The dates of celebrations and national events change annually. For the latest update on events contact the Belize Tourism Board, Gabourel Lane, Central Bank Building, Level 2, PO Box 325 Belize City; tel: +501 2 31910; toll-free in the US or Canada on 1800 624 0686; fax: +501 2 31943; email: btbb@btl.net; web: www.travelbelize.org

Natural History

GEOGRAPHY

The Belize River valley runs northeasterly, roughly dividing the country into equal halves. To the north lies a wide area of low tableland, much of it swampy coastal plain that once lay submerged beneath the sea. The western portion rises almost imperceptibly to a limestone plateau about 160m above sea level. To the south, the coastal plain narrows to a mere 16km-wide strip just south of Dangriga. Rising steeply from this plain, the Maya Mountains occupy nearly a third of Belize and include the National Monument Victoria Peak (1,120m). Underlain with granitic intrusions and ancient sedimentary rocks, mostly shale and sandstone, the Maya Mountains extend southwesterly into Guatemala where they merge with the highlands. On their southeastern flank lies the much smaller southern plain, also composed of sandstone, shale and limestone.

Rivers dominate the Belizean landscape, most of them running northeasterly along ancient fault lines to the sea. Swamps and shallow freshwater lagoons punctuate the area surrounding these rivers, as well as the northern coastal plain. South of the Maya Mountains, a series of short, swift rivers head toward the sea in a southeasterly direction. The upper tributaries of the Río Usumacinta originate on the southwestern slopes of the Maya Mountains; this is the only region of Belize draining into the Gulf of Mexico.

Offshore lies the second longest barrier reef in the world, an undulating coral curtain that extends nearly the length of the country and shelters in its lee hundreds of sand and mangrove cayes.

This varied topography – along with variations in rainfall – has fashioned a rich mosaic of habitats. Ecologists frequently divide the country into six major regions: Northern Hardwood Forest, with comparatively little rainfall but considerable aquatic habitat in the form of lagoons, swamps, and rivers; Southern Hardwood Forest, a wet sub-tropical 'jungle' in the classic sense; Mountain Pine Ridge, regions of sandy soil sparsely covered by southern pine forest; Coastal Savanna, including sedge marshes and lagoons; Mangroves and Beaches on the mainland; and the Cayes offshore. With apologies to the science of ecology, the following brief overview for travellers lumps all these regions into two categories, reef and rainforest.

The barrier reef, cayes, and atolls

Corals are minute, filter-feeding animals which live in colonies. Each individual coral, or polyp, resides inside a stony cup secreted by the animal itself. The gradual build-up of these rocklike colonies has, over the centuries, resulted in the largest structures ever created by living creatures: coral reefs.

Belize's coral barrier reef, stretching 306km along the country's coastline, is frequently cited as second only to Australia's Great Barrier Reef in terms of total length. Coral reefs are rather amorphous things, however, always broken at some point and therefore difficult to measure. Thus it turns out that New Caledonia and Fiji also line up behind Australia for longest-reef honours. It's safest to say that Belize's barrier reef is the longest in the Western Hemisphere.

The barrier reef runs nearly the entire length of the country, encompassing hundreds of islets called cayes (universally pronounced in Belize as *keys*, and variously spelled with or without an *e*). Some of these cayes lie well inside the reef, some make up the reef itself, and some sit in the more wave-tossed water outside the reef. The barrier reef itself lies less than 1km from Ambergris Caye in northern Belize, gradually veering away from the mainland; the southern tip of the reef, known as the Sapodilla Cayes, sits some 35km east of the Belizean mainland.

Far beyond the reef stand three coral atolls: Lighthouse Reef, Glovers Reef, and Turneffe Island. Atolls are coral reefs, more or less circular in shape, which rise from great depths – much deeper than those where reef-building corals can grow. Obviously, that can only happen when corals grow on a structure thrust up from the depths – a volcano, for instance. Charles Darwin showed that Pacific atolls could have formed when these volcanoes later sank, leaving a ring of coral surrounding a lagoon. Unlike Pacific atolls, however, the ten recognised Caribbean atolls formed not on volcanoes but on giant fault blocks thrust upward during the late Tertiary, some 70 million years ago.

Coral reefs, as almost everyone knows, support huge numbers and a spectacular array of marine life. But fewer people realise that these reefs are fertile exceptions in an otherwise impoverished environment – 'oases in the desert', as one famous ecologist puts it. Tropical seas, in general, lack the rich broth of organic material that characterise temperate oceans, and therefore run a very poor second in terms of marine life. Nutrient levels in tropical sea water could never support the fabulous web of life found on coral reefs, so what does?

The answer lies in the reef's remarkable recycling system. Corals play host within their tissues to microscopic plants called zooxanthellae. These tiny plants utilize carbon dioxide exhaled by the corals, and thereby assist the corals' ability to extract calcium and carbonate ions from the surrounding seawater; these form the basis of the corals' stony skeletons. In return, the coral reef supports the zooxanthellae near the sunny water surface, allowing them to photosynthesize. These and a host of other symbiotic relationships form a complex nutrient-sharing network, one that loses very little to the environment. Any food available is instantly taken up and recycled in this efficient natural system. You'll be hard pressed to find a dead fish, for example, while snorkelling the reef.

This amazingly efficient system is more than a little reminiscent of the rapid recycling that goes on in the mainland rainforest (see *Flora* below). Indeed, coral reefs are rivalled only by tropical rainforests in terms of species abundance and diversity. Snorkellers and scuba divers will find the reef and atolls alive with hundreds of species of fish, sponges, starfish, sea urchins, anemones, marine worms, gorgonians, crabs, lobsters and turtles.

Easily overlooked by snorkellers and divers is the rich marine ecosystem formed by red and black mangroves. Although admittedly not as colourful as the coral reef, mangroves harbour vast fish, invertebrate and bird populations, and they are particularly important as rearing areas for juvenile reef fish. Their prop roots also protect shorelines from erosion.

Good spots from which to reach and explore the barrier reef include San Pedro, Caye Caulker, Placencia, and Dangriga. By the time you reach Punta Gorda in southern Belize, the reef is farther offshore, less-visited, and consequently more difficult and expensive to reach. Scuba divers will find the very best Belizean seascapes on the three offshore atolls, and the southernmost portion of the barrier reef, the Sapodilla Cayes. Belize boasts several marine reserves open to snorkellers and divers, including Hol Chan Marine Reserve, Half Moon Caye Natural Monument and Glovers Reef National Park. For suggested trips, guides, boats and prices, see the appropriate area chapters as well as *Chapter 6, Scuba Diving and Snorkelling,* page 69.

Coral reefs worldwide are in trouble. Surviving only in clear water with few nutrients and even fewer toxins, coral quickly succumbs to sewage, agricultural runoff, petroleum products, siltation, pesticides, fertilizers, dredging and garbage. Mechanical damage from boat anchors, propellers and careless divers can destroy in a few seconds what nature took centuries to create.

And unfortunately, the death of coral reefs can even be part of a perfectly natural cycle. Some researchers point out that coral reefs have already undergone four worldwide collapses, and that what we are witnessing today may be nothing more than a fifth natural collapse. This may be comforting news for the few of us who live on an archaeological time scale, but the jury isn't in yet. And as long as the ultimate causes of reef destruction are still only dimly understood, we had better assume the responsibility and work to fix things ourselves. For more information – and conservation tips for snorkellers and divers – read *What you can do to help* below. *Appendix 2, Further Reading* lists several good books on reef life. A great additional source of information on Belize's marine life and conservation programmes is the Hol Chan Marine Reserve office in San Pedro, Ambergris Caye.

The rainforest

Tropical broadleaf forest of one sort or another still blankets nearly 45% of mainland Belize. That's a remarkable statistic within Central America, where ecologists are predicting that by the turn of the century only 10% of the original forests will remain.

As most people will have noticed, rainforests have become a cause célèbre over the last decade or so, with pleas for their conservation popping up on everything from T-shirts to candy bar wrappers. Obviously a good thing, but the tropical forests still remain cloaked in myth and mystery even among much of the concerned public. Belize offers the ideal opportunity to experience the rainforest close-up and first-hand. You have a number of options: guided trips with trained naturalists arranged through a tour company; more informally arranged trips, usually with local guides who've come to know the forest as woodsmen or hunters; hikes on your own, often along well-maintained paths, in Belize's many parks and reserves; staying at one of the 'cottage resorts' located in the rainforest itself; and canoe trips (guided or un-guided) down jungle rivers. Visits to several Maya ruins – including Caracol and Lamanai – necessarily involve a trip through the rainforest.

For those venturing into the forest for the first time, a few basic pointers:

First, the rainforest is not a dense, hostile environment teeming with menace. Virgin rainforest, like old-growth temperate forest, is easy to walk through because its canopy screens most light from reaching the forest floor. To avoid getting lost, stick with a guide, follow a well-maintained path or a waterway, use a compass, and/or mark your way with red plastic flagging (remove it on the way out, of course). Except for insects, forest animals aren't likely to bother you, let alone endanger you (see *Fauna* section below and *Chapter 5, Health and Safety*). In general, tropical rainforests are far more benign than the temperate mountains and forests that most of us hike around in at home.

Secondly, don't go into the forest expecting to see animals draped from every tree and vine. Even in the richest of forest habitats, that's a fiction fostered by movies and TV. You'll need time, luck, patience, and often a good guide to see many animals. Above all, keep as quiet as possible. The best times to see animal life are near dawn, dusk, and well after dark.

Don't miss an opportunity to spend a night in the forest exploring with headlamps. Nocturnal animals tend to be more sluggish than their diurnal brethren and thus more easily seen. It's natural to feel a bit nervous during your first night walk – just remember that you're undoubtedly far safer in the forest than at home on your local city streets. Stick to a trail or waterway that you've walked during the day and wait until well after nightfall to get started. This gives nocturnal animals a chance to 'wake up' and start about their business. Scan not only the trees and forest floor but also the twigs and branches at eye level; here you're likely to find arboreal frogs, snakes and insects. You'll see the reflective eyeshine of nocturnal animals all around. Take along a standard torch (flashlight) as backup in case your headlamp fails.

And finally, get to know the rainforest in stages, particularly if you're new to it. Take day hikes or an overnight trip before signing on for a week-long expedition. The forest can be hot, buggy, claustrophobic – and yes, even dull – for some travellers.

Where to find the Belizean rainforest? The broadleaf forest of northeastern Belize has been called 'quasi-rainforest' and, not too surprisingly, looks a good deal like Mexico's Quintana Roo just across the border. Much of it is second-growth forest, on land originally cleared and farmed by the ancient Maya. Although it supports a fascinating array of life, it's admittedly less luxuriant than the forests further south and west, and consequently doesn't hold quite the same appeal. Along the major rivers and lagoons, on the other hand, the northern hardwood forests become far more verdant. Areas to explore include the Community Baboon Sanctuary, Shipstern Reserve, the Maya ruin of Lamanai, and Crooked Tree Wildlife Sanctuary.

Wet, steamy, and lush, the rainforests of southern and western Belize are classic jungles right out of Conrad. Places to explore include the Cockscomb Basin Wildlife Sanctuary, the Río Bravo Conservation Area, much of Cayo District (particularly the Vaca Plateau, which includes the Caracol Maya site), and most of western Toledo District (including the Maya villages participating in the unique *Guest House Ecotrail Programme*, see *Chapter 12, Excursions*, page 204).

For details on these rainforest areas, lodging, guides, trip possibilities, and prices, see the appropriate area chapters. Also read *Chapter 4, Package tours*, page 42.

The sections below discuss some of the more interesting flora and fauna found in the Belizean rainforest, but a comprehensive overview of this fascinating ecosystem is clearly beyond the scope of a travel guide. You'll find a number of excellent books listed in the *Appendix 2, Further Reading*. My own favourite overviews include *Tropical Nature* by Miyata and Forsyth and *The Community Baboon Sanctuary* by Horwich and Lyon.

FLORA

Nowhere on earth has plant life reached such levels of diversity as in the tropical rainforests. The great paradox of this lush ecosystem is that all its verdant growth springs out of very poor soil. Those of us living in temperate climes – geologically young systems whose lands have been recently enriched by glaciers and mountain-building – rightly regard soil as the great reservoir of plant nutrients. But that's not the case in the rainforest, an ancient landscape battered by tropical downpours for over 200 million years.

Jungle soil is thin and nutrient-poor, and it's only by virtue of a remarkable group of fungi that it can support plant life at all. These fungi, called mycorrhizae, form a complicated network of fine white filaments just below the jungle floor topsoil. This mycorrhizal network quickly sops up decomposing nutrients and feeds them back to the forest via a series of shallow, intertwining rootlets. Aiding this process is the tropical heat, the humidity, and the action of ants, microbes, and termites, all of which speed the breakdown.

This high-speed recycling system keeps nutrients in the trees, plants, and vines themselves, rather than the soil, where they would be quickly washed away. And it works admirably, so long as all that vegetation is left standing. Tropical farmers worldwide are still learning a bitter lesson: clearing and burning the forest destroys both the standing 'nutrient bank' and the hidden mycorrhizal network upon which future crops depend. Slash-and-burn farming can be sustainable, but only when plots are kept small and rotated on a fairly long-term basis, roughly 15–30 years.

You don't have to be a botanist to notice some of the implications of nutrient-poor tropical soil on forest ecology. Over 700 tree species have been identified so far in Belize, but you'll be hard pressed to find two of the same species growing next to each other, as they do in temperate forests. This is an adaptation to the poor soil, preventing groups of trees with identical nutrient requirements from depleting the earth around them. This makes logging in rainforests a fairly wasteful proposition – loggers must sometimes cut down ten trees to reach a species with marketable wood.

Most of the large trees you'll see in the forest support themselves on thin topsoil with flange-like buttress roots. Plant life in the rainforest involves a manic competition for sun, and you'll find three, four, or even five 'stories' of trees vying for light. Towering above them all is the stately **ceiba**, known to Creoles as the cotton tree. The ancient Maya held this tree sacred, and you'll often see ceibas left standing on acres of cleared agricultural land. **Mahogany** was one of the economic cornerstones of British Honduras, so much so that the Belizean coat of arms still refers to it with the words 'Sub Umbra Floreo' – Under the Tree We Flourish. Unfortunately, by the time the Forestry Department was established in the 1940s, most of the prime mahogany trees, particularly along riverbanks, had long since been cut.

The **bullet tree**, still common along rivers, is prized for railroad ties, posts, and pilings; once cut and exposed to the elements, it becomes as hard as its namesake. Most **chicle** trees you see these days still bear the machete scars of *chicleros*, who periodically tapped them for sap used in making chewing gum. Although the chicle trade practically disappeared after synthetic petroleum-based gums came into use, it is picking up again in Belize; new markets for natural chewing gum have already surfaced in Italy and Japan.

Edible native trees include the **bucut**, or 'Stinking Toe', a common pink-flowered tree whose metre-long pods exude a strong smell but also a chocolaty liquid. The **suppa** palm provides a buttery edible nut as well as a sap used in making palm wine. The **pokenoboy** palm – frequently called pork-and-doughboy – yields a tangy, black-cherry flavoured pulp within its nut. Look for small specimens of the **jippy-jappa** palm, which contain a tender heart-of-palm you can eat on the spot. The best-known palm is the **cohune**, whose oil (used in cooking and cosmetics) supports one of Belize's most successful cottage industries. The thatch is widely used by the modern Maya in building houses, and cohune heart-of-palm is a delicacy.

The marble-sized yellow fruits sold in plastic bags throughout Belize come from the **craboo** tree. Everyone is familiar with **allspice**, the dried berries of the allspice tree, but few people know that the leaves make a sitz bath useful in easing menstrual cramps. Early settlers discovered the medicinal properties of **negrito** tree bark, which alleviated both diarrhoea and dysentery. For over 150 years in Paris and London, the bark sold for its weight in gold.

Trees to avoid include the **give-and-take** palm, whose needle-sharp spines give unwary hikers a painful wound; a cottony substance scraped off the inner bark, however, takes away the pain, staunches the flow of blood, and prevents infection. British soldiers must learn this bush remedy during their jungle training. Black sap from the **poisonwood** tree causes a painful burning sensation that lasts for weeks. This isn't likely to happen unless you're carelessly whacking away at trees with a machete, and even so there's a cure: the boiled bark of the **gumbo limbo** tree. The gumbo limbo is more popularly known as the 'tourist tree' owing to its red, flaky bark reminiscent of a sunburned foreigner.

Belize hosts several species of **heliconia**, the large and colourful ornamental flower with banana-like leaves. Hummingbirds, which feed voraciously on *Heliconia* nectar, often defend a single plant against all competition.

You'll see these and many other examples of Belizean flora – nearly 4,000 species of flowering plants have already been identified – along the self-guided nature trails at the Cockscomb Basin Wildlife Sanctuary, the Shipstern Reserve, the Ix Chel Farm, and cottage resorts such as the Maya Mountain Lodge and Chan Chich. Guides are available at these and many other locations for a more in-depth botanical tour. For that matter, just about any guided tour in wooded areas of Belize will include some discussion of the country's unusual flora. A guided orchid tour – Belize has some 250 species – is offered by the Godoy Brothers in Orange Walk Town (see *Chapter 10*). The best local printed references to Belizean flora include *The Community Baboon Sanctuary* by Horwich and Lyons and Miller and Miller's *Exploring the Rainforest: Chan Chich Lodge* (see *Appendix 2, Further Reading*).

FAUNA

Space permits only a brief discussion here of Belize's varied animal life. See *Appendix 2, Further Reading* for further references and field guides. One of the best books discussing the full range of Belizean fauna is Horwich and Lyons' *The Community Baboon Sanctuary*. And before going in search of Belize's often elusive wildlife on your own, get a close-up preview at the world famous Belize Zoo (see *Chapter 7*).

Mammals

Most visitors see Belize's national animal only on its currency, postage stamps and at the Belize Zoo. Despite the fact that the **Baird's tapir** (*Tapirus bairdii*, or 'mountain cow' to Creoles) is Central America's largest native land mammal, it's a shy, solitary vegetarian that frequently forages at night. Tapirs live in a variety of habitats, but always near water. You're likely to spot the imprint of a tapir's splayed feet along jungle riverbanks. Threatened by habitat loss and hunting, tapirs have disappeared from most of their former range in Central America and Mexico, and are listed as endangered by CITES (Convention on International Trade in Endangered Species). Public education has gone a long way toward bolstering tapir populations in Belize. 'April', the Belize Zoo's tapir, qualifies as a national celebrity and local schoolchildren celebrate her birthday each year with a massive vegetable cake.

The **Caribbean manatee** (*Trichechus manatus*) qualifies as another Belizean success story. These so-called 'sea cows', often weighing over 450kg, have been the victims of hunting, habitat destruction, water pollution and boat propellers over much of their former range. Bone mounds found on Moho Caye prove that even the ancient Maya slaughtered them by the thousands for meat, hides and oil. Yet while numbers continue to decline in most of the Caribbean, the Belizean manatee population appears relatively stable. Indeed, a census in 1989 turned up 55 manatees in Belize's Southern Lagoon alone, the highest count for a specific site anywhere in the Caribbean. This is undoubtedly your best bet for manatee viewing with a guide and boat (see *Chapter 11, Gales Point and Southern Lagoon,* page 172, for details). Other sites with healthy manatee populations include Four Mile Lagoon and the Lower New River (both in Corozal District), the lower Belize River (not far from the Municipal Airport!), the cayes near Belize City, and Placencia Lagoon. Canoeists on the Monkey River occasionally sight these gentle herbivores as well.

Belize, which permitted **jaguar** (*Panthera onca*) hunting until 1974, is these days synonymous with jaguar conservation worldwide. The Cockscomb Basin Wildlife Sanctuary (referred to by most people as simply 'The Jaguar Sanctuary'), the focal point of this effort, expanded in 1990 and again in 1998. It now protects some 120,000 acres of forest. Yet jaguars thrive in other parts of Belize, such as the Río Bravo Conservation Area, which boasts some of the highest jaguar track densities ever recorded in the country. Consider yourself extremely lucky if you actually see a jaguar – they're both wary and nocturnal – and comfort yourself with the fact that the biologist who founded the Cockscomb Sanctuary spent two months there before coming across his first jaguar. See *Chapter 11, Cockscomb Basin Wildlife Sanctuary,* page 176, for more information on jaguars and Belize's battle to save them.

Four other native cats live within Belize's borders: the **mountain lion** or **puma** (*Felis concolor*); the **ocelot** (*Felis pardalis*); the **margay** (*Felis wiedii*); and the **jaguarundi** (*Felis yagouaroundi*). All are listed along with the jaguar as threatened or endangered by CITES. And like the jaguar, they're all difficult to spot. Casual visitors to Belize are most likely to come across the charcoal-black jaguarundi, which hunts birds and small mammals during the day.

The cascading, thunderous roar of **howler monkeys** remains one of the most unforgettable of all jungle experiences. Black howler monkeys (*Alouatta pigra*), 'baboons' in Creole, now enjoy protection in a sanctuary of their own, this one privately owned and managed by Belizean farmers. The Community Baboon Sanctuary in Bermudian Landing isn't the only place to see and hear these noisy primates – the Monkey River, for instance, owes its name to the local howlers – but it's the easiest and best. See *Chapter 7, Community Baboon Sanctuary,* page 95, for more information on howlers.

Two species of **peccary** roam the Belizean forests and savannas. Peccaries are pig-like animals which feed mostly on roots, seeds, insects, fruits, and the occasional farmer's crop. Both the **collared peccary** (*Dicotyles tajacu*) and the **white-lipped peccary** or 'warrie' (*Tayassu pecari*) travel in herds of 15–30 animals, feeding during the daytime. These herds can turn nasty if threatened, and Belizean hunters generally shoot the last straggler in the group rather than face an oncoming horde of angry peccaries. It's difficult to imagine peccaries on the dinner table; scent glands on the back give both species (the warrie in particular) a pungent odour that's distinctly unappetising.

The **paca** or 'gibnut' (*Agouti paca*) finds its way onto the Belizean table more often than any other wild game. A cat-sized rodent with beautiful white spots on its coat, it was served to the Queen during her trip to Belize, and has ever since been nicknamed the 'royal rat'. Pacas spend their day in solitary burrows, emerging after dusk on well-defined paths to forage for leaves, roots, fruit and seeds. They hop about in a rabbit-like fashion, as do their close relatives, the **agoutis** (*Dasyprocta punctata*). Agoutis are smaller, lack the spotted coat, and feed strictly during the day. Both animals prefer forested areas but we've observed them on several occasions in the clearings surrounding Maya ruins.

The **coati** (*Nasua nasua*) is a member of the racoon family, which also includes the **kinkajou** (*Potos flavus*), called 'nightwalker' by Belizean Creoles, and the rare and endangered **cacomistle** (*Bassariscus sumichristi*). But unlike other members of the family, the coati is active mostly during the day. Like racoons, coatis sport a ringed tail and distinctive 'bandit mask' markings around the eyes. Their handsome, tawny red coat makes them easy to spot against the forest background, where they can usually be found rooting around for insects, scorpions, spiders, fruit, lizards and mice. The oft-heard name 'coatimundi' is a Guarani name meaning 'lone coati', a reference to the solitary males which were once mistakenly believed to be a separate species.

Reptiles and amphibians

Of the 51 species of snakes which inhabit Belize, only nine are venomous. Most notorious are the **tommygoffs**, a group of three closely-related pit viper species. All have arrow-shaped heads and fairly thick bodies. The **yellow-jaw tommygoff** (*Bothrops asper*) – or *barba amarilla* to Spanish-speaking Belizeans – lives in every district of the country and in a variety of habitats, including bushes and low trees. Inactive by day and seldom seen, the yellow-jaw is quite active at night, the most commonly encountered snake in many parts of Belize. Some specimens reach 2.5m in length. This snake goes also by the nickname *fer-de-lance*, although temperament-wise it has little in common with the true fer-de-lance (*Bothrops atrox*), a sluggish relative that I've approached and photographed eyeball-to-eyeball. The yellow-jaw is excitable, unpredictable, fast, outfitted with huge fangs and potent venom – an extremely dangerous snake.

The **jumping tommygoff** (*Porthidium nummifer*) enjoys a certain local notoriety for leaping great distances from trees to strike a victim. In fact, it can only extend its stout, muscular body about one-half its length, and lives mostly on the forest floor. Like the yellow-jaw, the jumping tommygoff is nocturnal. It has relatively short fangs, rarely grows much longer than 1m, and even its venom is fairly weak by pit viper standards.

The **green tommygoff** (*Bothriechis schlegelii*) lives in trees and boasts a set of raised supercilliary scales which resemble eyelashes. A fourth species, found only in Cayo District and sometimes lumped with the tommygoffs, sports an upturned snout which earned it the name **rhino viper** (*Porthidium nasutum*). Rounding out the pit viper clan in Belize is the **tropical rattlesnake** (*Crotalus durissus*) and the **Mexican water moccasin** or *cantil* (*Agkistrodon bilineatus*). Within Belize, you're not likely to run across a cantil, and then only in Corozal District.

The other three venomous Belizean reptiles are all **coral snakes**. Only one, *Micrurus diastema*, is common. All three species exhibit gorgeous rings of brilliant red, black, and sometimes yellow. This same brightly coloured pattern, however, is common in a number of harmless species. Coral snakes themselves don't deserve all the notoriety; although their venom is quite toxic, they're shy, nocturnal creatures with small heads and even tinier fangs. I consider myself lucky to have stumbled on one of these beautiful snakes by day, startling it from its sleep beneath a pile of leaves.

Precautions and first-aid advice for snakebite victims are discussed in *Chapter 5, Snakebite*.

The **common boa** (*Boa constrictor*), or 'wowla' in Creole, rarely grows much longer than 1.8m in Belize. Non-venomous, it asphyxiates rodents and small birds by coiling its powerful body around the victim.

Take most any canoe trip down a Belizean river and you're bound to see dozens of **iguanas** (*Iguana iguana*). Adults, most the size of your arm, clamber along tree branches and splash into the river. Individual iguanas have the ability to shift colours throughout their life. Depending on the season, food, age, and breeding condition, they span a spectrum from leafy green to rusty red to black. Belizeans eat iguana on occasion, giving rise to the nickname 'bamboo chicken'. A close relative, the **wish-willy** (*Ctenosaura similis*) is often seen by visitors to Half Moon Caye Natural Monument.

The **basilisk lizard** (*Basiliscus vittatus*), dashing about on its hind legs, has frequently been compared to a tiny *Tyrannosaurus rex*. Crossing small creeks and ponds in this manner has earned it the Belizean nickname 'Jesus Christ lizard'.

Four species of **sea turtles** inhabit Belizean waters and lay their eggs on local beaches, but only three of them – the loggerhead, hawksbill, and green sea turtle – are at all common. **Green sea turtles** (*Chelonia mydas*) often grow to 180kg or more, and have long been sought for their meat. The **loggerhead** (*Caretta caretta*), rarely heavier than 160kg, hasn't escaped intense fishing pressure despite its relatively sinewy, strong-flavoured flesh. **Hawksbills** (*Eretmochelys imbricata*) are the species most often spotted by snorkellers and divers. Yet these small sea turtles are probably the most threatened in Belize, where their eggs are destroyed by poachers and racoons. Their translucent shells were once exported from Belize to England in great numbers for use as jewellery. The fourth species, the **leatherback** (*Dermochelys coriacea*), has never been particularly common in Belize. These deep-water sea turtles qualify as the world's largest living reptile, and 725kg specimens have been landed by commercial fishermen. Except for their eggs, they have no commercial value.

Sea turtle conservation programmes involving Belizean volunteers are underway in San Pedro (Ambergris Caye) and near Gales Point, Stann Creek District. Visits to certain spawning beaches are possible at Gales Point (see *Chapters 11* and *13* for more information). Please help discourage the sale of turtle products and turtle meat.

Of the eight Belizean freshwater turtles, the **hickatee** (*Dermatemys mawei*) draws the most concern from environmentalists. Once common over a broader range, this nocturnally active turtle now can be found only in Belize – where it favours the deep, clear water of large lagoons and rivers – and isolated spots in Guatemala and southeastern Mexico. The hickatee can grow as large as 23kg, and its habit of drifting motionless on the water surface by day makes it easy prey for human predators.

Belize hosts small populations of the **American crocodile** (*Crocodylus acutus*) and the more diminutive **Morelet's crocodile** (*C. moreleti*). Locally known as 'alligators', both species inhabit rivers, creeks, mangrove swamps and lagoons. Guided boat trips on the Belize or New Rivers, particularly at dusk or after dark, provide the best chance of actually seeing crocodiles. Neither species is common (indeed, Morelet's crocodile is endangered), but they've been sighted in locales as distant as the offshore atolls. Northern Lagoon on Turneffe Island, in fact, is an important breeding ground for the Morelet's crocodile. The best opportunity for seeing crocodiles in Belize is offered by the Lamanai Outpost Lodge (see *Chapter 10, Lamanai*). They take guests aboard a pontoon boat in an extremely shallow lagoon near the Maya ruin site and drift among the crocs after dark.

Birds

Belize, with more than 500 species of birds, increasingly draws organised groups of birdwatchers to places like Crooked Tree Wildlife Sanctuary, Cockscomb Basin Wildlife Sanctuary, and Half Moon Caye Natural Monument. One party of three birders at Cockscomb, for example, checked off an average of 85 species each day. But avian life isn't restricted to a few nature reserves, and you don't need to be a fanatic birder to catch the birding fever in Belize. Binoculars and a field guide are musts for any trip (see *Appendix 2, Further Reading* for field guide suggestions).

Forests, lagoons and savannas play host to a huge variety of birds: herons, ibises, two stork species, ducks, vultures, eagles, hawks, ospreys, falcons, rails, the brilliant ocellated turkey, doves, pigeons, nine parrot species, cuckoos, swifts, kingfishers, woodpeckers, antbirds, flycatchers, swallows, jays, wrens, thrushes, warblers, vireos, tanagers, cardinals, sparrows, blackbirds, finches and 21 species of hummingbird. Birding is excellent even at night, when you're likely to see or hear nighthawks, pauraques, the boat-billed heron and ten owl species. On the beaches, cayes, and atolls you'll find pelicans, cormorants, the magnificent frigatebird, ibises, spoonbills, plovers, sandpipers, gulls, terns and two species of booby.

Rarely sighted birds include the jabiru stork, roseate spoonbill, scarlet macaw, chestnut-bellied heron, harpy eagle, black rail, Yucatan flycatcher and black catbird. Within Belize, the latter species is now found in significant numbers only on Caye Caulker, where a nature preserve is being proposed for it (see *Chapter 13* for details). A number of migratory birds visit Belize, including, on extremely rare occasions, snow geese and greater white-fronted geese which presumably are a bit off course.

You'll find more information on Belizean birds throughout this book. Only a few of Belize's more spectacular avian 'stars' are mentioned below.

Birders filling out life-lists invariably seek out the **jabiru stork** (*Jabiru mycteria*) when visiting Belize. Legally protected since 1973, the Belizean jabiru population now consists of nine to twelve breeding pairs. While still abundant in parts of South America – many hundreds can be seen in a day at places like Brazil's Pantanal – this magnificent bird is rare and endangered over most of its former range in Mexico and Central America. One of the largest flying birds in the Western Hemisphere, the jabiru stands nearly 1.5m tall with a wingspan of about 2.7m. Its white body feathers are offset by a naked black neck ringed at the base with a reddish collar. This featherless collar changes from pink to deep crimson when the bird is excited. Unlike most wading birds, which feed by sight, the jabiru feeds by touch. Periodically, it dips its huge open bill into the water and waits for a frog, fish, or snake to make contact, then snaps it shut and swallows. This form of feeding has obvious advantages in Belizean lagoons where the water is turbid and prey is plentiful. Jabirus nest in protected waterways from late December through early March. The best places to see them include Crooked Tree Wildlife Sanctuary and along the nearby New River in Orange Walk District. Hire a guide and plan to put some effort into finding this rare bird.

The **keel-billed toucan** (*Ramphastos sulfuratus*) is the national bird, and a good deal more common than the jabiru. Black, yellow and red plumage is complemented by iridescent blue feet and a bill that includes shades of crimson, blue, orange and lime green. The massive bill, used for eating rainforest fruits, is not as ungainly as it may appear; beneath the horny exterior lies a sponge-like network of fibres that lighten the owner's load considerably. In contrast to its gaudy plumage, the toucan's call is a monotonous, froglike croak. Belize boasts two other toucans, the **emerald toucanet** (*Aulacorhynchus prasinus*) and the more commonly seen **collared aracari** (*Pteroglossus torquatus*). Both are smaller and less colourful than the national bird. Look for all three species high in the largest of forest trees.

The **blue-crowned motmot** (*Momotus momota*) is a relative of the kingfisher, easily identified by its trademark tailfeathers. The vanes of the two longest tailfeathers are missing for about 2.5cm, so that the motmot appears to sport a pair of elongated, feathered darts for a tail. Some experts claim that the motmot barbers itself in this outlandish fashion, plucking the feathers out with its beak. But it's more likely that the loosely-attached barbs fall out of their own accord. In any case, the motmot is apparently aware of its flamboyant appearance, using the tail in courtship displays. These iridescent blue-and-green forest birds nest in holes dug in the ground. They use their powerful beaks to seize large insects. Belizeans sometimes refer to this species as the 'good cook', owing to its low, distinctive call – more a coo-coo to my ear. Two other close relatives – the **tody motmot** and the **keel-billed motmot**, both rarely sighted – make their homes in Belize.

Although worldwide the **red-footed booby** (*Sula sula*) is perhaps the most abundant of the booby species, it nests in only a few sites within the Caribbean. Half Moon Caye Natural Monument, established in 1982 and open to visitors, was largely created to protect these birds. Most adult red-footed boobies are a dull brown colour, while the Half Moon Caye population is composed almost entirely of pure white individuals. Although a long way offshore, this site is definitely worth visiting. You'll see not only the boobies (present year-round) but also a nesting colony of **Magnificent frigatebirds** (*Fregata magnificens*). See *Chapter 14* for more information on these birds. A related species, the **brown booby** (*Sula leucogaster*) can be seen on Man of War Caye (best visited from Dangriga or Tobacco Caye, see *Chapter 11, Tobacco Caye, page 169*).

Insects

Troublesome insects, including mosquitoes, 'doctor flies', and the Africanized 'killer' bee, are described in *Chapter 5, Health and Safety*.

Termite nests, built by worker termites which chew and glue tiny wood particles together, are a common site on tree trunks. By releasing nutrients into the impoverished rainforest soil that were formerly tied up in the trees, termites perform a vital function in the jungle's rapid recycling system.

You're unlikely to do much hiking in the rainforest without crossing a trail of energetic **leaf-cutter ants** (*Atta cephalodes*). Known to Belizeans as 'wee wee ants', these insects live in highly structured communities and practise an amazing form of agriculture. Hordes of specialized worker ants – the most numerous type you'll see along the trail – carry leaves and leaf fragments back to the colony. Along the way, they are protected and herded by larger soldier ants. In some areas, where tiny parasitic wasps attempt to lay their eggs on the backs of the workers, they are warded off by a third and much smaller ant which rides 'shotgun' on the leaf. Back at the colony, this third variety of leaf-cutter ant shreds the leaves and injects the resulting compost with fungal spores. Eventually, this fungus crop produces food for the entire colony.

A dazzling variety of **butterflies** and moths make Belize their home. These include the iridescent blue Morpho and the black, yellow and red Heliconius. Lepidopterists will want to visit the Fallen Stones Butterfly Ranch and the Chaa Creek Cottages Morpho Butterfly Centre, where butterflies are raised to the pupal stage and then sold to European butterfly houses and parks (see *Chapter 12, San Pedro Columbia, page 213* and *Chapter 8, Rural lodges and resorts near San Ignacio, page 114, for details*).

Marine fish and invertebrates

Belize's cayes, barrier reef, and offshore atolls provide habitat for hundreds of fish species, ranging from the tiny **neon goby** (*Gobiosoma oceanops*) to giants like the **hammerhead shark** (*Sphyrna sp.*) and the **manta ray** (*Manta hamiltoni*). An even greater variety of invertebrate life graces the reef. Besides at least 30 species of coral itself, you'll find colourful sponges, anemones, starfish, sea cucumbers, sea urchins, shrimp, crabs and lobster. Reef life is described in more detail in *Chapters 11, 13* and *14*. See *Chapter 6, Fishing, page 72*, for information on sport fish species.

CONSERVATION IN BELIZE

Particularly in the last decade, Belize has earned a reputation for its conservation stance that may be unmatched anywhere in the world. Government leaders, Belizean environmental groups, local landowners, and international conservation groups all deserve credit for that reputation. As travellers and world citizens, we all stand to benefit from it.

The conservation movement in Belize has focused on two main goals: preserving tracts of land and promoting environmental education. Early efforts by the Belize Audubon Society resulted in the designation of Half Moon Caye, a haven for the red-footed booby, as Belize's first Natural Monument. The movement has gained momentum ever since. Since 1990, 14 new national parks or nature reserves have been created. Faced with constant demands for development, the government of Belize has taken a firm stand for conservation and managed growth.

The Belize Audubon Society has been joined by other local conservation groups, such as the Programme for Belize. International organisations such as the World Wildlife Fund (World Wide Fund for Nature), Wildlife Preservation Trust International and New York Zoological Society have pitched in on projects ranging from the Cockscomb Basin Wildlife Sanctuary to the Belize Zoo.

Perhaps most inspiring has been the participation of private citizens. Belize's largest reserve, the Río Bravo Conservation and Management Area, was a gift from local businessman Barry Bowen. Farmers near Bermudian Landing set aside portions of their own land for the Community Baboon Sanctuary.

But there's more to conservation than setting aside land. From the start, Belize has recognised the need for environmental education and now boasts a school programme that is envied worldwide. The Belize Zoo and Tropical Education Centre, through the leadership of Sharon Matola, the work of former employees Amy Bodwell and recently retired Myrtle Flowers, and her replacement Celso Poot are instilling Belizean kids with a strong environmental ethic. For many schoolchildren, visits to 'April' (the zoo's famous tapir) and her cohorts are their only contact with Belizean wildlife. Local press such as the *Belize Report* (web: www.belizereport.com) and *Belize First* (web: www.turq.com/belizefirst) magazine constantly give conservation news a high public profile. The Programme for Belize involves itself regularly with education, such as developing lesson plans and hosting workshops for teachers and wildlands managers.

The outlook isn't all rosy. Illegal slash-and-burn farm plots encroach on protected lands. Marine reserves remain few and far between, even as tourism and residential development increase exponentially. There is constant pressure from agri-business, particularly the citrus industry, to clear land for cultivation. Immigrants from El Salvador, Guatemala and Honduras continue to stream across Belize's borders, adding to the pressure on this tiny nation's natural resources. The government has even been petitioned to reopen sport hunting for jaguar. And finally, the huge increase in tourism along the coast and cayes continues to cause problems with sewage, dredging and garbage. Your decision to travel responsibly in Belize helps, but if you want to get more involved, see *What you can do to help* below.

Parks and reserves

Reserved lands – those set aside for one or more specific purposes – make up about 35% of Belize's land area. These include national reserves, wildlife sanctuaries, forest reserves, natural monuments, parks, 'Crown Reserves', marine reserves, and privately owned reserves. A number of archaeological and Indian reserves have also been created. Not all of these reserves will be of interest to travellers. Forest reserves, for instance, include many thousands of acres of scrub, and are often managed for selective logging, erosion control, and watershed protection as well as recreation; Indian reserves are managed strictly for agriculture. And a couple of Belize's protected areas – Bladen Branch and Tapir Mountain Nature Reserves – are open only to visits from qualified scientists doing research.

Nevertheless, this still leaves visitors with eight government-managed reserves totalling over 230,000 acres and ten privately-owned reserves and research stations encompassing another 200,000 acres. Undoubtedly there will be more by the time you read this book. Each reserve has its own character and reason for being. Some cater more to birders while others draw botanists. Many offer lodging and/or camping, while others can only be visited on day trips. Some feature well-maintained trails or self-guided nature walks; in others, you'll need the services of a guide to steer you through mazy waterways or trackless jungle.

These reserves range in size from as small as 50 acres to as large as 265,262 acres, and span every type of habitat from coral reef to cloud forest. Many can be reached via public transportation; only a few, such as Río Bravo Conservation Area or Half Moon Caye, require the expense of a charter airplane or guided boat. Trips to most reserves are well within the means of budget travellers.

The accompanying map shows the reserves, protected areas, and research stations of interest to travellers; some of these are discussed in the appropriate area chapters of this book.

Few travellers have the time to visit all of Belize's nature reserves, parks and natural monuments. Read the descriptions of each in the area chapters and decide which suit your own interests. If I were limited to just three, my own personal favourites (in no particular order) would probably be the Cockscomb Basin Wildlife Sanctuary, Half Moon Caye Natural Monument and Community Baboon Sanctuary.

Finally, don't assume that nature reserves have a monopoly on Belize's flora and fauna. Areas such as the New River, Monkey River and Caracol Maya ruins – just to name a few – swarm with native wildlife and vegetation.

What you can do to help

Belize's natural splendours bring out the conservationist in even the most apathetic of visitors. Perhaps the single most important thing you can do to help at this time is simply this: go to Belize and spend money. The government of Belize has made a courageous bet – that preserving the country's natural heritage will eventually bring in more money than yielding to the pressures for unplanned development. That may seem like a logical and easy choice for those of us on the sidelines. But remember that the long-term economic benefits of 'ecotourism' are still something of an unknown. Consider the dilemma of a government official choosing between preserving land for 'green travellers' – and admit it, we often have a reputation as miserly skinflints – and the enormous, immediate cash flow offered by a multinational citrus company. Belize has clearly voted in favour of ecotourism and sustained resource development. We must now prove to them with our wallets that it works.

Naturally, you have to be somewhat choosy in where and how you spend your money. Insist that tour guides, for instance, follow conservation guidelines and treat the environment and local cultures with respect. When visiting places like Cockscomb Basin Wildlife Sanctuary, buy something from the local stores owned by villagers who moved to accommodate the park. Likewise, when touring the Community Baboon Sanctuary patronise local stores and lodging – they're the folks who voluntarily set aside former farmland as wildlife area – and pass up the hotel that

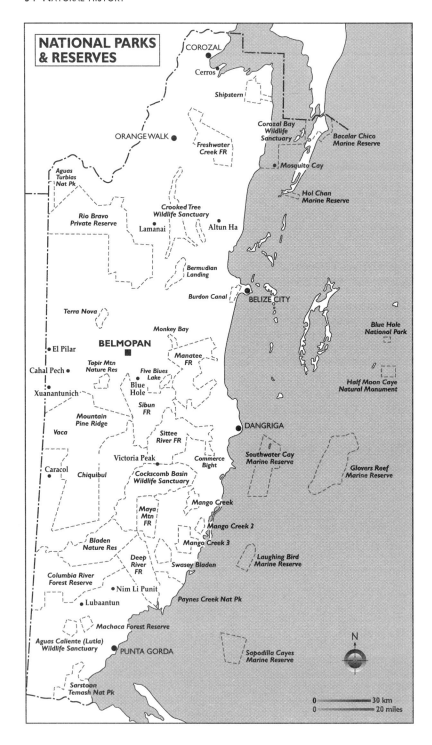

NATIONAL PARKS & RESERVES

COROZAL

Cerros

Shipstern

Corozal Bay Wildlife Sanctuary

Bacalar Chico Marine Reserve

ORANGE WALK

Freshwater Creek FR

Mosquito Cay

Aguas Turbias Nat Pk

Hol Chan Marine Reserve

Rio Bravo Private Reserve

Crooked Tree Wildlife Sanctuary

Lamanai

Altun Ha

Bermudian Landing

Burdon Canal

BELIZE CITY

Terra Nova

Blue Hole National Park

Monkey Bay

El Pilar

BELMOPAN

Manatee FR

Cahal Pech

Tapir Mtn Nature Res

Five Blues Lake

Blue Hole

Half Moon Caye Natural Monument

Xuanantunich

Sibun FR

Mountain Pine Ridge

Vaca

Sittee River FR

DANGRIGA

Victoria Peak

Commerce Bight

Southwater Cay Marine Reserve

Caracol

Chiquibul

Cockscomb Basin Wildlife Sanctuary

Glovers Reef Marine Reserve

Mango Creek

Maya Mtn FR

Mango Creek 2

Bladen Nature Res

Mango Creek 3

Laughing Bird Marine Reserve

Deep River FR

Swasey Bladen

Columbia River Forest Reserve

Nim Li Punit

Paynes Creek Nat Pk

Lubaantun

Machaca Forest Reserve

Aguas Caliente (Lutla) Wildlife Sanctuary

PUNTA GORDA

N

Sapodilla Cayes Marine Reserve

Sarstoon Temash Nat Pk

0 —————— 30 km
0 —————— 20 miles

has recently bulldozed mangroves to accommodate a 'beach view'. Don't patronise restaurants that serve undersized lobsters and conch, or offer seafood out of season.

Pick hotels, dive boats and tour companies that are Belizean-owned or employ Belizeans as much as possible. When dealing with foreign-owned companies, look for those that make regular donations to Belizean conservation programmes or otherwise contribute directly to the local economy. Be warned that even the most callous tour operators (fortunately, there aren't many in Belize) are now paying lip service to 'ecotourism'.

Secondly, encourage the government of Belize and Belizean conservation organisations in the work they're doing. Letters, phone calls, and even short personal visits are always appreciated.

Thirdly, practise responsible tourism yourself. Leave plants, animals and Maya artefacts where they are. Follow the *Coral reef etiquette* guidelines below. Allow animals their territorial space, admiring them from a respectful distance and passing them as quietly as possible. Don't poke your camera in the face of every 'colourful native' you run across. Pack out what you pack in.

Coral reef etiquette

On the grand scale of things, most experts agree that the major threats to coral reefs include things like industrial pollution, sedimentation and nutrient influx. But when they don mask, snorkel or scuba tank, even the most concerned 'green' travellers can unknowingly wreak havoc on coral reefs. Sadly, mechanical damage done by divers and snorkellers may rival other causes of reef death in some of the popular sites visited by tourists. Keep the following rules in mind at all times when you're in the water.

• Don't remove anything, living or dead, from the water. As Belizean Creoles say, 'Doan teef de reef, mon!' – Don't thief the reef!
• Don't touch anything. The slightest contact of your bare hand or glove can destroy delicate coral polyps. This happens when the polyps, only a few cell layers thick, are pressed against their own razor-sharp stony exoskeleton. Once dead, this bare spot can be colonised by algae that will kill even more coral. Don't wear gloves – it only encourages you to touch things. Gloves are not even allowed at the Hol Chan Marine Reserve and on many dive boats.
• Avoid wearing fins while snorkelling. If you feel they're necessary, be conscious of them at all times and use a shallow, light kick. Besides the obvious breakage of fragile corals done by fins, they can stir up sand and sediment which slowly smothers the reef. Like gloves, they constitute body armour that encourages standing on the reef, and many people are blissfully ignorant of the wake of destruction they leave behind them. Most competent swimmers don't really need fins in the commonly-visited snorkel sites in Belize. Divers, too, should stay conscious of their fins.
• Stay 1m or more from the reef. Currents and surge can suddenly push you into contact with living coral if you're too close.
• Divers should make sure that octopus regulators, consoles and gauges don't drag freely over the reef. Personally, I follow the French example and don't use an octopus or all that extraneous, potentially reef-destroying paraphernalia so popular with American divers these days. Unfortunately, some dive boats insist on octopus regulators, so make sure they don't dangle.
• Divers should also practise buoyancy control at all times. Keep your weights to a minimum, avoid freefalls, and stay well away from the reef until you've got your buoyancy completely under control.

Conservation organisations

Consider supporting one or more of the following organisations, all of which are actively involved in one way or another with the environmental movement in Belize. Write to them for more information. Also, when travelling you may find a particular issue that concerns or interests you – take time to write a letter expressing your anger or, equally important, pleasure. Writing letters can make a difference to people who otherwise have no way of gauging the opinion of visiting travellers.

Belize Audubon Society PO Box 1001, 12 Fort Street, Belize City, Belize; tel:02 35004/34987/34988; fax: 02 34985; email: base@btl.net; web: www.belizeaudubon.org. Since 1969, this is Belize's oldest conservation group and still one of the most active and helpful. They're involved with environmental education, development and management of nature reserves (including, among others, Half Moon Caye, Crooked Tree, Cockscomb, Guanacaste, Blue Hole and coastal bird sanctuaries covering over 150,000 acres), conservation publications, and the Christmas bird count. Various memberships are available.

Programme for Belize 1 Eyre Street, Belize City, Belize; tel: 02 75616/71248; fax: 02 75635; email: pfbel@btl.net; web: www.pfbelize.org. Formed in 1988, this group not only manages the Río Bravo Conservation and Management Area (over 260,000 acres making it Belize's largest reserve), but also undertakes education, training and research projects dealing with sustainable resource use and conservation. Work includes a tropical ecology teaching handbook, school lesson plans in conservation and environmental workshops for teachers and reserve managers. Programme for Belize also provides a number of ecotours in the areas they manage.

Belize Zoo and Tropical Education Centre PO Box 1787, Belize City; tel: 081 3004/3003; fax: 081 3010; email: belizezoo@btl.net or tec@btl.net; web: www.belizezoo.org/zoo/zoo.html. With over 500 Belizean schoolchildren visiting monthly, the Zoo and TEC may play the single most important role in underwriting the nation's environmental future. They also have a school outreach programme, captive animal breeding project, and one of the finest, most original zoos in the world. See *Chapter 7, page 90,* for more details. Individual memberships start at US$25.

World Wildlife Fund US 1250 24th Street NW, PO Box 97180, Washington, DC 20077-7180; tel: 1 800 2255 993 and **World Wide Fund for Nature** Weyside Park, Godalming, Surrey GU7 1XR, Great Britain. Active worldwide, WWF has supported a number of Belizean projects including Cockscomb Wildlife Sanctuary, Hol Chan Marine Reserve, Blue Hole National Park, the Community Baboon Sanctuary and the Coastal Zone Management Programme.

Lighthawk c/o Monkey Bay, PO Box 187, Belmopan, Belize; tel: 08 13032; fax: 08 23361; email: Mbay@pobox.com; web: www.lighthawk.org www.lighthawk.org. This non-profit group began in 1979 by flying volunteer 'missions' over environmentally-sensitive areas to call attention to problems and point out the need for protection. Among other accomplishments in Belize, this 'Environmental Air Force' helped convince government officials to designate the Bladen Branch of the Monkey River a nature reserve.

The Nature Conservancy 4245 North Fairfax Drive, Suite 100, Arlington, VA 22203-1606; tel: 1 800 628 6860; dan_campbell@TNC.org, or in Belize at PO Box 150, Punta Gorda; tel: 07 22503; email: will@btl.net. A partner organisation with Programme for Belize, the Nature Conservancy assisted in the purchase of 110,000 acres of rainforest as part of the Río Bravo Conservation and Management Area.

Planning and Preparations

RED TAPE
Visas and other entry requirements

All travellers entering Belize require a valid passport. At the time of writing, citizens of the USA and Canada do not require visas, neither do most Western European nations, with the exceptions of Poland and Switzerland, nor Australians or New Zealanders. Citizens of most East European, Asian, African and Latin American countries do require a visa. This may change, however, so check with your local embassy or consulate before leaving. In theory, travellers should also 'demonstrate that they have sufficient funds for their visit (US$50 pp per day) and have a ticket to their onward destination'. We haven't met anyone recently who's actually been required to produce either for a border official – but then we're travelling with an older crowd these days. We have, on one occasion, seen young backpackers asked to fill out a short government form describing their itinerary and financial status.

Visitors are allowed to stay for up to one month in Belize. After that, you'll need to apply for an extension from the Immigration Office at 99 Barrack Road, Belize City (BZ$25) or the offices in Punta Gorda, Dangriga, Belmopan, Orange Walk, Corozal or in Benque Viejo del Carmen at the immigration post. The sixth extension will cost BZ$50.

Even if you aren't planning a trip to Guatemala, consider getting a Guatemalan visa before leaving home. Although relations between the two countries have improved to the point that Guatemala now has an embassy in Belize City, you will usually save considerable time by getting a visa beforehand, in case you decide mid-vacation to visit Tikal or Livingston, for example.

If you're planning to drive into Belize, see *Chapter 6,* page 60, regarding special entry requirements.

No immunisations are required for entry, although you may want to play it safe on your own accord (see *Chapter 5*, *Before you go,* page 45).

GETTING THERE
Air

Flights to Belize from North America are getting more simple as airlines consolidate. **American Airlines** (tel: 1 800 433 7300; web: www.aa.com) provide daily flights from Miami and Houston. **Continental Airlines** (tel: 1 800 525 0280 in the US and Canada or 0800 776 464 in the United Kingdom; web: www.continental.com) provide one direct flight from Houston Monday to Friday, and a couple of flights on both Saturday and Sunday. **GRUPO TACA** (tel: 1 800 535 8780; and the - currently being revamped - website: www.grupotaca.com) is the consolidated airline of several Central American national airlines. TACA has daily flights from Miami and Houston in high season. Daily flights leave for Belize City from Los Angeles and San Francisco via El Salvador, and from New Orleans via San Pedro Sula, Honduras.

Flights from Miami start at US$365 return in the low season, but prices vary greatly so contact the airline or a tour operator to find out prices for the time you wish to travel.

There are no direct flights from Europe so you will have to stopover in North America – take your pick from Miami or Houston. Return flights link up without the loss of a day's travel.

A mid-season ticket from London costs £480 return.

Travel from neighbouring countries by air is limited to an on-off Saturday and Sunday service between Cancun, Mexico, and Belize City provided by AeroCaribe (41 Albert Street, Belize City, Belize; tel: 02 77185; fax: 02 75213), at US$189 return. The Belizean airline Tropic Air (PO Box 20, San Pedro, Belize; tel: 02 62012; fax: 02 62338; toll free in the US and Canada: 1 800 422 3435; email: tropicair@btl.net; web: www.tropicair.com) provide a daily service from Guatemala City and Flores, at BZ$300 and BZ$160 one way respectively.

Charter flights can be arranged with **Tropic Air**, **Maya Island Air** or **Javier's Flying Service** which all have offices at the Municipal Airport in Belize City (see page 84). Flights are paid for by the hour, but if you have a group prices can be competitive.

The only alternatives are to link up with the international flights travelling through Central American countries that originate in the US.

Overland routes

Although Maya Indians commonly cross the Guatemala–Belize border on a trail system as ancient as their culture, foreigners entering Belize by land may only do so at two locations: the eastern Guatemalan border town of Melchor de Mencos, adjacent to Benque Viejo del Carmen, Cayo District, Belize; and the Mexican crossing at Santa Elena, 15.5km south of Chetumal, Mexico and just 14.5km north of Corozal Town, Belize. You'll find information on the Guatemalan border crossing in *Chapter 8, To and from Guatemala,* page 111; look for details on the Mexican border crossing in *Chapter 9, To and from Mexico,* page 136.

By boat

Regularly scheduled boats link Punta Gorda in Belize's southern Toledo District with Puerto Barrios, Guatemala (itself about an hour's boat ride from Livingston, Guatemala). Requena's Charter Services (12 Front Street, PO Box 18, Punta Gorda, Toledo District, Belize; tel: 07 22070; email: watertaxi@btl.net) are based in Punta Gorda. Boats leave the Public Pier in Puerto Barrios, Guatemala daily at 14.00. The trip from Punta Gorda for Puerto Barrios leaves at 09.00 (BZ$25). Requena's can also arrange charters to and from Puerto Cortes in Honduras.

There is a weekly service to Puerto Cortes, Honduras, from Dangriga. The boat leaves from the Riverside Café, Dangriga, around 09.00 on a Saturday and calls in at Placencia en route if requested. If leaving from Placencia you will have to book before 17.00 on the Friday – see Charles Leslie in Placencia for information.

The cost is BZ$80 from Dangriga and BZ$100 from Placencia – the higher cost is due to having to send your passport to Dangriga for immigration formalities to be completed. The boat returns from Honduras on Monday mornings. You'll find details on this crossing in *Chapter 12,* page 201.

A resident of Mango Creek in Belize's Stann Creek District runs an informal boat service to Puerto Cortés, Honduras. His schedule is very irregular, and it would be entirely a matter of luck to find him in Puerto Cortés when you wanted to go to Belize. For details, see *Chapter 11, Independence/Mango Creek/Big Creek,* page 152.

There's a fair amount of commercial boat traffic between Chetumal, Mexico and ports in northern Belize, particularly the lobster village of Sarteneja. These aren't passenger boats, and schedules are irregular. I've never attempted this route into Belize myself, however, nor have I met other travellers who've used it.

Cruise boats stop in Belize. American Canadian Caribbean Line (ACCL) has a 12-day cruise that takes in much of the coastal area of Belize including the cayes, Placencia and Punta Gorda. The Niagara Prince has a capacity of 84 people, provides lectures on board and completes the trip every couple of weeks. Contact ACCL at PO Box 368, Warren, RI 02885 or on tel: 401 247 0955; fax: 401 247 2350 or on the web: www.accl-smallships.com.

You can, of course, sail your own boat to Belize. See *Chapter 6, Sailing* for details.

BELIZEAN CONSULATES/EMBASSIES
United States
Embassy of Belize, 2535 Massachusetts Ave. NW; Washington, DC 20008; tel: 202 332 9636; fax: 202 332 6888; email: belize@oas.org

Canada
Consulate of Belize, c/o McMillan Binch, Suite 3800, South Tower, Royal Bank Plaza, Toronto, Ontario, M5J 2JP; tel: 416 865 7000; fax: 416 864 7048.

Great Britain
Belize High Commission, 22 Harcourt House, 19 Cavendish Square, London W1M 9AD; tel; 020 7499 9728; fax: 020 7491 4139; email: BZHC-LON@tlk21.com.

Germany
Consulate of Belize, Lindenstrasse 46-48, 7120 Bietigheim, Bissingen; tel: 07142 3924, fax: 07142 33225

WHAT TO BRING
The standard rule of thumb for tropical travel applies in Belize: bring half the clothes you think you'll need and twice the money. In a country like Belize that offers everything from rainforest camping to scuba diving, it isn't always easy to pack lightly, but you'll be glad you made an effort as you crowd aboard that standing-room-only bus with your bag.

Most travellers should be able to get by with a nylon duffle bag and a small daypack. Any of the non-rigid nylon 'suitcases' will work, but we prefer the bags that convert to backpacks. Internal-frame backpacks are always a good choice; local prejudice against backpackers seems to be on the wane everywhere.

Clothes
It rarely gets very cold in Belize. Bring a couple of T-shirts and a light-fabric, long-sleeved shirt for the rainforest. For cold spells and camping, we've found that long underwear made of silk is ideal – amazingly warm, it takes up very little room in your bag. Shorts and/or a bathing suit are necessities. Lightweight rain gear or a plastic poncho can prove invaluable. Leave your blue jeans at home. They're hot, bulky, soak up water like a blotter, and don't wash or dry easily. Much preferable are loose-fitting athletic trousers made of synthetic fabric. Bring a hat or visor to shade you from the sun.

For tramping through jungle and across coral-strewn beaches, I recommend simple running shoes. Other travellers swear by army jungle boots, lightweight hiking boots or the short black rubber boots favoured by many Maya farmers.

Cheap sandals and/or a pair of 'reef walkers' are ideal for the cayes and atolls. Whatever shoes or boots you bring, break them in well before the trip – you'll be far better off in a comfortably tatty pair of shoes than in brand new ones which give you blisters. I sometimes bring an old pair of running shoes for muddy hikes, giving them away or discarding them just before returning home.

The most important thing to remember with regard to clothing is this: you can always buy extra if you find that you underpacked. The only exception is footwear, which you won't find in larger sizes.

Camping equipment

Internal frame backpacks are a must, along with a rain cover or poncho. If your hiking itinerary is limited, consider one of the fabric suitcases that convert into a backpack. A light sleeping bag is all you'll need. Particularly if you're coming to Belize via Mexico, you may want to buy one of the famous, lightweight Yucatecan hammocks that compress so well for travelling. Tents should also be lightweight, with a separate rain fly and plenty of ventilation. As for stoves, I recommend one of the multiple-fuel stoves such as the MXR X-GK, or kerosene-burning stoves such as the Optimus 00 (in a pinch, these will burn unleaded gasoline). Camping Gaz cartridges aren't readily available outside Belize City.

Bring plenty of strong nylon cord for tying and hanging things in camp. A small nesting set of aluminium cooking pots, along with plastic cups and cutlery completes your kitchen. Don't forget a small container of dish soap and a scouring pad. Bring lots of matches; the Toucan brand matches available in Belize are worthless.

You'll need some sort of water purification system, be it chemical treatment or one of the filter kits. See *Chapter 5, Water sterilisation,* page 53, for a list of options.

Miscellaneous

Malaria pills and other medicinals are mentioned in *Chapter 5*. Bring plenty of insect repellent – the best stuff contains 95% DEET (diethyl-meta-toluamide) but persistent use can be damaging to the skin and is now discouraged by many doctors. Many Belizeans highly recommend Skin-So-Soft hand lotion (an Avon product) to repel the sand flies that can ruin a stay in the cayes; we've tried it with mixed success. You may want to bring mosquito coils for camping as well as for the inevitable hotel room or cabin with a missing insect screen. Chinese-made mosquito coils, however, are also easy to find in Belize. If you're scuba diving and anticipate ear-clearing problems due to nasal congestion, bring along the sort of decongestant that doesn't make you drowsy (eg: Sudafed). Sea-sickness prevention (pills, patches or wristbands) may come in handy on long crossings out to the offshore atolls. Even non-hikers should bring a supply of moleskin or plasters for blisters – you'll probably be walking a lot in Belize.

Tampons and contact lens solutions aren't always easy to find in Belize. Bring spare glasses or contact lenses and your glasses prescription. You'll want plenty of sunscreen.

Definitely bring a mask and snorkel. Away from the main tourist circuits like Caye Caulker and San Pedro, they're not often for rent. I recommend that you leave your fins at home unless you're actually scuba diving (and even then I like to rent them). They're unnecessary, take up far too much room in your baggage, and can badly damage coral reefs in the wrong hands (feet, that is).

Serious anglers will definitely want to bring fishing gear from home. See *Chapter 6, Fishing,* page 72, for tackle recommendations.

Buy a fabric money pouch, the kind worn around the waist under clothing, and make sure your passport fits comfortably in it. You'll use a pocket-knife hundreds of times during a trip; try to get one with scissors. A small travel alarm will come in handy when you need to catch that early bus. Film can be quite expensive in Belize, so bring far more than you think you'll shoot. Pack a flashlight (torch). Anyone visiting the rainforest should also bring a headlamp for nature walks at night; they're also useful while camping, keeping both hands free to cook or pitch a tent. Bring plenty of spare batteries, particularly for your camera and headlamp.

Don't forget binoculars. We prefer the light-weight (0.5kg) 7x35 model, although serious birders may want an 8-power model. A compass could be a life-saver if you'll be doing much hiking in the forest.

Plastic water bottles are essential, even if you don't plan on camping a single night. You'll use them on day hikes and trips to deserted cayes. Another invaluable item for camping or long bus rides is an inflatable pillow, available at travel stores.

Finally, we've never brought too many Ziplock plastic sandwich bags, using them for everything from matches to pills to dishwashing equipment.

MONEY

How much to budget for expenses like hotels, meals, and transportation is discussed in *Chapter 6*. You'll want to bring virtually all of it in US travellers' cheques, preferably American Express, in denominations no larger than US$50. All banks accept travellers' cheques, as do local airlines and a growing number of guides. You may want to bring a small stash of US currency for those rare occasions when it comes in handy.

WHEN TO GO

Read the section on climate in *Chapter 1* before deciding on your itinerary. Broadly speaking, the dry season extends from December through May, and most travellers prefer this time for a visit. Yet even within a country as small as Belize, what kind of weather you're having can depend a great deal on which area you're visiting. You'll also want to consider your favourite activities; scuba divers, anglers, canoeists, and orchid lovers, for example, all have their own best seasons for travelling in Belize. Consult *Chapter 6, Activities*.

GETTING INFORMATION

The very latest information on entry requirements, hotels, tours, guides, transportation, events and a whole lot more besides can be obtained from the Belize Tourist Board, New Central Bank Building, Level 2, Gabourel Lane, PO Box 325, Belize City, Belize; tel: 02 31913; fax: 02 31943; toll free in the US and Canada: 1 800 624 0686; email: info@travelbelize.org; web: www.travelbelize.org.

In Germany, the Belize Tourist Board address is Bopserwaldstr, 40-G, D-70184, Stuttgart, Germany; tel: 711 233 947; fax: 711 233 954; email: BTB-GERMANY@t-online.de.

The Belize Tourism Industry Association has put a great deal of energy into promoting the use of the internet. Many regions have their own website domain which is mentioned in each chapter accordingly.

You may also want to consider joining the **South American Explorers Club** 126 Indian Creek Road, Ithaca, NY 14850, USA; tel: 607 277 0488; fax: 607 277 6122; web: www.samexplo.org. They offer trip reports written by members describing travel not just in South America but in Central America as well. The best single map of the country is the International Travel Map of Belize (scale 1:350,000) 4th edition 1998, published by International Travel Maps, 345 West Broadway, Vancouver, V5Y 1P8, Canada; tel: 604 897 3621; fax: 604 879 4521;

itmb@itmb.com; web: www.itmb.com. This map is also available from Stanfords, 12–14 Long Acre, London, WC2E 9LP, tel: 020 7836 1321, or all good map shops. Except for topographical maps, it is best to buy maps before going to Belize, since good ones are seldom available there. In Belize topographical maps are increasingly difficult to get hold of with many of the 1:50,000 maps produced by the Lands and Survey Department office in Belize City now out of print. (see *Chapter 7, Belize City, Information and useful addresses*).

PACKAGE TOURS

It's easy to see most of Belize on your own, arranging local transport and guides as you go. For English speakers there's no language barrier in Belize, making independent travel easier than anywhere else in Central America. Independent travel is almost always cheaper than a package tour and often more rewarding. Nevertheless, there are many situations where travellers will want to consider a package tour for at least part of their trip.

If you're considering a week of scuba diving on the offshore atolls, for instance, you'll often find it much cheaper to arrange a package tour through a dive shop at home or a travel agent specialising in dive travel. By buying large 'blocks' of airline tickets, hotel rooms, and boat space, these operators frequently get rock-bottom prices that you as a lone traveller can't possibly find. Kayak trips, as another example, can generally be done much cheaper through established tour operators than on your own.

But probably the two biggest factors that travellers should consider when weighing the benefits of a package tour are time and convenience. For travellers on a tight schedule, tours allow you to spend more time actually enjoying Belize and less time arranging guides, waiting for public buses, looking for hotels, etc. Besides your time schedule, consider your personal tolerance for these admittedly dreary aspects of travel. Package tours usually avoid the cramped bus ride, the small plane that was fully booked a week ago, the search for other travellers to fill a canoe trip, the house-to-house information gathering that independent travellers must often go through to find their way around a foreign country. For some, these are but minor hassles, an integral part of travelling that makes for good stories back home. For others, these are irritations which get in the way of their trip, irritations that they would gladly pay someone else to deal with.

Package tours invariably stick you with a group of strangers. This could turn out to be a real blessing, especially for travellers with similar interests. Avid birders, for instance, may welcome the chance to meet like-minded souls on a package tour led by an expert ornithologist guide. This may turn out far better than simply wandering the nature reserves on your own, or with a 'pick-up' group of travellers who don't know a toucan from a tanager. You always take your chances, however. Anyone who's done enough package tours will have a horror story or two about 'The Couple from Hell' who nearly ruined the trip for everyone else.

'Study tours' are becoming increasingly popular worldwide. For a price, you participate in a biological, archaeological, or related field study run by qualified university researchers. The fee helps support the research as well as your stay on the study site. In Belize, recent study tours have included coral reef fish research and coastal Maya archaeology. Some people love these trips while others come away disappointed. This all depends on the study itself, the lead researcher, and what kind of person you are. Some would-be scientists, for instance, quickly discover that real archaeology involves a lot more tedium than Indiana Jones would have you believe. Others feel that they're 'sitting on the sidelines' and not allowed to do real science. On the other side, I've heard research leaders complain of volunteers who would rather sunbathe than lend a hand in the research. Lots of travellers swear by study tours; just learn as much about the tour (and yourself) as you can before embarking on one. They're not particularly cheap.

Listed below are a few of the huge number of package tour operators doing trips to Belize. This is an admittedly subjective, abbreviated list of operators whom we've used or heard good things about. Most of these operators offer general-interest tours covering many of Belize's geographic areas. You'll find specialised tour operators for such activities as kayaking, diving, caving, bicycling, listed in *Chapter 6, Activities*. For tour operators specialising in certain areas of Belize, see the appropriate chapter. Again, this is an incomplete list that probably misses some very good operators; for a full listing, write to the Belize Tourist Board, PO Box 325, Belize City, for a copy of their brochure *Belize Visitor's Guide*. As of 1995, all tour guides in Belize must have and display a licence from the Ministry of Tourism and the Environment. Guides must be 18, fluent in English, must have completed a course in Belizean history, ecotourism, geography, art, folklore, first aid and CPR.

Belize

Global Adventure Tours PO Box 244, Belize City; tel: 02 77185; fax: 02 75213; email: bzadventur@btl.net

Jungle River Tours 20 Lover's Lane, PO Box 95, Orange Walk Town; tel: 03 22293.

Maya Travel Services Municipal Airport, Belize City; tel: 02 31623, fax: 02 30585, email: matatravel@btl.net; web: www.mayatravelservices.com

Melmish Mayan Tours PO Box 934, 44 Barrack Road, Belize City; tel: 02 35399.

Native Guide System Water Lane, PO Box 1045, Belize City; tel: 02 75819.

S & L Travel Services & Guided Tours 91 North Front Street, PO Box 700, Belize City; tel: 02 77593/75045; fax: 02 77594; email: sltravel@btl.net; web: www.belizenet.com/sltravel.html.

Travel & Tour Belize PO Box 42, San Pedro Town, Ambergris Caye; tel: 026 2031; fax: 026 2185; email: travltour@btl.net; web: www.belizenet.com/travltour.html

UK

Coral Cay Conservation 154 Clapham Park Road, London, SW4 7DE; tel: 020 7498 6248; fax: 020 7498 8447; email: ccc@coralcay.demon.co.uk; web: www.coralcay.org. Study tours.

Earthwatch 57 Woodstock Road, Oxford, OX2 6HJ; tel: 01865 311600; fax: 01865 311383; email: info@uk.earthwatch.org; web: www.earthwatch.org

Journey Latin America 12/13 Heathfield Terrace, London, W4 4JE; tel: 020 8747 3108; fax: 020 8742 1312; email: sales@journeylatinamerica.co.uk; web: www.journeylatinamerica.co.uk

Reef and Rainforest Tours Ltd 1 The Plains, Totnes, Devon, TQ9 5DR; tel: 01803 866965; fax: 01803 865916; email: reefrain@btinternet.com

USA

Earthwatch Expeditions, Inc Earthwatch Expeditions, 680 Mount Auburn Street, PO Box 9104, Watertown, MA 02471; toll free 1 800 776 0188. Study tours.

Great Trips 1616 West 139th Street, Burnsville, MN 55337; tel: 612 890 4405 or toll-free 1 800 552 3419.

International Expeditions, Inc One Environs Park, Helena, AL 35080; tel: 205 428 1700 or toll-free 1 800 633 4734; email: belize@ietravel.com; web: www.ietravel.com. One of the most highly recommended general tour operators in the US. Many guides are Belizeans, and the company contributes some profits to local conservation groups.

International Zoological Expeditions 210 Washington Street, Sherborn, MA 01770; tel: 508 655 1461; toll-free 1 800 548 5843; fax: 508 655 4445; email: ize2belize@aol.com; web: www.ize2belize.com.

Island Expeditions tel: 604 452 3212 or toll-free: 1 800 667 1630; email: info@islandexpeditions.com web: www.islandexpeditions.com. Specialise in kayaking and sailing in Belize.

Oceanic Society Expeditions Fort Mason Center, Building E, San Francisco, CA 94123; tel: 415 441 1106 or toll-free 1 800 326 7491. Study tours.

Sierra Club 85 Second Street, Second Floor, San Francisco, CA 94105-3441; tel: 415 977 5630.

Smithsonian Odyssey Tours and Research Expeditions Smithsonian Institution, 1100 Jefferson Drive SW, Washington, DC 20560; tel: 202 357 4700 or toll-free 1 800 443 2157 ext 500. Study tours.

University Research Expeditions Program University of California, One Shields Avenue, Davis, CA 95616; tel: 530 752 0692. Study tours.

Wilderness Travel 1102 Ninth Street, Berkeley, CA 94710; tel: 510 558 2488 or toll-free 1 800 368 2794.

Health and Safety

HEALTH

This section deals with health topics particular to travel in Belize and the tropics. All travellers, and especially those camping and hiking in the backcountry, should be prepared to deal with the whole spectrum of common ailments and first aid crises. *Appendix 2, Further Reading* lists several good reference books on staying healthy while travelling.

Before you go
Immunisations

Your preparations to ensure a healthy trip to Belize should include checks on your immunisation status and you'll also need to pack lotions and long clothes to protect you from insect bites and the sun. It is wise to go to a travel clinic a couple of months before departure to arrange immunisations. The only requirement for Belize is a Yellow Fever certificate if you are coming from a Yellow Fever infected area (certain countries in South America and Sub-Saharan Africa). However, for reasons of good health the following vaccines are recommended. Tetanus immunity needs to be boosted every ten years, as does diphtheria. Polio has been eradicated from the Americas (1999) and immunisation is therefore no longer necessary. The majority of travellers are advised to have immunisation against hepatitis A with hepatitis A vaccine (eg: Havrix Monodose, Avaxim). One dose of vaccine lasts for one year and can be boosted to give protection for up to ten years. The course of two injections costs about £100. It is now felt that the vaccine can be used even close to the time of departure and is nearly always preferable to gamma globulin which gives immediate but partial protection for a couple of months. There is a theoretical risk of CJD (the human form of mad cow disease) with this blood-derived product. The newer typhoid vaccines are about 85% effective and should be encouraged unless you are leaving within a few days for a trip of a week or less when the vaccine would not be effective in time. It needs boosting every three years. Immunisation against cholera is currently ineffective, but a cholera exemption certificate is not required in Belize.

Hepatitis B vaccination should be considered for longer trips or for those working in situations where contact with blood is increased. Three injections are ideal which can be given at 0, 4 and 8 weeks prior to travel or if there is insufficient time, then on days 0, 7–14, then 21–28. The only vaccine licensed for the latter more rapid course at the time of printing is Engerix B. The longer course is always to be preferred as immunity is likely to be longer lasting.

Rabies vaccine should be considered for travellers likely to be more than 24 hours away from medical help or who are specifically going to handle animals. Ideally three doses of vaccine should be taken over a four week period before departure, but two doses are better than one, and one is still better than nothing at all. Contrary to popular belief this is a relatively painless vaccination!

It is always wise to be up to date with BCG for tuberculosis (most people from the UK will have been vaccinated between the ages of 11-14). It is more important for trips of 8 weeks or longer, but note that it can take this length of time for the vaccine to be given. Another good reason to plan your trip well in advance.

Travel clinics
UK
British Airways Travel Clinic and Immunisation Service 156 Regent St, London W1, tel: 020 7439 9584. This place also sells travellers' supplies and has a branch of Stanfords travel book and map shop. There are now BA clinics all around Britain and three in South Africa. To find your nearest one, phone 01276 685040.

Nomad Travel Pharmacy and Vaccination Centre 3–4 Wellington Terrace, Turnpike Lane, London N8 0PX; tel: 020 8889 7014.

Thames Medical 157 Waterloo Rd, London SE1 8US; tel: 020 7902 9000. Competitively priced, one-stop travel health service. All profits go to their affiliated company InterHealth which provides health care for overseas workers on Christian projects.

Trailfinders Immunisation Centre 194 Kensington High St, London W8 7RG; tel: 020 7938 3999. Also 254–284 Sauchiehall St, Glasgow G2 3EH; tel: 0141 353 0066.

MASTA (Medical Advisory Service for Travellers Abroad) Keppel St, London WC1 7HT; tel: 09068 224100. This is a premium-line number, charged at 50p per minute.

USA
Centers for Disease Control 1600 Clifton Road, Atlanta, GA 30333; tel: 877 FYI TRIP; 800 311 3435; web: www.cdc.gov/travel. This organisation is the central source of travel information in the USA. Each summer they publish the invaluable *Health Information for International Travel* which is available from the Division of Quarantine at the above address.

Connaught Laboratories PO Box 187, Swiftwater, PA 18370; tel: 800 822 2463. They will send a free list of specialist tropical-medicine physicians in your state.

IAMAT (International Association for Medical Assistance to Travelers) 736 Center St, Lewiston, NY 14092. A non-profit organisation which provides lists of English-speaking doctors abroad.

Australia
TMVC Tel: 1300 65 88 44; website: www.tmvc.com.au. TMVC has 20 clinics in Australia, New Zealand and Thailand, including:

Brisbane Dr Deborah Mills, Qantas Domestic Building, 6th floor, 247 Adelaide St, Brisbane, QLD 4000; tel: 7 3221 9066; fax: 7 3321 7076

Melbourne Dr Sonny Lau, 393 Little Bourke St, 2nd floor, Melbourne, VIC 3000; tel: 3 9602 5788; fax: 3 9670 8394.

Sydney Dr Mandy Hu, Dymocks Building, 7th floor, 428 George St, Sydney, NSW 2000; tel: 2 221 7133; fax: 2 221 8401.

South Africa
There are four **British Airways travel clinics** in South Africa: *Johannesburg*, tel: (011) 807 3132; *Cape Town*, tel: (021) 419 3172; *Knysna*, tel: (044) 382 6366; *East London*, tel: (0431) 43 2359.

Malaria
Malaria is potentially fatal and is by far the most serious health risk to travellers in tropical countries. Every year the disease kills between one and two million people worldwide. No prophylactic drug will totally prevent the disease, but there are several that will severely reduce your chances of acquiring malaria, and are worth

taking. Check with a doctor specialising in travel health or tropical diseases before deciding on anti-malaria prophylaxis for your trip. Malaria is especially dangerous in pregnancy, so pregnant women should always seek advice before travelling. Drug-resistant strains of *Plasmodium*, the one-celled protozoan parasite that causes malaria, have not been reported in Belize yet. Consequently, chloroquine is still the drug of choice. Travellers from the UK will be given this in the form of two tablets (300mg base) taken at the same time weekly (branded Avloclor or Nivaquine). Travellers from Europe may be given daily nivaquine, which is not available in the UK. For those who are unable to take chloroquine (eg: epileptics or people with severe psoriasis), two tablets of proguanil (Paludrine) taken daily is an alternative. Ideally chloroquine should be started one week before departure, taken through the trip and for four weeks after arriving home (proguanil can be started just the day before). All malaria tablets are best taken with food and plenty of fluid in the evening to reduce side effects like indigestion and nausea. Since no drug is 100% effective, you should be vigilant for symptoms of malaria which can develop from seven days into your trip and up to one year after your return. You should go immediately to a doctor if you develop a temperature of over 38°C, regardless of any other symptoms that may be present. Some travellers who know they will be further away from medical help may wish to carry a treatment for malaria. The current recommended regime is Quinine with Fansidar, but specific up-to-date advice should be taken, and the drugs purchased preferably before travel. In Belize, the National Malaria Service can be reached at 02 44362 if you need advice while you are there.

Rabies

Rabies is carried by all mammals (beware the village dogs and small monkeys that are used to being fed in the parks) and is passed on to humans through a bite or a lick of an open wound. You must always assume any animal is rabid (unless personally known to you) and seek medical help as soon as possible. In the interim, scrub the wound with soap and bottled/boiled water then pour on a strong iodine or alcohol solution. This helps stop the rabies virus entering the body and will guard against wound infections including tetanus.

If you are exposed as described, then treatment should be given as soon as possible, but it is never too late to seek help as the incubation period for rabies can be very long. Those who have not been immunised will need a full course of injections together with rabies immunoglobulin (RIG), but this product is expensive (approximately US$800) and may be hard to come by. That is another reason why pre-exposure vaccination should be encouraged in travellers who are planning to visit more remote areas.

Tell the doctor if you have had pre-exposure vaccine as this will change the treatment you receive. Remember if you contract rabies, mortality is 100% and death from rabies is probably one of the worst ways to go.

Insurance

If you've got health insurance, ask your provider if you're covered while travelling in Belize. Write to IAMAT (International Association for Medical Assistance to Travellers), 417 Center St, Lewiston, NY 14092; tel: 716 754 4883; web: www.sentex.net/~iamat/index.html) for advice on this topic and a list of recommended doctors in Belize. Scuba enthusiasts should consider the divers' insurance plan offered by DAN (Divers Alert Network). This is a non-profit safety organisation located at The Peter B. Bennett Center, 6 West Colony Place, Durham, NC 27705, USA; tel: 1 800 443 2671; email: dan@diversalertnetwork.org; web: www.diversalertnetwork.org). It covers hyperbaric chamber treatment and emergency air evacuation to the chamber. See *Chapter 6, Scuba diving* for more information.

In Belize
Local medical facilities
Belize has reliable hospitals and clinics throughout the country. Services are, on the whole, far better than in neighbouring Central American countries, and outpatient care is free at the public hospitals. The few travellers we've met who needed medical help were satisfied with the doctors and facilities. Belize City General opened in 1995 with all new facilities. The major health care facility in each district is listed below, but there are also numerous rural and mobile health clinics:

Karl Heusner Memorial Hospital Belize City; tel: 02 77251
Belmopan Hospital tel: 08 22264
Corozal Hospital tel: 04 22076
Dangriga Hospital tel: 05 22078
Punta Gorda Hospital tel: 07 22026
San Ignacio Hospital Cayo; tel: 09 22066
Orange Walk Hospital tel: 03 22072
Caye Caulker Health Center tel: 022 2166
Lion's Clinic San Pedro; tel: 026 2073
Hyperbaric Chamber San Pedro; tel: 026 2854/2073

Insects and insect-borne diseases
Malaria, dengue fever and Chagas' disease aren't all that common in Belize, even among residents. Nevertheless, all three are reported in Belize, and all three are transmitted by insects. The protozoal disease, malaria, is transmitted via the bite of an infected female *Anopheles* mosquito. It is especially prevalent in the Cayo, Corozal, Stann Creek and Toledo Districts. Over 10,000 cases were reported in 1994, but no fatalities. Since then figures have decreased dramatically with just 1,936 cases in 1998. Dengue fever is a viral disease that is increasingly common worldwide, and is also transmitted by mosquitoes – in this case, *Aedes aegypti*. Chagas' disease, another protozoal ailment, is much less common, particularly in travellers. The parasite infects humans thanks to the messy eating habits of several species of reduviid bugs. The bug defecates as it bites, and parasites usually enter the bloodstream when the victim scratches the wound.

Avoiding contact with host insects is the most obvious way to stay healthy. Repellent with at least 50% DEET is best throughout Belize, including the cayes, rainforest, and towns (the Belize Zoo must surely rank as one of the world's all-time mosquito havens!). People who are especially prone to being bitten should consider 100% DEET (eg: Repel 100). You should cover up, particularly at night, with long-sleeved shirts and long pants. Mosquito coils, if you can stand the smell, work well in unscreened hotel rooms and even when camping; Chinese-made coils are widely available in Belize. Campers without a tent will need a mosquito net. The free-standing type is the most practical and can also be used in hotel rooms without insect screening. During the evening in the rainforest, wear long-sleeved shirts, long pants, and try tucking your pant legs into your socks.

Anopheles mosquitoes bite mostly at night (from dusk till dawn) and tend to fly low to the ground, but don't let your guard down during the day because that's when *Aedes*, the vector for dengue fever, likes to feed. *Aedes* is an urban insect, favouring towns and cities, but both mosquitoes live in a variety of habitats. Unless you spend a lot of time sleeping unprotected in mud huts, the favourite haunt of the nocturnal reduviid bugs, you aren't likely to contract Chagas' disease.

Thankfully, most of your insect encounters will be of the merely irritating kind. Sandflies ('no-see-ums') plague many of the cayes and coastal areas, and standard repellents don't seem to be of much use. Many Belizeans swear by Avon's Skin-So-Soft hand lotion, available in many local drug stores. A stiff wind deters them, but watch out for breezeless areas like mangrove swamps. It's unlikely you'll leave Belize without being bitten by at least one 'doctor fly'. A yellowish relative of the common horse fly, the doctor fly takes a big bite of flesh but is more a nuisance than a danger. As with all insect bites, avoid infection by trying not to scratch them; calamine lotion may help.

The macaw or warble-fly lays her eggs on mosquitoes so that when the mosquito feeds the warble infants can burrow into the victim's skin. Here they grow, feasting happily until they mature to cause a boil-like inflammation that will need surgical removal. Now there's another reason to avoid mosquito bites. Jiggers or sandfleas (niguas) are minute flesh-feasters, not to be confused with chiggers (see below). They latch on if you walk bare-foot in contaminated places (locals will know where), and set up home under the skin of the foot, usually at the side of a toenail where they cause a painful boil-like swelling. These need picking out by a local expert; if the distended flea bursts during eviction the wound should be dowsed in spirit, alcohol or kerosene otherwise more jiggers will infest you. Chiggers and chivacoa are both ticks and these pestilential little mites can be kept off by applying repellent (even on your boots) and tucking pants/trousers into socks. Chiggers are related to little red harvest mites that run around in the summer in Europe. The Central American version, though is incredibly irritating and the itching stays with you long after the mite has gone. Eurax cream (crotamiton) or calamine lotion is most likely to help, plus exposing the itchy part and cool sponging. Africanised honey bees ('killer bees') were first shipped to Brazil in 1957, and it's taken them two decades to expand their range as far north as Belize. Since their arrival in 1987, they've been blamed for the deaths of two Belizeans. Many people assume that Africanised honey bees pack a special wallop with their sting. In fact, their venom is similar to that of the North American variety – itself a European import – and they carry less of it. The crucial difference is that the Africanised bee colony, if provoked, can inflict up to ten times as many stings as their more docile northern neighbours. Most 'killer bee' reports come from Toledo District, although these are hard to confirm – telling the difference between the two honey bees requires laboratory dissection. There's not much you can do, except follow local advice on areas to avoid, and leave if you run into bees of any kind.

Travellers' diarrhoea (TD)

Many authorities claim that TD is due to faecally contaminated food or water, while a growing number suggest that the cause could be a simple change in diet, heat and humidity, and the stress of visiting a foreign land. (Witness the fact that visitors from Third World countries frequently get sick when they visit our own, spotlessly hygienic nations.) Realistically it is more likely to be a combination of the two. Everyone agrees on one point – sooner or later, you're bound to get a case of TD. Besides diarrhoea itself, symptoms may include stomach cramps, nausea, bloating, fever and a general malaise. It's not the end of the world, and the problem usually resolves itself without specific treatment within a few days. But to lessen the risks, doctors recommend that you follow these guidelines: PEEL IT, BOIL IT, COOK IT OR FORGET IT!

Don't drink tap water or even brush your teeth with it unless it's chlorinated and considered safe. When in doubt use bottled water if even mouth wash. Likewise, avoid ice cubes, iced drinks, ice cream, popsicles and dairy products. Don't eat uncooked or warmed-over food. Don't eat raw vegetables, especially unwashed salads, or any fruit you haven't peeled yourself. The prejudice against street vendors may well be unwarranted since their food is often freshly cooked, sells fast, and is visible at all times. Common sense tells you to avoid stalls that are surrounded by flies and stray dogs! Restaurant meals, on the other hand, are prepared out of sight, and are often reheated. Reject any meal that is not piping hot when it is brought to the table.

Remedies for TD abound. The trend nowadays is away from the old 'quick cures' like Lomotil, Imodium, Kaopectate, Enterovioform, Kaolin and the host of other medicines available in Central America. Most of these may prolong the problem and therefore make things worse. Enterovioform can have serious side-effects, and Kaolin apparently interferes with the absorption of the anti-malarial chloroquine. Only resort to the others if you really need a short-term 'cork', such as during a long bus trip.

Most doctors now recommend a simple regimen of rest and liquids. Avoiding dehydration and replacing body salts is paramount, so drink something even if you're not particularly thirsty. The USCDC recommends the following drink for sufferers of diarrhoea: Mix eight ounces of fruit juice with a teaspoon of sugar or honey and a pinch of salt. In a second glass, dissolve one quarter teaspoon of baking soda in eight ounces of water. Alternate sips from these two glasses, and repeat the ritual at least four times a day. Carry plastic sachets or film canisters of baking soda, salt and sugar, just so you're ready. Alternatively ready made rehydration sachets can be bought before you go, for example, Electrolade or Dioralyte.

Drink as much water and/or fruit juice as possible (at least 3 litres a day), but avoid alcohol (including beer), caffeine and foods that are spicy or greasy. Avoiding solid food for 24–48 hours often speeds recovery from TD. Cramps are normal during a bout of TD, but a high fever, extremely painful cramps and/or blood in the stool may signal dysentery usually requiring treatment with antibiotics. Wherever possible seek medical advice before starting them but if this is not possible then a three-day course of one of the antibiotics, ciprofloxacin (500mg twice a day) or norfloxacin can be used. Be careful about what you take from local pharmacies: drugs like chloramphenicol (sold as Chloromycetin, Catilan or Enteromycetin) and the sulpha antibiotics, (eg: streptomagma) have too many serious side effects to be worth the risk in treating simple diarrhoea. Do not take them!

AIDS
Safe sex

Travel is a time when we may enjoy sexual adventures, especially when alcohol reduces inhibitions. Remember that the risks of sexually transmitted infection are high, whether you sleep with fellow travellers or locals. About half of HIV infections in British heterosexuals are acquired abroad. Use condoms or femidoms and buy them before you leave, to ensure they are of a high standard. If you notice any genital ulcers or discharge get treatment promptly; sexually transmitted infections increase the risk of acquiring HIV. AIDS is known as SIDA in Spanish. HIV is not uncommon in the Americas and it is most prevalent in areas visited by tourists. As of 1996, roughly 100 Belizeans have died of AIDS, and some estimates put the number of HIV+ Belizeans at more than 3,000. While efforts are being made to counter the problem, getting an up-to-date picture of the current situation is difficult.

Other problems
Skin infections
Skin infections set in remarkably easily in warm climates and any mosquito-bite or small skin-nick is a potential entry point for bacteria. It is essential, therefore, to clean and cover even the slightest wound.

Creams are not as effective as a good drying antiseptic such as dilute iodine, potassium permanganate (a few crystals in half a cup of water) or crystal (or gentian) violet. One of these should be available in most towns. If the wound starts to throb, or becomes red and the redness starts to spread or the wound oozes, and especially if you develop a fever, five days of antibiotics will probably be needed: flucloxacillin (250mg capsules four times a day) or cloxacillin (500mg four times a day). For those allergic to penicillin, erythromycin (500mg twice a day) should help. See a doctor if it does not start to improve within 36-48 hours of starting treatment. Fungal infections also get a hold easily in hot moist climates so wear 100% cotton socks and underwear and shower frequently. An itchy rash in the groin or flaking or soreness between the toes is likely to be a fungal infection. This needs treatment with an antifungal cream such as Canesten (clotrimazole) or if this is not available try Whitfield's ointment (compound benzoicacid ointment) or crystal violet (although this will turn you purple).

Sun and heat
Prickly heat
A fine pimply rash on the trunk is likely to be heat rash; cool showers, dabbing (not rubbing) dry and talc will help; if it's bad you may need to check into an air-conditioned hotel room for a while. Slowing down to a relaxed schedule, wearing only loose baggy 100% cotton clothes and sleeping naked under a fan will reduce the problem.

Protection from the sun
The incidence of skin cancer is rocketing as Caucasians travel more and spend more time exposing themselves to the sun. Sun exposure also ages the skin, making people prematurely wrinkly; cover up with long loose clothes, put on plenty of suncream and wear a hat when you can. Keep out of the sun during the middle of the day and, if you must expose yourself, build up gradually from 20 minutes per day. Be especially careful of sun reflected off water and wear a T-shirt and lots of waterproof SPF 15 suncream when swimming; snorkelling often leads to scorched backs and thighs so also wear a T-shirt and Bermuda shorts.

Heat stroke
This is most likely within the first week or ten days of arriving in a hotter, more humid climate. It is important to slow down and drink plenty and avoid hard physical exercise in the middle of the day, particularly at first. Treatment for heat exhaustion is rest in the shade and sponging, plus lots to drink.

Sea and freshwater problems
Foot protection: If you wear old plimsolls sneakers or jellies on the beach or riverside, you will avoid injury and you are less likely to get venomous fish spines (and jiggers and geography worms) in the feet. If you tread on a venomous fish, soak the foot in hot (but not scalding) water until some time after the pain subsides; this may be for 20-30 minutes submersion in all. Take the foot out of the water to top up otherwise you may also scald the injured foot. If the pain returns re-immerse the foot. Once the

venom has been heat-inactivated, get a doctor to check and remove any bits of fish spines in the wound.

Snakebite

Of the 51 snake species found in Belize, only nine are venomous. And of these nine, the majority are either nocturnal, shy, or of such a small size that a bite isn't likely to penetrate clothing. Only one species is widely feared – the yellow-jaw tommygoff, or fer-de-lance (*Bothrops asper*). You'll find more information on these snakes and their habits in *Chapter 3, Reptiles*. Don't forget that many non-venomous snakes bite. Remember too that even the venomous species don't always inject poison with every bite; after feeding, for example, venom sacs are often depleted. In short, you need to be careful about venomous snakes, but don't let unwarranted paranoia keep you from enjoying Belize's rainforest. Encounters with snakes are rare, and most naturalists count themselves lucky when they've seen one.

Watch your step in the forest, especially near tree falls and large piles of leaf litter beneath trees. Be particularly cautious at night. If bitten, try to stay calm, remembering that most snakebite victims recover without treatment. Cleanse the wound, try to note the snake's characteristics for identification, and attempt to get to a doctor. Do not try to apply a tourniquet or open the wound with a razor – both can do far more harm than the bite itself. Many authorities now recommend the syringe-like suction devices (such as the X-Tractor). If used soon after the bite occurs, they help in removing some of the venom.

Scorpions, spiders, and ticks

Scorpions are common in most parts of the country, including the coast, and most rural Belizeans have been stung at least once. Just be careful when walking around in sandals (particularly under trees or near leaf litter), and follow the standard advice of checking shoes for sleeping scorpions before putting them on. Belize has black widow spiders and tarantulas, but bites are neither common nor particularly dangerous to healthy adults. After camping or hiking in the forest, check yourself for ticks. Some trails, such as the one leading to Victoria Peak, are real tick havens, and you'll be amazed at how these tiny arachnids can get inside your clothing despite tightly buttoned collars and long sleeves.

Sharks and other marine animals

Most experienced scuba divers and snorkellers in Belize consider themselves lucky if they spot a single large shark during their trip. In fact, there are only a handful of dive sites where guides can confidently assure divers they'll see sharks on a regular basis. Shark attacks are even rarer, and one expert has noted that many more sutures are expended on pop-top lacerations at beaches than on shark bites. Bleeding from a wound, diving solo, or spearfishing increase the risks, but presumably you won't be doing any of these. Ironically, recreational divers and snorkellers most often get in trouble with the docile nurse shark. Resting passively beneath coral ledges, nurse sharks seem to invite prodding, poking, and tail-grabbing. They'll only take so much abuse, however, so leave them to their slumber.

Moray eels commonly inhabit the reef, but they won't be a problem unless you stick a hand into their crevice or attempt to feed them. You'll see barracudas frequently while diving or snorkelling, but attacks are extremely rare. Don't wear shiny jewellery, which reportedly attracts barracudas.

Stingrays are common along particular stretches of shoreline. They lie buried in the upper layer of sandy or muddy bottoms, and can inflict an extremely painful wound if stepped upon. Locals invariably know these areas, so ask before taking a dip where you don't see any bathers. If there's no one about to ask, play it safe by shuffling your feet along the bottom; this will chase any stingrays away and eliminate the danger of stomping on one.

Stepping on sea urchin spines can cause a painful wound, but snorkellers and divers shouldn't be that close to the reef in the first place (see *Chapter 3, Coral reef etiquette*). Contrary to rumour, Belizean species aren't venomous, although the wound can easily become infected. Only *Diadema*, the long-spined black variety, is of any real concern and it isn't common following the recent (and mysterious) die-off that devastated Caribbean populations. Try to remove the spine fragments and treat the wound until healed with an antibiotic. Urchin spine infections can become quite serious, so see a doctor immediately if the wound doesn't heal quickly. Coral scratches can also become infected if not cared for immediately. But once again, you shouldn't be touching the reef; this advice applies as well to fire coral, a finger-like variety that causes a temporary burning sensation upon contact. Jellyfish larvae, sometimes referred to as 'sea lice', can cause skin rashes and itching. Wear a thin wet suit or Lycra body suit when snorkelling or diving.

Water sterilisation
If you're planning on camping, decide on a water sterilisation programme that suits your needs and budget (see below) and buy the necessary chemicals or equipment before you leave.

Much of the tap water in Belize is chlorinated and perfectly safe to drink. Exceptions have been noted in the sections on various towns throughout this book. Cisterns holding rainwater are usually safe, although some can become contaminated. Locals will usually learn this very quickly, so it's worth listening out for advice.

Only campers who plan to spend several days in the bush, or those visiting Maya Indian villages really need to worry about sterilising water in Belize. Hepatitis A, dysentery and giardiasis can all contaminate water in the backcountry. You can't tell by looking; the foulest swamp water may be perfectly safe, while that pristine, babbling mountain stream may harbour giardia.

Boiling water for 5–10min should destroy all viruses and bacteria. This method works without fail, but also puts a big dent in your fuel supply. A second option is chemical treatment with iodine. Iodine tablets such as Potable-Aqua, Coughlan's or Globaline have been proven to deliver 8ppm of iodine, which effectively kills all microorganisms. Many medical professionals now advise you to let the treated water stand for at least two hours before using; that's much longer than the usual 30 minutes the manufacturers recommend. Iodine leaves an unmistakable taste, neutralising

QUICK TICK REMOVAL
Ticks (*garrapatas*) transmit a variety of unpleasant infections, but if you get the tick off promptly and whole the chances of disease transmission are much reduced. Manoeuvre your finger and thumb so that you can pinch the tick's mouthparts as close to your skin as possible and slowly and steadily pull away at right angles to your skin. This often hurts. Jerking or twisting will increase the chances of damaging the tick which in turn increases the chances of disease transmission. Once the tick is off, dowse the little wound with alcohol (local spirit, pisco etc, is excellent) or iodine. An area of spreading redness around the bite site or a rash or fever coming on a few days or more after the bite indicates a trip to a doctor is required.

tablets are available, but are costly so try either a pinch of sodium thiosulphate (available in pharmacies and photographic equipment shops) or powdered fruit drink to make the water palatable. Using iodine is safe in the short term, but is not recommended throughout a long trip and is contraindicated in pregnancy.

Chlorine tablets such as Halazone disintegrate within a week of opening the container, and few medical authorities still recommend them.

A number of water filters are available and more recently have undergone rigorous field testing. Many experts advise a combination of filtration and chemical treatment. Take advice from a backpacking store or one of the travel clinics mentioned earlier.

Natural remedies
Within the last few years, Belize has become something of a world focus for natural plant-based remedies. Rainforest plants have been used for centuries, of course, to effectively treat everything from malaria to bleeding wounds (even the British Army teaches 'bush medicine' during its jungle survival courses in Belize) but only recently has Belize stepped into the media limelight. Much of the credit for this resurgence goes to the Ix Chel Tropical Research Foundation, a non-profit organisation that has rekindled interest in Maya bush medicine. The Foundation holds seminars and workshops on a regular basis, publishes a newsletter, and sells natural remedies on site and by mail. You can also visit the Ix Chel Farm and tour their nature trail of medicinal plants; see *Chapter 8, Excursions*. A number of natural healers (including 'snake doctors') ply their trade in Belize, and Ix Chel is a good place to start if you'd like recommendations. Having said this there is little or no hard data on the efficacy of some of the preparations, so doctors in the UK will still recommend traditional medicines and vaccines.

SAFETY
Outside of an actual war zone, there was a time when Belize City was regarded as the diciest 2,000 acres in all of Central America – a reputation that has managed to taint the rest of the country. We recently met a Dutch couple, nervously entering Belize's Cayo District from Guatemala, who were hell-bent on reaching Mexico before dusk via a non-stop bus. They clearly expected to be robbed the moment they stepped across the border into Belize!

It's no use denying that Belize City can be dangerous at certain times and places – or that crime hasn't spread to other parts of the country as well. Crime was very much on the increase in Belize in the mid-1990s, much of it linked to drugs and the economic recession. Travellers have been robbed at gunpoint in formerly placid spots like Caye Caulker. And Orange Walk didn't earn the nickname 'Rambo Town' because Sylvester Stallone paid a visit. But the bulk of the country – indeed, most places where travellers will want to spend their time – remained quite safe. Official figures now say crime levels are falling. That doesn't mean there are no problems in Belize, but travellers should have no problems if they use some common sense, read the tips in this book, and follow local advice.

See the section on Belize City in *Chapter 7* for a few cautionary tips.

Ask locals for advice before wandering around Orange Walk Town at night. Robberies and a rape have occurred at the Blue Hole National Park, but now a guard has been stationed there. In the past robbers have accosted hikers walking up the hill to Xunantunich Maya ruins (although a free guide now accompanies visitors). The dark beaches of San Pedro have been the scene of several robberies and a recent double murder. When visiting areas that are suspect, try to go with a group of three or more; it's probably no coincidence that the few travellers we've met who were robbed happened to be walking alone at night in Belize City. Wear a money pouch beneath your clothing, carry most of your money in travellers' cheques, and avoid carrying large amounts of cash. Don't wear expensive jewellery or watches. Take taxis after dark in Belize City, and don't change money on the street.

Simple theft can be a problem in any place where travellers congregate. Ask hotel owners to hold your valuables or place them in a safe. Be especially careful when camping in frequently-visited sites. In this case, try to leave someone behind to watch camp while you're exploring, or else carry virtually everything in your pack. Tents on seemingly isolated cayes like Laughing Bird have been ransacked while the owners were off snorkelling.

Be sure to keep a list of your travellers' cheque numbers and a photocopy of your passport's first page.

The government has recently stepped up the war on crime, with tougher criminal sentencing and a plan to conduct warrantless stop-and-search procedures in high risk areas, a controversial subject. Tourist Police have been introduced in many of the country's larger towns, along with some new measures that specifically address crimes against visitors, such as speedier trials and evidence gathering following thefts.

Drugs

Marijuana is as easy to come by in Belize City as a Belikin beer. That much hasn't changed since the mid-1970s, when hippies on the Gringo Trail made detours to Belize specifically to buy and smoke pot. Nowadays, however, cocaine and crack have entered the market in a big way, and the government is actively pursuing an educational anti-drug campaign. Posters quote the Belizean national motto – 'Under the Mahogany Tree We Flourish' – but add 'Under the Ganja Tree We Perish'. Drugs are especially common in Belize City, Orange Walk Town (the acknowledged capital of the Belizean narcotics trade), Caye Caulker, Ambergris Caye and Corozal. But we've also been offered cocaine in places as outwardly bucolic as Monkey River Town.

Belize now serves as a cocaine transhipment route from Colombia. Estimates on the number of planeloads leaving each month range from three to thirty. All sea plane traffic has been banned, several airfields closed, and steel posts were erected alongside stretches of the Northern Highway to discourage its use as a clandestine landing strip. (They were quickly bent aside by the traffickers.) In January 1995, a police raid in Belize City netted US$7 million worth of cocaine bound for the US via Mexico. The US Drug Enforcement Administration has pressured Belize into an aerial spraying programme for marijuana, one that reportedly damages many legitimate crops. Jail sentences and fines are stiff, but business appears to go on as usual in Belize City. Unless you're elderly or look like a DEA agent, it's almost impossible to walk the streets of the former capital without several offers. Pebble-sized balls of 'Belize Breeze', wrapped in aluminium foil, go for about US$0.50.

Harmless as such a purchase may seem – and granted that you're not likely to be caught – every conscientious traveller needs honestly to consider the long-term social and economic consequences that buying drugs has on people.

In Belize

COST OF LIVING/TRAVELLING

Belize remains for travellers the most expensive country in Central America. The difference in the cost of living will be most dramatic if you cross the border from Guatemala, but even Mexico's Yucatan Peninsula is noticeably cheaper than Belize. If it's any comfort, think of Belize as a displaced Caribbean isle rather than as part of Central America; in that sense it's a real bargain. The Belizean economy is also more stable than most of its neighbours' (particularly in regard to the US dollar), so you aren't likely to be in for any unpleasant surprises between planning your trip and taking it. The real cost of travel, for instance, doesn't appear to have changed dramatically in Belize since Jayne's first trip in 1975.

Obviously, how much you'll spend depends on your style of travel, so it's risky printing any sort of all-purpose cost-per-day estimate. For food and shelter, however, you probably can't get by on much less than US$35 pp per day, with about US$15 of that spent on food. That estimate assumes double-occupancy hotel rates at the cheapest joints; obviously, single travellers will spend a bit more. Add to that basic daily figure your cost estimates for transportation, guided trips, and special activities based on the sections below.

MONEY MATTERS

The Belize dollar, first issued in 1974, is stabilized at an exchange rate of US$1 = BZ$2. Notes of 1, 2, 5, 10, 20, 50 and 100 dollars have been issued, as well as coins worth 1, 5, 10 and 25 cents. You'll sometimes hear the 25-cent piece referred to as a 'shilling'.

New one and two dollar coins are being introduced and the notes are due to be phased out but no schedule has been put in place – both are accepted at the time of writing.

US dollars are frequently accepted, particularly in San Pedro and the dive/fishing resorts in the offshore atolls. Some hotels, tour operators and guide services quote their prices in US$. If you are uncertain make absolutely certain to find out if the price you're being quoted is in BZ$ or US$. We've known travellers who've had some unpleasant surprises when paying bills because of this misunderstanding. When seeking clarification you may be subject to a stern reproach. Quoting prices in US$ may make it easier for the international traveller but you are in Belize. Many travel guides, this one included, quote prices in US$. For the 3rd edition we have used Belizean dollars (BZ$) throughout unless no price is available in local currency.

Both US currency and travellers' cheques can be exchanged readily for Belize dollars at banks in all the major towns. The difference in exchange rates offered for cheques and cash is negligible, generally about 2% less for cheques. Bank opening hours vary across the country, but they are generally open Monday through Thursday from 09.00–13.00 and on Friday, 08.00–16.30. Some are beginning to open on Saturday mornings as well – the bottom line is go to the bank in the morning if you don't want to get caught high and dry. They'll want to see your passport when cashing travellers' cheques.

One way round the confusion – and the queues – is to take advantage of the ATMs popping up all over the place. VISA and MasterCard can be used at different banks and in the country overall there appears to be no preference at present.

Credit cards such as VISA or MasterCard are useful mostly when paying for such things as guided boat/fishing/diving/jungle trips. Although the expensive lodges and hotels accept credit cards, few budget hotels do, nor do most restaurants. A surcharge is added to credit-card transactions.

Many (but not all) hotels will accept your personal cheque through the mail as a deposit on a room reservation.

TRANSPORT
Road
There are only three main highways in Belize: the New Northern Highway, running from the Mexican border south through Corozal and Orange Walk to Belize City; the Western Highway, which heads toward the Guatemalan border from Belize City, passing Belmopan and San Ignacio (Cayo) along the way; and the Hummingbird/Southern Highway, which leaves from Belmopan, runs southeast to Dangriga, and finally to Punta Gorda, the southernmost town in Belize. Both the New Northern and Western Highways are mostly flat, well-paved, two-lane roads. The Southern Highway, however, is an unimproved road notorious for its potholes, deep furrows, and steep inclines. At times during the rainy season, it becomes a quagmire, virtually impassable for all but 4WD vehicles and some trucks and buses. As of 1995, all but about 40km of the Humminghbird Highway near Belmopan has been resurfaced. The drive from Belmopan to Dangriga, always the most beautiful in the country, is now pleasant except for a middle stretch of rubble of around 20kms which should be resurfaced soon. Financing for the Southern Highway south of Dangriga has been arranged and resurfacing has begun but will not be completed for several years.

In addition to these three main highways connecting the seven main towns, there are a number of unimproved roads serving the smaller communities. Only a few will be of interest to the traveller: the Old Northern Highway, a pot-holed blacktop road which accesses the Maya site of Altun Ha; the road to Bermudian Landing, home of the Community Baboon Sanctuary; logging roads in the Mountain Pine Ridge; a coastal route linking Placencia with the Southern Highway; the road from Orange Walk to the Sarteneja Peninsula; the New Coastal Highway, a badly washboarded 75km 'shortcut' from Belize City to Dangriga; and a series of dirt roads connecting Toledo District's Maya villages.

Buses
Within mainland Belize, the cheapest way to get from place to place is on public buses. Buses leave several times daily from Belize City for all of the six major towns in Belize: Corozal, Orange Walk Town, Belmopan, San Ignacio (Cayo), Dangriga and Punta Gorda. Departures are far more frequent for the towns served by good highways to the north and west. Buses on the tortuous runs south to Dangriga and Punta Gorda leave only a couple of times daily. Many buses to Corozal continue on past the border to Chetumal, Mexico. Four companies, all reliable, monopolise most of the major routes: Batty, Venus, Z-Line and Novelo's. A number of smaller, independent – and in some cases, highly unreliable – buses operate on the backroads to the less-travelled areas.

By Central American standards, Belizean buses (at least those of the major four companies) are models of cleanliness, roominess and efficiency. Gone are some of the charming Latin touches – the kitschy Saint Christopher statuettes and Christ medallions – as well as some of the less-than-charming ones. I have yet to see, for example, a live chicken ride a Belizean bus. Many Belizean buses, however, are surplus American schoolbuses, which means that room for luggage is very limited. Racks above the seats (when they exist at all) are too small for most large rucksacks. In many cases you'll either stuff your packs and bags in a big pile in the back of the bus or hold them on your laps. Except on the longer runs, you won't be allowed off the bus. Food and drink vendors are never far from a bus that's making even the briefest stop, however.

You can buy tickets several days ahead for most runs (although it often isn't necessary except during holidays). Sample prices and approximate travel times: Corozal-Belize City (BZ$8, 3hrs); Belize City-San Ignacio (BZ$1.90, 2hrs 30min); Belize City-Punta Gorda (BZ$22, 8-10hrs). Belizean buses generally run on time. Seats are reserved, although some buses adopt a rather laissez-faire attitude in this respect. You can expect service to be fast and efficient when travelling the well-paved Northern and Western Highways. Travel times south of Dangriga are entirely dependent on the rains. Bus schedules are listed in the appropriate area chapters, but service on Sundays is limited throughout Belize.

To reach more off-the-beaten-track destinations by bus, you'll be relying on small, independent companies. In many cases, local 'bus lines' consist of a single surplus school bus, owned and operated by a resident and his children. In other cases, you'll find yourself riding in the back of a flatbed truck recently outfitted with a canvas cover and makeshift benches. Schedules are rarely available (perhaps a good thing considering how frequently they change), but I've attempted to provide as much information as possible in the appropriate area chapters. For updates, your best bet is to call the local community telephone operator (see *Telephone* below).

Rental cars

Renting a car in Belize is expensive and seldom worth it. A standard 4WD vehicle, for example, will run you at least US$75 per day, often closer to US$100, and as much as US$125. This doesn't include petrol, which costs roughly US$0.69 per litre for regular (US$2.60 per US gallon). It also doesn't cover Collision Damage Waiver insurance. (Reserving in the US, however, can sometimes cut these costs in half, see below.) Rental cars, even from the big agencies, run the gamut from brand new to real beaters, and you seldom have much to choose from.

So before you rent, ask yourself if you really need a car in the first place. While it's true that public transport doesn't go to places like the Cockscomb Wildlife Sanctuary or the Mountain Pine Ridge, you'll find that the cost of hiring a taxi or guide to such places is often far cheaper than renting a car and driving yourself – not to mention the fact that you can relax and camp for a few days without paying a steep daily fee for a car that ends up being parked most of the time. Note also that no agency will permit you to take its cars across the border to Guatemala.

Still, a few destinations remain difficult to reach by public transportation and could be combined in a whirlwind rental car tour by those pressed for time. For instance, you could visit the Community Baboon Sanctuary, Altun Ha ruins, and Crooked Tree Lagoon – none of which are served by frequent scheduled bus service – quite efficiently over the course of a few days. And if your style of travel is to drive, stop for the night, and drive off the next day, renting a car may prove cost-effective.

If you do decide to rent a car in Belize, you'll want to pick up the car in Belize City, where all the major rental agencies are located. These are listed under the section *Belize City, Getting there*. Most of the agencies, both international and local, have an office at the International Airport. Try to make reservations in advance, however, especially during the tourist season. Reserving in advance from the US may also save you up to half of the price you'd pay at the counter in Belize, even at the same agency. Get telephone quotes from the big agencies in the US (Avis, Budget and Hertz) before you go. Reserving in advance not only may get you a cheaper rate and assure you a car on arrival, but it sometimes gets you a car with less mileage.

Presumably you'll be renting a car to see parts of Belize not served by frequent public transport, which means you should probably rent a 4WD vehicle. Isuzu Troopers, Jeep Cherokees, and Land Rangers are the most common 4WD rentals. But if you're planning to stick strictly to the Western and/or new Northern Highways, both of which are fully paved and completely flat, you'll save lots of money and do just fine renting a passenger car.

Before you can rent a car, you'll need to show a valid US or International Drivers Licence plus a credit card. You will be asked if you want Collision Damage Waiver insurance. This costs about US$16 per day, and there is usually a deductible of US$500–1,000. Many credit cards such as American Express provide primary coverage in Belize, but there are often catches that exclude 4WD vehicles or driving on unpaved roads.

And before you drive off in your rental car, be sure to check several important items. First, check the mileage and attempt to get the lowest-mileage car in the lot whenever possible. Second, check the tyres for tread and check that the spare is in good condition. Even if you haven't had a flat in years at home, be prepared for one on Belize's back roads. Finally, ask the agent what happens if you break down. Some agencies will send a mechanic, but many won't.

Some car rental agencies in Mexico will permit you to drive their cars into Belize. This may be a cheap alternative, but check first. And remember that you'll still have to buy Belizean insurance.

Be sure to read the section below (*Private Car*) for other tips related to driving in Belize.

Private car

Most US and Canadian travellers who bring their own cars to Belize do so as part of an extended trip through Mexico and Central America. Otherwise, there isn't much advantage in driving your own car all the way to tiny Belize, where you'll need 4WD to go most places not served by cheap public transportation.

There are now about 60 petrol stations in Belize (Shell, Texaco and Esso), and you'll be charged about BZ$5.25 per gallon. Premium costs a few pennies more, while unleaded fuel is not available anywhere in Belize. Credit cards are not accepted for petrol.

In Belize City, look for a copy of Emory King's *Driver's Guide to Belize* (see *Appendix 2, Further Reading*), an informal road atlas published annually. You can order this useful driver's guide through the mail from Equator Travel Publications, Inc. 280 Beaverdam Road, Candler, NC 28715, USA, or access it online at www.belizewheels.com. The best widely available map of the country is the International Travel Map of Belize (1:350,000) 4th edition 1998, published by ITMB, Vancouver.

A few driving tips: Top up your fuel tank regularly, especially when off the main highways. Don't drive at night if you can help it. Carry plenty of water with you in case of a breakdown in the backcountry, and be prepared to wait a long time for another vehicle to pass by. Your tyres should have plenty of tread, and your spare and jack must be in good condition. Six-ply truck tyres are best for driving Belize's backroads, rather than four-ply passenger car tyres. Watch out for speed bumps ('sleeping policemen'), especially on the outskirts of villages and towns.

You'll need a valid US or Canadian driver's licence and car registration papers to bring your car into Belize from either Mexico or Guatemala. Visitors may operate a vehicle in Belize for three months with a US or Canadian licence. After that, you'll need to obtain a Belize Driving Permit at the Belize Licensing Authority, Dean Street, Belize City. The permit costs US$20 (plus a medical examination form and two passport photos). At the border, you'll also need to get a permit allowing you to travel in Belize without paying duty on the car. When you leave the country, the authorities will want to see both your permit and the car. Finally, you'll need third-party insurance (roughly US$25 per week or US$90 per year for most cars) for the duration of your stay, available from the Insurance Corporation of Belize Ltd. at both Santa Elena (Mexican border) and Benque Viejo (Guatemalan border). Call them at 02 45328 or 02 45329 in Belize City if you'll be arriving late at night or on a Sunday to see if they'll be open. Exit fees (US$2.50) are charged when you leave Belize.

Taxis

Fortunately, most Belizean towns are small enough to be navigated easily on foot, even with baggage. This means that most travellers will seldom need a cab. One major exception, of course, is Belize City after dark.

Belizean taxis can be readily identified by their pale green licence plates. Fix the fare with the driver before setting out (and make sure there's no confusion about which currency you're discussing). Sample fares: Belize International Airport to downtown, BZ$30; Belize Municipal Airport to downtown, BZ$12-16; other destinations within Belize City, BZ$5 for one person, BZ$1 extra for additional riders; San Ignacio (Cayo) to Guatemalan border, BZ$4 per person.

Longer trips can be arranged either with green-plate taxis or with more informal 'cars for hire'. Ask around, particularly in places like San Ignacio which cater for travellers. In most cases, you'll save money by finding other passengers to split the costs.

Hitching

There's not much traffic on Belize's roadways, so don't expect to cover much ground hitching. But as one Garifuna woman advised us, 'Here in Belize, you can always request passage on any passing vehicle'. Indeed, many Belizeans hitch while waiting for the bus. Sometimes you'll be expected to pay, particularly on trucks which regularly ply the same route and act as informal buses.

Air

Particularly if you're short on time and travelling to the south of Belize, you may find flying advantageous. Compare, for instance, a 50-minute flight from Belize City to Punta Gorda for US$54 with the bus ride, which can take anywhere from 10–12 hours, for US$8.50. The planes are safe, reliable, and small – mostly eight-seaters – affording beautiful views of the cayes, barrier reef, mountains, and rainforests.

Between them, MayaIsland Air and Tropic Air offer regularly-scheduled daily flights from Belize City to the following towns within Belize: Corozal (via San Pedro), Dangriga, Big Creek, Placencia, Punta Gorda, San Pedro, Caye Caulker. Flights south typically stop at Dangriga, Big Creek, and finally Punta Gorda, picking up passengers along the way (in theory, at least – but ticketed passengers have been left standing at airstrips on occasion, so be sure to reconfirm shortly before the flight leaves Belize City to remind the pilot you're waiting). Fewer flights are available on Sundays, and no night flights are permitted in Belize.

Most flights leave Belize City Municipal Airport, but a few flights originate daily from the Belize City International Airport, stopping five minutes later to pick up passengers at the Municipal Airport before continuing. Sample one-way prices from Belize City Municipal Airport: Punta Gorda, BZ$135; Dangriga, BZ$55; San Pedro, BZ$47; Caye Caulker, BZ$47; Corozal, BZ$111. Return fares are often simply double the one-way fare, but are reduced for some destinations. Prices are about BZ$30 higher if you board the plane at Belize City International Airport. Children are offered reduced fares on some flights.

It's fairly easy to book most scheduled flights at short notice, but don't expect to show up at the airport and climb aboard at the last minute. You'll find ticket agents in all the Belizean towns served by MayaIsland and Tropic Air.

Charter flights can be arranged for other destinations. MayaIsland and Tropic Air offer charter flights carrying up to nine, five or three passengers to or from a number of airstrips, including Gallon Jug, Central Farm, Belmopan, Augustine Pine Ridge, Corozal, Hill Bank, Melinda, and Tower Hill. Finally, at least half a dozen other operators offer charters (see *Chapter 7, Getting there*).

For current schedules and fares, contact MayaIsland Airways, PO Box 458, Belize City; tel: 02 62435; toll free from US and Canada: 1 800 521 1247; fax: 02 62192; email: mayair@btl.net; web: www.mayaairways.com or Tropic Air, PO Box 20, San Pedro, Belize; tel: 026 2101 (San Pedro) or 02 45671 (Belize City Municipal Airport); fax: 02 62338; email: tropicair@btl.net; web: www.tropicair.com.

Javier's Flying Service, PO Box 301, Belize City, Belize; tel: 02 35360; fax: 02 31731, and Cari Bee Air Service, PO Box 308, Belize City, Belize; tel: 02 44253; fax: 02 31031, both have offices at the Municipal Airport and can organise national and international charters.

Sea and rivers

Regularly scheduled passenger boats leave Belize City daily for Caye Caulker and San Pedro; see those sections for details. A service between Belize City and Placencia running four times a week is being set up to operate in high season, see *Placencia, Getting there and away*, page 183. Most other boat traffic within Belize is fairly informal, requiring a bit of initiative (and patience) on your part. The routes most often used by travellers are from Dangriga to Hopkins or Tobacco Caye, from Corozal to Sarteneja and from Dangriga to Belize City via the Southern and Northern Lagoons. See these sections for details.

ACCOMMODATION

While it should be obvious that I haven't actually stayed in every hotel listed in this guide, I estimate that I've peeked in the rooms and run the water of at least 75%, gathering informal testimonials from fellow travellers on many of the others. My own wallet and preference run to the cheaper hotels, and although I've attempted to list every hotel in operation at the time of publication, the lion's share of the hotel reviews here are devoted to the more economical lodgings. In the more expensive hotels there is generally a difference in price between high (winter) and low (summer) season. Prices quoted, for reasons of brevity, generally indicate the average price. You may find there are some spectacular price cuts to be had either side of the high season and low season. Prices listed are valid as of December 1999 in most cases, and generally include all government and service taxes. Still, prices are likely to change, new hotels will open and old ones will close. Write to the Belize Tourist Board, New Central Bank Building, Level 2, Gabourel Lane, PO Box 325, Belize City, Belize; tel: 02 31913; fax: 02 31943; tollfree in the US and Canada: 1 800 624 0686; email: info@travelbelize.org; web: www.travelbelize.org for the latest edition of the *Belize Visitor's Guide*, which lists virtually all hotels in the country by price category.

Note All prices listed in this book are for double rooms unless otherwise stated. A single room usually, although not always, works out at about 75% of the cost of a double. There are, however, some hotel owners who charge by the bed or the person.

Hotels in Belize run the gamut from luxury five-star condominium to the plywood-walls-and-bare-light-bulb sort, but you're not likely to find a double room with shared bath for much less than BZ$20 anywhere in the country, with the more acceptable places starting at around BZ$40 per night. Travellers coming from Guatemala will find that those US$2-a-night hovels they're used to in the highlands cost five times that in Belize. From the standpoint of lodging, the two most expensive mainland towns are Belize City and Belmopan; there is simply no such thing as a budget hotel in the latter. San Pedro is frequently cited as expensive, based on its plethora of luxury hotels, but cheap lodging does exist there. Decent budget rooms are hard to come by in Orange Walk Town, but as with the case of Belmopan, few travellers feel the need to stay there anyway. Lodging on the three offshore atolls (Glovers Reef, Lighthouse Reef and Turneffe) is, with only an exception or two, very expensive. You'll find the widest choice of cheap hotels in Caye Caulker and San Ignacio (Cayo), the two most popular spots along Belize's 'Gringo Trail'.

The cheaper hotels throughout Belize generally have shared bathrooms down the hall and are cooled by fan. Air conditioning, though sometimes available in the pricier hotels, is noisy and ends up giving colds to more than a few tourists. Fans are quite adequate in most cases, but be sure they work before taking a room. Many hotels facing the sea rely quite nicely on nothing more than ocean breezes for cooling. Insects, spiders, frogs and lizards are almost unavoidable in most of the cheaper hotels, but unless you're particularly squeamish they won't be a problem. The main exceptions are mosquitoes and sandflies, both of which can be pesky in the cayes. Screened windows help, but a good fan makes a better deterrent. Mosquito coils – if you can stand the smell – are handy as a backup defence in the cayes and along the coast.

Many hotels add a 10% service fee and all registered hotels have to add a 7% government tax to your bill. Ask at the outset if these have been included in the price quoted you. This practice is more common in the pricier lodgings (where it can amount to a hefty surcharge after a few days), although some real flophouses have adopted it as well. Only the more expensive hotels and lodges accept credit cards. Finding a hotel in Belize's seven main towns is straightforward; you can step off the bus and canvass most of the town's hotels within a half-hour walk. Reservations are rarely necessary in the cheaper mainland hotels, but there are some important exceptions: Placencia fills up quickly at Christmas and especially during Easter, while Dangriga's hotels are fully booked up to a year in advance of Garifuna Settlement Day. During the winter holidays, you may want to make reservations for cheap lodging in San Pedro and Caye Caulker, both of which can become quite crowded. And finally, it's becoming increasingly difficult to show up unannounced at the few cheap and comfortable hotels in Belize City. You can write for reservations, but even the cheapest Belizean hotels usually have phones and often email accounts; this makes reservations a fairly easy matter, although in most cases you'll be asked to mail a deposit to hold your room. Reservations are virtually required at the better cottage resorts, jungle lodges, and diving/fishing hotels in the offshore atolls.

Outside Belize's seven main cities, formal lodging is quite limited or even non-existent – the notable exceptions being coastal resort towns such as Placencia, and the growing number of cottage resorts in the Cayo District countryside. Although most of these cottage resorts are relatively expensive, they're often set in pristine territory and offer all meals and a range of activities including horseback riding, nature trails, canoe trips and jungle excursions. Budget travellers will find that a few of these resorts are within their means for an occasional splurge, and that it's sometimes possible to bargain for much cheaper rates by showing up during the off-season (summer). See *Chapter 8, Rural lodges and resorts near San Ignacio* for a full listing.

Besides the cottage resorts, informal lodging is often available in Belize's backcountry by simply asking around. In most small towns there is at least one home that puts up travellers and will cook meals. Rather than take your chances in a small town with no formal lodging listed, you may want to call ahead to the community telephone operator, who can usually tell you if lodging is available with a family in town. Finally, an innovative programme has begun in Toledo District whereby travellers can arrange to spend a few days living with Maya or Garifuna villagers (see *Chapter 12, Village Guest House Ecotrail Programme*).

Camping offers a good way to cut back on your two biggest expenses, lodging and food. More or less formal campsites exist at a number of spots throughout the country, including the Cockscomb Wildlife Sanctuary, the Community Baboon Sanctuary, Toledo's Blue Creek, Douglas D'Silva Forestry Station (formerly Augustine, in the Mountain Pine Ridge), Sittee River, and various locations along the Macal and Mopan Rivers in Cayo District. Some of the classier lodges in Cayo such as Chaa Creek now offer camping nearby, with meals, at relatively cheap prices. Prices average about BZ$5 pp. You can sling a hammock without problem on many of the tiny offshore cayes and on some coastal beaches (e.g., Hopkins), but always check with locals first and bring all your own water. If planning to camp in government-regulated areas such as the Mountain Pine Ridge, be sure to check with officials of the Forestry Department beforehand. Camping near Maya ruins can be problematic. Officially it's forbidden, particularly at remote sites like Caracol, where looting has been common in the past. You may be able to convince caretakers at other sites (such as Altun Ha) to relax the rules a bit, but don't under any circumstance camp in archaeological zones without some kind of permission. More specific campsite information can be found in the chapters dealing with each region in Belize.

The general rules of tropical camping apply in Belize: avoid pitching a tent under palm trees (falling coconuts), agricultural fields (trespass and ticks) or on jungle river sandbars (flash floods).

FOOD AND DRINK
Food

No one goes to Belize for the food, and a Belizean cookbook – and there are a couple available – will be the work of an overzealous patriot rather than a gourmet. On the other hand, you won't go hungry in Belize – the food is hearty and ample. Prices vary widely, of course, but as a rule of thumb expect to pay about BZ$8–12 for a basic meal including beverage, and anything up to BZ$50 at some of the smarter places.

The standard Creole meal revolves around chicken, white rice, and beans, rarely prepared with the flair for seasoning that characterises Mexican food just a few kilometres to the north. Chicken, once virtually unknown in Belize, is now the unofficial national dish thanks to the Mennonites, who introduced poultry farming shortly after their arrival in the 1950s. Even in coastal fishing areas, chicken is the most readily available main dish, nearly always served deep fried. Fish or beef sometimes replaces the chicken, occasionally accompanied by fried plantain or French fries. The seasoning of choice is Melinda's Hot Sauce, made from Scotch bonnet peppers (the fiery *habanero* of Yucatan fame) in Dangriga. You may go days without seeing a green vegetable. American fast food in the form of hamburgers and hotdogs is ubiquitous.

Seafood can be quite good in Belize, although more often than not it's served up rather unimaginatively. Popular finfish include hog snapper, red snapper, shark, trunkfish and barracuda. The latter can sometimes harbour *ciguatera* fish poisoning, particularly in June and July. Fishwives say that you can detect *ciguatera* toxin if a silver ring tossed into the cooking pot with the 'barra' discolours. Spiny lobster (accompanied by French fries or mashed potatoes and coleslaw) costs as little as BZ$15 in Caye Caulker during the season (June 14 – February 15). Lobster is also easy to find – although somewhat more expensive – in Placencia and San Pedro. Conch, served in stews, fritters, or fried, is well worth trying during the season. Don't insist on eating lobster or conch out of season – there is always someone in Belize ready to accommodate you – and please don't eat sea turtle.

Fry jacks – deep-fried triangles of bread dough, usually served with jam – turn up frequently on Belizean breakfast menus. Children like to drench theirs in condensed milk. You'll sometimes be offered homemade coconut bread, powder buns, pumpkin cakes or other flavoured breads, usually sold from a basket by the baker's children. Good local bakeries exist in Placencia, Caye Caulker and Dangriga.

Traditional Garifuna food is definitely worth trying if you get the chance. *Hudut* (pronounced hooDOOT and referred to by Creoles as *foofoo*) is a savoury stew containing mashed plantain, coconut milk, fish broth, cooked breadfruit, okra and fish cooked in coconut. *Alabundigas* are dumplings made from green bananas cooked in coconut gravy and served with fish or conch on the side. Probably the most characteristic Garifuna food is cassava bread, fashioned into large thin rounds; cassava also figures prominently in Garifuna dessert puddings. Another Garifuna speciality worth trying is homemade ginger wine, strong and tangy. Unfortunately, there are very few restaurants serving Garifuna food, even in Dangriga. Try the Sandy Beach Women's Cooperative in Hopkins, or stay with a Garifuna family in Barranco (see *Chapter 12, Excursions*).

Other traditional Belizean foods more talked about than actually eaten these days include the game meats – deer, paca ('gibnut' in Creole, *tepezcuintle* in neighbouring Guatemala), armadillo and iguana ('jungle chicken'). Gibnut is technically a rodent, earning it the nickname 'Royal Rat' ever since it was served to Queen Elizabeth during her stay in Belize. As one of our Belizean guides advised us when serving gibnut, 'If it's good enough for the Queen, it's good enough for you, brudder!' Beyond the novelty, there's nothing special to recommend these dishes, although I haven't actually tried iguana yet. Game meat stews are frequently cooked with a savoury red paste made from achiote (recado or 'ricardo' sauce). Cowfoot soup, by the way, is simmered with a real cow's hoof, not the local plant of the same name.

Local fruits include a variety of delicious mangoes (my favourite is the so-called custard mango), papayas, bananas, watermelons, and oranges. You're most likely to find these at the public markets in the larger towns. Market day in many towns is but once a week, and the good produce is snapped up early in the morning.

Thick, homemade corn tortillas are the staple among Kekchi and Mopan Maya villagers throughout Belize. If you end up visiting one of the more remote villages close to the Guatemalan border, you may be served nothing but tortillas. Often, however, they serve to mop up a smidgen of scrambled egg or chicken.

Chinese and Mexican food are both by now fully integrated into the Belizean restaurant scene. In many towns such as Orange Walk and Dangriga, the vast majority of restaurants seem to be Chinese. Unfortunately, few of these Chinese restaurants are on a par with their counterparts in the States or Europe. Still, they're perhaps the only Belizean restaurants regularly serving crisp green vegetables, and they're usually cheap. Mexican restaurants tend toward snack foods like *salbutes* (small corn tortillas fried and topped with shredded chicken, onions, grated cheese, tomato and cabbage or lettuce); *panades* and *garnaches* are similar finger-foods, but order at least six of these per person if you're at all hungry. *Tamales* (corn dough enclosing shredded chicken, wrapped in banana leaves and steamed) are delicious and available everywhere; even Creoles are cooking *tamales* these days and selling them on buses. *Chilmole* (or *chirmole*) is a black-spiced chicken stew. *Escabeche* is another Mexican-style stew, heavy on the onions.

The larger towns all have supermarkets where you can stock up on tinned or packaged food for camping. Much of it is imported from Europe, the US, or Australia and thus fairly expensive. Don't expect to find much in the way of fruits or vegetables in the supermarkets. Your best bet is to visit the weekly market early in the day. Likewise, you can sometimes talk fishermen into selling you their catch directly, or even buy from the local fishing cooperative in places like Placencia or Big Creek.

Drink

Belize boasts two domestic beers, Belikin and Crown, both costing around BZ$1 a bottle. Within the last few years, Belikin has come out with a 'premium' brew which doesn't seem to merit the extra price. Both companies market passable stouts, although they're harder to find than the standard lager. Imported brands – Guinness, Sheafs and Heineken – are often available, and they cost roughly double what the domestic brews cost. Belizean rum is quite good and decidedly cheap. You can order a half bottle of rum (a 'chop' in local parlance) in many bars.

You can buy bottled mineral water in most towns, particularly those where the local tap water isn't chlorinated or considered palatable. Easier to find are bottled 'squashes' (concentrated citrus juices), soft drinks, especially Coca-Cola, Fanta orange, Sprite and the ever-mysterious 'red' Fanta (does anyone know what flavour this purports to be?).

'Seaweed' is a local speciality drink, properly made from dried agar seaweed, hot water, milk, sugar, nutmeg and rum. It tastes much like eggnog and is reportedly an aphrodisiac, but much of the stuff sold nowadays is thickened not with seaweed but with flour or cornstarch.

Coffee means Nescafé almost everywhere. Maya Indians make a delicious hot cacao drink.

HANDICRAFTS AND WHAT TO BUY

Sandwiched between Mexico and Guatemala, Belize is unaccountably poor in local handicrafts. In fact, you'll find many a Belizean gift shop stocked mostly with Guatemalan products.

Besides the usual assortment of T-shirts, gift shops typically sell carvings made from zericote (a dark, lustrous local wood), and Maya handicrafts (including baskets, slate carvings and embroidered wall hangings). For Maya artwork, your best bets are the small community store at Maya Center (the entrance to the Cockscomb Wildlife Sanctuary) and the Garcia Sisters shop in San Antonio (just outside San Ignacio). Proceeds from the former directly benefit the local Maya who were displaced during the creation of the Jaguar Sanctuary.

Dangriga offers a variety of traditional Garifuna handicrafts, including local wooden drums and the folk paintings of Belize's best-known artists.

Other gift ideas include Melinda's Hot Sauce and jams (made near Dangriga and available nationwide), cassette tapes of Belizean and other Caribbean music (see *Music* below), wildlife posters from the Belize Zoo and the excellent series of Belizean stamps depicting local birds, mammals, reef fish and flora (available at the post office in Belize City). Books by Belizean authors like Zee Edgell can be bought in several Belize City bookstores and at Sea-Ing is Belizing (Caye Caulker). Gift shops are noted throughout the chapters dealing with specific towns.

Don't buy products made of sea turtle or black coral (fortunately, much of the black coral sold throughout the Caribbean is fake, anyway!). Conservation concerns aside, you need a licence from the government to leave the country with either product.

MISCELLANEOUS
Telephone
The country code for Belize is 501.

Belize's reliable phone system makes both in-country and overseas calls easy. But few of the budget hotels have phones in their rooms, nor are pay phones very common. Either ask to use the hotel phone for a fee or make your call from the offices of Belize Telecommunications Limited (BTL), located in every major town. BTL's hours at most locations are 08.00-12.00 and 13.00-16.00 Mon-Fri. Some offices are open on Saturday morning. The main BTL office in Belize City (1 Church Street) is open daily 08.00–18.00. Depending on the particular BTL office, they'll either dial for you and have you pick up the phone when the party answers, or allow you to dial it yourself; pay when you're done.

When calling Belize from anywhere in the world follow with the area code for the town. Area codes consist of a zero followed by one or two digits, but when dialling from outside Belize omit the zero. Thus, a call to the Hol Chan Marine Reserve Office in San Pedro would be dialled from the US or Canada as 011 501 26 2247 but from Belize as 026 2247.

For Directory Assistance, dial 113.

International Direct Dialling (IDD) is now installed virtually everywhere in Belize. When making international calls from within Belize, dial 00 (giving access to the international service), followed by the country code, then the city or area code (if used) and finally the telephone number. Calls to the US, Canada, Caribbean, Central and South America cost US$1.60 per minute; to Europe, US$3 per minute; all other countries, US$4 per minute. If you need operator assistance for an international call, dial 115.

Within Belize, simply dial the area code for the appropriate city plus the number. National calls are not that cheap and quickly eat into your change. Phonecards work out to be more economical and less wieldy than a pocket full of change if you have to make many calls. Most BTL offices also offer fax, telex, and telegram services. The office in Belize City also provides internet access.

Smaller towns in Belize are usually served by a single community telephone. The people who staff these phones (numbers in any phone book) can be invaluable sources of information on local transport, lodging, even guide services. A quick call to Sittee Village, for example, will confirm the fact that a local woman has room in her house for travellers and that the boat to Glovers Reef is expected on Sunday. Likewise, a call to Guinea Grass can put you in touch with a guide to Lamanai. In virtually all cases, the community phone operators will be far better informed of these local titbits, schedule changes, etc than tourist agencies (or even guidebook authors!).

Email and internet

Belize is connected to the internet – in fact it is difficult to imagine a country more connected. Most hotels, jungle lodges and tour operators have email addresses and websites making it easy to make enquiries and book accommodation and services from anywhere in the world.

For people wanting to access their own email accounts, the relatively high cost of telephone calls in Belize has deterred the widespread creation of cybercafes. That said, in popular areas such as San Ignacio and Caye Caulker there are several tour operators and bars who have put a terminal in their office. For the time being, 60 minutes on the internet might cost as much as a night in a cheap hotel – the situation may change when BTL loses it's telecommunications services monopoly in 2001.

Tourist information

I don't generally recommend government tourist bureaux. All too often they steer travellers exclusively toward packaged tours and luxury hotels, with little to offer those on a budget or simply roughing it. The Belize Tourist Board (New Central Bank Building, Level 2, Gabourel Lane, PO Box 325, Belize City, Belize; tel: 02 31913; fax: 02 31943; tollfree in the US and Canada: 1 800 624 0686; email: info@travelbelize.org; web: www.travelbelize.org), however, does its best to cover all bases. By all means get a free copy of their yearly pamphlet *Belize Visitor's Guide*, which lists virtually every hotel from five-star to fleabag as well as tour operators, restaurants and other useful information.

For the latest information on lodging, transportation and local guides in the smaller villages, take advantage of the community telephone system (see *Telephone* above).

Visa renewals

If you decide to stay in Belize for more than 30 days, you'll need to get an extension (BZ$25) from the Immigration Office in Belize City (99 Barrack Road) or from their offices in Orange Walk, Corozal border, Dangriga, Punta Gorda, Belmopan or the Benque border.

Mail

Letters addressed to you care of the Poste Restante, Main Post Office, Belize City will be held for two months. The office is located just north of the Swing Bridge and is open Monday to Friday 08.00–16.30. A special desk sells the popular stamp sets depicting Belizean flora, fauna and folklore. Belize may also be the only country to immortalise a hurricane on a postage stamp. Letters and postcards to Europe cost BZ$0.75 and BZ$0.40 respectively; to the US, BZ$0.60 and BZ$0.30.

Newspapers, magazines, and books

The four leading newspapers, all weeklies, make little effort to disguise their political slants. Much of the reporting verges on slander, and even travellers without the slightest interest in Belizean politics may find some amusement here. The *People's Pulse*, for instance, referred to rival PUP leaders as 'moguls of the Perverted Useless Party'.

The official party organ of the UDP is the *People's Pulse* which, along with the pro-UDP *Reporter* does battle with the *Belize Times*, the PUP's mouthpiece. *Amandala* is perhaps the most politically independent of the bunch, owned and edited by a former leader of the United Black Association for Development; lately they've been reporting regularly on environmental matters.

The Belize Information Service publishes a bimonthly business-oriented magazine *Belize Today*, which is free. *Belize Currents* is a glossy, semi-annual general-interest magazine, while the *Belize Tourism News* and *Belizean Tourister* serve the growing travel industry.

For eco-tourists, potential investors and Belizephiles in general, the best of the nation's press is the occasional *Belize Review*. With a strong environmental bent, the *Review* prints up-to-date information on nature reserves, conservation efforts, and ecological education. You'll also find frequent news of Belizean literature, art and music. Like any good member of the Belizean press, the *Review* does its share of feisty political squabbling, but it's a good read for anyone with a long-term interest in the country. Although published in the US, *Belize First* magazine, published quarterly, is the best travel-oriented publication on the market (see *Chapter 4, Getting Information*).

Bookstores

Most of the few decent bookstores are listed in the Belize City section. Sea-Ing is Belizing on Caye Caulker and a few other gift shops in San Pedro carry books about Belize or by Belizean authors.

Electrical equipment

Voltage in Belize is 110 volts AC, 60 cycles.

Time

Belize is six hours behind GMT (the same as Central Standard in the US). Daylight Savings Time isn't observed.

Business hours and public holidays

Most businesses are closed on Sundays, and both bus and air transport are limited. Retail stores generally close for lunch from 12.00–13.00 and then stay open until 17.00. Businesses are usually open on Saturday only until lunchtime. Banks are open Monday through Thursday 09.00–13.00 and Friday 08.00–16.30.

Public holidays are described in *Chapter 1*. All banks and most businesses close on holidays.

ACTIVITIES
Scuba diving

Long before Belize was 'discovered' by most travellers, scuba enthusiasts were quietly making annual pilgrimages there, enjoying world-class diving on spectacular coral drop-offs with 30m or more of visibility. But you won't find the adrenaline-rush diving that Belize is famous for if you hug the country's barrier reef. For the truly breathtaking walls and near-virgin diving you'll need to expend the extra effort and money to reach one of the three offshore atolls: Lighthouse Reef, Turneffe Islands or Glovers Reef. True, it's far easier and cheaper to dive along the barrier reef near San Pedro, Caye Caulker, Placencia or Dangriga.

Indeed, the spur-and-groove coral formations here are worth a look for a few days if you've got the time. But unless you're new to the sport you won't be particularly awe-struck by dive sites so close to the mainland. Indeed, I've met a number of disappointed divers who left Belize wondering where all those luscious photos were taken that they'd been ogling for years in the dive magazines.

I can't stress this point enough: as long as you've come all the way to Belize, why not spend the extra few dollars to visit the Mecca of Belizean diving, the offshore atolls? On the barrier reef itself, only the 'outer reef' dives offshore of Placencia and the newly-visited sites at the Sapodilla Cayes can rival the atoll diving.

Belize offers fine diving for all skill levels, although some sites such as the Blue Hole on Lighthouse Reef and The Elbow on Turneffe shouldn't be attempted by beginners. Divers have three basic options: 1) day trips, mostly out of San Pedro, Caye Caulker, Belize City or Placencia, usually one- or two-tank dives along the barrier reef and cayes; 2) live-aboard dive boats, which offer everything from two-day to week-long trips out to the three offshore atolls; and 3) dive-oriented resorts located directly on the offshore atolls or nearshore cayes along the barrier reef. In all three cases, dives are made from a boat with a divemaster. There are no shore diving opportunities in Belize.

I have had good luck arranging live-aboard dive trips both from abroad and from within Belize. Be aware, however, that boats may be fully booked during the winter vacation period. If you've got the time, it's best to go directly to San Pedro and personally visit prospective boats and chat with the divemaster before signing on. Besides the obvious creature comforts – fresh water shower, bunks or mats, clean head – look carefully for such things as first aid kits, radios, fire extinguishers and an oxygen kit. No agency checks these things.

Good quality rental gear is readily available. I bring nothing more than my prescription mask, renting everything else to avoid lugging gear all over inland Belize. But if you're fussy about your gear or really need to economise, best bring your mask, regulator and BC from home for a short dive trip, and all your gear (minus cylinder and weights) for an extended trip. Bring your C-card, although not all guides demand to see them. Particularly if you plan on diving the Blue Hole, it's a good idea to bring your logs showing deep dives; some guides like to see them.

A number of resorts and dive shops offer instruction. My only advice here is to avoid the so-called 'resort courses', quickie one-day intro classes which do not lead to a diving certification. Your best bet is to learn at home and come to Belize with a C-card and some experience, comfortable with your diving skills. Failing that, take a bona fide certification class in Belize from a licensed instructor. Fred Good, longtime owner/instructor at St George's Lodge, has been highly recommended by many (see *Chapter 13, St George's Caye*). Becky Cabral at Glovers Reef Atoll Resort (see *Chapter 14, Glovers Reef*) has also been recommended. Other dive resorts offering full certification which have been recommended include Ramon's (tel: 026 2071; fax: 026 2214; email: ramons@btl.net; web: www.ramons.com) and Amigos del Mar (tel: 026 2706; fax: 026 2648; email: amigosdive@btl.net; web: ambergriscaye.com/amigosdive) in San Pedro, and Belize Diving Services (tel: 02 2143; fax: 022 2217; email: bzdiveserv@btl.net) and Frenchie's (tel: 022 2234; fax: 022 2074; email: frenchies@btl.net; web: www.belizenet.com/frenchies.html) on Caye Caulker.

Diving is possible year-round in Belize, although occasional strong northerly winds during November-February sometimes disrupt schedules and force boats to alternative dive sites. Visibility varies considerably with local weather conditions, but, in general, it improves as you move further from the mainland. 15–22m visibility is normal along the barrier reef at San Pedro, but at Lighthouse Reef and Glovers Reef, the two most distant atolls, you can usually count on 30m visibility or better. Water temperature near the surface varies from about 25°C (77°F) during the winter to about 30°C (85°F) in the summer. I've made repetitive dives during both seasons wearing only a swimsuit and T-shirt, but I'll admit to goosebumps afterwards. If you're going to spend more than a day or two diving, you'd be best to bring a ⅛-inch shorty top as 'thermal comfort insurance'.

Belize has one recompression chamber located at the San Pedro airstrip (Subaquatic Safety Services; PO Box 76, San Pedro; tel: 026 2854/2073 in case of emergency). If you're diving out of San Pedro or one of the live-aboards based there, you'll probably be asked to contribute a small fee per tank to help support the chamber. It's well worth it, especially since it buys you free treatment there should you need it. Check with DAN (Divers Alert Network), a non-profit safety organization, about their dive insurance policy covering evacuation and recompression treatment worldwide: DAN, The Peter B Bennett Center, 6 West Colony Place, Durham, NC 27705 USA, tel: 1 800 443 2671; email: dan@diversalertnetwork.org; web: www.diversalertnetwork.org.

Nitrox, the enriched air breathing mixture which adds an extra margin of safety to deep diving, is now becoming available in Belize. Fred Good at St George's Lodge not only encourages its use, but provides Nitrox certification.

You'll find detailed information on dive sites, guides, boats, equipment, and prices in the chapters dealing with the Offshore Atolls, San Pedro, Caye Caulker, and Stann Creek District. Other good sources of timely information include *Skin Diver Magazine*, which does a Belize feature annually. *Undercurrent* is a 'consumer review' publication for divers which publishes brutally frank, detailed reports on dive destinations, guides, and boats worldwide. Write to *Undercurrent*, PO Box 1658, Sausalito, CA 94966, for a subscription or back issues dealing with Belize.

Divers on the internet can look at www.scubadivingbelize.com for the very latest diving information about Belize. There is also general information on diving in Belize at the www.belizenet.com site, which will give a good overall guide to prices, boats and destinations.

Read *Chapter 3, Coral reef etiquette* and stay conscious of your impacts on the reef at all times. Note that it's illegal for visitors to spear fish or take lobster while using scuba. Say something to your divemaster if he or she encourages you to hunt for lobster.

Snorkelling

Unless you plan on spending your entire trip inland – or can't swim – you should definitely bring a mask and snorkel to Belize. Nearly everyone who visits Caye Caulker or San Pedro – where the barrier reef lies within sight – spends a day or two snorkelling among the bizarre coral formations and colourful reef fish. The price is well within the reach of the most miserly of low-budget of travellers, and virtually anyone who can swim can master snorkelling on the first day.

As you move south along the Belizean coastline, you'll find yourself farther from the barrier reef and cayes. The number of people travelling to Placencia has brought prices down to compete with those of the inner cayes. But at Dangriga you'll have to look a bit harder for snorkel trips, you'll pay more, and spend more time getting out to the reef by boat. In compensation, you'll escape the crowds farther north and often find more pristine reef conditions. By the time you reach Punta Gorda, the reef is so far offshore that expensive overnight trips are the only option – but in compensation you'll be camped in relative seclusion, the visibility is better and the reef much wilder.

The offshore atolls – Turneffe, Lighthouse and Glovers – offer some superb snorkelling. But while the very best Belizean scuba diving is found here, it's mostly wall diving in depths of more than 5m, so the opportunities for the average snorkeller are a bit limited. The live-aboard dive boats naturally favour these deeper dive sites rather than the shallower sites more suitable for snorkelling. One notable exception is the famed Blue Hole of Lighthouse Reef. Here, the shallow fringing coral reef and its attendant fish life nearly rival the eerie deep-water adventure below. Half Moon Caye on Lighthouse Reef, site of the red-footed booby sanctuary, also has a gorgeous snorkelling reef on its windward side.

As with scuba diving, snorkelling always involves a boat trip of some kind. Snorkelling directly from shore is rarely possible until you're actually out on the reef or coral cayes. The cayes very close to shore are generally mangrove cayes, a complex ecosystem of great interest to marine biologists but often with poor visibility and little to inspire most snorkellers.

You can rent mask and snorkel easily and cheaply in San Pedro, Caye Caulker and Placencia, but I advise bringing your own from home if you plan to do much snorkelling or if you're headed for more distant sites like Tobacco, Laughing Bird, Wee Wee or Hunting Cayes. Fins take up a lot of room in your baggage and they're best left at home. Experienced snorkellers will have no trouble getting around without them and fins on novice snorkellers are probably the number one cause of coral reef destruction at popular dive sites. Gloves, formerly favoured by some divers and snorkellers as protection against cuts and fire coral, are also superfluous; you shouldn't be touching coral, fire or otherwise, in the first place.

Detailed information on snorkelling opportunities, boats, equipment rental and guides can be found in the chapters dealing with San Pedro, Caye Caulker, Stann Creek District and Toledo District.

Fishing

Anglers, like divers, discovered Belize long before most travellers, and it's no wonder; the flyfishing, deepsea trolling and spincasting are all excellent for a variety of species in habitats ranging from jungle rivers to bonefish flats to the open ocean. The most sought-after species include bonefish, tarpon, permit, marlin, sailfish and snook, but there is also plenty of opportunity for kingfish, barracuda, jacks, grouper, wahoo, yellowfin and blackfin tuna, bonito, sharks and at least a half dozen species of snapper.

Travellers who might be interested in a little fishing but who have trouble reconciling it with eco-tourism will be glad to know that much of the best Belizean fishing is, by custom and general agreement, catch-and-release. This includes fishing for tarpon (virtually inedible, and rarely landed anyway!), bonefish and permit.

Low-budget travellers, however, aren't likely to include a great deal of sportfishing in their Belize itinerary. A full day of bonefishing out of Placencia, for example, will cost at least US$275 for up to four people (excluding gear rental), and you'll pay upwards of US$600 for a day-long, five-angler deepsea fishing trip out of San Pedro. Petrol is expensive in Belize, and the farther you must travel by boat to fish, the more expensive your trip will be.

Anglers have several options in arranging trips. It's fairly easy to arrange a half-day or full-day fishing trip out of San Pedro or Placencia on fairly short notice, but remember that you may have to wait a few days for the best guides to become available. Many of these guides will have long-time customers who will have made reservations months ahead. Most of the larger hotels in places like San Pedro and Dangriga offer half-day and full-day trips for a set rate. For serious anglers with more time (and money), a number of resorts on the mainland, cayes and offshore atolls offer special fishing packages that include lodging for two to seven days, all meals, airport transfers, fishing guides, boat and fuel. Some of these resorts cater to a wide range of tourists, while others specialise only in sportfishing. Particularly in the offshore atolls, you'll find resorts catering to both scuba divers and anglers.

Although some species such as bonefish (and certainly all the river fish) can in theory be stalked from shore, you really need a boat to get to the best spots, cover lots of ground and put you close to your prey. Even if you're an experienced tropical angler, you'll need the services of a guide who knows the local fishing spots and, more importantly, how to navigate through the tricky coral reefs and labyrinthine mangrove channels.

If you intend to do much serious fishing at all, bring your own tackle, flies, and plugs (except in the case of deepsea fishing for marlin, sailfish and tuna, where guides usually supply the heavy, specialised tackle and lures). You'll find some general tackle recommendations below, but phoning local guides before your trip for specific tips always helps. Guides in the offshore atolls, San Pedro and, to a lesser extent, Placencia, can usually come up with rental tackle, but they are accustomed to anglers supplying their own. Buying any kind of tackle in Belize is nearly impossible. Savvy anglers often buy new gear at home, fish it in Belize, then sell it to fishing guides at cost at the end of their trip. Rods and reels are especially hot items. Lures and flies make excellent tips at the end of your trip, far more welcome by most guides than mere cash.

Most guides take two anglers for a set price, so you'll need to find a fishing companion if you're alone. Guides usually have no problem with neophyte anglers and are more than willing to show you the basics of casting and playing a fish, but don't expect the same tolerance from a stranger in your boat. Expert bonefish and permit anglers, for example, won't have much patience with a beginner who spooks trophy fish. Be honest with any potential fishing companions (and the guide) about your fishing experience before you climb aboard.

In addition to fishing tackle, be sure to bring the following from home: Polaroid sunglasses (a must for stalking bonefish and permit in the shallows); old tennis shoes, neoprene booties or 'reef-walkers' (for stalking bonefish); a hat to shield you from the sun; plenty of heavy-duty sunscreen and lip balm; and rain gear (you may be warm in the rain on shore, but not in a moving boat!).

Belize is well-known for excellent bonefishing. This torpedo-shaped species schools in the shallow, gin-clear, sandy flats just offshore of Belize's mainland, cayes, and atolls. Bonefish aren't considered edible – this is a catch-and-release species – and in Belize they usually range in size only from 1 to 3kg. Their fame among light-tackle anglers rests on their ability to fight with the fury of a much larger fish. And larger, 'trophy' bonefish aren't uncommon; the world record bonefish (7.6kg) was landed off Turneffe Flats in 1991.

Bonefish must be stalked in the flats as they feed on molluscs and crustaceans. Experienced guides will spot them via the tell-tale mud they raise during feeding, or when their tails break the surface. Often guides will look for a trophy fish feeding away from the school. The boat will get you close. Then it's up to you to cast your fly to within a metre of the fish, sometimes requiring you to creep out of the boat and stalk your trophy on foot. The guide will suggest how close your fly should land – at times, a fly placed within 2m of a bonefish will spook the whole school into a frenzy of flight. Lightweight fly rods (2-2.7m) and reels able to hold lines from WF5 to WF8 are recommended, the longer rods are better in windy conditions. Floating line works best. Leaders should be at least 3m long (and preferably longer), with 4-8 pound tippets. Bonefish aren't as choosy about what they strike as permit, but bring a large assortment of 1-2 inch bonefish flies (tied on #4-#8 hooks) in all colours, both weighted and unweighted. Spinning gear also works for bonefish (2–2.1m rod, open face reel, 6-pound test line, $1/8$–$1/4$ ounce lures such as the Phillips Wiggle Jig in brown, black, white and yellow). Bonefishing is good all year, but best November–April.

Permit resemble large pompano, and 9kg specimens aren't uncommon. Particularly on incoming tides, you'll often find them sharing the flats with bonefish, but being deep-bodied, permit require deeper water than the slender bonefish. They also require considerably more skill from the guide and angler; permit spook easily, don't readily respond to flies, lures or even live bait, and veteran anglers may cast to scores of these fish without a strike. They have more stamina than bonefish, running for great distances and often snapping or fouling lines in the process. In short, you're likely to see hundreds of these fish on the flats and never hook or land a single one. The same flyfishing gear used for bonefish works well for permit, as does spinning tackle, but bring $1/8$-ounce lures such as the Blue Fox Vibrotail, crabs or other permit jigs. Fishing is equally good (or difficult!) year-round.

Snook haunt both marine and fresh waters in Belize, and adults are sometimes found quite a distance upstream from the nearest saltwater. Tides play a big role in fishing success near creek mouths; local guides will have the timing down. Fairly stiff, medium-weight spinning and baitcasting rods (2–2.1m) are needed to set the hook and wrestle these fish in the confines of a river and past mangrove roots; freshwater bass tackle works fairly well. Bring line in the 12–18 pound test class, 60# mono leader (a snook's gillcovers can cut line like a razor), and a variety of surface plugs (eg: Mirrolure 52M or 65M, Heddon Zara Spook or Lucky 13, Rebel), lipped diving plugs, jigs, poppers and spoons. Freshwater bass anglers will find most of their arsenal from home useful. Fishing for snook in Belizean rivers is best from February through August, although they're catchable year-round.

Tarpon are considered by many anglers to be the finest sportfish in the world, famous for their acrobatics when hooked. Like snook, they inhabit both saltwater and freshwater, although they're rarely found far from the shoreline and always in fairly shallow water. Tarpon (*sabalo* in Spanish) resemble mammoth herring, and coming across one of these blindingly silver giants while scuba diving is always exciting. In Belize, they'll range in size from 9kg to 40kg, with the average about 23kg. Landing a tarpon on flyfishing tackle is considered one of the sport's ultimate tests. You'll want a medium-weight rod (2–2.1m) and reel capable of holding 175m or so of line in the WF7-12S class, depending on the size of fish you're after. Bring streamer flies with 3–5 inch hackle feathers in yellow, red, orange, and white (and combinations thereof) tied on 1/0 to 5/0 hooks. A foot or so of 80-100# test leader prevents line chafing in the tarpon's mouth. For spinning tackle, use medium-weight rods (2–2.1m), 10–15 pound line and plugs such as the Heddon Zara Spook or Lucky 13, $6^{1}/_{2}$-inch Cisco Kid, Rapalas or Mirrolure 65M and 47M. Tarpon school from late February through August, making for the hottest fishing, but they are hookable year-round.

Out in the bigger water, both inside and outside the reef, guides can put you on barracuda ('barra'), kingfish, wahoo, jacks, bonito, tuna and a variety of snapper species. For inexperienced anglers, these species are relatively easy to catch (compared with bonefish, tarpon and especially permit), usually via trolling or jigging. They're often boated for eating rather than released. A medium-weight spinning rod (2.1m) with 15–25 pound line will suffice for most offshore trolling and jigging. Fishing is good year-round for all these species except wahoo (best November-February) and kingfish (best March–June). Deepsea fishing for blue marlin (all year), white marlin (best November–May) and sailfish (best March–May), requires heavy, specialised tackle and lures generally supplied by the guide.

Finally, if the high cost and competition involved in angling for the species listed above doesn't appeal to you – but you'd still like to hook a few fish in a more relaxed setting – consider striking up a conversation with a Belizean commercial fisherman. Occasionally you'll find one who will be willing to take you out for a day of commercial hook-and-line fishing for a small, easily negotiable fee. He'll also probably let you bring a small portion of the catch home. A friend of ours had one of his most memorable days in Belize fishing for small grunts with a Garifuna fisherman in Punta Gorda. Just remember that it's a day of work for the fisherman, not a picnic on the beach, and act accordingly.

Guides, fishing lodges and prices are listed throughout this book in the area chapters, particularly those on Stann Creek District, San Pedro and the Offshore Atolls.

Sea kayaking

The Belizean barrier reef provides kayakers with relatively protected waters for exploring hundreds of isolated cayes and mangrove islets. Most popular is the section of barrier reef running between Tobacco Caye (off Dangriga) and Ranguana Caye (southeast of Placencia). Three North American based companies (all with both North American and Belizean guides) operate kayak tours in this area, and more are bound to follow. One operator offers a trip which goes all the way from Belize City to the Sapodilla Cayes at the extreme southern end of the barrier reef. Another offers a side trip up the jungled Monkey River. Glovers Reef, the most isolated of Belize's three atolls, is now being visited by two kayak tour companies. Trips are generally a week long and are offered only during the calmer, drier months of February through May. They usually involve paddling from caye to caye, camping overnight on the cayes (bring your own camping gear), with food, drink, and all kayaking and safety equipment provided. First-time kayakers are welcome, and indeed make up the lion's share of the people on these tours. Detailed information on tour companies, itineraries and prices can be found in *Chapter 11, Placencia and Tobacco Caye.*

One of the above tour operators rents single and double kayaks in Dangriga to experienced paddlers and will ferry you out to the reef. See *Chapter 11, Placencia, Excursions* for details.

Sailing

Sailors, like kayakers, are increasingly discovering the charms of Belize's barrier reef, which provides a sheltered, though still breezy, haven from which to explore a chain of coral islets extending nearly the length of the country. Those who wish to charter a boat (crewed or bareboat) can contact TMM Bareboat Vacations who have a wide-range of catamarans for between four and 12 people. Prices vary greatly across the season. A four-berth catamaran is US$2,200 in summer and US$3,650 in winter. The 12-berth Bahia 46 is US$4,875 in summer and US$7,500 in winter. Full provisioning works out at US$22.50 per person per day, a skipper is US$100 a day.

Contact TMM Bareboat Vacations on tel: 026 3026 or toll free: 1 800 633 0155; fax: 026 3072; email: tmmbz@btl.net; web: www.sailtmm.com.

Sailing conditions: Easterly 10-15 knot trade winds blow steadily from January through April, and rain is at a minimum during this period. May and June offer only light breezes, followed by the hurricane season which runs from August through October. From November through February, the easterly trades are punctuated by 20-knot northerlies bringing rain squalls.

An invaluable reference for any sailor considering a cruise in Belize is the *Cruising Guide to Belize and Mexico's Caribbean* (1991), by Freya Rauscher, a large and meticulously detailed book showing anchorages, routes, points of interest and much more (see *Appendix 2, Further Reading*).

Windsurfing

Most boardheads make for San Pedro; in addition to the best selection of equipment and instructors, the nearby barrier reef acts as a natural breakwater, providing flat water and plenty of onshore breeze at the same time. Consult the chapter on San Pedro for details. Conditions are equally good on the eastern (ie: barrier reef) side of Caye Caulker, but the selection of boards and sails is quite limited. Corozal and Chetumal Bays seem perpetually windy, but once again, you're fairly limited in rental boards. See the appropriate chapters for rental operators.

Canoeing, river rafting and tubing

Belize offers almost unlimited opportunities for canoeing on calm, jungle-flanked rivers, either with guides or by yourself in rentals. Cayo District has by far the largest number of canoe rental operators and virtually all of the cottage resorts there offer canoe trips or rentals to their guests. Guided trips from San Ignacio range from day excursions to trips lasting several days, with guests camping on the riverbank all the way to Belize City. One operator is now offering guided raft trips in the area, including trips on the only safe stretch of white water (Class 2) in the country. Generally, the best season for canoeing Cayo's rivers is from November through January and again in late August-early September. See *Chapter 8, Macal River canoe and raft trips* for details regarding guides, rentals, and prices.

In southern Belize, probably the most popular stretches of water are the mainstem Monkey River and its two tributaries, the Bladen and Swasey branches. Canoeists can drift downstream for several days past thickly jungled banks, iguanas, herons, howler monkeys and the occasional manatee. See *Chapter 11, Monkey River* for details. Other canoeing possibilities in southern Belize include Joe Taylor Creek near Punta Gorda (see *Chapter 12, Excursions*).

Downriver tubing trips are possible on your own at the Cockscomb Wildlife Sanctuary, while guided tube trips through caves are now an option on the Caves Branch of the Sibun River near Belmopan. See *Chapter 11* and *Chapter 8* for details. Remember that rainfall (or the lack of it) can dramatically change river conditions. This means that even the most carefully planned canoe trip may have to be postponed or scuttled at the last minute.

Bicycling

Cycling, still not common in Belize, becomes more popular each year. The Western and Northern Highways, while flat and paved, aren't all that scenic and don't offer cyclists much of a shoulder. Possible day trips from Belize City include the Belize Zoo, Guanacaste Park and the Community Baboon Sanctuary (the latter taking off on a dirt road). The Hummingbird Highway, on the other hand, passes through some spectacular forested mountain country, and all but 20km section has been resurfaced. The Southern Highway is rutted, sloppy in the rain, and isn't particularly scenic. The Old Northern Highway is flat and pleasantly tree-lined, but potholed, with little vehicular traffic; day trips to the Altun Ha ruins are possible.

On Caye Caulker, you'll find rental bikes at Caye Caulker Gift Shop. Ambergris Caye offers more cycling possibilities, including a small Maya ruin. You can rent bicycles in San Pedro from Amigo Travel (tel: 026 2180). In Belize City, you can rent mountain bikes at Kevin's Store and Quans.

The best mountain bike country in Belize is in the Mountain Pine Ridge of Cayo District (see *Chapter 8, Mountain Pine Ridge and vicinity* for a list of the area's many attractions).You can rent bikes from the Crystal Paradise office in San Ignacio; see *Chapter 8* for details and prices. Best time of year for bike trips in Cayo is late January through October. November through early January is usually too wet and sloppy.

If you bring your bike to Belize, bring plenty of spare parts. The only stores stocking any parts and accessories at all are located in Belize City: Hop Sing (3 Orange Street; tel: 02 72089); Quan's (18 Orange Street and West Canal, Belize City; tel: 02 75774); and Kevin's Store (32 Euphrates Avenue and Cemetery Road, Belize City; tel: 02 73190). You'll be able to transport your bike atop most buses, and even in the rear of some. Likewise, passenger boats to Caye Caulker and Ambergris Caye can fit your bike aboard. You're not likely to need or want a bicycle on any of the other, smaller cayes.

Mountain climbing and hiking

The only climb of note is Victoria Peak at 1,120m. Even so, it's more an extended hike of several days through rainforest with a scramble at the end. See *Chapter 11, Cockscomb Basin Wildlife (Jaguar) Sanctuary* for details.

The possibilities for day hikes in Belize are practically endless, and you'll find suggestions throughout this guide. For extended, overnight backpacking trips without a guide, your best bet would be the Mountain Pine Ridge of Cayo District, which has a network of small dirt roads and tracks. Unfortunately, there aren't many legal camping possibilities here. See *Chapter 8, Mountain Pine Ridge and vicinity* for details.

Stop at the Lands and Survey Department office in Belize City to try and buy excellent topographic maps of the entire country, at 1:250,000 and 1:50,000. At the time of writing, there were no topographic maps available, and no plans to reprint them, but it may be worth trying. See *Chapter 7, Belize City, Information and useful addresses*.

Caving (Spelunking)

The limestone karst foundation of Belize's Cayo and Toledo Districts is pockmarked with caves of all sorts. Barton Creek Caves south of San Ignacio make for an interesting canoe trip (see *Chapter 8, Excursions*) Many – perhaps the majority – remain unexplored. Some can be easily visited on your own with no caving experience, such as Cayo's popular Rio Frio cavern or Che Chem Ha Cave, Toledo's Blue Creek (Hokeb Ha) Cave, or St. Herman's Cave and Mountain Cow Cave in the Blue Hole National Park. Underground rivers flow through a number of these caves and some – like Toledo's Blue Creek Cave – can be explored at certain times of the year by swimmers with headlamps! In the same vein, one tour operator runs tubing trips through the Caves Branch River south of Belmopan (see *Chapter 8, Other caves in Cayo* for details).

Real spelunkers will want to contact an experienced guide who can take them into Cayo District's cave country. Caves were considered sacred by the ancient Maya and many in the Cayo District still contain pottery shards or completely intact ceramics. The Belize Archaeology Department has wisely closed a number of these sites until more studies can be made, and responsible guides toe the

Department's line. Caves Branch Adventure Camp near Belmopan takes experienced cavers on extended tours of the Vaca Plateau which have been recommended. They also offer trips for first-time cavers (see *Chapter 8*). The Belize Tourist Board can also furnish a list of qualified spelunking guides in Cayo and other districts.

Horseback riding

As with so many of the inland activities, Cayo District leads the way. Many of the Cayo cottage resorts offer horseback day trips, including visits to Maya ruins such as Pilar and Caracol. See *Chapter 8* for details.

Maya ruins

Few travellers would think of visiting Belize and not taking in a ruin or two. There are at least a dozen major Maya sites at various stages of excavation, ranging from the massive Caracol to the tiny Cahal Pech, and many more sites throughout the country (see the map on page 7). Some are remote and difficult to reach – Pusilha, for example – while others like Santa Rita require only a five-minute stroll from town. Some are nothing more than unexcavated rock mounds overgrown with weeds, while others have been meticulously restored.

In general, Belize's ruin sites are far less developed and touristy than Mexico's. At Lubaantun, for example, you'll see more hummingbirds than tourists during most visits. Some, like Caracol and Lamanai, are not only magnificent in their own right but are surrounded by luxuriant rainforest. Wildlife, including tapirs and howler monkeys, are common at many ruin sites in Belize. Everyone has their own favourites, and it's difficult to make any recommendations. I've described all the major sites in this book, and most amateur Mayanists will also probably want a copy of *Warlords and Maize Men: A Guide to the Maya Sites of Belize* published in Belize by Cubola Productions and available at many Belize City bookstores.

The magnificent ruins of Tikal in Guatemala lie only a few hours by bus from Belize's western border. Many travellers claim that Tikal is the Maya ruin to see, and I won't argue. See *Chapter 8, Heading to Tikal,* page 130, for details.

Part Two

The Guide

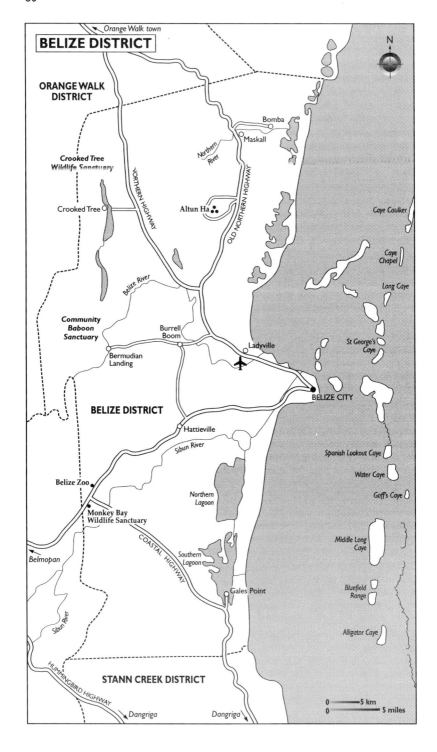

BELIZE DISTRICT

ORANGE WALK DISTRICT

Orange Walk town

Bomba

Maskall

Northern River

Crooked Tree Wildlife Sanctuary

NORTHERN HIGHWAY

OLD NORTHERN HIGHWAY

Crooked Tree

Altun Ha

Caye Caulker

Caye Chapel

Long Caye

Belize River

Community Baboon Sanctuary

Burrell Boom

Bermudian Landing

Ladyville

St George's Caye

BELIZE CITY

BELIZE DISTRICT

Hattieville

Sibun River

Spanish Lookout Caye

Water Caye

Goff's Caye

Belize Zoo

Northern Lagoon

Monkey Bay Wildlife Sanctuary

COASTAL HIGHWAY

Southern Lagoon

Gales Point

Middle Long Caye

Belmopan

Bluefield Range

Sibun River

Alligator Caye

HUMMINGBIRD HIGHWAY

STANN CREEK DISTRICT

Dangriga

Dangriga

0 ——— 5 km
0 ——— 5 miles

Belize District

Most visitors get their first taste of the country in Belize District.
Besides Belize City – which many people prefer as little more
than an overnight layover – the district includes a number of
natural attractions: Maya ruins at Altun Ha, the Belize Zoo,
Crooked Tree and Monkey Bay Wildlife Sanctuaries, and
the world's only howler monkey preserve. It was here that
Europeans made their initial attempts to settle the country,
first as pirates and later as loggers. Logwood and mahogany,
floated down the Belize and Sibun Rivers to waiting ships,
formed the economic backbone of the fledgling colony.
That legacy lives on in many of the district's place names:
villages like Flowers Bank, Bermudian Landing and Burrell
Boom. A 'bank' or 'landing' was the spot along the river where loggers first put
ashore. 'Booms' were those areas where they laid chains across the river to trap
floating logs. The district's Creole majority also traces its roots to the logging days,
when the English Baymen commonly took black women as mistresses.

Although technically part of Belize District, the Northern and Southern
Lagoons are usually accessed via Dangriga, and therefore are covered in *Chapter 11*.
Nearshore cayes such as Caulker and Ambergris are discussed in *Chapter 13*.

BELIZE CITY

> 'At seven o'clock the next morning we saw Belize, appearing – if there be
> no sin in comparing it with cities consecrated by time and venerable
> associations, like Venice and Alexandria – to rise out of the water.'

Those words were penned by veteran explorer John L Stephens in 1839, as his ship
lay at anchor outside Belize City. Stephens was quite probably the last person to
wax poetic on the subject of the former capital. Nowadays, by the time most
travellers reach Belize City, they've heard and read so many deplorable stories that
it's hard to be at all objective about the place. Indeed, many people avoid Belize
City altogether, hopping on the first plane, bus or boat to the country's more
bucolic hinterland. Within the former British Empire, Belize City enjoys a
reputation that is right up there with the Black Hole of Calcutta.

Yet most travellers manage to survive their stay in the city, and some even come
to like the place. Admittedly, it takes time. But there is a funky, unpretentious
charm to this bustling little city built on stilts that you won't find anywhere else in
Belize, perhaps the entire Caribbean. It will be a long time before anyone
complains that Belize City is too touristy.

The crime and street hustlers you've heard about aren't a myth. But with a little
common sense and knowledge of the city it's easy to avoid problems (see *A
cautionary word* below). Most of the city's inhabitants are friendly and cheerful, and

even the hustlers are, by and large, harmless pests. The notorious open sewers were replaced several years ago. In short, there is no reason to huddle in your hotel room as if it were a bomb shelter. For most travellers – especially those interested in the country's natural wonders – Belize City will forever remain a stopover on the road to more exciting destinations. But you cannot know Belize without at least sampling Belize City.

History

Most historians accept 1638 as the city's founding date, although the evidence is scanty. Also questionable is the claim that pirate Henry Wallace first set foot here, lending the area its name (some accounts hold that the name Belize is a Spanish corruption of the buccaneer's surname). But there is no doubt that the first Europeans to settle here were English sailors in search of logwood. Logwood chips had been used for some years as a deep blue woollen dye in Europe, but advances in the textile industry made it a particularly hot commodity in the mid-1600s. Selling for upwards of £100 per ton, logwood suddenly became sought after by buccaneers throughout the Caribbean. The suppression of piracy at about this time further convinced many English seamen that their future lay in logging.

The mouth of the Belize River provided a convenient place to export logwood, and so grew Belize City. Logwood (and later, mahogany) was floated down the river from inland camps. Unfortunately, the area surrounding the river mouth for many kilometres was also an insect-infested mangrove swamp resting only inches above sea level. So intolerable were conditions on the mainland that many early settlers moved their residences offshore to places like St George's Caye. These early English settlers became known as Baymen, and most historians harbour no illusions about them: they are invariably described as drunken, ungovernable wretches, and modern-day Belize City is said to rest on a vast platform of mahogany chips and rum bottles.

Slaves, of course, performed most of the labour. The Baymen frequently took the women as mistresses or even common-law wives, and it was common practice in this case to free them from slavery. Thus began the 'Creolisation' of Belize.

The prosperous logwood trade attracted the Spanish, who raided the settlement repeatedly, beginning in 1718. At one point in the late 1700s, Spaniards succeeded in driving off all the Baymen. The Treaty of Versailles in 1783 allowed English logcutters to return to the area, but conflicts continued until 1798. On September 10 of that year, logcutters, slaves and a small contingent of Royal Navy sailors vanquished the attacking Spanish fleet at St George's Caye. Spain never again attempted to dislodge the English from Belize.

Fires and hurricanes continued to take their toll on Belize City, however. Smallpox, yellow fever and cholera also devastated the area in the mid-1800s. During this time, Belize became the Crown colony of British Honduras, and Belize City boasted all the trappings of a British colonial town in the tropics.

When World War I broke out, patriotic Belizeans volunteered to fight for the motherland. But the black troops ended up as labourers in the Middle East, far from the battlegrounds, humiliated by their racist officers and fellow British soldiers. When they returned to Belize and faced further snubs, hundreds of troops and local citizens embarked on several days of looting and destruction. This, the so-called Ex-Servicemen's Riot of 1919, is generally considered to signal the start of both black and political consciousness in Belize.

A massive hurricane swept into Belize City on September 10 1931, even as citizens celebrated St George's Caye Day. The city was levelled, and nearly 15% of the population killed. Meanwhile, the independence movement grew, with Belize

City as the focal point for anti-colonial politics. Three years before internal self-government became a reality, however, Hurricane Hattie levelled the city, killing 262 and leading to plans to relocate the capital inland. But despite the capital's move to Belmopan, Belize City remains the cultural, political and economic centre of Belize. Nor has the orderly turnover of political power to Belizeans dampened affection for some aspects of British colonial rule: Queen Elizabeth's visits in 1985 and 1994 were occasions for massive celebrations in Belize City.

Getting there and away
By air
All international flights land at Phillip S W Goldson International Airport (tel: 025 2045), located in Ladyville about 17km north of the city centre. From here, you can catch internal flights to Punta Gorda, Dangriga, Big Creek, Placencia, Caye Caulker, Ambergris Caye, Caye Chapel and Corozal with either Maya Island Air or Tropic Air. These flights originate at the Municipal Airport a few miles away, but will land at the International Airport for ticketed passengers. Note, however, that fares often run about 20–50% higher if you get on at the International Airport; consequently, it may be cheaper to take a cab for BZ$30 and catch your internal flight at the Municipal Airport. Some internal flights, however, originate at the International Airport. Maya Island Air (tel: 02 62435 in Belize or 1 800 521 1247 toll-free in the US and Canada) and Tropic Air (tel: 02 62012 in Belize City or 1 800 422 3435 toll-free in the US) both operate ticket booths at the International Airport. Both airlines have daily flights to San Pedro, Ambergris Caye. You'll find more information on internal flights in *Chapter 6, Transport*, and in the chapters dealing with your destination.

You'll be stamped into Belize at the Customs Desk. It's a good idea to make sure they give you the standard 30-day stay. One of our travelling companions found out only as he tried to leave the country three weeks later that he'd been given (for some unfathomable reason) only a week-long visitor's permit. Since he'd overstayed the permit, there was serious talk of detaining him! I've only heard of this one instance, but it's a good idea to watch carefully what gets stamped in your passport.

Belize Bank, located just outside the airport doors, is open daily 08.00–10.30 and 12.00–16.30. They change cash and travellers' cheques.

There are several shops selling crafts and T-shirts in the departure lounge to help you spend the last of your currency.

Most international and local car rental agencies have booths at the car rental row opposite the International Airport entrance. These include: Hertz (tel: 025 3300 at the airport or 02 30886 downtown; fax: 02 30268; email: safarihz@btl.net); Pancho's Auto Rental (tel: 025 2540 at the airport or 02 45554 downtown, fax: 02 31504); Avis (tel: 025 2385 at the airport or 02 34619 downtown at the municipal airstrip); Crystal (tel: 025 2139 at the airport 02 31600 downtown; fax: 02 31900; email: crystal@btl.net; web: www.crystalbelize.com); Jaguar Auto Rental (tel: 025 2747 or 02 73142 downtown, fax: 02 70397; email: jaguarrent@btl.net); Budget (tel: 02 32435; fax: 02 30237; email: jmagroup@btl.net; web: www.budget-belize.com) and Jabiru (tel: 02 44680; fax: 02 34136; email: jabiru@btl.net). Be sure to read *Chapter 6, Rental cars,* page 59, before deciding to rent a car in Belize.

In the same strip there is Margie's Travel Service (tel: 025 2016) and G&W Holiday Travel Agency (tel: 025 2461) which can help you out with any last minute questions.

The Embassy Hotel (tel: 025 3333; fax: 025 2267; email: embassy@btl.net; web: www.belizeweb.com/embassyhotel) is right alongside the airport. Conveniently located for business meetings, but there is little other reason to recommend staying in the overpriced, yet comfortable rooms – a double is BZ$100.

A taxi from the airport to the downtown hotels or anywhere else within the city costs a set fee of BZ$30. You can share the cab and fare, of course, with other passengers even though the cab drivers will discourage you.

A cheaper option, depending on the amount of luggage you are carrying, is to walk for about 30 minutes to the main highway and take a bus downtown from there. Turn left out of the terminal building and just keep going. You may by lucky enough to hitch a ride all the way into town as that is where most people will be going. There used to be a shuttle bus running from the International Airport to downtown, but this has been discontinued. The airport departure tax when leaving Belize is BZ$30.

The **Municipal Airport** is about 3km north of the downtown hotels, facing the water. Here you'll find not only Maya Island Air and Tropic Air (which provide scheduled flights to major towns and cayes), but also a couple of charter companies: Javier's Flying Service (tel: 02 35360; fax: 02 31731) and Cari-Bee Air Service (tel: 02 44253; fax: 02 31031). It's not likely you'll need to fly charter unless you're headed for difficult-to-reach spots like Gallon Jug (the heart of the Río Bravo Conservation Area, see *Chapter 10*). Maya Travel Services (tel: 02 31623, fax: 02 30585; email: mayatravel@btl.net; web: www.mayatravelservices.com) have their office at the Municipal Airport. There is a small restaurant next to the terminal building.

By bus

At least half a dozen bus companies operate out of Belize City, serving all the major towns and many of the smaller ones. Buses run almost hourly throughout the day to all destinations north and west, with fewer departures headed south. For more information on bus schedules, see the chapter describing your destination or call the numbers listed below. Bus schedules change frequently. The four biggest companies are Batty Bus (tel: 02 72025/73929), Venus (tel: 02 73354), Novelo's (tel: 02 77372) and Z-Line (offices in Dangriga tel: 05 22160). Fortunately, all four are located within a few of blocks of each other, making connections easy. Z-Line and Venus share the same terminal near Magazine Road and Vernon Street. Nearby, on West Collet Canal Street, you'll find Novelo's terminal. On the other side of Collet Canal, Batty's Bus terminal is on Mosul Street just off Orange Street. James Bus , travelling to Punta Gorda via Dangriga, operates off the street on Cemetery Road opposite the Texaco gas station. Ritchie's Bus, travelling to Dangriga and onto Placencia, operate off the street on East Collet Canal Street, opposite Novelo's. All the bus services are located in the area of town called Mesopotamia, about 0.7km from the town centre and the Swing Bridge. It's not the safest part of town at night, so definitely take a cab if you arrive at night. During the day we've had no problems walking from terminal to terminal or into the centre; if you've got lots of luggage, however, you may still prefer to take a cab.

By taxi

Taxis within the city (excluding the International Airport, see above) cost BZ$5 for one passenger, BZ$1 for each additional passenger. The taxis have no meters, and you're best off making sure both you and the driver know exactly how much the fare is. Also be sure that to establish whether the fare quoted is in US$ or BZ$. Extra stops within the city cost extra, and drivers will frequently have an excuse handy for why they must charge you more than the standard fare for your particular trip.

By boat

Boats run daily from near the Swing Bridge in the city centre to Caye Caulker, San Pedro (Ambergris Caye) and Caye Chapel. See *Chapter 13* for details. Boats leave from the petrol station on North Front Street, from the Marine Terminal by the swing bridge or near the Bellevue Hotel

Where to stay

The range of accommodations in Belize City, as you might expect, covers 5-star luxury hotels down to the hostels in the 'budget' category (less than BZ$25). For a complete, updated list, contact the Belize Tourist Board New Central Bank Building, Level 2, Gabourel Lane, PO Box 325, Belize City, Belize; tel: 02 31913; fax: 02 31943; toll free in the US and Canada: 1 800 624 0686; email: info@travelbelize.org; web: www.travelbelize.org.

The listing below is obviously only a partial one, concentrating mostly on cheapies that we've tried or have been recommended. In general, you get very poor value for your hotel dollar in Belize City compared with the rest of the country. Many hotels are dark, dingy, and not particularly cheap. The few places that are both pleasant and cheap are often solidly booked. Therefore, I've listed a few nicer, albeit more expensive, options. To get a room in the recommended cheaper places, which you may want to do if you are flying in, you usually have to reserve well in advance and send a deposit. It's always worth dropping by, however.

Considering the prices and options, you're often better off hopping on a boat to Caye Caulker, where you'll find plenty of lodging at much cheaper prices. Some travellers like to do this even if they're taking a bus from Belize City the next day, since the combined cost of a round- trip boat fare and hotel in Caulker is frequently less than a hotel in the city, and a good deal more relaxing.

Seaside Guesthouse 3 Prince Street, PO Box 2060; tel: 02 78339; email: friends@btl.net. Six rooms. Friendly, pleasant location south of the river, consistently packed. A rustic, two-storey wooden building that is Quaker-owned and non-profit (only the Belizean staff is paid). BZ$48 with shared bath, fan. BZ$20 for a bed in the 7-bed dormitory.

Hotel Mopan 55 Regent Street; tel: 02 77351; email: hotelmopan@btl.net. Also south of the river, somewhat overpriced, but pleasant inside and out, with a bar for guests. 16 rooms, with private bath, air conditioning or fan. BZ$80. Takes credit cards.

Bellevue Hotel 5 Southern Foreshore; tel: 02 77051/2; fax: 02 73253; email: fins@btl.net; web: www.belize.com/bellevue.html www.belize.com/bellevue.html. The best of the bunch south of the river, but pricey, but then it does have a pool! Right on the harbour. 35 rooms at BZ$130 with AC and TV.

Glenthorne Manor 27 Barrack Road; tel: 02 44212. 7 rooms. A lovely Victorian house, friendly, safe and conveniently located in the centre of town. Unfortunately, all this is hearsay, because it's always solidly booked! BZ$75 with breakfast.

Golden Dragon 29 Queen Street; tel: 02 72817. 27 rooms. Somewhat dark and depressing, but a friendly staff, safe and very close to the Swing Bridge, boats and restaurants. There's also a passable Chinese restaurant downstairs. US$25 with private bath and fan.

Hotel Estefan 11 Handyside Street; tel: 02 30797. Eight rooms. Originally Mom's Triangle Inn, one of the most famous gringo hotels in all of Central America, Mom's has closed down ending nearly three decades of tradition. The new owner has kept some of the atmosphere but there is still a long way to go. BZ$50 with private bath, air conditioning or fan and TV.

Fort Street Guesthouse 4 Fort Street; tel: 02 30116; fax: 02 78808; email: fortst@btl.net; web: www.fortst.com. 6 rooms. Two American sisters run this popular, charming and airy house in the classy Fort George part of town towards the end of the peninsular. Even if you don't stay here, the excellent restaurant is worth a splurge for breakfast, lunch or dinner. Unlike some of the classier hotels in town, the owners don't snub budget travellers who drop by, and will go out of their way to help with storing bags, travel advice, taxis, etc, even for non-guests. BZ$110 with private bath, fan, including a delicious breakfast.

Dim's Mira Río Hotel 59 North Front Street; tel: 02 44970. 6 rooms. Close to the boat dock for Caye Caulker, with a restaurant and bar, serving seasonal food and BBQs. BZ$30 with shared bath and fan.

North Front Street Guesthouse 124 North Front Street; tel: 02 77595. 8 rooms. Basic, but very popular with budget travellers, and conveniently located near the Caulker boats. BZ$27 with shared bath, fan. BZ$12 on the dormitory.

Bon Aventure Hotel 122 North Front Street; tel: 02 44248. 9 rooms. Next door to North Front Street Guest House. Basic but clean and safe. BZ$26 with private bath, fan.

Colton House 9 Cork Street; tel: 02 44666; email: coltonhse@btl.net. 5 rooms in total, all with ceiling fans and one with AC. A beautiful, well-maintained home typical of colonial Belize City right out on the end of the peninsular, run by a former British soldier and his Belizean wife. BZ$120 with private bath.

Chateau Caribbean 6 Marine Parade, PO Box 947; tel: 02 30800; fax: 02 30900; email: chateaucar@btl.net; web: www.belizeweb.com/~chateau or www.chateaucaribbean.com. Old colonial house on the sea front. Romantic, elegant and a little pricey (US$86) but a good place to relax before flying out.

Bakadeer Inn 74 Cleghorn Street; tel: 02 31286; fax: 02 36506, email: mcfield@btl.net. 12 rooms. Not far from Municipal airport with guarded parking. The restaurant serves excellent meals. From BZ$80 with private bath, AC, TV, and refrigerator. A popular place with conservation workers and the only member of the Belize Ecotourism Society in Belize City.

Freddie's Guesthouse 86 Eve Street; tel: 02 33851. 3 rooms. A cheapie that gets lots of recommendations. Close enough to be central, far enough away to be quite. BZ$45 with a shared bathroom.

If you pull into town on the Venus or Z-Line buses late at night and don't want the hassle of finding a hotel, you can always try the hotel directly above the Venus Terminal (tel: 02 77390), 8 rooms, US$25 with private bath. There's a restaurant in the terminal.

Places to eat

Most restaurants are closed on Sundays, and many close Saturday as well. Even many of the hotel restaurants close on Sunday, a notable exception being the **Bellevue Hotel** restaurant at 5 Southern Foreshore.

Besides those mentioned above (Fort Street Guest House, Dim's Mira Río, the Bakadeer Inn and the Golden Dragon), you'll find dozens of acceptable places to eat in town. **Pearl's**, on Handyside, serves good pizzas and Italian food. **Macy's Café** (18 Bishop Street) serves good, cheap Belizean Creole food, often including such game meats as gibnut and armadillo. There are a score of Chinese restaurants, all pretty much serving the same dishes (**Caribbean Restaurant** on Regent Street). For classier eats, **The Grill** (164 Newtown-Barrack Road) and **Three Amigoes** (King Street) have been recommended. The **Sea Rock Café** near the post office serves good East Indian food at budget prices. The **Hard Rock Café** near the Estefan serves steaks and seafood. One cheapy with good Belizean food is **Mar's** at 118 North Front Street near North Front Street Guest House. DIT's south of the river at 50 King Street is also excellent, open at weekends and has

A typical Caribbean beach in Belize, near Placencia (JN)

THE CAYES
Belize at its most relaxed and the focus for visitors attracted by the excellent diving and snorkelling around the coral reef.
Above: *Out Island Beach Club, Caye Caulker (TC)*
Below: *Ambergris Caye (AG)*

Above: *The dock – heart of Belize City* (JB)

Below: *San Ignacio, gateway to the Maya* (AG)

CHILDREN OF BELIZE
Above: *Maya youngsters* (JN)
Below: *Girls at Punta Gorda* (SB)

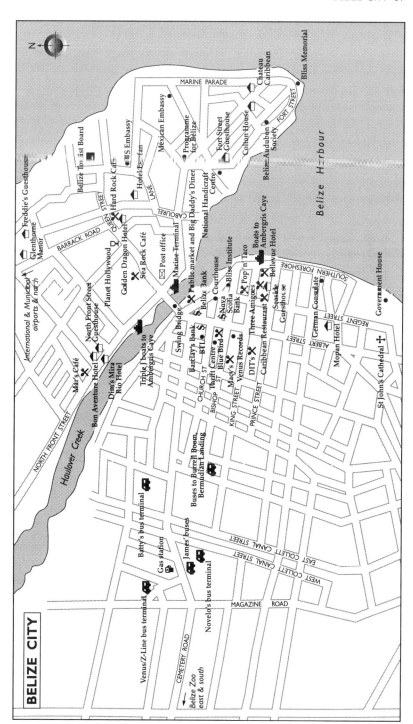

BELIZE CITY

fantastic cakes and pastries. Across the street from Nova Scotia Bank is Blue Bird Café which has good food and ice cream. Big Daddy's on the second floor of the market is cheap, excellent value and has a view over the river. Pop'n'Taco on the corner of King and Regent Street has good, cheap food.

What to see

You can easily see the city in an hour or two and most travellers end up stuck for at least that long in town, awaiting buses, planes, or boats. Unfortunately, the old-style wooden colonial homes with latticework, balconies and broad porches are few and far between these days, many of them the victim of hurricanes.

From the famous Swing Bridge in downtown, you can walk to the outskirts of the city in 20 minutes. Not that you'd want to – everything worth seeing is close to the centre – but that gives you an idea of the city's size. The **Swing Bridge** itself opened in 1923, and for travellers, it marks the centre of town. The bridge, constructed in Liverpool, spans Haulover Creek, the mouth of the Belize River. Twice daily, at 05.30 and 17.30, the bridge is manually cranked around to let boat traffic pass by. Meanwhile, traffic comes to a halt on either side. It's a nostalgic little ritual, popular with tourists and citizens alike; plans to replace the bridge with a mechanically operated one have met with stiff local opposition.

Just on the south side of the Swing Bridge, you'll find the newly restored **public market**, selling the produce of inland Belize and fish from the cayes. Commercial boats crowd the area near the bridge, and you'll often see turtlers slaughtering their catch. Refuse from the market and fish boats goes into Haulover Creek, where vast schools of catfish prowl the impossibly murky waters. The funky ambience of the riverfront was put to film in Peter Weir's 1985 version of Paul Theroux's *The Mosquito Coast*. Belize City also doubled as an unnamed African capital in the film version of Frederick Forsyth's *Dogs of War*.

Continuing south on Regent Street, you'll find the **Court House** complex, some of the few well-preserved pieces of colonial architecture in the city. Closer to the water on Southern Foreshore is the **Bliss Institute**. Named for 'Baron Bliss', a wealthy benefactor of the city who never actually left his yacht anchored offshore, this building houses the National Library, some stelae from the Caracol ruins, and a number of cultural events. At the very southern end of Regent Street lies **St John's Anglican Cathedral**, the oldest Protestant church in Central America. Nearby is **Government House**, former residence of the Governor in colonial day, where there is a small museum. If you are looking for somewhere to quietly sit and read for a couple of hours, pop along to the Government House.

The Fort George area north of the Swing Bridge offers a pleasant, breezy walk to the **Bliss Memorial** next to the water. This neighbourhood is one of the older, elite parts of the city, with a few remaining wooden homes with shutters, balconies, and latticework. Recent building work has added an atmosphere of prosperity to some of the district.

Special events

The big blow-out in Belize City spans the period from September 10 (St George's Caye Day) to Independence Day (September 21). The festivities actually start a few days early and include parades, music, food and plenty of rum. The highlight of Baron Bliss Day (March 9) is the big sailing regatta coinciding with the arrival of La Ruta Maya Belize River Challenge that sails from San Ignacio for 170 miles. (see *Chapter 8, Macal River canoe and raft trips*).

Information and useful addresses

All of Belize's conservation organisations are headquartered in Belize City and they're a good source of information on the nature reserves and current environmental news. Particularly helpful are the **Belize Audubon Society** at 12 Fort Street; tel: 02 35004 and the **Programme for Belize** at 1 Eyre Street; tel: 02 75616. Stop in for a visit, their enthusiasm is infectious. You'll find addresses, phone numbers and brief descriptions of their goals in *Chapter 3, Conservation organisations*.

While you're in that area, the **National Handicraft Centre** on Fort Street is a cooperative run by producers for producers that has a wide range of gifts and souvenirs. If you're looking for gifts to take home, buying from here gets more of your money out to the producers.

Change cash or travellers' cheques at the conveniently located **Belize Bank** on Market Square (just south of the Swing Bridge). There's also the **Bank of Nova Scotia** on Albert Street, **Barclays Bank** at 21 Albert Street and **Atlantic Bank** at 6 Albert Street. All three banks have ATMs taking VISA and/or MasterCard.

The **BTL** office for making phone calls is at 1 Church Street, open daily from 08.00–18.00.

The **Belize Tourist Board** has an office in the New Central Bank Building, Level 2, Gabourel Lane; tel: 02 31913 that's open daily during the week, 08.00–12.00 and 13.00–17.00. They can supply you with a list of hotels and services countrywide, as well as suggestions for guides.

Many foreign embassies are headquartered in Belmopan rather than Belize City. The **US Embassy** is at 29 Gabourel Lane (tel: 02 77161), the **German Consul** at 57 Southern Foreshore (tel: 02 77282), the **Mexican Embassy** is at 20 North Park Street (tel: 02 30194), and the **Guatemalan Embassy** can be reached at 8A Street, King's Park (tel: 02 33150; fax: 02 35140.).

If you're looking for books, the **Thrift Center** is at 4 Church Street on the second floor, opposite the BTL office. You'll also find books, especially those by locally renowned author Emory King, at **Admiral Burnaby's Art Gallery**, 9 Regent Street.

The post office has a special storefront just north of the Swing Bridge on Queen Street. Here you can buy sets of the popular stamps depicting Belizean flora, fauna, and folk characters.

Hikers and backcountry travellers will want to buy the excellent topographic maps of the country available at the Lands and Survey Department, on the second floor above the post office (Paslow Building, use the Front Street entrance just north of the Swing Bridge). Two maps on a scale of 1:250,000 cover the country (BZ$10 each), and there are some 30 more detailed topographic maps at 1:50,000 selling for BZ$1.50. Unfortunately, you'll probably have to wait in line behind Belizeans settling land taxes, something which could take an hour or more, and even then you may find there are none in stock. When researching this edition there were no 'topos' in stock and no plans to print new ones.

The best selection of Belizean music on cassette tapes can be found at **Venus Photos and Records**, 33 Corner of Albert and Bishop Streets. They'll play tapes for you if you're not sure what you want.

Those who want nightlife need to be careful. There are several bars in the central and outer lying districts, but caution should be your guide. On Queen's Street you can find the Belizean version of **Planet Hollywood** or you can take a cab out to the Lumberyard on the Western Highway. One quiet, sea-front bar is **Lindsburg Landing** out of town on Barrack Road.

The **Hard Rock Café**, near the Estefan Hotel, is an air-conditioned nightclub and bar which also serves steak and seafood dinners.

Try to avoid being in Belize City on a Sunday, when the whole place shuts down.

A cautionary word

When my wife first stepped off the bus in Belize City in 1975, she and her companion were immediately set upon by a pair of young touts, each determined to take them to different hotels. Unable to settle their business differences in a more diplomatic way, the touts pulled knives on each other – one brandished a Swiss Army knife! – and Jayne and her friend managed to slip quietly away.

Street hustles and hassles haven't changed much in the past 25 years. The streets may be a bit meaner now; Belizean versions of the Los Angeles Crips and Bloods gangs have sprouted here and there, and crack has joined pot in the local drug market. Armed robbery still takes its toll of tourist dollars; on one trip, we met two travellers who'd been shaken down in separate incidents as they walked the city on their own at night.

Yet most travellers come away from Belize City vaguely wondering if the bad publicity isn't a bit overblown. Unless you blockade yourself in a luxury hotel room day and night, there's no way to avoid the hustlers trying to sell you a little Belize Breeze. But that's about all that you're bound to face if you follow a few common sense precautions.

First of all, don't wander around town at night, especially alone. If you must walk, go with a group of fellow travellers. A safer bet is to always take a cab at night. Certain areas of town should definitely be avoided on foot after dark: the district known as Mesopotamia, which stretches from the Southside Canal to the Collet Canal near the bus depots; and the Southern Foreshore, particularly behind the Bliss Institute. Stay clear of the alley just to the west of Handyside Street. These same areas, incidentally, are fairly benign by day. Crack dealers and their clientele move around, however, so it's best to ask the people who run your hotel about which areas to avoid.

Secondly, wear a money pouch beneath your clothing. Robbers know this trick, of course, but it may slow them down a bit, long enough for them to get nervous and take off; that's exactly what happened to one traveller we met. Don't carry much money when you're out at night, but always have something on hand, just in case.

Thirdly, don't wear expensive watches or jewellery, and don't flash money around.

Finally, be prepared to be hustled. In most cases, this amounts to being approached by Pseudo-Rastas selling 'smoke', or offering to change money. Persistent, yes, but seldom are these pitches threatening, and sometimes they can even be amusing. Look on the bright side: you rarely see a beggar in Belize City. Walk away with a smile and they will too, eventually. It's a little tougher at bars; try not to leave an empty seat for someone bumming drinks. Women, particularly those travelling alone, can expect a fair amount of verbal harassment. It's no worse than in other parts of Central America, but here you might have a harder time convincing them you don't speak the language.

Keep in mind that most residents are honest, friendly people who are more than a little embarrassed at their city's reputation for street hassles. And remember that the vast majority of travellers have no trouble here.

Excursions
Belize Zoo

Veteran travellers in most Third World countries have long since learned to give wide berth to the zoos – tawdry little places where wild animals pace sullenly in cramped cellblocks. Belize's Zoo, on the other hand, has become something of an international model as a sensitive, truly educational facility, and it's well worth a visit.

The Belize Zoo is privately financed, the brainchild of Sharon Matola, an American expatriate who became a Belizean citizen in 1990. Although she qualifies as a genuine Belizean celebrity these days, the path that led her there was more than a little circuitous. During the late 1970s, she left graduate school in Florida to take a job as a dancing girl and lion tamer in a Mexican circus. When British filmmaker Richard Foster offered her the animal-handling duties for a wildlife series, she left the circus for Belize. The documentary – *Amanti* – had to be abandoned when funding fell through, and for a time it seemed as if the tamed 'wildlife' would face the same fate.

Matola made the best of a bad situation. Rather than releasing her charges into the forest – where their domestic habits made them ill-suited for survival – she turned the outdoor holding area into a public zoo in 1983. She raised money for the fledgling venture in any way possible: from raising chickens to tapping celebrities for donations (the producers and actors of the movie *The Mosquito Coast* made sizeable gifts to the zoo). A number of conservation groups, most notably Wildlife Preservation Trust International, were instrumental in making the Belize Zoo a reality.

For eight years, the zoo remained on Foster's property west of Belize City. In late 1991, Matola moved the zoo to its new location on a 30-acre site just west of the old one. Seattle architectural firm Jones and Jones, award-winning designers of progressive, habitat-conscious exhibits at the San Diego Zoo and Seattle's Woodland Park Zoo, donated the master plan for the new facility. Actor Harrison Ford, who first became enchanted by the Belize Zoo during the filming of *The Mosquito Coast*, was among those who donated money for the construction of the new Gerald Durrell Visitors' Centre.

The new zoo retains the funky, natural feel of the old place. Simple wire barriers surround existing forest, connected by pathways that wend their way through the bush. This is clearly a zoo designed first with the animals' comfort in mind; aesthetics are, thankfully, a secondary consideration. The aviary, for instance, consists of nothing more elaborate than netting stretched over a group of trees. Signs are handmade, with informal and humorous texts that belie their educational content. Deer roam freely on the same trails as visitors, while toucans fly into and out of the zoo grounds at will.

The animals themselves are mostly the original bunch, representing some 70 indigenous species. The list includes spider monkeys, giant anteaters, kinkajous, a jaguar, two species of peccary, howler monkeys, pacas ('gibnuts'), coatis, foxes, ocelots, jaguarundis, curassows, vultures, butterflies, hawks, owls and wading birds. The individual attention lavished on the animals is reflected in the fact that the staff has named many of them. Celebrities include Rambo the keel-billed toucan, Sally the crocodile and April the tapir. Matola and her staff point out that none of the animals has been captured in the wild for exhibition at the zoo. Those not born in zoos were 'pets' which were later abandoned and would face no chance of survival in the wild.

The Belize Zoo would be noteworthy even if it were nothing more than a well-tended collection of indigenous animals in a near-natural setting. But the foresight of Matola, her staff and Belizean educators has made it much more. Over the years, the zoo has gradually become the single most important tool of environmental education in Belize. A regularly-scheduled programme brings Belizean schoolchildren to the zoo, where they learn not only about their tiny nation's biological wealth but also how to conserve it. A whole generation is growing up with a new perspective on habitat and wildlife, much of it thanks to the Belize Zoo. This becomes particularly important in a poor country like Belize, where poaching and habitat protection laws can't realistically be enforced without grass-roots community support.

And the zoo gets its environmental message across in typical Belizean fashion. The handpainted signs steer clear of scholarship or high-handed lectures. Instead, the animals 'speak' for themselves, in colloquial Creole-style English, describing in jocular fashion the problems they face, and the way in which ordinary Belizeans can help.

The living symbol of this new conservation-based ethic is April, the resident Baird's tapir, Belize's national animal. Schoolchildren learn about the tapir's endangered status, the need for protection and the myths that have encouraged its decline in the past (for example, the notion that tapirs enjoyed skinning people alive with their snouts). April's birthday is now celebrated by children throughout the country. Gifts include carrots, bananas and a vegetable birthday cake several feet tall.

These educational efforts received a major boost in 1989 with the purchase of 140 acres of forest across the highway from the old zoo. The land was formerly owned by a founding member of the Belize Audubon Society and a pioneer in local conservation, Dora Weyer. With donations from private citizens, the USAID, and pop singer Jimmy Buffett, among others, Environmental Education Committee Chairperson Amy Bodwell – who also works as Assistant Director of the Zoo – and the rest of the zoo staff have transformed the area into the Tropical Education Centre. The Centre features nature trails, a library, lecture rooms and a dormitory for visitors, all power supplied via solar energy.

Finally, the zoo is actively involved in a captive breeding programme. Breeding will not only provide a continued supply of animals for the zoo (precluding the need to remove them from the wild), but may help bolster wild populations of some threatened or endangered species. When the Los Angeles Zoo agreed in 1990 to donate a newly-born captive male tapir as April's future mate, the news made the front page in Belizean newspapers. US zoos have been highly successful in tapir breeding, and they expect April's second-born young to help diversify the captive gene pool there. Meanwhile, the Belize Zoo plans eventually to reintroduce tapirs in suitable habitat throughout their former range in Central America.

The Belize Zoo is located 47km west of Belize City (or about 32km east of Belmopan) on the well-paved Western Highway. There are mileposts along the highway and a sign at the zoo turnoff itself, on the northern side of the highway. To reach the zoo via public transportation from Belize City, take any of the numerous daily buses headed for Belmopan, Dangriga or Cayo (San Ignacio). Ask the driver to put you off at the turnoff to the zoo, after which you'll have a ten-minute walk to the site. Wait along the highway and flag down any bus headed east to get back to Belize City. Buses run by about once an hour during daylight. Most of the Belize City travel agencies offer day trips to the zoo.

The zoo is open daily from 08.00 to 17.00. Admission for non-Belizeans is BZ$15.00, concessions BZ$7.50 and this includes a personalised tour of the facility with a well- informed local guide. An informal gift shop sells T-shirts, postcards and wildlife posters. In the unlikely event that children get bored watching the animals, there's a playground. Be sure to wear long pants, shoes, socks, a thick long-sleeved shirt and plenty of insect repellent on anything left exposed. The zoo may have the most voracious mosquitoes in all Belize, converging in great swarms on T-shirted backs and deftly drilling right through the fabric.

The Belize Zoo still needs and welcomes donations. The mailing address is PO Box 1787, Belize City. For information call tel/fax: 081 3004/3003; email: belizezoo@btl.net.

Monkey Bay Wildlife Sanctuary

This privately owned sanctuary lies 2km west of the Belize Zoo at mile marker 31 along the Western Highway. Fronting the Sibun River for nearly 3km, the area takes in 1,070 acres of wetlands, pine ridge, and cohune ridge. Visitors report sighting 250 species of birds, as well as jaguars, peccaries, deer, crocodiles, iguanas, and mountain lions. The entire area was once logged, but the American who purchased the area in 1990 has since been reintroducing native fruits and vegetation as wildlife habitat. Biologists now use the sanctuary as a research base, but visitors are welcome. Write to the manager, PO Box 187, Mile 31 Western Highway, Belmopan or tel: 081 3032; fax: 08 23361; email: mbay@pobox.com; web: www.watershedbelize.org. Monkey Bay has opened one segment of the planned Mesoamerica Trail at Indian Creek. It is a beautiful, relatively easy two-day guided hike with primary forests and wildlife linking Monkey Bay and Five Blues Lake National Park in St. Matthews Village. Room and board accommodations are available at both ends of the trail segment. Contact Monkey Bay to arrange trail access, guide and food provisions for the trek.

To reach the sanctuary, hop on any bus headed west from Belize City and ask the driver to let you off at the access road; it's a short hike to the headquarters. There's a small camping area, a swimming hole on the Sibun River, and drinking water from cisterns.

Altun Ha

Altun Ha is one of only two Belizean Maya sites north of Belize City that will impress non-archaeologists (Lamanai in Orange Walk District is the other). A major ceremonial and trading centre, Altun Ha was apparently first settled around AD150, flourished during the Late Classic, and was abandoned under mysterious circumstances around AD1000. Many of the ceremonial tombs bore unmistakable signs of desecration, signs that couldn't be attributed to latter-day looters. This led archaeologist David Pendergast to suggest that Altun Ha may have been brought to its feet by a violent peasant revolt. Other, less dramatic, theories have been put forth and it's not likely that the riddle around Altun Ha's downfall will be solved any time soon.

Belize's first Archaeological Commissioner, A H Anderson, learned of Maya remains at Altun Ha as early as 1957. But it wasn't until 1963, when local quarry workers found a jade pendant at the site, that archaeologists launched a full-scale investigation. David Pendergast of the Royal Ontario Museum began work the following year, leading the first intensive, long-term archaeological dig in Belize's history. Following restoration work by Belizeans Joseph Palacio and Elizabeth Graham in the 1970s, Altun Ha became the country's second Maya site opened for tourism (Xunantunich in Cayo District was the first).

Pendergast found Altun Ha unusual in several respects. First, the Maya erected no stelae here, a common feature at many other sites. Secondly, the tombs in the main temple are not those of warlords or dynastic rulers, but priests. And finally, he found remains of a unique sacrificial offering at one of the temples: charred bits of jade and copal resin jewellery, which had first been smashed to pieces, thrown into a fire, and then scattered ritually just before new construction was built atop the older altar. The ritual significance of these unusual features has never been explained.

The most spectacular find lay deep within one of the tombs in the so-called Temple of the Masonry Altars, alongside the remains of a priest: a massive carved jade head of the Maya Sun God, Kinich Ahau. Standing 14.9cm high and weighing 4.42kg, it was the largest carved jade artefact ever uncovered in the Maya world. Jade doesn't occur naturally in Belize, and researchers suggest that the stone

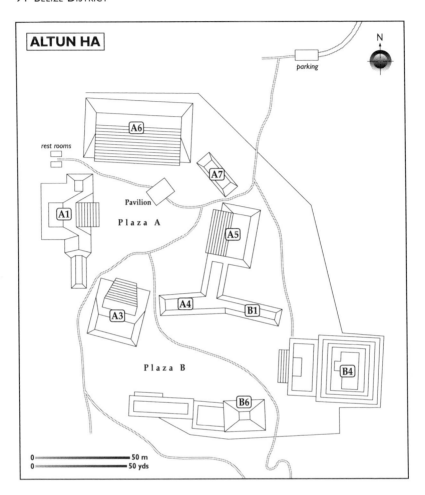

originated in Guatemala's Motagua River valley. It won't be on display until Belize can afford a proper archaeological museum, being housed for the time being in a vault in Belize City. Pendergast also found artefacts of a distinctive green-gold obsidian at Altun Ha, some 1,100km from its origin in Mexico's Teotihuacán area.

The site consists of 13 structures surrounding two main plazas. Entering the site, you'll find yourself facing Structure A-1, in which archaeologists uncovered a single tomb containing over 300 pieces of jade, and the overgrown Structure A-6, possibly a residence for the elite. Structure A-4, at the far end of the plaza, is also badly overgrown. Researchers found shells from the Pacific Ocean here, further evidence of Altun Ha's importance along the Maya trade routes. Continue south past A-4 and you enter Plaza B, built as an extension to Plaza A during the Early Classic. At the far end of the plaza stands Structure B-4, known alternatively as the Temple of the Masonry Altars and the Temple of the Sun God. Rising 18m above plaza level, it is the largest of the pyramids at Altun Ha, and the burial site of the Kinich Ahau jade head.

A trail beginning at the base of B-4 leads through the bush a short distance to Rockstone Pond, Altun Ha's water reservoir. Originally a much smaller natural pool, the reservoir was gradually enlarged by quarrying, lining the sides and bottom with clay to prevent seepage.

Altun Ha lies about 53km north of Belize City, just off the Old Northern Highway. It's one of Belize's most pleasant roadways, narrow and full of turns, shaded in spots by encroaching forest, seldom travelled nowadays with the availability of the newer, wider, and straighter Northern Highway. Nevertheless, it's flat and well-paved south of Maskall. If you've got a rental car, turn right off the Northern Highway onto the Old Northern Highway just past Sandhill, some 27km northwest of Belize City (the sign reads Maskall). Follow the Old Northern Highway for another 18.5km, at which point you'll see the dirt road turnoff to Altun Ha on your left. About 2.6km from the turnoff, the dirt road forks; stay to your right and follow this fork 1km to the site. About 2.3km before the turnoff to Altun Ha, on the west side of the Old Northern Highway, you'll pass a small wooden shack where woodcarver Alston Burgess sells his zericote carvings. Prices here are much lower than at gift shops.

There is very limited bus service on the Old Northern Highway. On weekdays at 13.00, 15.30 and 17.30 you can catch an independently-owned bus for Maskall at the Belcan Bridge leading out of town (call the Maskall community telephone, 031 2058, to make sure that the bus is still operating). Hitchhiking is a possibility but there's not much traffic.

There are no overnight accommodations at Altun Ha and camping is technically forbidden. Ask the caretaker, however, about camping possibilities nearby. Near the town of Maskall, 15km north of Altun Ha, you'll find the Maruba Resort and Jungle Spa; tel: 03 22199. Their mailing address in the US is PO Box 300703, Houston, TX 77230; tel: 713 799 2031; fax: 713 795 8573; email: maruba@flash.net; web: www.maruba-spa.com. They've got nine rooms, all with private bath, fans and partial air conditioning, pool, Japanese tub, restaurant, bar, horseback riding and tours. Upwards of US$230 a night. A much cheaper alternative, the Nago Bank Guest House, located at 2.4km on the Bomba Road just north of Maskall, had closed its doors at the time of printing. Check with the Maskall community telephone operator to see if it's reopened.

The Altun Ha site is open daily 08.00–16.00, and admission costs BZ$10. Wallace's Beer Parlour, a house at the site entrance, sells soft drinks, beer and snacks. Toilets and a picnic shelter are available.

COMMUNITY BABOON SANCTUARY

When Belizean Creoles talk about 'baboons', they're referring to the black howler monkey (*Alouatta pigra*). The black howler is one of only three primates in Belize, the others being Geoffroy's spider monkey (*Ateles geoffroyi*) – a much smaller primate which Creoles simply call 'monkey' – and the capuchin monkey (*Cebus capucinus*). Black howler populations in southern Mexico and Guatemala have declined precipitously in recent years, as farmers clear forest for agricultural land. But 42km west of Belize City, local farmers are themselves preserving howler habitat, active participants in a unique conservation programme that's become something of an international showcase.

History

Dr Robert Horwich, a Wisconsin ethologist, first approached the villagers of Bermudian Landing with his plan in 1985. A howler monkey expert, Horwich had studied the noisy primates in both Mexico and Guatemala before landing in Belize, where populations seemed healthier. Howlers are sometimes hunted as food in Belize, but Horwich found that farmers along the Belize River not only tolerated the monkeys but respected them. Perhaps as a result, villagers readily bought into Horwich's proposal: that they spare the howlers' favourite food trees, saving small corridors of forest along the edges of their farmland and the Belize River to be used as howler 'freeways'. The loss to villagers, in terms of crop-growing potential, is small. And, with an increased ratio of forest 'edge' to cleared agricultural land, villagers can expect their soils to make a speedier recovery following slash-and-burn farming. Other benefits include stable stream banks, reduced erosion and improved riverine habitat for fish.

The final incentive for villagers – an option they themselves suggested to Horwich and his botanist colleague Jon Lyon – is the potential for tourism. In addition to providing cabanas for accommodation, several residents offer overnight rooms and meals in their homes. For travellers, it's one of the few chances to really spend time with rural Belizeans on their own turf. In addition to lodging, villagers offer guided river trips and extended nature walks in the forest. Recently the Protected Areas Conservation Trust, a Belize-based charity focussing on environmental and conservation issues, has provided office equipment and a telephone allowing the Sanctuary to compete in an ever-electronic tourism world.

Established in February 1985, the Sanctuary involves eight farming villages along the banks of the Belize River: Bermudian Landing, Big Falls, Double Head Cabbage (just plain 'Double Head' to locals), Isabella Bank, Flowers Bank, St Pauls, Willows Bank and Scotland Halfmoon (so named because of the Scottish immigrants who originally settled the village). Perhaps the most exciting aspect of the Sanctuary is that it involves private land only. Villagers themselves volunteered to save portions of the forest for the howlers. While they had help, advice and encouragement from biologists and government officials, it is the community that deserves credit for the Sanctuary's success. Not only did villagers agree to spare certain trees that provide food for howlers – among them sapodilla, trumpet trees, wild figs, bucut, bri bri, ramon, roseapple and hogplum – they suggested some improvements of their own. The aerial 'baboon bridge' across the roadway is reportedly a villager's innovation.

Howler counts testify to the success of the programme. Over 1,500 adult howlers are now estimated to make their home within the Sanctuary. The population continues to expand, so much so that some of the 'surplus' monkeys may be relocated to the Cockscomb Basin Wildlife Sanctuary (where yellow fever and hunting wiped out the original population) and the Shipstern Nature Reserve (where hurricanes did the same). The high density of howlers means that visitors are virtually guaranteed a sighting even during the briefest of stays. Indeed, if you get there at dusk and hit the trail immediately, you'll probably be standing beneath a troop of howlers within minutes of your arrival.

Another testament to the Sanctuary's success is the fact that it's become an international model for community-based conservation programmes. Inspired by the Bermudian Landing example, residents along the lower Wisconsin River near Sauk City, Wisconsin, USA, have set aside winter roosting areas for the American bald eagle. A sea turtle sanctuary has sprung up in northern Ambergris Caye, Belize (see *Chapter 13*). And most recently, the community of Monkey River Town is in the planning stages of their own village wildlife sanctuary.

The local 'baboon' is one of only six species of howler in the world. Adults weigh 6.8–9.1kg and are completely black; infants are a reddish brown colour. Howlers live in troops, usually an adult male accompanied by females and their young. Most troops consist of four to eight howlers. Although other howler species frequently band together in larger groups, troops of this particular species never contain more than ten members. The troop feeds and sleeps together, roaming over a home territory of about 12-15 acres.

It is this territorial instinct which impels howlers to howl. Perhaps the most unforgettable sound the jungle has to offer, it is a thundering roar which can carry for over 3km in dense forest. An enlarged bone in the howler's throat serves as a sounding box which amplifies the call. You're most likely to hear howling at dusk and dawn, although calling bouts can erupt at any time during the day. Rainfall, the sound of car engines, or any other loud, repetitive noise is likely to set howlers to howling. In the rainy season, the dawn and dusk calling periods aren't as pronounced, and howling during the middle of the day is common.

Getting there

Although many travellers (particularly those on package tours or guided sightseeing trips from Belize City) visit the Baboon Sanctuary for only a few hours, an overnight stay is highly recommended. Not only does this give you time to take extended walks in the forest and wake to the sound of howlers outside your window, but it allows you more than a cursory visit with the local people. Villagers are proud of their little community and they'll admit to being disappointed with travellers who rush into town just long enough to snap a few monkey photos before racing off again in their rental cars. Remember that overnight visitors contribute more money to the community, a community that elected to protect the howlers at some personal expense to themselves. Remember, as well, that this is one of the few chances you'll get for an intimate glimpse of rural Belizean life. If you do choose to visit for just a day, Chau Hiix Lodge and Paradise Inn, both in Crooked Tree Village, offer tours (see *Crooked Tree Wildlife Sanctuary* below).

If you go to Bermudian Landing via public transportation, an overnight stay is mandatory. Public buses leave Belize City in the afternoon (except Sunday) and return early the following day between 05.30 and 06.30. Mr Oswald McFadzean's bus leaves from the corner of Cemetery Street and Amara Avenue at 12.30 and 17.30. Mr Leonard Russell leaves from the corner of Cairo Street and Euphrates Avenue 12.00, 16.00 and 17.00. (Times are approximate, so you can check with the Community Baboon Sanctuary; tel: 021 2181 ahead of time.)

By private car, Bermudian Landing is roughly 42km west of Belize City. Head out of Belize City on the Northern Highway, past the airport, turning left toward Burrell Boom at 21km. The turn to 'Boom' (as locals call it) is well marked. You'll cross the Belize River just before entering Boom; continue west on a good, level dirt road, crossing Mussel Creek and, 4.8km later, the Belize River again just prior to entering Bermudian Landing. A second route is possible by turning off the Western Highway at Mile 15.5 and heading north, but this road is not quite as good as the route from the Northern Highway. The Sanctuary office and museum is past the school and clearly marked on the left. If you've got the room, stop and give lifts to pedestrians, most of whom are residents of Bermudian Landing or 'Double Head'.

Whether going by private vehicle or public bus, try to call ahead so that the Sanctuary staff can arrange a guide, meals, and lodging. Contact details are Community Baboon Sanctuary, PO Box 1428, Belize City; tel: 021 2181; email: baboon@btl.net. The Belize Audubon Society; tel: 35004/34987 will be able to help if there are problems with the newly installed telephone link. They'll want to know how many people are in your party, when you expect to arrive, and whether you'll want any meals or lodging.

Where to stay

Sanctuary staff will arrange overnight lodging for you if you call ahead announcing your arrival. You can pitch your tent outside the headquarters for BZ$5. They have an outhouse and a drinking water cistern. Most overnight visitors stay at the house of Alexandrina Young, a few steps from the Sanctuary office. Mrs Young has two rooms to rent, charging BZ$25 pp, and meals can be arranged. The Youngs also have three double cabanas charging BZ$40. Lodging in the village is basic: drinking water comes from rain water cisterns and outhouses serve as bathrooms. Howler Monkey Lodge, formerly Jungle Drift Lodge, PO Box 1442, Belize City; cellphone: 021 2158; fax: 02 78160; email: jungled@btl.net offers somewhat more formal lodging in screened cabins near the Belize River. Eight cabanas with shared bath, fan. US$50. Another lodging option for those with private transportation is El Chiclero; tel 0280 2005 in Burrell Boom, 14.5km east of Bermudian Landing. It's a comfortable bed and breakfast in the home of American expatriates. Rooms cost BZ$120.

What to see

When you get to the Sanctuary, ask for the manager. He, or one of his staff, will take you through the Sanctuary, on either the 'short walk' (which begins directly across the road from the Sanctuary office) or the 'long walk' (which starts along the banks of the Belize River at Isabella Bank, 3.8km from the office; you'll probably have to walk to Isabella Bank unless you hitch a ride with other travellers). Try to take both walks; your guide will point out not only the howlers, but allow you to sample some of the edible forest plants, including suppa palm, bucut, and pokenoboy palm. There is a registration fee of BZ$10 for everybody entering the sanctuary. You can walk the 8km of trails on your own but you will see far more with a guide – prices vary depending on how long you want to hike for but a half-day trek is about BZ$30 pp. You can also go for guided night hikes (highly recommended if you've never experienced the forest after dusk BZ$20 pp) and a canoe trip lasting nearly all day which takes you down the Belize River followed by a leisurely paddle upstream for BZ$50 pp. Horse riding is also an option.

Bermudian Landing goes to sleep early. There are a couple of rustic, friendly little bars where you can sit and contemplate the stresses of travel..

Information

Bring insect repellent. Mosquitoes can be fierce on the trails, particularly at dusk. If you're staying in a local home, you may want to burn a mosquito coil at night, since the screens aren't always an effective barrier. Bring binoculars for close-ups of the howlers and a torch (flashlight) for finding your way to the outhouse. You'll want comfortable hiking shoes that can afford to get thoroughly muddy, as well as a day pack for all-day hikes in the forest. Finally, bring plenty of drinking water; the local cisterns sometimes run dry or become contaminated.

For BZ$30, the Belize Audubon Society (see page 89) an excellent guide book to the howler reserve and to Belizean natural history in general: Horwich and Lyon's *A Belizean Rainforest: The Community Baboon Sanctuary* (see *Appendix 2, Further Reading*).

CROOKED TREE WILDLIFE SANCTUARY

For serious birders, no trip to Belize is complete without several days at Crooked Tree Wildlife Sanctuary. The Sanctuary, just 53km northwest of Belize City, consists of a vast network of inland freshwater lagoons. These lagoons, mazy waterways and swamps become home and feeding ground during the dry season to thousands of birds, both residents and migrants. For sheer numbers of birds – not to mention a spectacular diversity of species – Crooked Tree can't be matched anywhere else in Belize.

Crooked Tree Wildlife Sanctuary was established in November 1984, with funding from the Wild Wings and Underhill Foundations of New York. Crooked

Tree was one of Belize Audubon Society's first attempts at sanctuary development and management. They built the visitor centre, hired two park wardens and continue to develop educational, scientific and visitor programmes.

The Sanctuary encompasses the massive Crooked Tree Lagoon, as well as the Western Lagoon, Southern Lagoon, Revenge Lagoon, Calabash Pond, Black Creek and Spanish Creek. Local guides concentrate on Crooked Tree Lagoon, the Western Lagoon, Spanish Creek and heavily forested Black Creek for most of their birding and nature tours. In addition, the Sanctuary takes in Jones Lagoon and Mexico Lagoon, on the eastern side of the Northern Highway; neither of these two areas is open to visitors.

Getting there

Crooked Tree is located 5.4km off the Northern Highway, some 53km northwest of Belize City. If you're driving, turn left off the highway (the turnoff is well-marked) and proceed across the causeway to Crooked Tree Village and the visitor's centre. There are four buses a day to Crooked Tree, BZ$3.50. Batty Bus runs daily (Mon–Fri) to Crooked Tree Village, departing at 16.00 and making the return trip the following morning village at 06.00. Things change a little at weekends; buses leave at midday on Saturday and 09.00 on Sundays. Jex Buses also works the line providing three buses at day at 10.30, 16.30 and 17.30 from the Pound Yard Bridge, Belize City, leaving Crooked Tree the following day at 30-minute intervals from 06.00. Any bus between Belize City and the Mexican border, of course – including the frequent daily buses to Orange Walk and Corozal – can drop you off at the junction of the Crooked Tree road and the Northern Highway. From here it's a 5.4km walk to Crooked Tree Village across the causeway.

The best time to visit Crooked Tree is during the dry season, from approximately November through June most years; April, May and June are usually the driest. You'll witness far more birds during the dry season, and it's unlikely that the causeway connecting Crooked Tree Village to the Northern Highway will be impassable due to flooding. (When this occurs – as it has recently during the rainy season – the only option is to hire a boat to the village. The town is looking into ways to prevent the flooding, but not at any environmental cost to the area.)

Before making plans to visit Crooked Tree, contact the Belize Audubon Society (tel: 02 35004). They'll be able to tell you if the causeway is flooded, what lodging is available, the current bus schedules, tour guides offering trips from Belize City, and which local guides will be available once you reach Crooked Tree.

Where to stay

Whether you go with a guide or on your own, allow yourself an overnight stay at the least. This gives you an opportunity to see birds during the peak hours at dawn and just before dusk.

Crooked Tree Resort PO Box 1045, Belize City; tel: 02 77745; fax: 02 74007; cellphone: 014 9896. 8 thatched cabanas, US$95 with private bath, all meals included. The cabanas face the Northern Lagoon, and the resort features a bar and restaurant, both open to non-guests.

Bird's Eye View Hotel Crooked Tree Village, PO Box 1976, Belize City; tel: 02 32040; fax: 02 24869; email: birdseye@btl.net, web: www.belizenet.com/birdseye.html. 5 rooms, US$65 with private bath, fan or US$95 with all meals. Also located on the shore of the lagoon, and just opened in 1992. Owner Verna Samuels and her staff also offer a half-day bird and nature trip by boat within the lagoon for US$70 (1-4 persons) and US$1520 for each additional person. A 2hr guided nature walk through the village costs US$40 (1-4 people) or US$8 pp (groups of 5-8 people). They'll rent you a canoe for the day for US$40 (1-4 people) or US$60 (5-8 people). They also offer horseback riding and guided trips to Altun Ha (US$120 for 1-4 people, US$25 pp for groups of 5-8 people). Try calling the hotel's agent, S&L Tours (tel: 02 77593 in Belize City) if the hotel staff aren't near the phone, or write for reservations.

Paradise Inn Crooked Tree; tel/fax: 025 7044, mailing address in the US is Wildside Birding & Photo Tours, 14 Marchwood Center, Exton, PA 19341; tel: 888 875 9453 or 610 363 3033; fax: 610 363 3056; email: advcam@adventurecamera.com; web: www.adventurecamera.com. 6 thatched cabanas on stilts overlooking the lagoon, US$50, with private bath, fan, and hot water. Breakfast costs US$3–6, lunch US$4–6, dinner US$7–20. Owner Rudy Crawford and his family offer tours of the lagoon, birdwatching, horseback and carriage rides, and tours of the Chau Hiix archaeological site, Altun Ha, the Baboon Sanctuary, Belize Zoo, Lamanai, and other custom tours.

Chau Hiix Lodge PO Box 215 in Belize City, mailing address in the US is PO Box 1072, Sanford, FL 32772, USA, toll-free in the US, 1 800 654 4424; fax: 407 322 6389; email: chauhiix@belize-travel.com; web: www.belize-travel.com. The most secluded of the Crooked Tree lodges, often accessible only by boat. 4 rooms and 3 cottages, all with private bath and fans (cottages also have air conditioning). A 3-night stay in the rooms costs US$575, including transfers from Belize City, three meals, guided tours and snacks. A similar package week in one of the cottages costs US$1,100. Tours include Lamanai and the Baboon Sanctuary. There are canoes available and a swimming pool.

You can find cheaper and simpler accommodations with villagers. Ask at the visitor centre or call the community telephone at 021 2084 for any of the following: **Sam Tillet**, the well-known Crooked Tree birding guide, rents three budget rooms in the village (tel/fax: 021 2026). **Alma's Inn**, run by Alma Smith (tel: 021 7006) and located near the post office, comprises three rooms with shared bath and fan. **Molly's Rooms** (two rooms, US$15 with shared bath) is located nearby, just beyond the post office on the Trogon Trail; horseback riding is available. **Rhaburn's Rooms**, located next to the village school, offers four rooms with shared bath and fan. All of these homes in the village can provide meals. For an up-to-date list contact the Belize Audubon Society.

What to see

Just on the far side of the causeway, you'll see the visitor's centre on the right; check in here with the Sanctuary manager before proceeding. Inside the visitor's centre you'll find displays that explain both the Sanctuary itself and Belizean wildlife. Just past the centre, you'll enter **Crooked Tree Village**. For a short walking tour of the village, continue about 0.5km to a fork in the road and turn right. After another 0.2km, turn right again and continue for 0.2km to a fork in the road; turn right again. In 0.2km you'll come across the Riverview Beach Club (a bar) and after a further 0.3km, the road dead-ends at the water and the Crooked Tree Resort.

Three nature trails near the village provide shore-bound visitors with a chance to see a little of Crooked Tree's bird life: the Jacana trail (1hr walk); the Trogon trail (2hr); and the Kiskadee trail (1hr). During low-water periods, you can also walk along the shoreline of the lagoon. Even so, be prepared for some muddy hiking.

The best way to see Crooked Tree is with a guide. On foot, you won't be able to see nearly as much bird life or cover more than a minuscule bit of the sanctuary itself. In this watery ecosystem, a boat is practically essential. A guide will furnish not only the boat, but his or her knowledge of the local waterways and bird life.

One excellent local guide is Sam Tillet. He paddles rather than using a motor boat. Sam, like all the best guides, will insist that you be up early for the good birding at dawn.

At least a hundred bird species make their homes permanently or temporarily at Crooked Tree. Visiting birders seem especially intent on adding to their life-list the jabiru stork (*Jabiru mycteria*), one of the largest flying birds in the New World. Except for locally-abundant populations in Brazil's Pantanal, jabirus are now rare throughout their range, which extends from Mexico to northern Argentina. Belize boasts the largest nesting population anywhere in Central America (between nine and 12 pairs), but that doesn't mean they're easy to see. Your best chance is with a guide during the breeding period (December through March). They normally begin arriving, probably from Mexico's Campeche region, in late November and leave Belize when the rains flood the lagoon in May. See *Chapter 3, Birds* for more on the jabiru.

Equally uncommon in Belize, but occasionally sighted at Crooked Tree are the roseate spoonbill (*Ajaia ajaja*), the American white pelican (*Pelecanus erythrorhynchus*) and the jabiru's much smaller and homelier cousin, the wood stork (*Mycteria americana*).

Other, more commonly sighted species include the snail kite, another permanent resident, which feeds exclusively on the locally-abundant apple snails, the shells of which you'll find all along the lagoon's shoreline. Look in mango trees during the day for the boat-billed heron, one of the few nocturnal herons. One of the favourite roosts for these comical, broad-billed herons is practically within sight of the Sanctuary headquarters; ask the staff. Both snowy and great egrets gather by the hundreds to wade the shallow waters of Crooked Tree Lagoon. Ospreys ride thermals overhead before plummeting feet-first into the water for fish. North American ducks, like the blue-winged teal, American widgeon, lesser scaup and northern shoveler, make Crooked Tree a layover stop during their annual migrations. All five species of Central-American kingfishers – ringed, belted, Amazon, green and American pygmy – find niches at Crooked Tree. The coffee-coloured northern jacana ambles across the flimsiest marsh vegetation without sinking, supported by outlandishly oversized toes; this ability to 'tread water' has earned the jacana the nickname 'lily-trotter'.

Birds remain the top draw at Crooked Tree, but the Sanctuary also provides habitat for howler monkeys ('baboons'), iguanas, Morelet's crocodiles, turtles and basilisk lizards. The latter are known locally as 'Jesus Christ lizards' because of their curiously human way of dashing about on their hind legs at high speed, appearing to walk on air, if not water.

The closest archaeological site is Chau Hiix (the Maya word for jaguarundi), the most obvious feature being a 25m-high pyramid called Kinich-ku. Access to the site is by boat, about 45 minutes (motoring) or three hours (paddling) west of Crooked Tree Village in a cohune palm forest called Blackburn Ridge. All the local lodges can provide guides, and most will take a boatload to Chau Hiix for around US$60. Both the site itself and the surrounding area provide great birding, so bring binoculars.

Crooked Tree Village celebrates the local **Cashew Festival** on May 7–8.

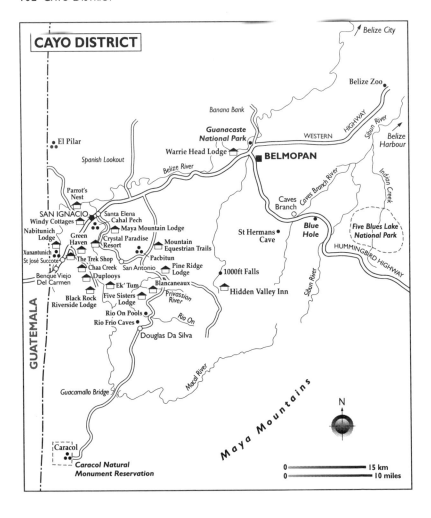

Cayo District

With the possible exception of the offshore cayes, Belize's tourist epicentre has to be Cayo District. Indeed, saltwater and coral reefs are about the only Belizean attractions lacking in Cayo. Archaeology buffs will find in Cayo not only the country's largest Maya site – Caracol – but also the most-photographed – Xunantunich. Even Tikal is more easily visited via Cayo than from most parts of Guatemala. Central America's highest waterfall plunges from a Cayo pine forest into pristine jungle 480m below. And the nearby Chiquibul cave complex is believed to be the most extensive in Central America, with the largest single subterranean 'room' (La Cebada) in the Western Hemisphere. Cayo offers the best 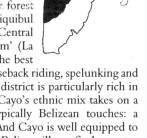 canoeing, river rafting, hiking, cave river tubing, horseback riding, spelunking and mountain biking in Belize. The western half of the district is particularly rich in birds and other wildlife. This close to Guatemala, Cayo's ethnic mix takes on a decidedly Maya and Latino flavour, but with typically Belizean touches: a smattering of Creoles, Mennonites and Garifunas. And Cayo is well equipped to handle the increasing stream of tourists; nowhere in Belize will you find a greater concentration of isolated 'cottage resorts' catering to adventure travellers and eco-tourists.

Cayo District's economy once relied on mahogany and chicle, the sap of the sapodilla tree used in chewing gum. But the mahogany was overharvested, and Americans lost their fondness for gum just as synthetics began to replace chicle. The hardy chicleros of Cayo's rough-and-tumble past have moved on to jobs in agriculture and cattle ranching, although chicle is suddenly experiencing a minor revival here. Belize's first cattle ranch was established in Cayo District by an American in 1950, and much of the country's beef and milk products now come from Cayo. Mennonite truck farmers from Spanish Lookout (an extensive, fairly modern settlement just northeast of San Ignacio) sell their produce, milk and eggs at markets nationwide.

Note When Belizeans speak of 'Cayo' they are generally referring not to the District, but specifically to the town of San Ignacio. Even bus placards reflect this usage. Travellers likewise think of Cayo as San Ignacio and vicinity. Although the district encompasses the nation's capital of Belmopan and its grassy flatlands, it is the mountains, jungles, caves, waterfalls and Maya ruins of Cayo's more westerly portion that lure visitors.

BELMOPAN

Belmopan is something of a miniature Brasília without the impressive architecture. Like Brasília, Belize's capital city of Belmopan was plopped down in the middle of the country; a modern, planned community meant to lure the masses from the squalor of hurricane-bedevilled Belize City. And, like Brasília, Belmopan succeeded in attracting only a handful of bureaucrats, many of whom returned on weekends to the former capital. The town is growing now, but away from the hubbub of the market place it's still very much a sleepy burg.

You'll rarely meet tourists who have spent the night in Belmopan. That's because there are precisely two points of interest to travellers: Guanacaste Park and the Archaeology Department's vault, both easily visited in a day from either Belize City or San Ignacio.

History

Even in the late 1950s, Belize City was bulging at the seams with new immigrants from the hinterlands. When Hurricane Hattie levelled the city in 1961, planning for a new inland capital began in earnest. By 1968, nearly three-quarters of Belize's entire capital-expenditure budget was being funnelled into the construction of Belmopan. The name itself combines the 'Bel' of Belize with the name of a major Maya group, the Mopan. In keeping with this theme, a number of the government offices were given the 'neo-Maya' look. It's an architectural style that blessedly hasn't caught on outside of Belmopan. On a more utilitarian level, Belmopan builders designed the concrete capital to withstand winds of at least 110 miles an hour. The new capital officially opened in 1970. Government officials predicted the population to grow within twenty years to 30,000. But ten years later, the city was still less than a tenth that size.

In October 1998 Hurricane Mitch gave Belize an abrupt reminder of why Belmopan was founded. As the strongest hurricane on record paused off the Belizean coast to gather strength, thousands of Belizeans headed for the highlands and Belmopan. A relaxed city of some 7,000 people was suddenly engulfed with 25,000 new residents arriving almost overnight. Water systems were stretched to capacity as the nation collectively monitored Mitch's movements.

While Honduras took the brunt of the hurricane, Belize issued a sigh of relief. Since then the University of Belize, the headquarters of Belize Telecommunications Ltd and a host of international organisations have relocated to Belmopan.

This flurry of investment and interest is unlikely to make Belmopan a destination of great interest to visitors, but it does add a little drama to a place that, apart from the bus station, seems to lack anything of interest to all but the most dedicated of urban planners. Nevertheless, you have to go via Belmopan to reach most places west and south of Belize City, and you may find yourself there for reasons outside your control, so…

Getting there

Centrally located between Belize City and all major towns south and west, Belmopan is a busy hub for buses. Between Batty, Novelo's and Carmen's bus companies, there's generally an arrival from either Belize City or San Ignacio every 30 minutes. From the south, all buses headed to Belize City stop in Belmopan. From Belize City, the trip takes one hour 15 minutes and costs BZ$4. From San Ignacio, the bus takes one hour and costs BZ$2.50.

Buses leaving Belize City for Dangriga, Independence or Punta Gorda are often full by the time they reach Belmopan. You may actually have to take a bus to Belize City and hop on one to Dangriga there, riding back through Belmopan en route! (See *Chapter 11, Dangriga*).

Belmopan has an airstrip, but there are no scheduled flights.

Where to stay

Belmopan is a city of bureaucrats, and lodging is expensive. As noted above, most travellers rarely have reason to spend the night here. The only exception is the Banana Bank Ranch, a cottage resort in the countryside some miles outside Belmopan.

Circle A Lodge 35-37 Halfmoon Avenue; tel: 08 20679; fax: 08 22309. 14 rooms, with private bath, fan. Restaurant/bar. BZ$64. About 1km east of the bus stop.

Belmopan Convention Hotel 2 Bliss Parade, PO Box 237; tel: 02 22130/22340; fax: 08 23066. 20 rooms, BZ$100 with private bath, air conditioning, TV and phone. Swimming pool, restaurant/bar and laundry service. Accepts MasterCard, VISA, Diners Club and American Express cards.

Bull Frog Inn 25 Half-moon Avenue, PO Box 28; tel: 08 22111/23425; fax: 08 23155; email: bullfrog@btl.net.. 24 rooms, with private bath and air conditioning, TV. An open-air restaurant/bar. They accept MasterCard and VISA. Near the Circle A, about 1km east of the bus station. From BZ$80.

El Rey Inn 23 Moho Street; tel: 08 23438; fax: 08 29915. 12 rooms, with private bath, fan. About 0.75km northeast of the bus stop. BZ$40.

Outside Belmopan

Banana Bank Lodge PO Box 48, Belmopan, Belize District; tel: 08 12020; fax: 08 12026; email: bbl@btl.net; web: www.bananabank.com. 14 rooms, 4 of which are in the main house, and 5 thatched guest cabanas. A working cattle ranch and farm on the left bank of the Belize River, a few kilometres north of Belmopan on all-weather road. John and Carolyn Carr, expatriate Americans, have lived in Belize for 23 years. The speciality here is horseback riding. The Carrs maintain 20–25 saddle horses (US$20 for 2–3hrs, guided) and a 5m boat for river trips (US$25 for 2½hours). Day trips arranged, including Tikal, Belize Zoo, and the Cockscomb Wildlife Sanctuary. There are several tours ranging in length from 3 to 7 days that use the Lodge as a base. The Carrs will pick up guests in Belmopan if you call in advance. Cabanas are US$95 for a double, a triple is US$127, a quad is US$149. The cabana rate includes a full breakfast. Rooms in the lodge are US$52 for a single(with private bath), US$63 for a double (private bath) and US$74 for a triple, with shared bath. Meals are served in a family style atmosphere and the cost is US$11 for breakfast and lunch and US$16 for dinner.

Warrie Head Ranch and Lodge Teakettle Village, PO Box 244, Belize City; tel: 02 75319; fax: 02 75213; email: bzadventur@btl.net; web: www.warriehead.com. 10 rooms, US$70 with private bath, hot water, fan. Located 9.7km west of the Belmopan turnoff, this lodge lies on the site of an old mahogany logging camp along the banks of the Belize River. It's now a 137-acre working farm. Breakfast costs US$5, lunch US$10 and dinner US$17.50 pp. They offer canoe rentals for trips down the Belize River, from Iguana Creek (near Spanish Lookout) to the lodge, for US$20 per canoe, including transport to Iguana Creek, life jackets and cushions. With a guide, the same trip runs US$30 per canoe. Either way, the trip lasts about 1hr 30min. They also offer the usual range of Maya ruin site trips, bird watching and horseback riding.

Where to eat

All the hotels listed above except the El Rey have their own restaurants. Right next to the bus stations you'll find the **Caladium Restaurant**, good for breakfast and lunch, and very popular with government employees. Close by is the International Café which serves fantastic coffee, pastries and meals throughout the day. There's also the Little Dragon (Chinese) and Yoli's. The New Capitol Chinese Restaurant (next to the Bullfrog Inn) serves good meals in a pleasant atmosphere. But probably the best place to eat – certainly the cheapest and liveliest – is the marketplace surrounding the bus stop area. Several stalls sell burritos which can be wrapped to

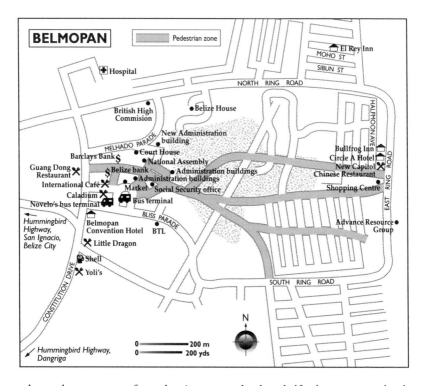

take on the next stage of your bus journey, and at least half a dozen women hawk steaming hot chicken tamales, and you'll find a fair selection of fresh fruit.

What to see
The Archaeology Department's vault was formerly the only real tourist attraction in Belmopan itself, but it has now been closed to visitors and there are no plans to reopen it in the immediate future.

Information and useful addresses
Money and travellers' cheques can be changed at either **Belize Bank** or **Barclays**, both located in the public market square near the bus station. The BTL telephone office and post office are across from each other on Bliss Parade, just south of the market. Email services are springing up. The **International Café** has a send and receive service (email: intlcafe@btl.net) but no Internet-based accounts can be accessed yet. **Advance Resource Group** 88 Ring Road; tel: 08 23267; fax: 08 23283; email: resource@btl.net – above Lopez Pharmacy – near the Circle A Hotel, on the East Ring Road, provides internet services. **El Caracol Gallery and Gift Shop**, 32 Macaw Avenue offers Maya-influenced arts and crafts, including slate carvings, baskets and ceramics.

Excursions
Near town
Guanacaste Park
The Belizean government purchased this 50-acre site in 1973, on the urging of the Belize Audubon Society. Seventeen years later, the government changed

Guanacaste's status from National Reserve to National Park. A little over 3km north of Belmopan, the park lies along an oxbow section of the Belize River, and was named for the massive guanacaste tree (*Enterolobium cyclocarpum*) which stands just west of the entrance. Thirty-five species of aerial plants, including orchids and bromeliads, adorn the upper branches. Belizeans also know the guanacaste as the tubroose, or 'monkey's ear tree' because the seed is a brown, flattish affair coiled and folded into an ear-like form. They also prize the tree as raw material for dugout canoes. This particular specimen probably escaped the saw and axe because of its unworkable, misformated trunk.

In 1989, the Belize Audubon Society, with a grant from the MacArthur Foundation of Chicago, created over 3km of nature trails within the park. It's an ideal spot for a stroll, swim and picnic. Visitors to the park have occasionally spotted tree-dwelling iguanas, howler monkeys, pacas ('gibnut'), agoutis, kinkajous ('night-walkers'), armadillos, white-tailed deer and jaguarundi. Bird sightings are more dependable, and birders have recorded over 100 species within park boundaries, including the blue-crowned motmots for which a short trail was named. North American species arrive during the winter months. Signs along the trails point out some of the park's more notable flora. Besides the stately guanacaste, there is a ceiba tree ('cotton tree' to Creoles and sacred to the Maya), mahogany (planted since 1973), bucut, mammee apple, quamwood and hundreds of cohune palms. Orchids bloom in the spring months, February through May.

A civilised little piece of forest, Guanacaste offers seating areas along the trails, drinking water, and pit toilets. Camping isn't allowed. The park entrance is located along the Western Highway at the junction with the Hummingbird Highway. You can either walk the highway for 3km from Belmopan, take a cab, or ask any bus travelling east or west from Belmopan to drop you off.

Further afield
Blue Hole National Park and St Herman's Cave
Established in 1986, Blue Hole National Park comprises 575 acres of primary and secondary growth tropical forest some 18km south of Belmopan. The entire area is pockmarked with sinkholes, underground streams, cenotes and extensive cave systems.

The big draw here is the namesake **Blue Hole**, not to be confused with the Blue Hole at Lighthouse Reef first explored by Jacques Cousteau (see *Chapter 14*). From this collapsed karst sinkhole, roughly 30m deep and 90m in diameter, gushes forth a tributary of the Sibun River. The stream runs above ground for about 45m before disappearing again into a subterranean labyrinth of caverns. Steps lead from the parking lot down to the Blue Hole, named for the water's aquamarine colour as it emerges from the earth. It's a popular picnicking and swimming spot for locals and tourist alike. A cabana for changing into swimwear is located by the main entrance.

Leading from the picnic area is a self-guided trail with explanations on how to recognise and use different rainforest plants and trees. The leaflets are in limited supply but be persistent and see if you can borrow the guards.

About 1km down the road you'll find a nature trail leading to the area's second attraction, **St Herman's Cave**. The trail, through secondary hardwood forest, is roughly 2.5km long and will take about half an hour to negotiate. There's another, much shorter trail to the cave (1km) which takes off from the Hummingbird Highway about 3km north of the Park's main entrance. Both trails involve some steep ups and downs; if you prefer to avoid these, follow the road by the pasture on the Park's southeast side. The forest here is home to tapir, collared peccary, coati, armadillo and white-tailed deer, among others. Three of Belize's five species of wild cats have been sighted here: jaguars, ocelots and jaguarundis. Bird sightings include the national bird, the keel-billed toucan, as well as many other species. Iguanas, coral snakes, tommygoffs and boa constrictors also live within the Park boundaries.

St Herman's Cave has three known entrances, the nearest of which is a 60m-wide sinkhole narrowing to an entry that is 20m wide. Concrete steps overlay those built by the ancient Maya and lead into the cave itself. Ceramic urns dating from the Classic Period have been found here, presumably used to collect cave water drippings.

This cave gets a lot of foot traffic and is perfectly safe to explore on your own. But bring sturdy walking shoes and a good flashlight or headlamp. Because it lies within Park boundaries, no special permission is required to visit St Herman's Cave.

The Park entrance is located at Mile 11.3 of the Hummingbird Highway. In the past, car break-ins were common here, and at least one robbery and rape were reported. More recently, a guard has been hired to watch the parking area. The site is easily visited via public bus; any bus travelling between Belmopan and Dangriga will drop you off at the entrance, but check to make sure when the next returning bus will pass on the Highway.

If you are looking for somewhere to stay in the area Caves Branch Adventure Co and Jungle Lodge is across the road from the Blue Hole car park. In addition to the adventures (see below) they have a variety of accommodations ranging from cabana suites (BZ$194), jungle cabanas, a bunkroom and camping facilities (BZ$10 pp). The setting is idyllic and the food is reported to be very good.

Other caves in Cayo District
A number of caves punctuate the karst limestone landscape surrounding Blue Hole National Park, but most are outside the national park so you will need permission to enter. Permission is obtained from the Department of Archaeology (tel: 08 22106; fax: 08 23345) but is a complex and time-consuming process that usually results in a 'no'. But in recent years options for visiting some of the many caves has increased. For those who make the effort the karst geology have carved out subterranean rivers, waterfalls and left crystal formations sparkling in the torch beams

Che Chem Ha is a Maya ceremonial cave, active from 1000BC to AD500, and still contains many pottery pieces. This cave is on land near the Maya Mountain Lodge, and owner Bart Mickler can arrange to take you there. The trip involves a 45-minute drive and a 4km hike (see entry for Maya Mountain Lodge in *Rural lodges and resorts* below).

The most popular cave trip for non-spelunkers in this area, although not technically in Cayo district, is run by Ian Anderson of Caves Branch Adventure Co and Jungle Lodge Mile 41.5 Hummingbird Highway, PO Box 356, Belmopan, Belize; tel/fax: 08 22800; email: caves@pobox.com; web: www.cavesbranch.com. He offers all-day inner tube float trips on the Caves Branch River. These trips are open to anyone, involving a leisurely float through a series of caverns, punctuated by open stretches of water and rocky beaches. An underground waterfall spills into one of the caves, while another side channel is littered with thousands of Maya pottery shards. There are several trip options which include the **Black Hole Drop** – a descent of 300ft into one of the region's sink holes. Prices average around BZ$150 pp and include all equipment and guides fully trained in cave rescue. These prices are considerably higher than those paid in San Ignacio, 'but,' Ian says, 'safety cannot be compromised.'

Anderson can also arrange for pickups from Belize City or anywhere else in the country, but it is so easy to get to the site using public buses the extra cost is not really justified. There is, however, a 20-minute walk down the dirt track to the Jungle Lodge so call ahead saying what bus you'll be on and Ian will arrange for someone to pick you up from the end of the road.

Actun Polbiche Cave is located on the southern bank of the Sibun River near Church Yard village. Turn south off the Western Highway just before JB's Place. This cave was used extensively by the ancient Maya and you'll need permission from the Department of Archaeology to enter. The Indian Creek Caves lie within the newly created Five Blues Lake National Park, and local guides should be available at the Park or in at by St. Margaret's Village (see *Five Blues Lake National Park* below).

Further west in Cayo District, there are literally hundreds of caves and sinkholes, few of them fully explored. The best known and most easily accessed is the **Río Frio Cave** (see *Mountain Pine Ridge and vicinity* below).

Except for this popular cave, however, most require some caving experience, and even avid spelunkers should hire a guide before entering them. For one thing, subterranean floods are more common in the high country of western Cayo. They can turn dry caverns into watery graves without warning. Secondly, the Department of Archaeology has restricted access to a number of caves throughout the area to protect Maya artefacts until they've been properly investigated. The ancient Maya often worshipped in caves, and even many of those caves open for exploration contain massive piles of pottery shards. Others contain scores of intact pots, some more than 0.3m in height.

With these caveats in mind, western Cayo District offers a host of possibilities for spelunkers of all experience levels. Ian Anderson of Caves Branch Jungle and River Camp (see above) runs trips into seven or eight caves within the Maya Mountains. Caving experience is not necessary, although participants should be in reasonably good shape. Anderson also offers a seven-day spelunking tour through three or four caves in the Vaca Plateau; this trip is for expert cavers only, and rope work is required.

A new cave suitable for non-spelunkers was recently discovered in the Mountain Pine Ridge by Luciano Santos, an employee of Pine Ridge Lodge. The cave entrance is reportedly no more than 1m high, rapidly opening into a much larger chamber with stalagmites and stalactites. Jim Bevis of Mountain Equestrian Trails can also lead travellers through this cave (see *Rural lodges and resorts* below for more information on these two tour operators).

Finally, two more caves have recently been opened to visitors near the Maya ruin of Pacbitun (see *Mountain Pine Ridge and vicinity* below for details).

Five Blues Lake National Park

This 4,200-acre national park is one of Belize's newest, dedicated in 1992. The park is located near the village of St. Margaret's Village (aka Santa Marta) along the Hummingbird Highway, roughly 45km from Belmopan. The park is so new that many Belizeans haven't heard of it yet, and you'll often see it mistakenly referred to as 'Five Blue Lakes'. Actually, there is but one main lake, an impressive limestone cenote plunging to depths of 70m. The 'five blues' refers to the various shades of water colour. You can wade to tiny forested **Orchid Island** near one shoreline. Local farmer Leon Wengrzyn, director of the Friends of Five Blues National Park, recently secured a United Nations grant to improve the park's infrastructure. The group is committed to maintaining community control over tourism in the area, which is under heavy pressure by agro-business and a burgeoning population of citrus farm workers.

Beside the lake itself, other attractions include the cave-ridden limestone karst country nearby, especially the **Indian Creek Caves**. These are prosaically known as Number 3, Number 4, and Number 5, and are strung out along the east side of the creek. There are now numerous hiking trails in the park, maps are provided, and birding is excellent.

A newly-surfaced, all-weather road turns off the Hummingbird Highway at the Over-the-Top Cool Spot restaurant, continuing about 7km to the park. Coming by bus from either Belmopan (BZ$3) or Dangriga (BZ$4), have the driver let you off at Over-the-Top, from where you can arrange transport.

You can stay with villagers by contacting the **Women's Rising Bed and Breakfast Association**. This is a cooperative homestay organization made up of women from St Margaret's Village. So far, about 12 homes are set up to receive guests. The villagers provide not only budget rooms (around BZ$10 pp) in their homes, but they also cook and offer guided day trips, birding tours, overnight jungle trips, even Spanish classes. Write in advance for reservations to Mrs Barbara Borland, Saint Margaret's Village, or simply call the community telephone (081 2005), and the operator will be happy to arrange a homestay for you.

A second lodging option is the **Tamandua Jungle Experience**, Mile 32 Hummingbird Highway, PO Box 306, Belmopan (tel: 08 23182; fax: 08 22458). Located about 4km from the park, Farm owners Janet and Bernard Dempsey only get into Belmopan once every few weeks to pick up messages, so it's best to write or leave a message at the Belmopan phone number well in advance if you want to be sure of reservations and to check for rates. Six cottages with private bath, fan.

SAN IGNACIO (CAYO)

Less than a decade ago, San Ignacio and its sister town Santa Elena were virtually unknown to travellers in Belize. If they saw the town at all, it was from a bus headed for the Guatemalan border just 13km west. These days, San Ignacio is no longer a mere stopover on the gringo trail to Tikal, but a destination in itself. The only place in Belize where you're likely to see more backpacks on the street is Caye Caulker. San Ignacio has somehow managed to retain its particular brand of funky charm despite all the recent popularity.

In a nation of drab little towns, San Ignacio is a picturesque blend of American Old West and tropical backwater. Khaki-clad archaeology students trudge down the hill from a day's work at the Maya ruins, machetes and canteens dangling from their belts. Mennonite farmers from Spanish Lookout peddle their milk and eggs alongside Mopan Maya women at the marketplace. Backpackers fresh from Guatemala sip Belikin beer on the wooden balconies of cheap hotels. A family of Sri Lankans, the women in saris, head up the main street to open their restaurant for dinner. And everywhere, taxi drivers hustle you good-naturedly for rides to the border, the Maya ruins of Xunantunich, Cahal Pech, Pilar, the rainforest, the Mountain Pine Ridge.

Besides these attractions, San Ignacio offers horseback riding, canoeing and river rafting, mountain biking, caving, birding along jungle trails and botanical tours. The town is also the ideal gateway to the magnificent ruins of Tikal in Guatemala and Belize's own Caracol ruins.

The town itself sits on the left bank of the Macal River, a tributary of the Belize River. Hawkesworth Bridge, the highest suspension bridge in Belize, has spanned the river since 1949 and links San Ignacio with its sister town, Santa Elena.

San Ignacio, surrounded by forested hills, is itself built on seven hills. The narrow streets are jam-packed with cheap hotels and restaurants. You can easily walk anywhere in town. Rains are more common in the afternoon, so plan your outings accordingly, particularly during the wet season. The 11,500 inhabitants of the twin towns include Creoles, Mestizos, Mopan and Yucatec Maya, a few Garifunas, Lebanese, and Sri Lankans, as well as a growing contingent of Guatemalan and Salvadorean refugees. Spanish is widely spoken.

Just a short word of warning. As with any popular stop-off point on the gringo trail, hoods and phonies that have crawled out from the woodwork will try to sell you short, but keep your head about you and all will be fine.

History

Spanish soldiers and priests arrived at the Maya village of Tipu (probably 8km south of present-day San Ignacio, near Negroman) in the mid-1500s. Their attempts at turning the local Maya into good Catholics – including the rather ungracious threat of death to non-believers – were not entirely successful. Repeatedly, the inhabitants of Tipu showed signs of reverting to their idolatry'. And by 1638, Tipu became the focal point of anti-Spanish rebellion, expelling the Europeans for almost 60 years. Even so, the rebels of Tipu held on to certain Catholic traditions, blending them with Maya customs when it suited them. Apparently much of the hatred for the Spanish stemmed not from their Christianity but from their insistence on heavy tribute, in the form of cacao and forced labour. Eventually the Spanish regained sway in Tipu, forcibly moving the Maya to Lake Petén Itzá in 1707. Since the Maya of that period erected few masonry buildings, nothing remained of Tipu and archaeologists were forced to locate the probable site using old Spanish documents.

Much later, San Ignacio served as the collecting point for mahogany and chicle harvested in the nearby forests. The town was known by then as El Cayo, a term still commonly used by locals. The Spanish word for small island, 'Cayo' takes on more meaning if you see the town and neighbouring area from a plane; it's sandwiched, island-like, between the Macal and Mopan Rivers. Since no road existed between San Ignacio and Belize City before the 1930s, 'pit-pans', long boats hewn from local wood, transported products up and down the Belize River. The journey upriver could take between ten and 20 days.

Getting there

The bus trip from Belize City over good roads takes only 2 hours 30 minutes and costs BZ$5. Between Novelo's, Batty, and Carmen bus companies, a bus runs just about every 30 minutes throughout the day. Coming from Dangriga or Punta Gorda, get off in Belmopan, since all the Cayo-bound buses stop there. Many will be full, but it takes only slightly more than an hour to reach San Ignacio from Belmopan so having to stand isn't the end of the world.

An airport is under construction, but most travellers won't be terribly interested, considering how fast, pleasant, and cheap the bus trip is to Cayo.

The Bus Station is right in the centre of town and just one block from Burns Avenue where most hotels are found.

To and from Guatemala

The Guatemalan border is about 13km from San Ignacio, and 1.5km from the Belizean border town of Benque Viejo del Carmen (see below). Every day – particularly in the mornings – you'll find a crowd of travellers in San Ignacio on their way to the border via taxi or bus. Taxis between San Ignacio and the border cost BZ$4 pp one-way, and they'll generally try to fill the taxi before leaving. You can find taxis either in the San Ignacio marketplace or at the taxi stand across from the police station. But if you're toting a backpack or a suitcase anywhere downtown, the taxis will find you. Almost all buses from Belize City to San Ignacio continue on to Benque Viejo after a brief stop, with many of them continuing to Melchor de Mencos. Ask at Eva's for the latest information on bus schedules.

The border station itself lies between Benque Viejo del Carmen and Melchor de Mencos, Guatemala. The border is officially open 24 hours a day, but in practice you probably won't find anyone to let you across between midnight and 06.00.

Exiting Belize is generally a routine affair. You'll show your passport and the Belizean officials will fill out a simple departure form. Belize charges a BZ$7.50 exit fee for land travellers.

Before and after entering the Belizean Immigration/Customs office, you'll be besieged by money changers offering quetzales in exchange for US dollars, Belize dollars and travellers' cheques. They generally offer the same amount for cash and cheques. If you're in a hurry, go ahead and exchange money – rates don't vary among the money changers, they're honest and fast. If you're concerned about getting the best exchange, however, walk over to the Guatemalan customs office (after passing through Belizean customs and just before you get your passport stamped to enter Guatemala) and check the rate being offered inside by the Banco de Guatemala. The bank frequently offers a slightly better rate than the money changers. If the bank is closed, the line long, or the rate unattractive, you can always stroll back to the money changers before passing through Guatemalan customs. Asking travellers who have come from Guatemala should give you the very latest exchange rate. At the time of writing the rate was US$1 to Q$7.20.

If at all possible, arrange for a Guatemalan visa before reaching the border. Guatemalan visas and tourist cards are now issued at the border, but it's easier to have them in hand. Guatemalan customs rarely checks baggage, passing visitors with visas through quickly and efficiently. You'll be asked how many days you intend to spend in Guatemala. When crossing into Guatemala a discretionary fee of Q$30 is often charged. This is not an official charge but seems to be applied by all customs officials across the board. You are perfectly within your rights to refuse payment but run the risk of being refused entrance into Guatemala. Asking for a receipt works sometimes but if you're not trying to test the system there is little point in running the risk.

Outside Guatemalan customs you'll be besieged by minivan operators rounding up customers for the trip to Tikal. The public bus for Flores, a cheaper alternative, also passes by. For details on getting to Tikal, see the box *Heading for Tikal* below. From Guatemalan customs it's an easy stroll across the river into Melchor de Mencos, where you'll find cheap lodging and simple *comedores*.

Entering Belize from Melchor de Mencos is equally easy. If you are young and/or hauling a backpack, Belizean officials may have you to fill out a one-page form and ask about your money situation before passing you through. The money-changers hanging around Belizean customs are reliable, honest, and all offer the same rates. You're unlikely to get a much better deal by waiting until you reach San Ignacio. Collective taxis wait outside Belizean customs, charging BZ$4 pp for the ride to San Ignacio.

Most buses to Belize City leave from San Ignacio without making the sidetrip to the border, so unless you're lucky enough to find a bus waiting at the border, you're better off taking a cab to San Ignacio. If you're in a hurry to reach Belize City from Flores, catch the first morning bus (Transportes Pinita) from Flores to Melchor de Mencos, leaving from the San Juan Hotel in Santa Elena at 05.00. Depending on road conditions, this usually gives you time to clear the border, catch a taxi to San Ignacio and board the 09.00 bus to Belize City.

Where to stay

For budget lodging, you won't find a better selection anywhere in Belize. The hotels listed below are those directly in town or neighbouring Santa Elena. See also Rural lodges and resorts near San Ignacio below.

Central Hotel 24 Burns Avenue; tel: 09 24179. 8 rooms, US$11 with fan, clean bathrooms down the hall, friendly owners. A couple of the rooms are tiny and stuffy. A pleasant little covered balcony with hammock and chairs overlooking the main street. They accept travellers' cheques.

Tropicool Hotel 30 Burns Avenue; tel: 09 23052. Clean, good-sized rooms, friendly, safe and good value. Shared bath, ceiling fans and TV in communal area. The owner, Andrew, will store luggage. BZ$25.

Pacz Hotel 2 Far West Street; tel: 09 24538. 5 good size rooms sharing 2 bathrooms. A good communal area and a homely feel if you're looking for somewhere to relax. The proprieter, Diana, lives next door. BZ$35.

Venus Hotel 29 Burns Avenue; tel: 09 23203; fax: 09 22225; email: daniels@btl.net. 34 rooms. A fairly new hotel in town, with views toward the river from some of the rooms. Popular with archaeology students, expeditions and groups. The owners accept travellers' cheques and credit cards. Rooms are currently undergoing renovation and should be finished by the time you read this. BZ$42 with bath, fan, TV; BZ$28 with shared bath, fan, hot water.

Hi-Et Hotel 12 West Street; tel: 09 22828. 6 rooms, with fan, shared bath. An attractive, homey little place with very friendly owners. There is a kitchen you can use. They accept travellers' cheques. BZ$20

Budget Hotel 22 Burns Avenue. 6 rooms, with fan, shared bath. Directly above Eva's Restaurant, basic and very much in need of a lick of paint, formerly called the Imperial Hotel. Some travellers have reported trouble sleeping when the drinking crowd in Eva's is on a roll. BZ$20

The New Belmoral Hotel 17 Burns Avenue, PO Box 9; tel: 09 22024; fax: 09 23502; email: belmoral@btl.net. 11 rooms, with private bathroom, hot water and cable TV. Some with fans others with AC. Recently remodelled. travellers' cheques accepted. BZ$35.

Riverview Hotel 1 Wyatt Street. 7 rooms with fan, shared bath. Some rooms have private baths. A bit seedy, and the river view here in town is not particularly inspiring. Has a bar downstairs. BZ$26.

A little further out of town
Piache Hotel 18 Buena Vista St, PO Box 54; tel: 09 22032; email: piache.hot@btl.net; web: www.belize.com/piache.html. 12 rooms, with fan, bath, hot water, breakfast included. Some rooms with air conditioning. A quiet location, just a few minutes walk up the hill from town. There's a thatched bar and restaurant. Run by Godsman Ellis, one of the few Garifunas in town, and a scholar well-versed in Garifuna history and culture. (He sells a detailed little pamphlet for BZ$4.) Ellis can also arrange trips to Maya ruins, including Tikal. He accepts travellers' cheques. BZ$58
San Ignacio Hotel 18 Buena Vista Street, PO Box 33, San Ignacio; tel: 09 22034/22125; fax: 09 22134; email: sanighot@btl.net; web: www.sanignaciobelize.com. 24 rooms, with air conditioning, private bath, hot water, phone, TV and outdoor swimming pool. San Ignacio's single luxury hotel, with a good restaurant, bar and weekend discotheque, located up the hill leaving town, just before the Piache Hotel. The hotel stands above the left bank of the Macal River, but the forest prevents a view. BZ$100.

Across the river in Santa Elena
Aguada Motel Santa Elena; tel/fax: 09 23609; email: aguada@btl.net; web: www.belizex.com/aguada.htm. 20 rooms with private bath, fan. The pricier rooms have air conditioning and TV. The restaurant serves good Belizean fare. About a 20min walk past the suspension bridge and off the main highway on Aguada Avenue. From BZ$40.
Snooty Fox 64 George Price Av, Santa Elena; tel: 09 22150; fax: 09 23556. 6 rooms, all with hot water and private bath. With open bar overlooking the river. Owners also organise trips to Barton Creek Caves and canoeing on the Macal River.

San Ignacio features two private camping grounds, both of which are 'building' to take advantage of San Ignacio's popularity: **Midas Campsite**, tel: 09 23172; fax: 09 23845, about 0.8km outside town on the road to Branch Mouth. The owner, another former British soldier, charges BZ$8 pp to camp, and he'll watch after your valuables in his house. He's also got seven huts which rent for BZ$63. The site overlooks the Macal River, and has toilets and showers. The other option is **Cosmos Camping**, tel: 09 27755, 0.4km past Midas, also overlooking the river. Cosmos also has five budget cabanas with shared bath and a dormitory. Camping costs BZ$5.59 pp, and they rent tents. The cabanas are BZ$7.50 pp and the room is BZ$10.70 pp. Chaa Creek Cottages has now developed a tent campsite downriver from their plush lodge. Several of the lodges outside of San Ignacio also provide camping facilities including The Trek Stop.
　　Rural accommodations are available in the myriad of lodges and resorts hidden away in the countryside surrounding San Ignasion.

Rural lodges and resorts near San Ignacio
Call them what you will – cottage resorts, lodges or guest ranches – Cayo has more of them than anywhere else in Belize. They're all rural, located some distance from San Ignacio, but beyond that it's hard to generalise. Some are located in rainforest, others on farmland, still others in pine ridge. Some specialise in horseback riding, some stress ecological education, and a few offer nothing but pure bucolic sloth. Prices are generally on the high side, but even here there are exceptions. Some travellers swear by them, spending their entire vacation at their favourite lodge and taking side-trips arranged by the management. Some folks, on the other hand,

prefer the 'gringo trail' bustle of San Ignacio. There's no reason you can't do both if you're so inclined. It's best to write or phone ahead for reservations, particularly at the more famous lodges like Chaa Creek.

Many of the lodges listed below offer trips to Tikal, Mountain Pine Ridge, Xunantunich, the Panti Medicinal Trail and Caracol. None of the lodges are accessible via public transportation, but Nabitunich, Windy Hill Cottages and Maya Mountain Lodge can be reached after a short hike from either San Ignacio or the Western Highway. Most will pick you up at Belize Airport for an extra fee. All the resorts below are located in the hillier portion of Cayo closer to San Ignacio; two other rural lodges, Banana Bank Ranch and Warrie Head Ranch and Lodge, are situated closer to Belmopan (see above). If you are on a budget and you fancy splashing out, most of the resorts take credit cards.

Maya Mountain Lodge PO Box 174, San Ignacio; tel: 09 22164; fax: 09 22029; email: jungle@mayamountain.com; web: www.mayamountain.com. Located about 0.8km up the Cristo Rey Road from Santa Elena (1.6km from San Ignacio). 14 rooms, price range US$43–106 depending on whether you're in a regular room, hillside room, or cottage and the difference between high and low season. Breakfast, lunch, and dinner cost US$8, US$8, and US$16, respectively. Owners Bart and Suzi Mickler have been in Belize for over 20 years. They call their beautifully located lodge an 'educational field station', and they stress natural history tours of the area. The Micklers offer a signed nature trail through the nearby rainforest, a staff naturalist/ornithologist, a lush garden featuring local plants, as well as an impressive reference library on Belizean culture, natural history and archaeology. Bart runs trips, involving a 4km hike, to Che Chem Ha Cave, a ceremonial Maya site which still contains pottery. They host study groups; the veranda serves as classroom, with occasional disturbances whenever sweet 'lady-finger' mangoes drop onto the corrugated steel roof. Tours throughout Belize and to Tikal, along with canoe rentals, horseback rides and mountain bike rentals. Highly recommended by many travellers.

Crystal Paradise Resort Cristo Rey Village; tel/fax: 09 22772/12014; email: cparadise@btl.net; web: www.crystalparadise.com. 20 rooms, some with thatched roofs. Run by the friendly Tut family who built all the rooms and still own the resort. A beautiful spot with options for rafting, horse riding and the usual tours in the Cayo district. Excellent food. Rooms start at US$86 with private bath, fans, and breakfast and dinner included.

Mountain Equestrian Trails Mile 8 Mountain Pine Ridge Road, Central Farm Post Office, Cayo; tel: 09 23310 (radiophone); email: aw2trav2bz@aol.com web: www.metbelize.com. In the USA tel: 1 800 838 3918; fax: 941 488 3953. 10 rooms in cabanas and 3 rooms in the main house La Casa Visa (US$85–120). Meals work out at US$35 per day. Located just east of the junction of the Cristo Rey Road and the Mountain Pine Ridge Road, about 12km from Georgeville. MET specialises in horseback riding, with nearly 100km of trails nearby. Indeed, the hotel, called Casa Cielo Hotel, is a relatively recent addition to what was once strictly a riding stable. 4 thatched stucco cabanas, all with private bath and hot water. The restaurant is open to the public. In addition to horseback rides throughout the Mountain Pine Ridge – including Caracol – MET offers cave trips, vehicle tours, horse-drawn cart trips, freshwater fishing, swimming, hiking and inland and caye tours. Horse trips are designed for all ages and experience levels.

Pine Ridge Lodge PO Box 128, San Ignacio, Cayo; tel: 08 23180; email: PRLodge@mindspring.com; web: www.PineRidgeLodge.com. 6 cottages, all with private bath. Pine Ridge Lodge welcomes small parties and individual guests. The lodge is 11 miles from 1,000-Foot Falls, 10 miles from Río Frio Cave, seven from Río On Pools and 33 miles from Caracol. Swimming is possible in the nearby mountain stream. US$90 including continental breakfast, tax and service charge. Lunch and dinner are extra.

Blancaneaux Lodge Mountain Pine Ridge, PO Box B, Central Farm; tel: 09 23878; fax: 09 23919; email: blodge@btl.net; web: www.blancaneauxlodge.com. A former hunting lodge deep in the Mountain Pine Ridge, now owned by Francis Ford Coppola, this is the closest lodging to Caracol. The site overlooks the Privassion River, and offers 6 2-bedroom luxury villas. Rates vary from US$295–400. There are also 6 thatched cabanas with screened porches, ranging from US$85–180). Breakfast included in price, lunch and dinner US$40 extra pp. The restaurant features wood-fired pizzas, pastas, and a slate bar carved by the Magana Brothers. The 100% organic three-acre fruit and vegetable garden supplies the restaurant with produce. The lodge has its own airstrip and charter plane. Trips to nearby Caracol as well as to other local attractions are available. There are stables on site for horse riding. Mountain biking and hiking is also catered for.

Five Sisters Lodge PO Box 173, Mountain Pine Ridge Forest Reserve, San Ignacio; tel/fax: 09 12005; email: fivesislo@btl.net; web: www.fivesisterslodge.com. Near Five Sisters Falls, a series of five waterfalls which empty into the Privassion River. Cabanas with private bath, from US$105, balcony and non-balcony rooms with shared bath US$70, breakfast included. Bar, restaurant, gift shop, and bike rentals on site. Dinners cost US$17.50, lunch US$6. Trips arranged to all the Pine Ridge sights plus Caracol. Cave and ruin trips also conducted on horseback, full day costs US$120 for two people.

Hidden Valley Inn 4 Mile Cooma Cairn Road, Mountain Pine Ridge; tel: 08 23320; email: HiddenVi@btl.net; web: www.hiddenvalleyinn.com. Mailing address for reservations C.W. Maryland and Co., 835 East Park Avenue, Suite A, Tallahassee, FL 32301, USA (tel: 800 334 7942; fax: 850 222 1992). Turn off to head south from the main highway at Georgeville about 45 min from San Ignacio. After an hour, or 25 miles, you'll find the turnoff on your left, just before the turnoff to Hidden Valley (1,000-Foot) Falls. Don't try to drive this 3.2km entrance road without 4WD. This is one of the most luxurious of the Cayo resorts, stunningly situated in the pine forest. 12 rooms, all with private bath and fireplace, US$192 including three meals daily (cheaper weekly rates available). Transportation to or from the Belize City Airport costs US$100 (1-2 people). In the past, it was sometimes possible to drop in unannounced and, with a bit of discrete haggling, to halve the pricey cost of lodging. They offer the full range of Cayo trips, plus Caracol and the Guatemala Cave.

Green Heaven Lodge PO Box 155, San Ignacio; tel: 09 12034; email: ghlodge@btl.net; web: www.ghlodgebelize.com. One of the newest lodges in the area, Green Heaven is one mile down the Chial Road west of San Ignacio. All the private cabanas have two double beds, ceiling fans and private bathrooms. US$90. Hammocks on the veranda are perfect for relaxing, or take time out in the bar and Belizean/French restaurant. Alternatively the more active can take part in aqua aerobics, volley ball and swimming followed by a massage.

Chaa Creek Resort & Spa and Inland Expeditions PO Box 53, San Ignacio, Cayo; tel: 09 22037; fax: 09 22501; email: chaacreek@btl.net; web: www.chaacreek.com. Located about 13km outside of San Ignacio; the turnoff is roughly 8km from town on the road toward the Guatemalan border. 21 cottages, BZ$320 with private bath. The cottages perch on a hillside overlooking the placid Macal River. Probably the best-known of Belize's cottage resorts, the place was originally a farm. Owners Mick and Lucy Fleming bought it in 1979 and eventually built 21 gorgeous thatched cottages. Directly next door is Ix Chel Farm and the Medicinal Trail (see *Excursions* below). They offer canoe trips on the Macal River, plus all the usual tours within Belize. About 1km downriver, the owners have set up the Macal River Jungle Camp, a tiny 'village' of 10 casitas, or small bungalows, each on a raised platform with two comfortable beds. Each casita has a private sheltered porch for quiet relaxation and peaceful views into the undisturbed jungle habitat. There are hot water showers, bathrooms and a private swimming and canoe landing. US$42. Chaa Creek also opened a blue Morpho butterfly breeding centre in 1995. The centre is open to visitors and a trip round the Chaa Creek Natural History Centre provides an excellent overview of the regions natural richness.

duPlooys Riverside Cottages and Hotel PO Box 180, San Ignacio; tel: 09 23101; fax: 09 23301; email: duplooys@btl.net; web: www.duplooys.com. On the same road and just upstream of Chaa Creek Cottages (see directions above), follow the signs to duPlooys. 9 jungle lodge rooms in 3 tile-roofed cottages, all with screened porches, private bath with hot water. US$115. There is also a 7-bedroom guesthouse with shared bath. US$40. Like Chaa Creek, duPlooys is a former farm, a 20-acre site located high above the Macal River. Ken and Judy duPlooy opened the resort in the mid-1980s, and they now offer both local tours and trips throughout Belize, including diving, canoeing, horseback riding, hiking, fishing, and swimming in the Macal River. Ken is a renowned orchid grower, and his gardens have over 300 species of trees and a wide variety of tropical flowers. Hot water and fans from 06.00–22.00, then the generator is turned off and kerosene lanterns are lit.

Ek'Tun Macal River, Cayo; tel: 09 12002; email: info@ektunbelize.com; web: www.ektunbelize.com. Also through Top Cat Copy Center at #8 Hudson Street, San Ignacio. 2 beautifully appointed thatched cabanas with a double bed and a double and a single in the loft. A spectacular setting overlooking the Macal River, isolated from the rest of Belize and seemingly the world. Activities include walks through the forest looking out over the valley below, exploring cave systems used by the Maya, relaxing in the stream-fed mineral pool and horseriding. Bird life in the area is spectacular and includes a pair of spectacled owls and the rare orange-breasted falcon. The food is personally prepared by the owners Ken and Phyllis Dart. When you arrive at Ek'Tun you will be amazed, when you leave you'll be sad and invigorated. US$215 pp includes all meals, transportation from San Ignacio is US$30.

Black Rock Riverside Lodge PO Box 48, San Ignacio; tel: 09 22341; fax: 09 23449; email: blackrock@btl.net; web: www.blackrocklodge.com. Located 29km upstream from San Ignacio on the banks of the Macal River, just below Vaca Falls. A recently completed road means you can now drive all the way to the secluded lodge. 12 stone cabanas, US$36 with shared bath, US$65 with private bath.

Windy Hill Cottages Graceland Ranch, San Ignacio; tel: 09 22017; fax: 09 23080; email: windyhill@btl.net; web: www.windyhillresort.com. On the outskirts of San Ignacio, about 2.4km west of town. 25 cottages decorated with exotic hardwoods, local art and hand-woven rugs. Hot water and ceiling fans in all the rooms. US$80. Rooms are half price off season. The restaurant is superb and serves three meals a day. Breakfast costs US$9, lunch US$11 and dinner US$19, but you must tell the owners if you wish to dine so they can plan ahead. There is also a swimming pool. Nature trails weave through the resorts 100 acres of manicured flowers and fruit trees. Horse riding, canoeing on the Macal River and local trips with guides to Caracol (US$300), Mt Pine Ridge (US$200) and Xunantunich (US$80) are available. Trips further afield can also be arranged.

The Trek Stop Mile 71 Western Highway, San José Succotz, nr San Ignacio, Cayo; tel: 09 32265; email: susa@btl.net; web: www.tbcnet.com/dyaeger/susa/trekstop.htm. Ideally located for trips to Xunantunich, this environmentally-friendly site is proving popular with budget travellers. Cabins, tents and tent site are available for rent, with kitchen facilities and solar-heated showers. Cabins start at BZ$20 pp, camping is BZ$7 pp.

Parrot's Nest General Delivery, Bullet Tree Falls; tel: 09 37008; email: parrot@btl.net; web: www.parrot-nest.com. If you haven't been in a tree house since you were a kid, here's your chance. 2 tree houses perched 22ft up in a 100ft Guanacaste tree overlooking the Mopan River give the place its name. There are also two thatched cabanas. Prices range from US$25–32.50 with shared bath. Breakfast is US$3 with dinner at US$7. Located about 6km outside San Ignacio on the Bullet Tree Falls road, there is a free shuttle service from town. They offer horseback riding and good swimming in the river.

Nabitunich Lodge San Lorenzo Farm, Benque Viejo del Carmen; tel: 09 32096, email: rudyjuan@btl.net. Nabitunich sits on 400 acres of farmland, producing beef cattle, coconuts, bananas, oranges, grapefruit, tangerines, pineapple, watermelons and sousop. They offer 7 cottages with two bedrooms, each bedroom with two twin beds and private bathroom. Extra beds are no problem. All cottages are thatched, with verandas, tile floors, hot water and locally-made mahogany furniture. Rooms alone cost US$50 for a double. Room and two meals costs US$74; MAP and B&B rates are also available, as are sack lunches. Xunantunich ruins are visible from all the cottages. A 30-min hike will get you there or you can hire horses for the journey. Discounts available for groups over ten. Indeed, the UCLA archaeologists excavating the ruin for the next six years have made their camp at Nabitunich. Canoeing in the nearby Mopan River and horseback riding throughout the area is available. A small nature trail cuts through the bush, mostly used by local hunters and fishermen. The owners can also arrange all the usual local day tours, including Tikal. The turnoff road to Nabitunich lies 8.4km west of San Ignacio, about 0.8km past the Chaa Creek/duPlooy's road. You can ride the local bus toward Benque Viejo (BZ$0.50) and have the driver put you off at the turnoff. From there, it's an easy 1.6km hike to Nabitunich. Or, they'll pick you up at the border for BZ$22. All in all, one of the cheaper alternatives among Cayo resorts, and highly recommended.

Where to eat

Eva's Restaurant 22 Burns Avenue; tel: 09 22267; email: evas@btl.net; web: www.evasonline.com . As much a Cayo landmark as Xunantunich, Eva's dispenses beer, liquor, standard Belizean fare and a wealth of advice for travellers. The owner – Bob Jones, a former British soldier who settled in Belize after his hitch – seems to spend most of his day informally planning Cayo travel itineraries and putting like-minded souls together to share trip expenses. His recommendations on everything from day-trips to guides to lodging are honest and objective; he won't try to steer budget travellers toward pricier alternatives. Eva's draws locals, archaeology students, Mennonite farmers from Spanish Lookout and hordes of travellers. The walls are festooned with postcards from all over the world, and there's a corner of the place set aside as a gift shop. Breakfasts include the standard eggs, beans, coffee and toast or tortillas (BZ$4). Lunch and dinner specials change every few days; chilimole (chicken, peas and onion in a pepper sauce, served with tortillas), chicken curry and tamales are frequent specialities, plus the usual burgers and sandwiches. Also has an internet and email service.

The **Happy Iguana** opposite the Venus Hotel. With the usual offerings of Belizean and international food it's the incredibly friendly service, outdoor restaurant and occasional live music at weekends that makes the Iguana stand out… and the lemon cake!

Serendib Restaurant 27 Burns Avenue; tel: 09 22302. A spotlessly clean, popular eating place, perhaps San Ignacio's best, featuring Sri Lankan and Belizean food. A small patio-garden at the back for enjoying the weather. Chicken, beef, or shrimp curries with rice, potatoes, salad, BZ$12. Good chow mein, ice cream, a surprisingly well-stocked bar and excellent service.To the right of the front door, a small store serves takeaway cakes and coffee.

Maxim's Chinese Restaurant Corner of Waight's Avenue and Far West Street. Huge portions at cheap prices and much better food than is usual in Belizean Chinese restaurants.

Other Chinese restaurants include the **Tai-San Take Away** (Savannah Street behind the Belmoral Hotel) and their restaurant on Burns Avenue.

Try also the **Ice Cream Paradise** at the corner of Burns Avenue and Waight's Avenue. In addition to cones, sundaes, banana splits and milkshakes, they serve burgers, nachos, french fries and popcorn. Inside seating and carry-out.

Just across the suspension bridge, and within easy walking distance from San Ignacio proper, Santa Elena offers several cheap eating spots: **Huada Chinese Restaurant**; and **Joe's Cool Club**, where saucy chicken is barbecued outside on a 55-gallon oil drum grill. The **Aguada Motel**, about a 20-minute walk past the bridge, offers very good food.

What to see
Much of Belize's finest produce originates in Cayo, and it's on display every Saturday morning in San Ignacio's marketplace (just behind the Belmoral Hotel facing the river).

Information and useful addresses
Scotia Bank, **Belize Bank** and **Atlantic Bank** are clustered together at the top end of Burns Avenue. Opening hours vary – your best bet is to get there in the morning. Few visitors to San Ignacio ever need to cash travellers' cheques at either bank, however, as most hotels in town cash them readily

There is no need to change money in San Ignacio before leaving for Guatemala. Wait until the border, where you'll find the Banco de Guatemala as well as a horde of money-changers. For details of this border crossing, see *To and from Guatemala* above.

The **BTL** telephone office is located on Eve and Church Street. You can also make calls throughout Belize from pay phones outside the Venus Hotel and the roundabout near the banks. The **post office** is in the centre of town next to Court's furniture store.

Several shops along Burns Avenue offer gifts, postcards, T-shirts and other souvenirs. Most offer a good selection of books by Belizean authors and maps of Belize and Guatemala. If you're heading for Guatemala many of the textiles will be better there but you probably will not have time to buy them if you're just going for a day trip. **New Hope Trading Company**, 0.4km past the San Ignacio Hotel on Buena Vista Street, (tel: 09 22188), sells furniture made out of local wood and a few carvings.

Tour operators and guides are numourous. **International Archaeological Tours** is at West Street, San Ignacio; tel: 09 23991; fax: 09 22760; email: iatours@btl.net; web: www.interlog.com/~nc/vacation, is well organised, very informative and friendly. **David's Adventure Tours** (tel: 09 23674; email: jet@btl.net) down by the Bus Station, is popular with backpackers and has a variety of tours including the Barton Creek Caves. David has a campsite on an unexcavated Mayan site. **Eco Jungle Tours** (tel: 09 23425) opposite the post office, above Crystal Bar offers all the standard tours and has an email and internet service.

Internet services and a good book swap are available at **Top Cat Copy Center**, 8 Hudson Street run by Phyllis Dart. Next door at #6 is **Venus Photos & Records** where you can buy print, slide and APS film and local music – advice on good local bands is lacking, ask Godsman Ellis at Piache Hotel if you want the very latest advice. Round the back of Martha's Guest House is the **Martha's Laundromat**. If you're going camping or need to stock up on some of the basics you can get absolutely everything you might need from **Celina's Superstore** at 43 Burns Avenue.

El Cenote is a sports bar close to the Bus Station. Hamburgers, sandwiches to eat while playing pool and darts. Open all day, the music gets loud in the evenings. **Third World Productions**, upstairs, has live music from local bands at weekends. The name changes regularly but the live music is a permanent offering.

Excursions
Near town
Cahal Pech

Cahal Pech isn't likely to lure visitors with its name – 'Place of the Ticks' – a moniker bestowed on the area in the 1950s when the place served as cattle pasture. Neither is it a particularly imposing Maya site. Real excavation only began in 1988, and although the ancient Maya undoubtedly had a panoramic view from their hilltop acropolis, that view is today blocked by trees. Still, Cahal Pech is worth a visit for several reasons: it's easy to reach – a 20-minute walk from downtown; it's amazingly serene and secluded despite its proximity to town; and, you'll have a chance to see archaeological work in progress.

That work has been funded since 1988 by Trent University and the Canadian Commission for UNESCO. You'll frequently run into Trent students at the site, excavating, surveying and recording data under the direction of Belizean archaeologist Jaime Awe. They're usually more than glad to answer a few questions. Prior to Awe's investigation, archaeologists had made only limited surveys of the site. Looters, on the other hand, frequently raided Cahal Pech.

As Maya sites go, Cahal Pech is a small one. Its 34 structures are jammed within two acres of densely wooded hilltop. Awe's work suggests that Cahal Pech was founded around 1000BC and abandoned during the Late Classic (AD800).

Visitors enter the site in the broad, cleared Plaza B. It was here, in 1969, that Peter Schmidt, Belize's second Archaeological Commissioner, uncovered a burial cache placed alongside the remains of a Late Classic noble. Along with pottery and objects of shell and obsidian, Schmidt found a rare mask of jade and shell in the form of a Maya god. Jade, the most valuable of Maya products, was associated with fertility and was often buried with important people to guarantee their spiritual life after death.

Moving up the broad stairway at the west end of Plaza B, visitors can climb the steps to the top of Structure A-1, the tallest of Cahal Pech's buildings at 23m. The pyramid looks down on two smaller plazas, D and E, with glimpses through the trees of the valley below. To the southeast, Plaza G is currently being excavated.

To reach Cahal Pech on foot from downtown, walk up the hill on either Benque Viejo Road or Buena Vista Road to where the two roads meet. Take a left on the signposted pit-holed road, which winds steeply up the hill to Cahal Pech ruins. At the top of the hill in addition to a few resorts and restaurants that don't appear to be interested in benefiting from the impressive view, you will find a small museum. A short path through forest leads to the secluded and very peaceful ruins. Entrance is BZ$10 but there is no water at the site and no other refreshments. At the time of writing none of the restaurants signposted at the bottom of the hill were serving either.

At the moment, the objects discovered at the Plaza B burial site by Peter Schmidt are in the archaeological vault in Belmopan and there are no plans to allow access to visitors.

Barton Creek Cave

One of the most popular half-day trips from San Ignacio, this tour takes travellers by canoe first into a huge cathedral-like cavern, and then into a claustrophobic (but entirely safe) cave so low that one has to lie down and tip the canoe to shimmy through. Car batteries power the bulbs needed to see the cave, and bats abound. The journey to the caves also takes you through some small Mennonite communities. Although you don't stop, it does give you something interesting to see along the way. Most guides charge BZ$50.

Branch Mouth

A leisurely half-hour stroll north of town brings you to Branch Mouth, where the Mopan and Macal Rivers meet to form the Belize River. It's a popular picnicking and swimming spot for both locals and tourists. A massive shade tree overhangs the river, fitted with an iron ring once used by commercial boats for mooring. Simply walk out of town on Savannah Street, past the sports field, and keep going.

Macal River canoe and raft trips

The Macal River – formerly known as the Eastern Branch Belize River – provides both the backdrop for San Ignacio and its most popular day trip. There are now a number of canoe and rafting guides, offering everything from short day trips to extended runs all the way downstream to Belize City.

Don't expect to duck hanging vines on a mazy, claustrophobic jungle river. The Macal is a wide river with expansive views. And you won't be alone; besides other canoeists and rafters, you'll find the shores dotted with villages, resort lodges and homes. But there are also stretches of breathtaking beauty, walls of jungle rising steeply from the river banks and dwarfing the canoes beneath them. Here and there, guanacaste trees spread majestically above the canopy, vying for space with trumpet trees, wild figs and bullet trees. Locals value this last tree for bridge footings because the wood becomes 'hard as a bullet' when in contact with water. You're likely to see toucans, motmots, wood rails, kiskadees, brown jays, painted herons and parrots along the way. Birders occasionally spot a trogon, a close relative of the quetzal. Rock outcroppings along the riverbank provide a cave-like resting spot for hundreds of bats which flutter downstream at the approach of a canoe. Iguanas, some green, some grey-brown, some a surreal orange, line the shoreline, blinking lazily from their perches in overhanging trees.

The river rarely gets too low for canoe travel, but it does get too high during the rainy season. In June 1990, for example, the Macal rose almost to the level of the Hawkesworth Bridge. During the wet season you may have to wait several days to make a canoe trip, while the river subsides to a safe level.

The most popular river guide in Cayo is **Tony's River Tours** (tel: 09 23292 or contact him through Eva's). Tony's relaxed manner belies his powerful paddle stroke, which propels his aluminium or fibreglass canoes up the Macal River from the Hawkesworth Bridge to Chaa Creek, the Ix Chel Farm, and the Medicine Trail. Naturally, you're invited to paddle as well, particularly in the faster riffles. Tony charges BZ$25 pp, lunch not included. You'll leave around 09.00, swim along the way, visit Ix Chel, and return to San Ignacio around 16.00.

Snooty Fox (tel: 09 22150 or through Eva's) can also arrange canoe rentals with or without guides.

It is also possible to arrange longer trips along the Macal River and, if you want, all the way down to Belize City. Tony charges US$50 pp per night for four people including all food and equipment. You camp on sand bars and low banks for about four or five days, depending on the flow.

A major sports event has developed out of the river. **La Ruta Maya Belize River Challenge** starts beneath the Hawkesworth Bridge in San Ignacio. Paddlers and amateur strokers test themselves and their endurance, for three and a half days over the 170-mile jungle course of the Belize Old River. En route to the finish line in Belize City, racers overnight at Banana Bank, Bermudian Landing and Burrell Boom. And the timing puts the victory celebrations right in the middle of the Baron Bliss Day Celebrations in Belize City.

The race runs from March 3–6. Categories include 'Professional', a new Kayak and Dugout Class and an 'Amateur' Class. Watching is fun if you can see the race on the river, and if you want to enter the fee is US$200. Visit the website on www.bighjuices.com for more details. If you fancy entering, tel: 092 2646; fax: 092 3075; email: bighjuices@btl.net .

Ix Chel Farm and Medicine Trail

While there are now a number of botanical trails in Belize – including those at the Shipstern Reserve, the Cockscomb Wildlife Sanctuary, and the Maya Mountain Lodge – the Trail concentrates almost exclusively on the medicinal properties of jungle flora. The trail lies within Ix Chel Farm, adjacent to the Chaa Creek Cottages a few kilometres west of San Ignacio. Both the farm and trail are owned by a pair of American expatriates, practising herbalist Rosita Arvigo and her husband, Greg Shropshire. I had heard only a little about Arvigo before visiting Ix Chel, and somewhat expected to meet a trendy, New Age healer-mystic. But this is Belize, after all, and Arvigo turned out to be a thoroughly practical jungle doctor with a delightful, irreverent sense of humour.

Arvigo's own trail to Belize, every bit as circuitous as the Ix Chel Trail, began in her home town of Chicago. There she studied at the National College of Naprapathy, a drug-less therapeutic system based on traditional Czechoslovakian chiropractics. By 1969, she had left her naprapathic clinic in Chicago to study plant medicine with the Nahuatl Indians of Guerrero, Mexico. After seven years among the Nahuatl, Arvigo came to Belize in 1976. She left three years later and returned in 1982 with her husband and family. Searching out native healers, she met Cayo's most renowned *hierbatero* (herbalist), Don Eligio Panti. Panti, then in his mid-80s, had learned Maya medicine from a *chiclero* some fifty years earlier in the Petén rainforest of Guatemala. He was initially reluctant to pass on his knowledge to a woman, and a foreigner at that. Arvigo tramped through the jungle after Panti, collecting roots, leaves and bark, and he eventually acknowledged her stamina. But there was still the matter of her foreign status; would his life's work end up benefiting clients in a Chicago clinic? Arvigo agreed to stay on in Belize.

Twenty years later she's still in Cayo. And while she's kept her pledge, tending to the health of the local population, the world of mainstream medicine has, perhaps inevitably, beaten a path to her door. In 1986, The US National Cancer Institute (NCI), headquartered in Bethesda, Maryland, began funding the New York Botanical Garden to collect Central and South American plants that might prove useful in the fight against cancer and AIDS. Similar funding goes to the University of Illinois and the Missouri Botanical Garden to collect plants in southeast Asia and Africa. The New York Botanical Garden contacted Arvigo and Shropshire, who subsequently formed the Ix Chel Tropical Research Center to begin collections of promising Belizean flora. Since then, additional funding has come from the US National Health Institute, USAID, the Metropolitan Life Insurance Company and private donations.

At this writing, Arvigo and her team of local native healers have sent samples of over 1,700 species to the NCI laboratories. There the plants are being tested on two AIDS viruses and 100 types of tumour. Time is short; even as cancer and AIDS claim more victims worldwide, the forests which may hold a potential cure are being burned and bulldozed.

In the meantime, visitors to Ix Chel Farm can see and learn about plants whose medicinal properties have been known for centuries. The Ix Chel Medicine Trail – formerly named the Panti Trail in honour of Arvigo's mentor – winds through 1.5km of jungle behind her house. You can choose to tramp the trail with a guide – sometimes Arvigo, sometimes Shropshire, sometimes a local *hierbatero* – for

BZ$17.50 or see it on your own. For BZ$5 pp, Arvigo will provide you with a series of cards which guide you along the trail, explaining the medicinal use of each featured tree, root, vine or leaf.

While you're on the trail, keep an eye out for examples of one of Maya herbology's guiding principles, the 'Doctrine of Signatures'. The doctrine holds that useful plants tend to resemble in some way the body organs which respond to their medicinal powers. The wild yam, for instance, is shaped like a heart, and happens to supply a potent blood tonic. Likewise, the peeling red bark of the gumbo limbo tree suggests its use as a bath for skin ailments.

When you've returned from the trail, Arvigo or a colleague will show you through a 'healer's hut' built in the old Maya style following Don Eligio's own plans. Thin trees are lashed together with vines to form walls, logs have been hand split to make benches and tables, the roof is thatch, the sink mahogany. There is a 1,000-year-old tortilla stone, hammocks, and a thatched bed useful for both massage and herbal steam baths. The Maya bush doctor would place a pot of hot water and herbs beneath the bed, allowing the steam to filter up through the palm fronds, while the patient lay on top under a wool blanket.

Several of Arvigo's herbal remedies are available in packet form at the Ix Chel Farm. The list includes a salve for itchy insect bites, jackass bitters tea (for parasites, amoebas, malaria, fungus, ringworm and yeast conditions), man vine tea (for gastritis, indigestion and constipation), and female tonic tea (a thoroughly distasteful combination of man vine, contribo, guaco and copalchi that you let steep in vodka and drink monthly to ease menstrual cramps; I've been told it's fairly effective after the first couple of months). You can also mail-order these packets direct; a list and prices are available from Dr Rosita Arvigo, DN, Ix Chel Farm, San Ignacio, Cayo, Belize.

Arvigo and her staff also hold three seminars in herbal medicine several times a year: Natural Healing for Health Care Professionals, Healthful Living for All, and Herbology North and South. Prices range from US$295–395 pp, including all activities, lectures, snacks and lunch. Write to Arvigo at the address above for more information.

Guests can now stay at Ix Chel Farm Guest House – simple rustic, clean rooms in a cabin. Rates are BZ$46.80 for a single and BZ$56.80 for a double including breakfast.

There is also a vegetarian restaurant serving organic salads, sandwiches and pesto on the veranda overlooking the river.

Ix Chel Farm and the Medicine Trail are open to visitors daily from 08.00–12.00 and 13.00–16.30. There is no public transportation, but it's easy enough to hire a taxi in San Ignacio. If you're driving yourself, follow the Western Highway about 8km west of San Ignacio before turning south toward duPlooys Resort and Chaa Creek. You can also let Ix Chel Farm arrange your transport and tour of the grounds (tel: 09 23870; email: ixchel@btl.net). But perhaps the best way to visit Ix Chel and the Panti Trail is via canoe from San Ignacio; most day-trips on the river stop at the Chaa Creek dock, allowing visitors to have lunch at Ix Chel Farm (see *Macal River canoe and raft trips* above).

Don Eligio Panti, by the way, died at the age of 103 in Feburary 1996.

Further afield
Pilar
Although one of the largest Classic Maya sites in Belize – it encompasses an area of some 50 acres – Pilar remains unexcavated. It wasn't until reports of looting reached the Archaeology Commissioner in 1972 that the site was officially

'discovered'. But locals were undoubtedly aware of this vast city long before that, and looting continues to this day.

Pilar consists of at least 15 courtyards, a ball court, and a number of palaces and temples, the tallest reaching 21m above the plaza. The city's most unusual feature is a low-lying stone wall which runs west toward Guatemala. Its purpose, like much of Pilar, remains a mystery.

Low-lying and completely unexcavated, Pilar will appeal only to the most avid Mayaphiles. The city lies at the end of a very poor dirt road, a few kilometres north of Bullet Tree Falls village.

Public transportation won't get you very close to Pilar. One option is to walk from San Ignacio to Branch Mouth (20–30 minutes, see *Branch Mouth* above), and from there to Bullet Tree Falls. Ask villagers in Bullet Tree about transportation to Pilar. They can usually arrange a truck or 4WD vehicle to the site. Weekdays are best for arranging this kind of ride; on a Sunday you'll find it hard to rouse the citizens of Bullet Tree at any price. A second and easier option is to hire a taxi in San Ignacio which will cost you about BZ$70 return.

Mountain Pine Ridge and vicinity

In Belize, the term 'ridge' has nothing to do with elevation or relief. It simply means an area characterised by a particular type of vegetation, such as the perfectly flat Southern Pine Ridge in Toledo District. Cayo's Mountain Pine Ridge, however, happens to combine a southern pine forest with spectacular highland scenery, including waterfalls, limestone caves and lofty peaks. Most of the area is a Forest Reserve where only selective logging is allowed, and it's ideal for mountain biking, horseback riding, spelunking, hiking and picnicking. Although not actually in the Pine Ridge itself, the gateway village of San Antonio attracts travellers because of its ancient Maya site (Pacbitun) as well as contemporary manifestations of Maya culture (the Garcia Sisters craft shop).

Mountain Pine Ridge covers some 170,000 acres on the northwestern flanks of the Maya Mountains, with elevations ranging between 300m and 915m above sea level. Most of the ridge is pine barren country, *Pinus caribaea* savanna strikingly similar in appearance to the pine forests of the southern United States. Some oak, rosewood and cedar (*Cedrela mexicana*) also grow here. Locals used to make the dugout canoes called 'pit-pans' from single cedar trunks. The soil underneath is siliceous sand, supporting only thin, wiry grasses. This thin layer of poor, sandy topsoil has kept the Pine Ridge fairly pristine and unpopulated for centuries, since it virtually precludes agriculture. At the same time, it makes the roads impassable after even modest rains. At lower elevations, however, the vegetation becomes more luxuriant, eventually merging into quasi-rainforest. This gradual transition from palm and mahogany jungle to pine barrens alone is worth a trip to Mountain Pine Ridge.

Most visitors to the Pine Ridge enter via the Cristo Rey road through San Antonio village. San Antonio (not to be confused with the village of the same name in Toledo District) is a large Mopan Maya village situated in the lowlands just 13km southeast of San Ignacio. Just before reaching the village you'll find the **Garcia Sisters Craft Shop and Museum** on the left. The five sisters – Maria, Piedad, Aurora, Carmelita and Sylvia – produce intricate slate carvings based on Maya glyphs, masks and stelae designs. Inspired at an early age by the nearby excavations at Pacbitun (see below), the sisters begged their father for sculpting lessons. You can usually find at least one of the Garcias carving under the thatched 'studio'. Inside their thatched shop, the sisters sell not only slate glyphs, but also inexpensive Maya-inspired slate jewellery.

About 3km east of San Antonio lies the Maya ceremonial site of **Pacbitun** ('Stones Set in the Earth'). First settled in 900BC and flourishing until the Maya collapse in the 10th century, Pacbitun is one of the oldest known Preclassic sites in western Belize. Although the site comprises some 75 acres, the ceremonial centre lies within a 0.8km radius. There are 41 major structures, including two dozen temples (the tallest one 16.5m above plaza level), a ball court, a pair of raised causeways for irrigation and a handful of stelae. Two caves with artefacts also exist nearby, but they have been off-limits to visitors until the landowner opened both caves to visitors in June 1992.

Archaeologists have excavated at the site since 1981, although systematic work only began in 1986 under the direction of Paul Healy from Trent University. Among the finds have been Maya musical instruments and objects of green obsidian, suggesting a trade connection with Teotihuacán, Mexico.

Pacbitun is located about 3km northeast of San Antonio, on private land. Contact Mr José Tzul (tel: 09 22322), the owner, at the turn-off road 0.8km past town before entering. Mr Tzul can also arrange horse riding tours that take in the ruins. The trip to Pacbitun can also be arranged with taxi drivers or guides in San Ignacio, but is best done as part of an all-day trip to Mountain Pine Ridge.

About 5km past San Antonio, you'll pass the junction of the road from Georgeville, an alternative route into the Mountain Pine Ridge. Here the road starts climbing, still in moist tropical forest. The Forest Reserve gate and guard station is 1.6km further on. The guard will allow you to camp here; the other legal camping site within the Reserve is at Douglas D'Silva (formerly Augustine) Forestry Station near the top of the Ridge. The first pines begin appearing within 3km. Heavy rains drench the Pine Ridge, and often the small 'trails' leading off the main road are nothing more than ditches to drain water from the roadway.

Roughly 4.8km beyond the Reserve entrance gate, the road forks. The left fork leads to **Hidden Valley Falls** (also known as 1,000-Foot Falls), the highest waterfall in Central America. Four miles down this track the road forks again; the left fork takes you to the Falls (a rustic sign points the way), while the rough track straight ahead leads to Cooma Cairn, a British Army training area.

This track to the falls ends abruptly at the brink of a spectacular canyon. On the far side of the canyon, Hidden Valley Falls plummets 480m (1,600-Foot Falls would be a more accurate name) into the forest floor below. Walk down a few steps from the parking area to the lookout for the best view. Also scan the nearby pine trees; many of them, unexpectedly, sport bromeliads more often associated with jungle trees. There is a toilet and an outhouse at the lookout, as well as a few small buildings. The largest of these belongs to the Hidden Valley Falls Environmental Studies Institute, a private research group. From this vantage point there are views north to the Mennonite community of Spanish Lookout and, on clear days, Belmopan. A trail descends steeply from here to the base of the Falls; a guide is recommended for this trip, which reportedly takes a full day on a poorly marked trail.

The main road continues south through pine forest for 13km after the Hidden Valley Falls cutoff, crossing at least four creeks: Little Vaqueros, Privation, Oak Burn and Pinol. The next flowing water is the **Río On**; a sign marks the turn off. Here the river cascades down a series of smooth rock chutes and placid bathing pools, a popular swimming spot for locals and travellers alike. At the end of the track, take the path to the right, which leads to the upper pools and waterfalls.

Most day trips to the Pine Ridge take visitors another 4.8km up the road, to the **Douglas D'Silva Forestry Station** (the station was previously known as Augustine). Douglas D'Silva is a large government forestry workers' settlement among sparse pines. There's a dry goods store with cheese, crackers, cold soft drinks, etc, and two thatched picnic tables conveniently located nearby. Off to one side are mobile drying-rack roofs which cover pine seeds used in reforestation. If you've come without a guide, it's a good idea to check in with headquarters, especially if you plan to camp. However, you can no longer get passes here to travel by car to Caracol; call the Department of Archaeology (tel: 08 22106). To reach the bunkhouse camping area, follow signs to the right past the schoolhouse playground. The camp area, an open-sided, covered wooden hut with hard wooden bunks, is on the right, just past the turnoff to the school and Río Frio Caves.

Follow the track to the schoolhouse and then downhill to the parking area for the **Río Frio Caves**. The main cave is nestled amid beautiful jungle. Clouds of big white butterflies dance through the hanging vines and lianas. Lizards scamper through the underbrush; what little sound they make is completely muffled by the electric hum of cicadas. A nature trail winds through the forest, many local trees identified with plaques along the way. Step carefully up the slippery mud trail to the largest of the caves, through which runs the Río Frio. Coarse sand 'beaches' line the creek's path. The massive cave itself – the largest river cave in the country – is open at both ends, providing just enough light to pick your way past the stalactites and bizarre limestone formations. Regrettably, there is now some graffiti, litter and a faint odour of urine in the cave.

The ancient Maya used the Río Frio and other nearby caverns as ceremonial sites during the Middle and Late Classic. Archaeologists have found pottery offerings scattered at the base of rock formations in these caves. At least one researcher has suggested that these formations might have served as symbols of the Maya deity Chac, although a dry cavern seems an unlikely spot to worship a rain god. In any case, the pottery shards found in these caves point to a close tie with the ancient city of Xunantunich (see below).

The road degenerates past Douglas D'Silva, continuing south for another 8km before reaching San Luís. This logging settlement was once larger than Douglas D'Silva, but is now all but abandoned. A sawmill remains on the site. It doesn't seem possible, but the road becomes worse 8km further on at the Guacamallo Bridge. Improvements have been made to the road, but it still gets very slick and dangerous after rains. The Belize Department of Archaeology is concerned with the damage done to the road by too many vehicles attempting this trip.

Another 25km past the Guacamallo Bridge lie the ancient remains of Caracol – the largest, most important and most difficult of Belize's Maya sites to access (see below). Road work is in progress between the Guacamallo Bridge and Caracol. The plans are to dump the 16km road, leaving 4.8km as is (ie: 4WD territory only).

There is no public transportation within the Mountain Pine Ridge Forest Reserve. A number of guides provide day trips from San Ignacio, including stops at the Río Frio Cave, Río On bathing pools and Hidden Valley Falls.

If you're driving yourself and coming from the east, a second route into the Pine Ridge may prove faster: turn off the Western Highway at Georgeville, heading south past Mountain Equestrian Trails Resort; just beyond the resort, this road joins the Cristo Rey-San Antonio Road.

One note of caution in planning trips to Mountain Pine Ridge: it frequently rains heavily up on the Pine Ridge when things in San Ignacio are dry. Guides and tour operators call the forest station to check on local conditions.

International Archaeological Tours (see page 119) and **Eco Jungle Tours** (San Ignacio, tel: 092 3425) offers trips to Mountain Pine Ridge and the Hidden Valley Falls with prices starting at BZ$75 pp. These trips can be tailored to incorporate trips to any other sites of interest in the area so just ask for what you want.

Cyclists can rent mountian bikes at BZ$5 an hour of BZ$30 a day from the Crystal Paradise office near the bus station in San Ignacio.

Caracol

Few visitors to Tikal – the 'supreme Maya centre' according to archaeologist William Coe – realize that just 80km to the southeast, deep in the Belizean forest, stand the remains of the mighty city that many scholars now believe conquered Tikal.

Despite its relative anonymity, Caracol is the largest known ancient Maya ruin in Belize. At the height of power, Caracol was larger than Tikal, home to perhaps 100,000 Maya. Yet the site's importance wasn't known until after full-scale excavation began in 1985. And despite Caracol's growing fame, it will likely remain the least-visited of the major Belizean ruins for some time to come. Lying at the end of a deeply-rutted, frequently impassable logging track, Caracol is both difficult and expensive to reach.

A logger named Rosa Mai first stumbled upon the ruins in 1937. His discovery lured British Honduras' first Archaeological Commissioner, A H Anderson, to the site that same year. Anderson named the city Caracol – Spanish for 'snail shell' – and briefly explored the area. University of Pennsylvania's Linton Satterthwaite removed stelae and altars during three expeditions in the early 1950s. The three finest are on display at the Bliss Institute in Belize City. Satterthwaite was followed in the mid-1950s by A H Anderson, this time leading a team from Harvard's Peabody Museum to excavate a masonry chamber. Caracol was then largely abandoned for almost two decades. In 1978, Paul Healy of Trent University studied the Maya farming terraces at Caracol, and Elizabeth Graham recovered a well-preserved stela now on display at the archaeological vault in Belmopan.

But the researchers most identified with Caracol are the husband-and-wife team of Arlen and Diane Chase, from the University of Central Florida in Orlando. In 1986, just a year after beginning work at the site, the Chases were excavating a ballcourt when they came upon a round commemorative stone in the middle of the playing field. They summoned project epigrapher Stephen Houston to translate the 128 glyphs adorning the stone's upper surface.

Houston was quick to realise the importance of the find. The glyphic text described the aggressions of Lord Water, a 6th century ruler of Caracol, a story that shook the foundations of the archaeological community. Lord Water apparently carried out an 'axe-war' – a preliminary, non-fatal military strike – against Tikal in the spring of AD556. Five years later, he struck again, delivering the coup-de-grace (the so-called 'star war') that silenced mighty Tikal for more than a century. Caracol ascended to a supreme position in the Classic Maya heartland.

For many archaeologists, the discovery at Caracol supplied the answer to a puzzle posed, some 36 years earlier, by the great Mayanist Tatiana Proskouriakoff. She noted the curious absence of monuments at Tikal between AD534 and AD593, and suggested that some cataclysmic event had befallen the Maya world during this period of 'hiatus'. Archaeologist Gordon Willey even compared the event to a 'rehearsal' for the great Maya collapse of the 9th century. Many researchers now accept the Chases' hypothesis: that Tikal was silenced by Lord Water's 'star war', and the city's ruler, Double-Bird, was publicly humiliated and put to death.

(It is only fair to note, however, that the archaeological community isn't unanimous on this point. Dr William Haviland of the University of Vermont, for instance, believes that Tikal retained both Double-Bird and some political clout following the 'star war'. And Dr Richard Leventhal of UCLA argues that Caracol's victory, as recorded in the glyphs, might have been wishful thinking on Lord Water's part, a Maya version of locker-room boasting.)

Still, the ballcourt glyphs weren't the only discoveries found beneath Caracol's overgrown limestone mounds. The Chases unearthed the bones of a woman in a royal tomb near the top of Caana, Caracol's tallest temple. Bedecked with jade ear flares, beads, jade-studded teeth and other jewellery, she was clearly royalty, perhaps a ruler. Women, once disregarded by archaeologists as mere bystanders in the Maya world, are now being seen in an increasingly important light. Palenque was ruled by at least two women. Other sites where women played important, possibly supreme roles, include Yaxchilán, Dos Pilas, Calakmul and Cobá.

Considering the size and importance of the site, Caracol is bound to yield further surprises. The Chases and their colleagues are currently funded by USAID and the government of Belize. The country's Archaeological Commissioner, Harriot Topsey, sees Caracol as a future tourist destination on the order of Tikal. The 41,000-acre national park would cover not only the archaeological site itself but the surrounding rainforest, teeming with wildlife and tropical flora. With the growth in popularity of the Cayo district and the proven success of Tikal as a regional magnet for Guatemala, the Belizean authorities have committed to developing the site over the next few years with more excavation and improved access routes. But until more of Caracol is excavated, visitors should not expect another Tikal, with distinct pyramids and manicured plazas. Most of Caracol's great temples remain jungle-infested mounds at this point.

The site itself covers 1,120 acres, although the ceremonial centre is roughly half this size. Most of the temples are of Early Classic vintage and, as at Tikal, the highest ones extend above the forest canopy. Caana – 'The Sky Palace' – is now known to be Belize's tallest building, rising 41m above plaza level. The research team's campsite, powered by solar panels, is located nearby, as is the ancient Maya reservoir. This reservoir is still in use, providing water today even as it must have during the drought-plagued dry months in ancient times. (There's only enough to go around for the archaeologists and caretakers, however; bring your own water if you go.) This complex of buildings once served as an observatory. Paths lead to four other main plazas, containing 32 large buildings and a number of smaller satellites.

Caracol lies within the Chiquibul Forest Reserve. Mammoth 'cotton trees' – the ceibas held sacred by the ancient Maya – vie with Caracol's temples for dominance of the jungled landscape. Ocellated turkeys poke among the clearings, as they do in Tikal, and several bands of howler monkeys claim the area with their thunderous roars. Tapirs often graze right in the main complex.

Researchers work at Caracol during the dry months, usually mid-January through May or June, but caretakers now safeguard the ceremonial centre year-round. They can sell you a map of the site and are responsible for giving tours during the off-season. When the dig is on, tours are given by University of Central Florida archaeology students. Both the student-run and caretaker tours are excellent.

Reaching Caracol is neither easy nor cheap. There is no public transportation, and most San Ignacio taxi-drivers balk at going anywhere past the Douglas D'Silva Forestry Station even in the dry season. Likewise, travellers aren't advised to attempt the trip on their own with a rented 4WD vehicle. From Georgeville, the trip involves 75km of rough road and about 3hrs. Recent improvements have been made to the road between Douglas D'Silva and Caracol, but it is still very slick and dangerous following rains. You must first obtain a pass from the Department of Archaeology in Belmopan. Passes are no longer given at the D'Silva ranger station. Your options come down to either a knowledgeable guide with a reliable 4WD vehicle, or packing in on horseback. Even so, trips aren't always possible during the rainy season, when the Guacamallo Bridge occasionally floods. And remember that even during the 'dry season', the Pine Ridge can be drenched with rains that never reach San Ignacio. Following such storms, it can take two rainless days for the river to subside.

Three other tour operators offer horseback trips into Caracol, some with overnight camping options in the surrounding rainforest (although no camping is allowed within the archaeological zone): Mountain Equestrian Trails, Maya Mountain Lodge and Chaa Creek Resort. Blancaneaux Lodge also offers trips to Caracol, and is the nearest lodging. See *Rural lodges and resorts* (page 111) below for addresses and phone numbers.

If you attempt to reach Caracol on your own, you must get permission in advance to visit the site from the Belize Department of Archaeology in Belmopan (tel: 08 22106). They will issue one-day permits only. Absolutely no overnight stays are allowed at Caracol. Also check to see if a special permit is required to photograph the site. A fee of BZ$10 pp is charged to enter the site.

Archaeology buffs will want to schedule their visit to Caracol during the dig, generally mid January through June. The rainy season is better for wildlife; tapirs frequently graze right in the main complex at Caracol, and some guests have reported jaguar sightings on the road between Douglas D'Silva and San Luís. Birding is good year round.

Xunantunich

Xunantunich is arguably the country's finest Maya ruin, and undoubtedly the one most often visited and photographed. It was the first Maya ruin opened to the public and, until fairly recently, locals boasted that Xunantunich's El Castillo was the tallest building in Belize; that honour now goes to Caana at Caracol. Only 12km west of San Ignacio near the Guatemalan border, this hilltop citadel is an easy day trip via public transportation.

As Maya ceremonial centres go, Xunantunich is quite compact. Located at the top of a natural limestone ridge, the site commands a spectacular view of the neighbouring forest. It was occupied during the Classic, and probably abandoned following an earthquake in AD900. It has been suggested that such an event prompted the Maya collapse, a highly unlikely scenario considering the vast geographic range of Maya influence.

Dr Thomas Gann made the first investigations of Xunantunich in 1894, returning in 1924 to excavate and remove burial goods. In the meantime, Harvard's Teobert Mahler had photographed and mapped a portion of the site. J Eric Thompson excavated an outlying group of mounds in 1938, and Xunantunich's famed stucco frieze was uncovered in 1949 by Belize's first Archaeological Commissioner, A H Anderson. Small-scale excavations and restorations continued throughout the 1950s and 1960s. Yet it is ironic that Belize's best-known Maya site has never been extensively studied. The site's reconstruction also rankles many professional archaeologists. The renovated frieze often gets poor marks, along with the exposed steel bolts dripping rust. To a rank amateur like myself, this seems to be quibbling – Xunantunich remains mightily impressive, as it must have been during the Classic Period.

The site itself is dominated by El Castillo (more prosaically known as Structure A-6), which looms 39m above plaza level. Two temples, one built atop the other, adorn the top of the pyramid. Except for these temples at the summit, the trademark stucco frieze and a stairway or two, El Castillo remains mostly unexcavated, its contours softened by a green cloak of vegetation. To reach the

HEADING TO TIKAL

The fabulous Maya ruins of Tikal lie 108km west of the Belize border by road, deep in Guatemala's Petén rainforest. It seems as if every traveller in San Ignacio is either headed to Tikal or just getting back from a trip there. Indeed, San Ignacio was regarded for years as nothing more than the Belizean gateway to Tikal. Budget travellers still consider the overland bus route from San Ignacio, Belize, far superior to the horrendously cramped, bone-crunching bus trip from Guatemala City to Flores, a trip that used take up to 24 hours – now closer to ten – and readily transforms even seasoned bus nomads into zombies.

The easiest way to reach Tikal, of course, involves flying to the Guatemalan city of Flores via either Belize City or Guatemala City. From Flores, you can catch ground transport to Tikal. See *Chapter 4, Getting there* for information on flights to Flores.

Overland from Belize you have several options. Not included among these is travelling to Tikal in a rented car. I know of no Belizean rental company that will permit you to take their cars into Guatemala, period.

Budget travellers will probably want to take a Guatemalan public bus from the border town of Melchor de Mencos to Flores. This takes most of a day, so that you'll spend the night in Flores and take either a public bus or van to Tikal the following morning. A quick glance at the map shows that this route involves some backtracking. Unfortunately, there is no completely reliable way to go from Melchor de Mencos to Tikal on public transport without going first to Flores (although I mention a somewhat chancier alternative below).

To reach the Guatemalan border and Melchor de Mencos from San Ignacio, you can simply get one of the buses leaving the bus station every 30 minutes from San Ignacio. If you are already on the road between San Ignacio and the border, just flag one of the bus drivers down. (see *San Ignacio, To and from Guatemala* in this chapter for more details).

Once in Melchor de Mencos, head for the central bus stop (it couldn't be called a station), a short walk from the border. Buses with Transportes Pinita or Rosita leave for Flores at 08.00 and 10.00 and then every couple of hours until 17.00. (Q$10 or roughly US$1.40). The trip takes about 3-4 hours when the road is dry; the bus makes a 20-minute stop near El Cruce, about half-way to Flores.

Once in Flores – a town built on an island in Lake Petén Itzá – you'll find plenty of lodging possibilities. The cheapest hotels are not in Flores itself, but rather in the mainland sister city of Santa Elena. But Flores is a far more pleasant place to spend a couple of nights. Most buses travelling from the border pass through Santa Elena before crossing the causeway to Flores.

Public buses (fare Q$7/US$1 one-way) leave Santa Elena daily for Tikal around midday, returning late in the afternoon. The disadvantage with the public bus (besides being slower) is that time at Tikal is limited to the bus timetables. (If budget is a real concern, you could take the public bus to Tikal and haggle with private minivan operators at the site for the return trip.)

Private minivans are altogether a much better bet. They leave outside the Hotel San Juan (in Santa Elena) and Hotel Petén (in Flores) daily from 04.00 until midday. They also meet all incoming flights at the Flores airport. The fare costs Q$30/US$4.20 pp round-trip, and they'll have you to Tikal within an hour. The minivans leave the ruins hourly from 11.00 until 17.00 for the return trip to

Flores, although you can certainly stay the night in Tikal and redeem your return trip the next day (but be sure to arrange this ahead of time with the driver). Staying at either hotel makes this slightly easier but most hotels will be able to arrange for you to be picked up. Inquire at the desks of either hotel named above for current schedules.

A second option involves taking a Melchor-Flores bus and having the driver let you off at El Cruce, also known as Puente Ixlu. This is the cutoff to Tikal, and every public bus, car or minivan headed to Tikal has to pass by. These are often full, however, and you aren't guaranteed a seat. There is meant to be a daily bus to Tikal from the border that leaves Melchor around midday. This would be a great option for people tight on time if it were reliable. In reality you're just as well off taking a bus to El Cruce and taking a ride from there.

A third overland option involves a private minivan direct from Melchor de Mencos to Tikal. As soon as you cross the border at Melchor you'll be besieged by minivan operators, most of whom want about US$125-US$150 for six to eight people round-trip. This generally includes the option to spend the night in Tikal, although be sure to discuss this before setting out. Pricey, but reportedly worth it if you're in a hurry and don't want to spend a night in Flores.

Finally, a number of tour operators, hotels, resorts and guides throughout Belize offer minivan trips to Tikal. These trips can be arranged to leave directly from hotels in Belize City, San Ignacio or rural lodges in Cayo. These generally cost US$75 pp for a day trip. Check whether the price includes fees for border crossings and entrance to Tikal. Overnights can also be arranged.

There are several cafes and restaurants close to the entrance providing reasonable food at reasonable prices. If you want to spend a lot of time in the site you may want to take a packed lunch. The walk from the centre to the restaurants is about 20 minutes each way.

Accommodation is available within the site complex but the options are limited and quite expensive. The Jaguar Inn (tel: 502 926 0002) has rooms at US$45 and the Hotel Tikal Inn (tel/fax: 502 926 0065) is slightly more expensive at US$50 but has a pool. Camping is not allowed in the site itself but you may be able to organise a spot to pitch your tent with the hotels or one of the restaurants. Although more expensive, staying the night does allow you to relax a little more in the ruins and enjoy the site with very few people in the area.

Note Although improvements have been made, the road from Melchor de Mencos to Flores is often impassable during and after rains. This happens mostly during the rainy season, but can occur any time of year. When this happens, your only recourse is to fly. Also, be aware that none of the bus or minivan fares quoted above include the cost of admission to Tikal (which in late 1999 was Q$50/US$7 pp per day) nor the cost of a guide should you want one. Finally, be prepared to have your bus boarded by Guatemalan soldiers along the Melchor-Flores route. At one of the larger military camps, you'll notice the word KAIBAL spelled out in painted rocks across the hillside. Readers of Ronald Wright's *Time Among the Maya* (see *Appendix 2, Further Reading*) will remember the Kaibal as Guatemala's elite anti-communist force, responsible for scores of atrocities against the civilian population. The *Kaibales* that pass down the bus aisle are mostly pimply-faced teenagers, dressed in camouflage fatigues, self-consciously fingering their automatic rifles.

uppermost temple of El Castillo, use the steep stairway on the back (southern) side. Views from the top extend over the Guatemalan forest.

You'll find the famous stucco frieze on the east side of El Castillo, about midway up the pyramid (accessible again from the pyramid's southern stairway). The frieze features an astronomical theme, with masks of the sun, moon, Venus and, curiously, a decapitated head. The frieze was restored throughout the 1970s, which will be readily apparent. Neatly plastered over the original, it's too slick for those of us who like our ruins a bit more ruinous.

Flanking the plazas leading up to El Castillo are a series of unexcavated mounds, probably minor temples. Behind the group of mounds on the west side of the plaza, and just across the path from the outhouses, lies a small Maya ballcourt, one of two such sporting fields at Xunantunich.

Underneath a thatched picnic hut at the base of El Castillo lie three stelae in fair condition. These were apparently moved to the site by Maya who occupied Xunantunich after its collapse as a major citadel in AD900.

Xunantunich can be easily reached from San Ignacio by taxi (roughly BZ$5 pp) or public bus (either Batty or Novelo, BZ$1). Catch any bus headed for the border and ask the driver to put you off at the ferry in San José Succotz village. As you approach town, watch for El Castillo, which dominates the forested hilltop to the right. Succotz is a small Yucatec Maya village, used as a base camp in the 1930s by the renowned archaeologist J Eric Thompson (who refers to it as Socotz). The town has no hotel, but **The Trek Stop** with cabins and a campsite is just east of the town. And about 1km east of town, along the highway, you'll find the **Stone Maiden Arts and Craft Shop**, which offers artwork in the Maya style by the Magana family. The free ferry across the Mopan River is hand-cranked along a steel cable, and can't always be depended on to carry cars or taxis across. If are driving, the car park for the ruins is about 250m before the site entrance. Hours for the ferry are 08.00 to 17.00; the ferrymen take an hour-long lunch break around noon.

On the far side of the Mopan River, a 1.6km-long trail heads uphill to Xunantunich. Talk to the ferrymen before heading off up the trail to find out what the situation is along the trail. In the past there have been robberies along the trail. The danger seems to have passed now but avoid walking on your own. The uphill walk takes roughly half an hour. Keep your eyes open for agoutis scampering across the road, and the occasional snake.

At the site itself you'll find a drinking water cistern, picnic shelter, outhouses and a caretaker's hut. Entrance costs BZ$10, and guides are available, free of charge, to show you the ruins and explain the stelae.

Returning to San Ignacio, you can wait for buses either at the covered bus stop near the ferry.

BENQUE VIEJO DEL CARMEN

Most travellers merely pass through Benque on the way to Guatemala, a short walk west of town. Indeed, there's not a great deal to see or do here. Some travellers like the relaxed pace and relative lack of tourists compared to San Ignacio; the Latin festivities during Christmas, Easter and feast days are reported to be colourful.

Getting there

Frequent buses shuttle between San Ignacio and Benque, as do taxis on their way to the border. Novelo's runs a direct bus to Belize City almost hourly from 04.30 to 11.00 daily except Sunday. See *San Ignacio, Getting there* above for details, including information on the border crossing.

Where to stay/eat

Lodging is far cheaper across the border in Melchor de Mencos, Guatemala, and the choices far more numerous in San Ignacio, Belize.

Maya Hotel 11 George Street; tel: 09 32116. 14 rooms, BZ$20 with shared bath, fan; BZ$35 with private bath. They have a restaurant/bar. Located near the Novelo Bus terminal and public market.
Okis Hotel 47 George Street; tel: 09 32006. 12 rooms, US$10 with shared bath, fan. Cheap, simple, and close to the town square. They serve food.
Maxim's Palace 41 Churchill Street; tel: 09 32360; fax: 09 32259. 10 rooms, US$45 with private bath, fans, some rooms air conditioned. Relatively new, and definitely Benque's nicest hotel.

Restaurants include the **Los Angeles**, the **Riverside** and the **Hawaii**. Here too, it's cheaper to cross the border and eat at the *comedores* in Melchor de Mencos.

Information and useful addresses

See *San Ignacio, To and from Guatemala* above for information on crossing the border, changing money, etc. See *Heading to Tikal*, page 130 for tips on reaching Tikal.

134

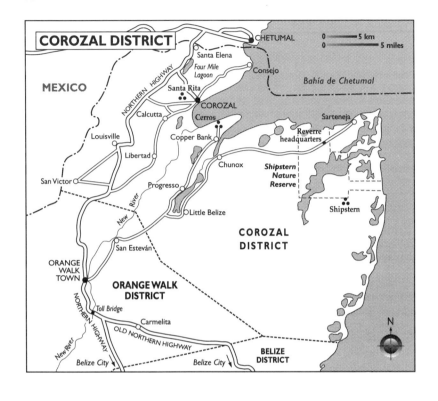

Corozal District

Heading southbound from Mexico, bus travellers get their first taste of Belize in Corozal Town, a mere 14.5km from the border. The sudden appearance of black faces, the sound of English spoken as a first language, and the sight of whitewashed clapboard houses on stilts, all underscore the striking differences which set this former British colony apart from the rest of Central America. Even so, Corozal District remains the most *latino* area of Belize; Spanish is widely spoken, and you'll eat tortillas more often than try jacks. Thousands of *latinos* and *Mestizos* fled Mexico during the bloody Caste War which erupted in 1848 in the Yucatan, and most of the refugees settled near present-day Corozal Town, farming small plots or cutting timber. Still other parts of the district – Sarteneja, for example – served for years as Mexican fishing camps, with little or no connection to the rest of Belize. More recent immigrants from Mexico were the Mennonites, who settled on farms in Little Belize (see *Chapter 10, Mennonites*).

The land is level, ringed on the eastern edge by vast mangrove lagoons which give way to the type of scrub forest found in Mexico's Yucatan. For travellers, the main draws include the Shipstern Nature Reserve and Butterfly Sanctuary, Maya ruins (the most important being Cerros) and the breezy, palm-fringed coastline. With the country's lowest rainfall – Corozal Town gets barely a sprinkling with 1,270mm a year compared to Punta Gorda's 4,320mm – this northernmost district often provides a dry refuge for travellers when the rest of the country is drenched.

Originally brought to Belize by Mexican refugees from the Caste War, sugar cane still dominates the economy of Corozal District. Due to the unique soil and climatic conditions, cane grown here has one of the highest sucrose contents in the world. Sugar from Corozal and Orange Walk, processed at two factories owned by the British sugar giant Tate and Lyle, became the country's number one export in the 1960s. But falling prices, beginning in the 1980s, have since driven out many cane farmers. In 1985, Tate and Lyle finally closed the large sugar factory in Libertad, 12km south of Corozal Town. Marijuana has taken up some of the slack; it's big business in Corozal these days, as is traffic in cheap Mexican gasoline smuggled across the border.

COROZAL TOWN

Corozal is a breezy, pleasant town with a distinctly Latin flavour. There isn't much at all to do in the town itself, but it makes a good base camp for outings to the Shipstern Peninsula and the Cerros ruins. Most travellers find it a considerably more pleasant – and certainly cheaper – place to stay than Orange Walk Town, making it a good base camp also for trips to Lamanai and the New River.

History

Corozal Town occupies what scholars suspect was once the site of the great Maya city of Chetumal. Within the town lies the single remaining piece of that legacy, the tiny Santa Rita site (see below). Much of Corozal was originally built from stones taken from nearby Maya mounds, as was the road which finally linked Corozal with Belize City in the 1930s.

Corozal, as the closest settlement to the Mexican border, was threatened with Maya attacks throughout the War of Castes in the mid-1800s. In 1858, the last Mexican stronghold in the Yucatan, Bacalar, fell to a surprise attack by Santa Cruz Maya. The Maya victors killed every adult male in the town. The Mexican commandant fled to Corozal Town, where British and Mexican officials attempted to bargain with the Santa Cruz leaders for the lives of the remaining women and children. The Santa Cruz announced they would only be satisfied by the return of the Mexican commandant, a provision the British obviously could not meet. That evening, the Santa Cruz Maya, inspired by their sect's belief in the 'Talking Cross', massacred the women and children of Bacalar.

As a result of the Bacalar massacre, the British fortified Corozal Town's defences with troops from Jamaica. After a series of minor skirmishes, the Santa Cruz and Icaiche Maya attacked Corozal Town in 1864, killing three citizens and taking 24 hostages. Three years later they returned, this time demanding ransom for the return of nearby San Pedro Village. The attackers retreated across the border, but not before disgracing the 4th West India Regiment, whose commander was accused of cowardice. And in 1870, the Maya again successfully attacked and ransomed Corozal Town. Maya raids on the British settlement only ceased in 1872, following the defeat of Icaiche forces at Orange Walk Town.

Getting there

The New Northern Highway is an excellent all-weather road, making bus travel from Belize City to Corozal fast and efficient. Between the Venus and Batty bus companies, there are departures hourly from Belize City to the border throughout the day, all of them stopping in Corozal. The trip takes three hours with a stop in Orange Walk Town and costs BZ$7.50.

Both Tropic Air and Maya Island Air fly twice daily from Belize City to Corozal via San Pedro (Ambergris Caye), the flight taking 1 hour 20 minutes and costing BZ$111 one-way from the Municipal Airport or BZ$144 from the International Airport. Because of the detour and stop in San Pedro, this flight is hardly an advantage over a bus from Belize City (unless, of course, you're already in San Pedro or like to fly).

To and from Mexico

Travellers entering Belize from Mexico by land do so via Chetumal, about 15km from the border and 30km from Corozal Town. Both Venus and Batty operate ticket booths at Chetumal's modern bus terminal, with buses to Belize City leaving every hour or so from 04.00 through 18.30 daily. The fare to Belize City (roughly 4 hours including border crossing formalities) is BZ$12. To Corozal (about an hour) the fare is BZ$3. The Batty ticket booth accepts Mexican pesos, US dollars or Belize dollars.

The border crossing itself is usually quick and painless. Buses from Mexico stop at the border outpost of Santa Elena, discharging passengers with their passports and Mexican tourist cards. Leave your luggage on the bus. Inside the Mexican immigration office, there's sometimes a separate line for tourists. Once you're stamped out of Mexico, re-board the bus, which will take you across the Rio Hondo to the Belizean immigration office. Here the procedure is the same.

If you're a young backpacker, you may be asked to fill out a short form describing your travel plans in Belize. Customs officials occasionally look at bags. Directly outside the office, moneychangers will offer to sell you Belize dollars in exchange for US dollars, US travellers' cheques or Mexican pesos. They all give the identical rate and I've never heard complaints of rip-offs. Pockets bulging with Belizean cash, you're ready to re-board the bus. Travellers staying at the Capri Hotel, Hotel Maya, Caribbean or Tony's in Corozal should inform the bus driver; these hotels are south of the main town and he'll drop you off outside their doors.

Entering Mexico from Belize, the routine is much the same. First the bus without baggage on the Belize side, where you can change US cash, US travellers' cheques or Belizean dollars into Mexican pesos at a good rate with any of a score of local money changers. After checking out of Belize, return to the bus, cross the river and go through Mexican immigration. Once again, passports only; you'll receive a Mexican tourist card to fill out. Back aboard the bus, you'll go a little further on before a stop at customs. You may have to open bags here, but it's not likely. The next and final stop prior to Chetumal is a fumigation station, where the outside and undercarriage of the bus are sprayed.

The border at Santa Elena is open 24 hours daily. Taxis are available in either direction.

Where to stay

Hotel Maya PO Box 112; tel: 04 22082; fax: 04 22827; email: hotelmaya@btl.net; web: www.corozal.com. 20 rooms, with private bath, hot water, fan. Some of the rooms have a balcony and/or sea view. The owners, Sylvia and Rosita Mai and family, are extremely friendly, helpful and can assist with any enquiries you may have about the area. Rooms are clean and pleasant. Restaurant on site. BZ$50.

Nestor's Hotel 123 Fifth Avenue South; tel: 04 22354; email: nestors@btl.net. 18 rooms, BZ$40 with private bath, fan. Located downtown, the rooms are small but clean. The restaurant/bar downstairs serves cheap, tasty meals.

Tony's Inn and Beach Resort South End, Corozal Town; tel: 04 22055; fax: 04 22829; email: tonys@btl.net; web: www.tonysinn.com. 24 rooms, with private bath, air conditioning in some rooms, fan. Corozal Town's nicest (and priciest) hotel, located a little bit off the highway on the very southern edge of town. All white stucco and balconies, on manicured grounds at the very head of Corozal Bay. The palapa bar on the beach is a pleasant place for a drink (beers are cheap, all other drinks fairly expensive). The food was Corozal's best, but is now rivalled by Le Café Kela. The snacks start at BZ$5 with meals up to BZ$20. On Sundays, they feature a large and mouth-watering 'Belizean Plate' (fry chicken, coconut rice, beans, potato salad and plantain). The hotel can arrange fishing and tours to Cerros, down the New River to see manatee and as far Lamanai. From BZ$120 for a room with two double beds.

Caribbean Village PO Box 210; tel: 04 22725; fax: 04 23414. 5 rooms, BZ$40 with private bath, fan; BZ$66 for a cabin sleeping five. They'll also let you camp for BZ$5 pp. Located on a breezy, tree-lined stretch of grass across the highway from the sea, this has long been a popular spot with RV owners on vacation from the States. Their rooms are less inviting but usually adequate.

Hotel Posada Mama 77 G'Street South; tel: 04 22107. 7 rooms, BZ$70 with private bath, air conditioning, phone and TV. On the northern side of 7th Avenue.

Central Guest House 22 6th Avenue, Corozal Town; tel: 04 22358; fax: 04 23335; email: cghczl@yahoo.com; web: www.corozal.com/tourism/cgh/default.htm. 3ree rooms, shared bathroom. Friendly environment with lots of good information about the area and Belize. Close to the bus terminal. BZ$30.

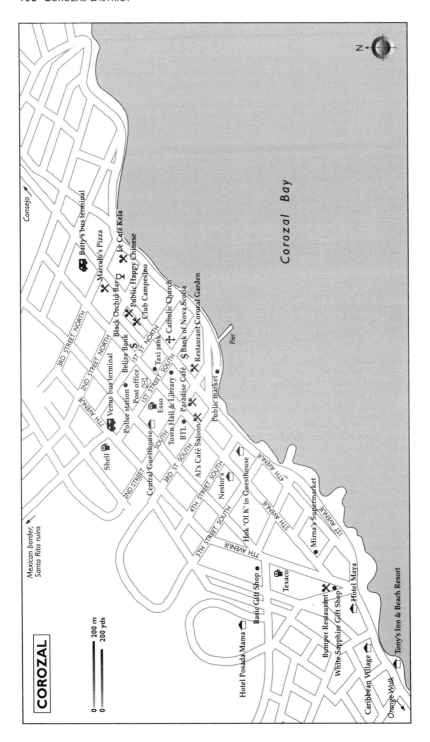

COROZAL

0 —— 200 m
0 —— 200 yds

Corozal Bay

N

Mexican border,
Santa Rita ruins

Consejo

Batty's bus terminal

Marcelo's Pizza

Le Café Kela

Black Orchid Bar

Public Happy Chinese

Club Campesino

Catholic Church

Bank of Nova Scotia

Restaurant Corozal Garden

Belize Bank

Taxi rank

3RD STREET NORTH

2ND STREET NORTH

1ST ST. NORTH

Venus bus terminal

Police station

Post office

Esso

Paradise Café

Public market

Pier

7TH AVENUE

Town Hall & Library

BTL

Al's Café Saloon

Shell

Central Guesthouse

Nestor's

Hok 'Ol K' in Guesthouse

2ND STREET

3RD ST. SOUTH

1ST STREET SOUTH

4TH STREET SOUTH

5TH STREET SOUTH

6TH STREET SOUTH

7TH AVENUE

4TH AVENUE

5TH AVENUE

1ST AVENUE

Mima's Supermarket

Hotel Maya

Texaco

Bumper Restaurant

White Sapphire Gift Shop

Hotel Posada Mama

Basic Gift Shop

Caribbean Village

Tony's Inn & Beach Resort

Orange Walk

Hok'Ol K'in Guest House PO Box 145, 4th Avenue and 4th Street South; tel: 04 23329; fax: 04 23569; email: maya@btl.net; web: www.corozal.net. A smart, new hotel facing the sea with clean, well-appointed rooms. Staff and management are very friendly and helpful. The Guest House runs tours in the local area using independent guide Stephen Moerman (tel: 04 22833). BZ$85.

If you're looking for something more secluded (albeit more expensive), try the **Hotel Casablanca** in Consejo Shores, about 12km north of town (see below).

Where to eat

The hotels listed above are probably the best places to eat in Corozal. There's also **Le Café Kela**, on the seafront between 2nd and 3rd Street North, which serves beautifully presented Belizean and international fare in the intimate surroundings of a *palapa*.

The search for the best burrito in Belize ends in Corozal. Visit **Restaurant Corozal Garden** on 4th Avenue one block south of the main plaza. Cheap and cheerful but oh so tasty. Incidentally the runners-up awards are found in Caye Caulker and Punta Gorda.

Al's Café, on 5th Avenue between 2nd and 3rd Street North is popular with the locals, as is the **Marcelo's Pizzas** next door. **Paradise Café** on 2nd Street South between 5th and 4th Avenue is often full.

What's left are typically Belizean Chinese restaurants such as the **Public Happy Chinese** (corner of 2nd Street North and 4th Avenue) and **Bumper** (Seventh Avenue). Other eating spots include the **Campesino Club** (47 4th Avenue).

If you fancy a drink try the **Black Orchid Bar** on 4th Avenue between 2nd and 3rd Street North. A relaxing atmosphere with friendly staff.

What to see

Sadly, there is little left to see of Santa Rita, once an important Maya city which controlled trade routes on the Rio Hondo, the New River and along the coast. The site, which archaeologists presume to be the ancient Maya city of Chetumal, at one time stretched from Paraiso (3km north of town) to the southern limits of modern-day Corozal. Today there remains but one structure of interest to travellers. Located in the midst of Corozal's residential area, the site has taken on the aspect of a sleepy city park. Children park their bicycles and play among the doorways and small rooms, while their older siblings shoot baskets down the street. Santa Rita dates from the Early Preclassic period (approximately 2000BC), the very beginning of Maya civilisation. The city was still thriving in 1531 when Spanish troops led by Alonso Davila attacked and conquered it. The Maya chieftain Nachancan recaptured the city, but the Spaniards were eventually able to sever Santa Rita's trade routes from their Mexican colonial stronghold in Bacalar. The Maya abandoned the city, and since then much of the stonework has been dismantled piecemeal and used in the building of Corozal.

Thomas Gann, the ubiquitous explorer and exploiter of Belizean Maya sites, first explored Santa Rita in 1896. He returned 20 years later for more excavation. He uncovered and painstakingly copied a fabulous series of stucco murals which, unfortunately, haven't survived. One night after Gann had copied half a mural, local Maya raided the site and carted off the stucco layer of the entire wall to distribute as medicine. This portion of the mural contained the only glyphs, which were never recorded. More than half the original 32 mounds at Santa Rita were subsequently destroyed for building stone.

Considering the site's pre-eminence in trade, it isn't surprising that the murals copied by Gann emphasize Ek Chuah, the most important Maya merchant god.

Gann also unearthed pottery figures, including lizard-like creatures which probably represent Itzam Na ('Iguana House'), the greatest god of the Yucatec Maya. Two important burial tombs were subsequently unearthed, both dating to the Early Classic. Both the murals and burial artefacts suggest trade links with the Guatemalan highlands and Mexican sites much further inland. Excavations in the 1980s led by Arlen and Diane Chase uncovered, among other things, a skeleton buried with jade and mica jewellery.

Santa Rita is an easy 15-minute walk from the plaza in downtown Corozal. Head north out of town on the highway; at the first fork in the road, stay to the right, remaining on the main road. Then take the first left; walk past the basketball court to the ruins on the right. Only one structure remains, and you can easily see the entire site in 15 minutes. Sr Wiltshire is the site caretaker and will be able to give you extra information about Santa Rita.

In town itself, pop into the Town Hall to see the mural by Manuel Villamor depicting area history in the style of the great Mexican muralists. Villamor has managed to include everything from Maya temples to Hurricane Janet.

Special events
Columbus Day (October 12) brings out the locals in a rollicking display of Latin gaiety. Christmas is likewise celebrated in typical Mexican fashion, with piñatas, parades and family get-togethers.

Information and useful addresses
Many of the hotels listed change cash and travellers' cheques, as does **Belize Bank** (corner of 5th Avenue and 1st Street North) and **Bank of Nova Scotia** (near the corner of 4th Avenue and 1st Street South).

Basic Gift Shop, on the highway just south of town, sells zericote woodcarvings as well as T-shirts and the usual souvenirs. **White Sapphire Gifts and Jewelry** (at the intersection of 7th Avenue and 9th Street South) offers similar items.

Mirna's Supermarket (5th Avenue between 7th and 8th Streets South) maintains a good stock of groceries and supplies for camping, picnics.

Phone calls can be made at the BTL office near the corner of 5th Avenue and 2nd Street South.

Excursions
Near town
Four Mile Lagoon
This privately owned picnicking and swimming spot lies 12km north of Corozal and 7km south of the Mexican border. The freshwater lagoon is popular with locals on weekends, and camping for a small fee is possible. This is a good place for swimming. Buses between Corozal and the border will drop you off at the turnoff, from where you'll have a 0.4km walk to the lagoon. Incidentally, there is another 'Four Mile Lagoon' south of town.

Consejo
Consejo lies 12km northeast of Corozal, and a mere 5km across the water from Chetumal, Mexico. It is a tranquil area of palms, well-manicured vacation homes owned by Americans, Canadians and Europeans, a resort hotel, customs dock and a nondescript but friendly little seaside village. There is no public transportation apart from the twice-daily school bus from Corozal. You may be able to hitch a ride with the bus or with locals making the seven-mile journey from town. Walking the dirt road is best done early in the morning when you might see

animals alongside the road; but in the day it is a hot, uninspiring journey. A taxi from town is US$10 one way.

The only lodging is at the **Hotel Casablanca**, next to the customs dock; tel: 04 38018; fax: 04 38003; email: info@casablanca-bythesea.com; web: www.casablanca-bythesea.com. The hotel has eight rooms, with AC, TV private bathroom with a view of Consejo Bay. From US$55. The restaurant has Belizean and international cuisine using local seafood. Trips throughout Belize can be arranged.

Just north of the now-closed Adventure Inn (stay on the road closest to the water) you'll walk past another hotel that is also presently closed, the white-stucco Don Quixote Hotel. Rumours are that both places may be opening in the future but nothing concrete to report at present. You'll find spots to swim directly past the Don Quixote Hotel grounds, but watch for rocks.

Smugglers Den is an informal restaurant and bar serving Belizean food.

The wide, tree-lined roadway continues north to Consejo Village, a 15-minute walk from the old Adventure Inn. The way is lined with holiday homes. For food, drink and friendly conversation, try **Derrick's Country Club**, a small screened-in wooden building where the locals and workers hang out. Derrick can also put you in touch with one of the two local taxis if you need a ride back to Corozal.

From the Consejo Custom Dock, a long cement affair, you can see Chetumal, Mexico. The dock is a good spot for a swim.

Public phones are available in the village square.

Cerros (Cerro Maya)

Located directly across the bay from Corozal, Cerros played an important role as a maritime trading centre during the Late Preclassic Period (100BC to AD250). It now consists of unexcavated or partially excavated mounds, although the pleasant boat ride and its coastal setting make Cerros a worthwhile day trip from Corozal.

Thomas Gann briefly explored Cerros ('hills' in Spanish) while he was practising medicine in Corozal, but it wasn't until 1969 that the area was officially registered as a Maya site. David Friedel of Southern Methodist University surveyed Cerros from 1973 to 1979, concluding that the site was originally founded as a fishing, hunting and farming village. Only later did it flower as an import centre for jade, obsidian and other goods. The location was fortuitous, just 2.4km from the mouth of the New River, giving access to Lamanai, and within 18km of the Rio Hondo, providing access to the Yucatan. The Maya believed that edges – caves, seashores and mountain tops – held great power, so that Cerros' location directly on the shores of Corozal Bay lent it a supernatural as well as economic advantage.

Friedel's superb book *A Forest of Kings* (co-authored with Linda Schele, see *Appendix 2, Further Reading*) concludes that Cerros and other Late Preclassic sites first saw the emergence of Maya kings as a social institution. Jade jewels carved in the images of gods, the magical tokens of kingship, have been found ceremoniously buried in at least two of Cerros' temples. Friedel hypothesizes that Cerros was abandoned during the Early Classic when its citizens turned their backs on the kings, returning to a less complicated way of life. Maya kingdoms, after all, never had standing armies to enforce their rule; they maintained power solely by virtue of their charisma and performance. Friedel suspects that either dissatisfaction with a weak king, or in coping with a large-scale society caused the citizenry of Cerros to opt out of kingship. A shift in trade routes during the Early Classic may have contributed to Cerros' abandonment.

This experimentation with kingship nevertheless produced a remarkable city within the space of a few generations. Beginning about 50BC, Cerros transformed itself from a small village into a city of impressive architecture. Villagers began by moving their homes to the town perimeter and systematically burying their former village under broad, plastered plazas. Upon these they built a series of royal temples, acropolises, and ballcourts.

The main site itself consists of four temples, the tallest of which stands 22m above the surrounding plaza. The Archaeological Reserve surrounding the ceremonial site takes in 53 acres, but the original city was somewhat larger; portions of the site are now under water.

The smallest temple (Structure 5C) stands directly on the water's edge, and was erected by the first king of Cerros. The stone panels on the terrace were adorned with magnificent stucco masks, divine images which prominently featured the Jaguar Sun God. These huge masks have been covered, at least temporarily, with plaster to prevent further erosion from the sea breezes. The second temple (Structure 6) lies just southwest of the first. Built by the second king, it rises 16m above plaza level and at its base is three times larger than the first temple. To invoke the power of his predecessor, the new king buried the former's jade jewellery near the summit of this temple. Just east of here lies the largest of Cerros' temples, an east-facing acropolis called Structure 4. Twenty-two metres high, it was the third great building constructed in Cerros. A sepulchre near the summit was clearly meant to house the remains of the king, but was never used; archaeologists surmise that he was taken captive during a battle far from Cerros. The temple directly south of the east-facing acropolis was the final one built at Cerros. Shoddily built and containing no buried offerings, it marks the end of kingship at Cerros.

To reach Cerros, ask around the Corozal marketplace and docks for a boatman willing to take you across the bay. If this doesn't work (finding boats in Corozal is not as easy as some guidebooks would have you believe), ask for Romeo at the central park cab stand. His wife is related to a boatman who does Cerros trips. Most boats can make the trip across the bay in half an hour, the price is normally around BZ$35 pp, although this reduces with larger groups. During the dry season (January through April), you can drive to Cerros via Orange Walk, Progresso, Chunox and Copper Bank (see *Shipstern Peninsula* below for details). There have been reports that you can walk to the site along the coast from Corozal, a distance of some 9km, via San Roman Village; this would still require hiring a boat to cross the New River. Whether this is possible or not, plans to develop a walk to Cerros should be in place by early 2000. Contact Rosita Mai at the Hotel Maya (see above) for details. Tony's Inn and Hok'Ol K'in Guest House can also arrange day trips by boat to Cerros.

Wear long pants, long sleeves, and bring plenty of insect repellent. Insects swarm all over the site.

Be sure to read Schele and Friedel's masterful *A Forest of Kings* – at least the chapter which brings ancient Cerros to life – before visiting the site.

Further afield
Shipstern Peninsula
Almost all of Corozal District's population squeezes itself into the western third of the region; the vast Shipstern Peninsula to the east of the New River remains largely uninhabited and seldom travelled. The area consists mostly of sub-tropical moist forest and northern hardwood forest, with wide belts of coastal savanna along the Shipstern Lagoon. There are only a handful of settlements – Progresso, Chunox, Little Belize, Copper Bank and Sarteneja – as well as the privately-operated Shipstern Nature Reserve and Butterfly Breeding Centre.

Until 1988 there was no all-weather road cutting through the Shipstern Peninsula. The Placid Oil Company improved the existing dirt track from San Estevan so that it could handle heavy oil-drilling equipment, and the legacy today is a pot-holed but generally passable dirt road all the way to the lobster-fishing village of Sarteneja near the peninsula's tip. During the wet season you should only attempt it with 4WD. Even so, it is impassable at times, especially in the wettest month of September. During the rest of the year it's bumpy and dusty. There are a couple of ways to access this road, and both require that you travel south into Orange Walk District before heading northeast again into Corozal District.

The first route takes off about 9.7km north of Orange Walk Town on the Orange Walk-Corozal highway. Here you'll head east toward San Estevan Village. Just before reaching San Estevan, you'll cross the New River on a hand-cranked ferry (pay for a round-trip fare and they'll write your name down or, in the case of most foreigners, they'll simply remember you). You can usually cajole the amused operator to let you crank the ferry across. The only other customers when we crossed were hunters and their hounds. Keep to your right in the village, following the paved road out of town. Some 11.3km later the road branches right toward Chunox and Sarteneja. Following the road straight ahead another 4.8km leads to Progresso, a small village on the western bank of picturesque Progresso Lagoon, where it's possible to camp for a fee.

Another 14.5km drive puts you in Copper Bank (San Fernando) on Lowry's Bight, within 5km of the Cerros Maya site (see above). The road to Chunox and Sarteneja heads north along the eastern shore of Progresso Lagoon. Just as you come within sight of the lagoon on your left, you'll enter Little Belize, a tidy Mennonite community. Blond farmers in straw hats and bib overalls often travel these roads in characteristic horse-drawn carriages. Here, even the billboards asking farmers to help in the eradication of cattle screw worm are written in the Plattdeutsch (Low German) spoken by Mennonites. About 12.9km later, the road enters Chunox, a neatly manicured village of Maya-style huts and clapboard buildings on the eastern shore of Laguna Seca. The Shipstern Nature Reserve headquarters is on the right 17.7km past Chunox, and Sarteneja lies another 4.8km further on.

The second route begins in Orange Walk itself. Leave town via the pontoon bridge near the Police Station (see the Orange Walk map) and head toward San Estevan. Once in San Estevan, follow the directions above.

Sarteneja

As travel clichés go, this quaint tropical fishing village remains one of the most elusive; by the time most travellers find their way to such spots, the local fishermen have long since chucked their nets to become tour guides. Sarteneja, on the other hand, remains a simple village whose only nod to tourism is a single, unpretentious hotel and café. Located at the tip of the Sarteneja Peninsula, the town is home to a fleet of lobstering boats which languish during the off-season along a breezy, palm-lined stretch of coastline facing Mexico. Until the road from Progresso was completed Sarteneja was to all intents and purposes a Mexican town on Belizean soil. The town was founded by Yucatecan immigrants in the 19th century, and they traded almost exclusively by boat with Chetumal and other Mexican ports. Hurricane Janet destroyed the entire town except the school and Health Department building in 1955. The rebuilt Sarteneja is surprisingly large, with some 1,500-2,000 residents, mostly boatbuilders, lobster fishermen and farmers. Spanish remains the primary language.

Although Sarteneja is a sleepy, pleasant spot, there isn't a great deal to do in town beside stroll the waterfront and admire the local lobster boats. The village is an ideal base camp for visits to the nearby Shipstern Nature Reserve (see below). Local guides can also take you to see two minor Maya sites, Chacan Chac Mol and Shipstern. The latter site is located about 1km southeast of the abandoned village of Shipstern, on the eastern side of the lagoon. Duncan Pring and Raymond Sidrys partially excavated the site beginning in 1974. Shipstern apparently became a major population centre during the Classic, when probably 1,000 people lived here, declining later during the Postclassic. The tallest structure stands 15m above plaza level, and has been heavily looted.

A bus run by Castillo's leaves Corozal Bus Station for Sarteneja every day at 14.00, although the bus takes a circuitous path through town for some 20 minutes, drumming up customers. The trip costs BZ$8, and generally takes 4 hours, including a stop in Orange Walk. If you want to catch Castillo's bus in Orange Walk, it stops just down the street from the Zeta's Store on Main Street, leaving town at around 15.30 and arriving in Sarteneja about 17.30. The return bus leaves Sarteneja at 06.00, arriving in Corozal at around 08.00.

Boat traffic from Corozal to Sarteneja is extremely informal and in reality quite unlikely. Ask around at the marketplace and the nearby docks. Skiffs make the trip across the bay in 45 minutes, while the sailboats used by Sarteneja fishermen take 1 hour 30 minutes. Boats also run from Sarteneja to Chetumal, Mexico (only 30 minutes in a skiff), although I've never made the trip myself and cannot guarantee travellers that they'll be allowed to enter Mexico this way.

If you plan on driving to Sarteneja, you have three options, all beginning near Orange Walk (see *Shipstern Peninsula* above for specific directions). Note that the road can be tricky or impassable during the wet season, particularly in September.

There is no shortage of accommodation in Sarteneja, the problem is finding the location. **Fernando's Seaside Guest House**, North Front Street, on the shore; tel: 04 32085, on the shore. New, clean and carefully put together, each of the four rooms has hot water, fan and a fridge. BZ$50. There are plans for a restaurant. Fernando arranges fishing tours as well as snorkelling, diving and trips to nearby ruins. He can also take you over to Ambergris Caye for a tour of the Bacalar Chico National Park and Marine Reserve (see, *Chapter 14, Ambergris Caye*).

At the time of writing **Krisami's** (tel: 04 32283) was under construction. Three rooms with a view over the bay, with private bathrooms and air conditioning. A quiet spot which also has plans for a restaurant.

Diani's Hotel, a long-time favourite, was closed for refurbishment at the time of writing.

The cheapest accommodation going is with **Daniel Andrade**. Just BZ$10 for a room and Daniel can make food for you as well.

Richie's serves basic food in a seafront palapa and there are several bars dotted around the town, most of which will serve food.

Shipstern Nature Reserve

Managed by the Swiss-based International Tropical Conservation Foundation (ITCF), the reserve is located on 22,000 acres at the northern end of the Shipstern Peninsula. The reserve takes its name from the abandoned village of Shipstern near the eastern shore of the lagoon. Approximately one-third of the Reserve is comprised of sub-tropical moist forest; one-third is water (the vast, shallow Shipstern Lagoon); and the final third is coastal savanna bordering the lagoon. Associated with the Nature Reserve is the Chiclero Botanical Trail (a path through the forest with signs marking the more notable plants) and the former Butterfly Breeding Centre, where pupae were raised and sold to European butterfly houses for live display.

A casual visitor with limited time will probably want to put Shipstern fairly low on his or her list of Belizean nature reserves. Although vast, much of the Reserve is fairly inaccessible, with no trails outside the forest and few within. Visitors hungering for a 'jungle' experience will likely be disappointed by the environment here, which is far more akin to the scrub forest of the Mexican Yucatan than the lush, moist rainforests of central and southern Belize. However, the flora of Shipstern Nature Reserve is absolutely unique for mainland Belize and relatively rare on the Yucatan Peninsula. Camping is not allowed anywhere within the Reserve, making daily access somewhat difficult for those without a vehicle (although the rule is undoubtedly a wise one). Two observation towers, one at the edge of the savanna and one at the Xo-Pol ponds, are ideal for observing wildlife. Dusk trips to these towers can be organised by the staff of the reserve.

These slight misgivings aside, Shipstern remains a unique and extremely valuable nature reserve. Alone among the other protected areas in Belize, Shipstern includes not only northern hardwood forest, but also saline lagoons and mangrove shorelines. Most of the trees are young, regenerating after Hurricane Janet and subsequent fires levelled much of the area in 1955. Characteristic trees include the Kuka-palm (*Pseudophoenix sargentii*), the Tuc-tree (*Beaucarnea ameliae*), the gumbo limbo ('tourist tree', *Bursera simaruba*), the sapodilla (*Manilkara zapota*), many wild figs (*Ficus sp.*), the last remnants of mahogany stands (*Swietenia macrophylla*), and the black poisonwood (*Metopium brownei*). The lagoon itself is extremely shallow, with a salty bottom overlying limestone bedrock, and mangrove 'cayes' dotting the vast watery landscape. Savanna borders the lagoon, comprised of grasses, mangrove and isolated limestone hillocks overgrown with palms and broad-leafed trees.

This diversity of habitats accounts for the staggering variety of wildlife reported in the Reserve. Virtually all the Belizean mammal species live here, the single notable exception being the primates (Hurricane Janet apparently wiped out the local howler monkey population). The jaguar population appears healthy; different animals are regularly sighted within an 8km radius of the headquarters, including a female last seen with cubs in 1999. Over 60 species of reptiles and amphibians – half the total species count in the entire country – have been recorded within the Reserve. Both Belizean crocodile species may live here, but so far only the endangered Morelet's crocodile has actually been spotted. One of the amphibian stars of the Reserve is the casque-headed frog, *Triprion petasatus*. The reserve participates in the Saltwater Crocodile Recovery Programme, started in 1999. The Crocodile Nursery can be visited, but arrangements must be made through the reserve staff.

Shipstern is a birder's paradise, with 201 species sighted until recently; biologists from the US Fish and Wildlife Service, led by Chan Robbins, added 19 previously unrecorded species to this list. One of these was the black catbird (*Melanoptila glabrirostris*), previously seen in Belize only on Caye Caulker and Ambergris Caye, and then but rarely. Wood stork colonies, mostly destroyed by local and Mexican fishermen who stole the young, are apparently making a comeback in Shipstern. Other specialities of the Reserve, uncommon in other parts of Belize, include the yellow-lored parrot (*Amazona xantholora*), white-winged dove (*Zenaida asiatica*) and Yucatan jay (*Cyanocorax yucatanicus*). Shipstern Lagoon is one of the most important feeding grounds for the reddish egret (*Egretta rufescens*), a bird which is uncommon or even rare throughout the rest of Central America. Virtually the entire Belizean population of this species resides in the extreme northeast portion of the country.

The **Chiclero Botanical Trail** provides easy access to the forest and an opportunity to learn about locally important plant life. Approximately 80 species of trees along the trail bear numbered signs listing Latin names, common names and local names in the Yucatec Maya tongue. The wardens of the reserve are excellent and knowledgeable guides, and a visit to the trail is included in the tour given to all visitors. Continuous botanical work is being carried out and Reserve staff keep expanding the trail every year.

The reserve headquarters and visitor centre are located on the right side of the road, about 4.8km before Sarteneja village. Any bus headed to Sarteneja will drop you off if you notify the driver (see Sarteneja for details). Unless you are driving yourself, you'll have to walk the 4.8km to Sarteneja; hitchhiking is possible, but there's little traffic on the road. The centre is open daily (except Christmas, New Year, and Easter Sunday) from 09.00–12.00 and 13.00–16.00. Admission to the visitor's centre and the butterfly display with a guided tour through the Chiclero Botanical Trail cost BZ$8 per person. The whole tour lasts little more than 2 hours.

If you want to see more of the Reserve, speak to the assistant manager Juan Aldana or any of the staff. It takes about 2 hours to reach the Shipstern Lagoon via trail from the Reserve headquarters.

Tours can be arranged to see the woodstork colonies from February through to May, and to observe wildlife at the tree-tops. All treks through the reserve must be made with a guide. There are no lodging facilities except for scientists, and food is not available at the Reserve. The nearest food and lodging is in Sarteneja village (see above). The International Tropical Conservation Foundation encourages all visitors to make use of the bed and breakfast facilities in the village, in order to promote eco-tourism in the area. No camping is allowed within the Reserve.

The ideal time to visit the Shipstern Reserve is in January, just following the rainy season. New foliage at this time should be lush, and the butterflies at their most active. A sunny day is best for butterfly viewing both along the trail; rains keep them from moving, feeding or mating. Naturally enough, winter months are best if you're interested in seeing North American migrant waterfowl which spend the colder months in the Shipstern Lagoon.

Bring insect repellent, long pants, a long-sleeved shirt, socks and footwear when visiting the Reserve. Mosquitoes may be fierce, particularly along the Botanical Trail and the trail to the lagoon. Also consider taking along water bottles, lunch and binoculars. More information may be obtained online at itcf@papiliorama.ch. Also visit www.papiliorama.ch for information on Shipstern Nature Reserve and Bacalar Chico Forest and Marine Reserve.

Fireburn Forest and Wetlands and the surrounding area
South of Shipstern Nature Reserve, the proposed Fireburn Forest and Wetlands Reserve is slowly opening up to visitors. Environmental, conservation and research work is still being carried out in the area. Development work involves the community but in the meantime communication regarding transport, accommodation or voluntary work is best through one of the assisting organisations such as Wildtracks (email: wildtracks@btl.net) in advance of arriving in the area.

Belizean and international student groups are actively involved in documenting and studying the area, working towards establishing a 1,750 acre reserve focusing on environmental education and sustainable development for members of the nearby community of Fireburn. This project has been assisted greatly by contributions from international volunteer organisations. It is expected that by the end of 2000, accommodation for visitors will be in place. Two cabanas have been built, educational trails and observation platforms are being constructed, and guides and supporting materials are being developed.

This is one of the best areas in Belize for wildlife. The forest in the proposed reserve is very different from that at Shipstern, it's much taller, more lush, and with a structure and species composition not unlike the forest at Rio Bravo. Visitors wanting to travel further afield can visit Bacalar Chico Marine Reserve as Lincoln Sealey from Fireburn can carry guests to and from Ambergris Caye. Contact him through Wildtracks. It is planned to establish trekking facilities, along biological corridor routes, visiting some of the sustainable development projects.

An archaeological reserve of at least 375 acres is also to be established around the Fireburn Ruins – a Maya site bigger than Altun Ha. Current research has revealed at least 165 structures.

Keel-billed toucan

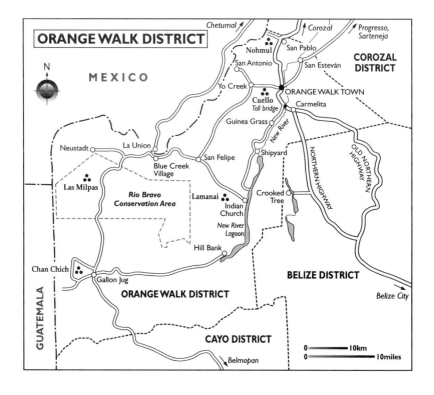

ORANGE WALK DISTRICT

N

MEXICO

Chetumal

Corozal

Progresso, Sarteneja

Nohmul

San Pablo

San Antonio

San Estéván

COROZAL DISTRICT

Yo Creek

ORANGE WALK TOWN

Cuello
Toll bridge

Carmelita

Guinea Grass

New River

Neustadt

La Union

San Felipe

Shipyard

Blue Creek Village

Las Milpas

Rio Bravo Conservation Area

Lamanai

Crooked Tree

Indian Church

NORTHERN HIGHWAY

OLD NORTHERN HIGHWAY

New River Lagoon

Hill Bank

Chan Chich

Gallon Jug

ORANGE WALK DISTRICT

BELIZE DISTRICT

Belize City

GUATEMALA

CAYO DISTRICT

Belmopan

0 — 10km
0 — 10miles

Orange Walk District

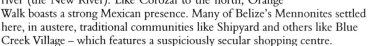

Orange Walk may get fewer travellers per square kilometre than any other district in the country. Much of the land is agricultural flatland, given over to the sugar cane that is still Belize's major export, while a good deal of the rest remains trackless jungle. It doesn't help tourism that the district is entirely landlocked and that its only major town has a reputation as the drug capital of Belize. On the positive side, Orange Walk District offers one of Belize's newest and most remote nature reserves (the Río Bravo Conservation and Management Area), a major Maya ruin on the banks of a forested lagoon (Lamanai), and a mazy, orchid-laden jungle river (the New River). Like Corozal to the north, Orange Walk boasts a strong Mexican presence. Many of Belize's Mennonites settled here, in austere, traditional communities like Shipyard and others like Blue Creek Village – which features a suspiciously secular shopping centre.

ORANGE WALK TOWN

Orange Walk Town, with 15,500 residents, is the largest settlement in northern Belize. It stands on the left bank of the New River, 106km north of Belize City and 48km south of Corozal. Orange Walk is a bustling agricultural centre with a pronounced Latin ambience. Mexican refugees from the Caste War of the mid-1800s have left their mark on the town. Many locals speak only Spanish, and street food runs to tacos, *salbutes*, and *tamales*. But this is still Belize, with its incongruous mix of cultures; bargaining with the *Mestizo* majority on market days are blond Mennonite farmers, in bib overalls and straw hats, switching adeptly between Spanish, English and their own low German dialect.

Many travellers never get to Orange Walk Town, and those that do rarely spend more than a night or two. The town is landlocked, nondescript, relatively expensive and has only a few nearby attractions: the Maya ruins of Lamanai, a minor Maya site at Cuello and the jungled banks of the New River. Moreover, bus service is so frequent that travellers can use either Belize City (1 hour 45 minutes) or Corozal (1 hour 15 minutes) as a base camp for the Lamanai, Cuello and New River trips.

Partly as result of the sugar depression, Orange Walk has lately become the acknowledged centre of Belize's marijuana traffic. Locals often refer to Orange Walk as 'Rambo Town' due to a continuing rash of drug-related violence. Travellers don't seem to be at any particular risk of this violence, although cabbies and other locals will warn you that the town can be risky after dark. And foreigners – even non-Americans – who spend more than a few days in Orange Walk have on occasion been verbally harassed, suspected of working undercover for the US Drug Enforcement Agency.

History

Orange Walk was one of the original logging camps in Belize. Like Corozal, the tiny settlement experienced an explosion of immigrants in the mid-1800s as Mexican Mestizos fled the bloody War of Castes in the Yucatan. Maya raiding parties continued to plague the settlers, however, and the British built Fort Cairns and Fort Mundy (now both ruins) to fend off attacks. In 1872, a huge army of Icaiche Maya led by Marcus Canul crossed the Río Hondo from Mexico and attacked Orange Walk. The town was defended for six hours by the 4th West India Regiment, which succeeded in killing Canul and driving off the Maya. The unsuccessful raid on Orange Walk marked the last armed resistance by the Maya in Belize.

The Mexican refugees mostly tended *milpas*, growing corn and chicle. A few farmers brought sugar cane cuttings, however, and by the late 19th century the face of agriculture in Orange Walk was changing. In 1967, British sugar giant Tate and Lyle built a major sugar factory at Tower Hill, 6km south of town, expanding and modernising it ten years later. As the sugar industry declined in the mid-1980s, Tate and Lyle turned over the Tower Hill factory to employees, retaining only a 10% interest. Although the market remains depressed – as Belizeans say, 'Sugar is no longer sweet' – the roads leading to Orange Walk are still clogged by trucks top-heavy with cane.

Getting there

All Venus and Batty buses operating between Belize City and Corozal (including those from Belize City to Chetumal, Mexico) stop in Orange Walk. Between the two companies, a bus leaves Belize City northbound and Corozal southbound about every hour. From Belize City, buses take 1 hour 45 minutes to reach Orange Walk, and the fare costs BZ$4.50. From Corozal, it's only 1 hour 15 minutes, costing BZ$3. All buses stop for about 20 minutes in Orange Walk, discharging and taking on passengers across the street from the northern corner of the central park. There is no bus station in Orange Walk; just wait on the corner with the rest of the crowd and pay your fare aboard the bus.

A daily bus to Sarteneja from Corozal, stops for about an hour in Orange Walk, generally around 15.30. Buses leave from outside Zeta's Store on Main Street. See *Chapter 9*, *Sarteneja* for details.

Where to stay

Lodging in Orange Walk is surprisingly expensive. Budget hotels are either located in the noisiest section of town, rundown, or both. Depending on your itinerary, you may be better off spending the night in Corozal Town, which is only 1hr 15min away by frequent bus and is much more pleasant.

St Christopher's Hotel 10 Main Street; tel: 03 21064; fax: 03 21064. 11 rooms with private bath, fan and cable TV. Very clean and friendly staff. Close to the river. The best in town. BZ$59.

Mi Amor 19 Belize/Corozal Road; tel: 03 22031. 12 rooms, with private bath, fan. A big concrete building located in the heart of downtown, with a discotheque below. BZ$48.

D Star Victoria Hotel 40 Belize/Corozal Road; tel: 03 22518; fax: 03 22847; email: dvictoria@btl.net; web: www.d-victoria.com. 31 rooms, BZ$48 with private bath, fan; BZ$84 with air conditioning. They offer protected parking, a swimming pool, laundry service and the Miami Nites discotheque below. Recommended, considering the options.

Jane's Guest House 6 Market Lane; tel: 03 22526. 6 rooms, with shared bath, fan. A simple clapboard building, located down a quiet lane one block east of the Belize Bank. A dubious part of town at night. BZ$20.

Jane's Hotel 2 Baker's Street; tel: 03 22473. 8 rooms, with shared bath, fan; some rooms have private bath. An only slightly more upscale version of Jane's Guest House (above), but in a much safer location. BZ$20.

A little out of town there are a couple of other options. **Chula Vista Motel Trial Farm** (tel: 03 23413). 7 rooms, with private bath, fan. Located next to the Esso petrol station in Trial Farm, roughly 1.5km north of town on the highway; not too convenient unless you've got a car. BZ$50.

Near the Toll Bridge on the Northern Highway heading south out of town is **New River Park** (PO Box 34; tel: 03 23987; fax: 03 23789; email: newriver@btl.net. Rooms with hot water and a fan are BZ$107, or with AC and TV for BZ$114. The restaurant serves Belizean and American cuisine. The hotel offers trips to Lamanai Maya ruins by covered boat. Trip leaves about 09.00 returning around 16.00. The package includes a guide, lunch and soft drinks provided. BZ$80 pp with $5.00 entrance fee.

Where to eat
Besides **D Star Victoria** listed above there are several other places to eat in town. 'Spanish' food – tacos, salbutes and excellent chicken tamales – is best had from the street vendors around the central park. Chinese restaurants are everywhere and besides those listed below, you'll find the **Happy Valley** (38 Main Street), **Jane's Chinese Food Center** (21 Main Street), and the **Sing Wang** (Main Street near St Christopher Hotel) among others. **HL's Burgers** serves Belizean and 'Spanish' food.

Hong Kong Restaurant 21 Belize/Corozal Road. Located next to Mi Amor Hotel. Typical Belizean Chinese fare.
Happy Days Chinese Restaurant and Ice Cream Parlour Sandwiches, burgers, beer and soft drinks in addition to the obvious.
Lover's Café 20 Lovers Lane. Belizean food, soft drinks. Also the home of the Novelo brothers, who run Jungle River Tours (see below). Nicely decorated with maps of Belize and wildlife posters.
The Diner Clark Street. About 1.6km north of town near the hospital, but probably the nicest restaurant in Orange Walk. US and European fare.

Information and useful addresses
Jungle River Tours, 20 Lovers Lane, PO Box 95; tel: 03 22293; fax: 03 23749, located inside the Lover's Café, serves as headquarters for Antonio and Herminio Novelo, brothers with extensive knowledge of the Lamanai and New River areas (see *Excursions* below). While they're obviously in business to promote their own guided trips, they welcome the chance to talk about the Orange Walk area, wildlife and eco-tourism in Belize. A good place to get your bearings and in reality you're unlikely to find somebody who knows more about the local area.

Godoy and Sons offer local tours and sell the orchids they cultivate. If you're interested in buying orchids to take home, Luis and Carlos can help with customs and inspection formalities. They also host an orchid tour on a newly-completed trail near the New River, as well as trips to the Lamanai ruins (see *Excursions* below). Their store (tel: 03 22969) is located on the east side of the highway at 4 Trial Farm, roughly 2km north of town.

Cash and travellers' cheques can be changed at **Belize Bank** (34 Main Street) or **Bank of Nova Scotia** (Park Street just east of the central park).

The **BTL** telephone office is in a second floor office on Park Street where it meets the central park. Internet services are available from midday until 21.00 in an office next to the Municipal Palace.

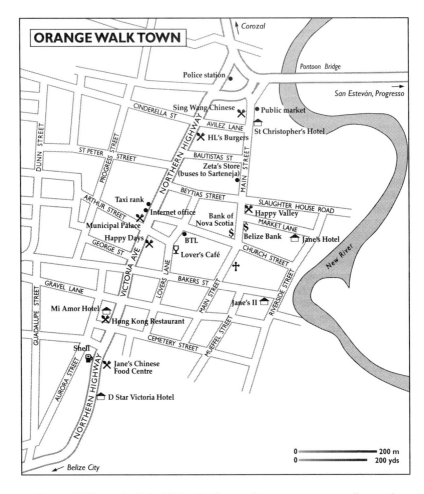

Orange Walk can be intimidating in the evenings so try not to walk round on your own.

Excursions
Near town
Cuello

Cuello is a relatively recent discovery. Although locals no doubt knew of the Maya site for years, it was Cambridge archaeologist Norman Hammond who first picked out Cuello from aerial photographs in 1973. The site takes its name from the family which owns the land and nearby rum distillery.

Hammond and his students worked sporadically at the site for the rest of the decade. The archaeological community was initially thrilled when materials found at Cuello were radiocarbon dated as originating around 2000BC, perhaps even earlier. Until that time, archaeological evidence suggested that the Maya civilisation originated around 1500BC. More recently, however, Hammond himself favoured redating the Cuello settlement roughly a millennium later, sometime in the Middle Preclassic.

There isn't much actually to see at Cuello beyond a few earth-covered mounds. Most of Hammond's work has focused not on these above-ground structures – remains of a later ceremonial centre – but on the stratified underground layers. Beneath one ceremonial platform erected in 400BC, Hammond found evidence of a mass human sacrifice; the Cuello priests killed and dismembered 26 victims, presumably to sanctify the new site.

Cuello is located within a pasture on distillery-owned grounds. It is about 6.4km west of Orange Walk on the Yo Creek Road (known as the San Antonio Road closer to town). Visitors can either walk, drive, or take a cab from town. Remember that the site lies on private land; call the Cuello Rum Distillery during normal business hours on 03 22141 for permission to enter. You can also arrive at the distillery and simply ask workers there for the manager, who will give you permission to see the site. The nearby swamp is good for birdwatching.

Nohmul

Nohmul's main pyramid not only dominates the surrounding plaza but is the highest landmark in the Orange Walk/Corozal area – mostly by virtue of its location on a limestone ridge. As with Cuello, there is little actually to see here beside the mound itself; the surrounding area is grassy and cultivated with sugar cane. But Nohmul ('Great Mound' in Mayan) once stood as a regional centre of government, surrounded by 4,800 acres of settlement. The area was occupied during the Preclassic, largely abandoned during the Classic and resettled during the Late Classic and Early Postclassic.

Thomas Gann was once again first on the site, working periodically from 1897 through 1936. He unearthed bones, jade, mollusc shells, polychrome vessels and obsidian, much of which he sent to the British Museum. Three tombs uncovered in the 1940s during roadwork were looted before archaeologists could recover much. Norman Hammond began extensive work in 1982, discovering, among other things, offerings of a distinctive green obsidian from Teotihuacán, near present-day Mexico City. The same obsidian has been unearthed at Altun Ha, signalling an extensive trade network that moved goods not only within the Maya world, but throughout Mesoamerica. Arlen and Diane Chase reported a special style of elite residence, known to archaeologists as Patio Quad, at Nohmul; the few other structures of this style exist only in Mexico, at Chichén Itzá and Cozumel Island.

The site, which charges no fee, stands on private farmland about 11.3km north of Orange Walk, just 1.6km west of the Northern Highway near the twin villages of San Pablo and San José. Any of the many buses between Orange Walk and Corozal can put you off in San Pablo. A round-trip taxi directly to the site from Orange Walk is a better option, since most casual visitors will be satisfied with a few minutes at Nohmul.

Orchid tour

Godoy and Sons at 4 Trial Farm (tel: 03 22969), roughly 2km north of town on the east side of the highway, recently completed an orchid trail at a site near Orange Walk Town along the New River. For US$200, Carlos Godoy will take a group of four to the site by boat, but prices vary greatly depending on the number in the group and the level of support you want – call for details. You'll see both wild and cultivated orchids, including the national flower, the black orchid. Also noted along the trail are medicinal plants and a number of trees that have played a role in Belize's history. Tours are offered daily, and take about 4 hours.

Further afield
Lamanai

Among the Maya sites of Belize, Lamanai is one of the most noteworthy and unusual. It commands the shoreline of the New River Lagoon, surrounded by 950 acres of protected forest. The site was occupied much longer than most Maya centres – from roughly 1500BC (Early Preclassic) to about AD1650 (the Colonial Period). Lamanai's history includes an amazing span of events: the period of early power and greatness, when its main temple was the largest known Preclassic structure in the Maya world; a minor collapse paralleling the catastrophic end of Maya civilisation in other parts of Central America; the Spanish conquest and colonisation, during which time Lamanai successfully teetered between two worlds; the Maya rebellion, when the old ways briefly returned; and the coming of British rule. A bizarre array of archaeological remains testifies to this varied history: European, North American and Mexican trade items, Maya effigies incorporated into Catholic churches and a 19th century sugar mill.

Even the name is unusual. The real names of Maya cities are usually lost in antiquity, and most sites were subsequently renamed by Spanish conquerors or well-intentioned archaeologists. Lamanai, on the other hand, is what the citizens actually called their great city, as recorded by Franciscan missionaries in the 17th century. The name means 'Submerged Crocodile'. The big reptiles seldom cruise the shores of New River Lagoon, but Lamanai is rife with crocodile figures, including ceramic decorations and stylised limestone headdresses. Among lowland Maya, there was a widespread belief that the world rested on the back of a crocodile, and crocodiles figure prominently in Mesoamerican myths of creation.

Pollen studies suggest that corn was being grown at Lamanai as early as 1500BC. The first stone structures and ceramics date from between 800BC and 500BC. Building reached a crescendo during the Preclassic period, when Lamanai's most magnificent structure, N10-43, was erected. It towers nearly 33m above the plaza, dominating an ancient city of some 700 buildings – mostly overgrown with jungle at this point.

Lamanai at its peak served as an important hub in the extensive trade network of the Maya, with links to Mexico, Guatemala and Honduras. As with other cities in the northern lowlands, Lamanai did not suffer the same stunning collapse of civilisation which befell those in the southern lowlands in the 10th century. Still, there is evidence at Lamanai of labour shortages and a decentralisation of power late in the Classic period. And by the time Spaniards colonised the Yucatan peninsula in the mid-1500s, the Maya were far fewer than in their Classic Period heyday. Epidemic disease, perhaps smallpox, is suspected as at least one cause.

Once-mighty Lamanai now became part of the colonial world. But this was still the frontier of Spanish rule, and the Crown's power here was tenuous. Anthropologists Elizabeth Graham, David Pendergast and Grant Jones believe that Lamanai and other Maya sites in present-day Belize were spared the heavy colonial hand that gripped most of Mexico. And the Maya, for their part, devised subtle ways to retain their cultural traditions. Graham and her colleagues found that in Lamanai and Tipu (in Belize's Cayo District), pre-Columbian traditions in the manufacture of ceramics, tools and weapons changed little after Spanish contact. While the Maya of Lamanai adhered to Catholic burial customs, for example, they continued to paint animal deities on their ceramics. And although the Spanish built two churches at the site – the crumbled remains are still visible – a sly Maya artisan managed to slip a bat effigy into the first, appeasing the old gods and his new colonial masters at the same time.

Subtle resistance turned into open rebellion in 1638. Lamanai and Tipu expelled the Spanish for almost 60 years, during which time the citizens reverted to many of the traditional Maya ways. They burned the Catholic churches and other European buildings and worshipped at pre-Columbian altars. Yet the Maya of Lamanai willingly held on to certain European traditions – Catholic burials, for instance – suggesting that they were more anti-Spanish than anti-Christian. Indeed, many Catholic beliefs nicely dovetailed with ancient Maya rituals.

But here the archaeological record at Lamanai lapses. Epidemics may have scattered the local Maya, because the site was largely deserted when the British arrived to set up logging camps in the 18th century. A sugar mill, its machinery imported from New Orleans in 1869 by expatriate Confederates following the Civil War, survives today as a boiler and flywheel.

Thomas Gann, who made the first excavations in 1917, uncovered in 1925 a massive serpent column virtually identical to those used by Maya architects at Chichén Itzá and other Mexican cities. The site was then known as Indian Church, a name which persisted until 1978, when the Lamanai-crocodile connection was made. Famed British Mayanist J Eric Thompson stopped by in the 1930s, followed by at least two minor expeditions in the 1960s. But it was David Pendergast of the Royal Ontario Museum (Toronto) who began the first large-scale excavations in 1974. Pendergast's studies continue at the site, and you may well see his students at work when you visit.

The site remains largely unexcavated, and casual observers will find it hard to believe that archaeologists have identified more than 700 buildings. Vines and philodendrons creep over the once-mighty city, now shaded by a forest of second-growth palms and hardwoods. The centre is concentrated within 320 acres along the lagoon's shoreline, but minor buildings and residential structures fan throughout the 950-acre Archaeological Reserve.

You can climb three structures, including the massive N10-43, which rises 33m above plaza level and can be seen over the treetops from the river. The ball court, sandwiched between buildings just south of N10-43, is far smaller than those at other Maya sites; archaeologists unearthed a covered clay pot filled with liquid mercury beneath the stone marker in the court's centre. Just beyond the ballcourt, at the base of a temple, lies an unusually well-preserved stela commemorating a ruler known as Lord Smoking Shell. Archaeologists believe that the ancient Maya built a fire at the stela's base, an offering to Smoking Shell. But the stela cracked, falling forward on its face, which would account for the high degree of preservation. The Maya apparently abandoned both the stela and temple, fearing the incident as a portent of doom. In the temple itself, investigators unearthed the remains of five young boys, the only evidence of human sacrifice at Lamanai.

Continuing south past the acropolis – the administrative centre of the city – you'll come across pyramid N10-9, flanked with jaguar masks. Further south lie the ruins of the two Spanish churches.

Structure P9-56 lies on a path north of the museum, and is notable for its masks, 4m in height, including those of a ruler with crocodile headdress. Artisans carved these masks from solid limestone blocks, rather than from plaster over a stone core, the more usual Maya technique.

The site is open 08.00–17.00 daily, with the standard entrance fee of BZ$5. Pay Guadelupe, the caretaker. There are restrooms, a picnic area, and a tiny hut of a museum crammed with artefacts found at the site. The reserve is now the only intact forest for many miles and is home to three troops of howler monkeys.

The cheapest way to reach Lamanai, but certainly not the easiest, is to catch a ride to Guinea Grass, and from there hire a skiff to take you 20km upriver to the site. Before going to the trouble of getting there, try to line up a guide. Atilano Narvallez charges BZ$175 for a boatload of up to four people. You can reach him in Guinea Grass on 03 31042; he's generally available in the evenings. Santiago Cima also reportedly runs a boat to Lamanai from Guinea Grass. Trucks leave for Guinea Grass daily (except Sundays) from the Municipal Palace in Orange Walk Town around 10.00.

The boat trip upriver from Guinea Grass takes about 1hr 30min, twisting through a maze of mangrove channels, past trees dotted with orchids. Many of the same birds which inhabit nearby Crooked Tree Wildlife Sanctuary can be seen along the way: jacanas, egrets, snail kites, cormorants, purple gallinules, limpkins, even the rare jabiru stork. Crocodiles are occasionally spotted, but outboard motors tend to spook them.

Jungle River Tours, 20 Lovers Lane, (see *Information and useful addresses*, page 151), runs highly recommended trips boat trips to Lamanai via the New River. The Novelos charge BZ$100 pp for a day trip to Lamanai, with lunch included. The trip leaves Orange Walk around 09.00 so either spend the previous night in Orange Walk, or else take a morning bus from Corozal or Belize City. Travellers are usually taken to the Carmelita toll bridge 9km south of town to meet the Novelo's boat, powered by a 40hp motor. The boat wends its way slowly up the New River, reaching Lamanai in about 1 hour 30 minutes. After a guided tour of Lamanai itself, the Novelo brothers show guests the deserted sugar mill and the remains of the old Spanish fort. Herminio is soft-spoken, friendly, fluent in English, and knows his birds well (including, for serious birders, the Latin names). Both brothers are members of the Belize Tourism Board, and have been committed to cautious eco-tourism since long before the term became shopworn.

An overland route to Lamanai exists, via a potholed red dirt road from San Felipe Village. This route is best done during the dry season and at other times only with a 4WD. Leave Orange Walk headed west on the San Antonio Road (the one which goes to Yo Creek). At Yo Creek, head south for some 30km; the red dirt road begins just north of San Felipe Village, where you'll turn southeast toward Indian Church. There is no good reason to visit Lamanai this way – it's rough, more expensive (assuming the cost of petrol and a rented 4WD vehicle) and you'll miss the forest and birdlife along the New River.

There is a bus that leaves Orange Walk three times a week at 16.00 making it essential to stay the night in Indian Church, where you can get some accommodation with local people or camp.

The best option if you plan to spend a few days in the area is to stay at the **Lamanai Outpost Lodge** located on the southern border of the archaeological zone (PO Box 63, Orange Walk Town; tel: 1 888 733 7864; tel/fax: 02 33578; email: lamanai@btl.net; web: www.lamanai.com). It is ideally suited for both amateur Mayanists and naturalists, 27m above the New River Lagoon. They offer 18 thatched-roof cabanas with fans, hot water, verandas and 24-hour electrical power (US$115dbl, US$95s). Three full meals run US$42 pp per day. The lodge owners put full emphasis on eco-tourism – this is no party resort. Besides tours of the ruin site, they offer birding trips (over 300 species have been reported), orchid tours and night walks in the jungle. The most unusual offering is the night-time tour of a smaller lagoon just behind the New River Lagoon. Guests aboard the pontoon boat can watch crocodiles glide through the extremely shallow (less than a metre) waters of the lagoon, their eyes lit by the guide's torch.

Programme for Belize can line you up with a guide to Lamanai at La Milpa Field Station (see *Río Bravo Conservation and Management Area* below) that will take you to Lamanai via road and boat.

Maruba Resort and Jungle Spa near Maskall (see *Chapter 7*) offers days trips to Lamanai for US$80 pp, lunch included.

Paradise Inn in Crooked Tree Village also runs recommended day trips to Lamanai. Also based in Crooked Tree, the **Chau Hiix Lodge** offers Lamanai trips as part of their package (see *Chapter 7*).

Carlos Godoy of **Godoy and Sons** in Orange Walk (see *Information and useful addresses* above) charges US$150 for a boatload of four passengers to Lamanai via the New River.

Río Bravo Conservation and Management Area

Located in the westernmost portion of Orange Walk District, the Río Bravo Conservation and Management Area spans 260,000 acres of tropical forest. The conservation area represents approximately 4% of Belize's total land area and is home to a rich sample of biodiversity including 400 species of birds, 200 species of trees, 70 species of mammals and 12 endangered animal species.

The area is privately owned and managed by the Programme for Belize, a consortium of Belizean and US-based environmental groups, including the Nature Conservancy and the Massachusetts Audubon Society. In October 1990, Programme for Belize purchased 110,000 acres of forest owned by Belizean businessman Barry Bowen. Coca-Cola Foods got into the act with a portion of their vast holdings in the area. Coke's original plans – clearing some 30,000 acres in order to plant oranges – met with the opposition of both environmentalists and Florida citrus growers. Insurance problems later sealed the project's fate, and Coca-Cola donated 42,000 acres. Bowen agreed to place another 130,000 acres of his adjacent land, centred around the logging camp of Gallon Jug, under conservation guidelines which allow only limited cutting, clearing and development.

In spring 1992, Coca-Cola donated another 52,000 adjoining acres, thanks to the efforts of Programme for Belize, The Nature Conservancy and the Belize Ministries of Natural Resources and Finance.

Most of the Río Bravo Conservation Area remains lush forest, wetlands, and savanna. This diversity of habitats supports a huge variety of plant and animal life, including all of Belize's large mammals. The area is being managed on a 'multiple-use' basis. That term may rankle environmentalists, particularly in the US, where it is little more than a euphemism for clear-cut logging on public lands. But Programme for Belize is under no pressure to sell timber. The experimental programme is conducted in the Hill Bank area, in a special zone covering less than 20% of the RBCMA and buffering the fully protected core that constitutes the majority of the area. Programme for Belize points out that through the Experimental Timber Programme, they are helping to resuscitate an industry that literally created the nation of Belize and sustained it over much of its life. Only time will decide how well the experiment works, but for the moment, scientists are busily mapping the area's soils and vegetation types with an eye for a truly compatible mix of low-impact tourism, research and sustainable timber harvest. Cynics would do well to remember that the area was once a private mahogany estate with no formal protection whatsoever.

Río Bravo adjoins Guatemala's Maya Biosphere Reserve, and plans are afoot to merge the two, along with Mexico's Calakmul Biosphere Reserve, in a tri-national Maya Peace Park. For more information on the area, contact the director, Joy Grant, at **Programme for Belize**, PO Box 749, Belize City; tel: 02 75616; fax: 02 75635; email: pfbel@btl.net; web: www.pfbelize.org or drop in at 1 Eyre Street, Belize City. They can always use donations to help defray the loans needed to purchase and manage these areas.

At present, there are three ways to visit the Río Bravo Conservation Area, one up-scale and the others slightly more economical.

The expensive option involves a stay at **Chan Chich Lodge**, Barry Bowen's luxurious yet low-key jungle resort built in one of the plazas of a Maya site of the same name. Chan Chich is near the Conservation Area but not actually within it. Surrounded by forest, Chan Chich offers 12 Maya-style thatched cottages, US$145 with private bath, hot water, ceiling fans, 24-hour electricity, polished hardwood interiors and wrap-around verandas with hammocks. Three meals daily cost US$40 pp for adults, US$30 pp for children under 12; hosts Josie and Tom Harding offer two entrees at each meal. A package plan including room, hotel tax, all meals, all activities (except the Las Milpas Maya site tour), beer and soft drinks

MENNONITES

Belize's ethnic and cultural mosaic became richer still with the arrival of Mennonite immigrants in 1958. In Plattdeutsch, the Low German dialect that the Mennonites speak amongst themselves, they are known as die Stillen im Lande – 'the unobtrusive ones'. Indeed, since the Mennonites neither proselytise nor seek political influence, it is only their physical appearance that calls attention to them in Belize – the men in their denim overalls and straw hats, the women in modest print dresses and wide-brimmed bonnets.

Mennonites are members of one of the earliest Protestant sects, tracing their ideological roots back to the Swiss Alps during the 16th century. There, a pacifist group of Anabaptists known as the Swiss Brethren formed their own church, which by the 1540s came under the leadership of a Dutch priest, Menno Simons. The Mennonites, as they were soon called, drew disciples from throughout Germany, Switzerland and the Netherlands. Then as now, they refused to bear arms or take oaths, renounced participation in secular governments, stressed adult baptism upon confession of faith and dressed plainly.

Fleeing persecution for their beliefs, they formed close-knit farming communities in Poland, the Netherlands, the United States and southern Russia. When Russia threatened the Mennonites with a military draft in the 1870s, thousands left for the Canadian provinces of Manitoba and Saskatchewan. But soon enough their autonomy was challenged by the Canadian government, which insisted that they send their children to public schools to be taught English, pledge allegiance to the Union Jack, and study 'worldly' subjects such as history and geography. By 1920, many fled Canada for Mexico and South America. But after three decades in Chihuahua, Mexico, the Mennonites were again displaced, this time by their need for more farmland and the Mexican government's sudden decree that they join the social security system.

At the time, British Honduras was desperate for agricultural colonists, and in 1955 they invited a delegation of Mennonites to visit Belize. The government drafted an agreement that granted Mennonites the right to run their own churches and German-language schools. Moreover, church members were promised permanent exemption from the military draft, social security and oath-taking in court. In return, the Mennonites agreed to produce enough food for export outside their own communities.

The first Mennonite settlers left Chihuahua in March 1958, some 350 families arriving in British Honduras during an horrendous rainy season. They bought large tracts of uninhabited land near Orange Walk and Cayo, land that must have appeared incredibly fertile to farmers from temperate climes, with lush, costs US$175 pp per night (double occupancy) or US$240 pp (single occupancy). For reservations, write to Chan Chich Lodge, PO Box 37, Belize City, tel/fax: 02 34419 or 1 800 343 8009 toll-free in the US; email: info@chanchich.com; web: www.chanchich.com). The US booking office is at PO Box 1088, Vineyard Haven, MA 02568.

Surrounding Chan Chich there's a well-marked trail system that covers some 15km. The trails range in length from 0.4km to 4km, and cover a variety of habitats. Many of them, including Temple Loop, Norman's Temple Loop and King's Tomb, skirt small Maya sites, some looted and some intact. Over 130 trees, plants and Maya ruins have been marked with wooden plaques allowing a self-guided tour. The lodge sells an excellent booklet by naturalists Carolyn Miller and

virgin stands of tropical forest. But they quickly learned the harsh lessons of impoverished tropical soil; rain, heat and malaria also took a toll during the colonists' early years.

Those that remained, however, established themselves before long as British Honduras' most productive farmers. Today's visitor to Belize – where 'fry chicken' is the unofficial national dish – may find it difficult to believe that poultry products were virtually unknown here prior to the arrival of the Mennonites. Experienced chicken farmers, the Mennonites started the country's first hatchery in Spanish Lookout, quickly driving the price of eggs – imported up until then – down by two-thirds. Mennonite farms were soon producing much of the fruits, vegetables, milk and cheese in the country.

Then as now, Mennonites did not subscribe to a single, all-inclusive set of values. Almost without exception, the colonists of the late 1950s came from two of the church's more conservative sects: the Altkolonier and the somewhat more liberal Kleine Gemeinde ('little congregation'). The former settled in Blue Creek and Shipyard near Orange Walk, while the latter colonised Spanish Lookout in Cayo. Even within these groups, schisms existed, with the most rigidly conservative members settling in Shipyard. Contrary to popular opinion, not all Mennonites eschewed mechanised equipment. Even the conservative Altkolonier embraced the use of farm tractors, but balked at rubber tyres because many believed this made tractors equivalent to automobiles, which the sect had banned since 1916. Steel-wheeled tractors had their limitations in the tropical mud of Belize and consequently many of the Altkolonier went back to using horses. Today, church members from more liberal communities such as Spanish Lookout rank among the nation's top farm mechanics; local wags dub them 'Mechanites'. Even so, you'll find that the town's river ferry is still cranked by hand.

Mennonites today work about 150,000 acres of land in Belize. Besides their contributions to agriculture, Mennonites are well known for their furniture. Understandably, 'the unobtrusive ones' would prefer not to be gawked at and photographed like picturesque oddities, nor are their simple communities particularly compelling as tourist destinations. If you'd like a chance to meet them – particularly the younger Mennonites who often speak good English and Spanish – visit instead the public markets in Orange Walk, Corozal, and Cayo Districts, where Mennonites sell their fresh produce. Shipyard and Little Belize remain the most conservative communities, while Blue Creek and Spanish Lookout are home to many Progressive church members. The Linda Vista Shopping Centre in Blue Creek, for example, is Mennonite-owned.

Bruce Miller, *Exploring the Rainforest – Chan Chich Lodge, Belize* (see *Appendix 2, Further Reading*) which includes maps of the trails and descriptions of the flora and fauna. Two local guides are available (at US$12 per hour) for both night and day trips to see plants, birds and mammals. Horseback riding costs US$18 pp per hour, canoeing US$12 pp per hour. Additional short tours (3-4 hours) include the Punta de Cacao Maya ruins, Laguna Seca bird area and 'Tapir Hole', each tour costing US$50. An all-day trip to the Las Milpas Maya site, including lunch and entrance fee, costs US$135 (four person minimum).

The lodge's location, in the courtyard of the Maya site itself, still stirs controversy. Owner Bowen argues convincingly that the lodge provides badly-needed protection for an area that was being constantly looted. The lodge lies in the middle of the 130,000 acres which Bowen has placed under stringent conservation guidelines, and just south of the Río Bravo Conservation Area itself. Neither area can rightfully be called virgin forest; first the ancient Maya and then the British logged the site. Over the years, however, both areas have been reclaimed by lush jungle, and species like the ocellated turkey (*Agriocharis ocellata*), threatened in much of its former range, roam peacefully outside the lodge just as they do at Tikal.

Most visitors to Chan Chich take a plane to Gallon Jug (about 30min from the Belize City airport with Javier's Flying Service in Belize City; tel: 02 35360). Javier's will also fly one-way charters to Gallon Jug for US$150 pp. The airstrip is about 5km from Chan Chich. Two overland routes also exist for those with rented 4WD vehicles. The first runs northwest from Belmopan, the second runs south from Blue Creek Village in Orange Walk District. From Blue Creek, the dirt road heads south for some 56km (no gas, food or lodging anywhere along the way past Blue Creek). Neither of these routes is passable during the rainy season, nor are they particularly recommended even when dry. With the road in good condition, it takes about 3 hour 30 minutes to reach the lodge from Belize City. From Orange Walk Town via Blue Creek, the route is about 100km and 3 hours to Chan Chich. If you can take the journey, travelling by land through the Río Bravo Conservation Area and flying out is probably the best combined way of seeing the area. Site preparation was underway at Bowen's Gallon Jug property for a more deluxe lodging.

A second, cheaper and less luxurious option involves a stay at **Las Milpas Field Station**, built and operated by the Programme for Belize. The station is located within the Conservation Area itself, north of Gallon Jug and Chan Chich Lodge. They've built two cabanas on the site, and there are also two private rooms in the main lodge as well as a dormitory that sleeps 24. A bank of solar panels and batteries supply electricity, and water comes from a cistern. The food is simple (rice and beans). Programme for Belize encourages naturalists, students, and anyone with a serious interest in rainforest ecology or archaeology to visit. Price is US$76.55 pp in the dormitory with meals and two-guided activities, US$92.60 pp in a cabana with all meals and tours.

The field station is three miles from the third largest archaeological site in Belize – Las Milpas Archaeological Site. Las Milpas is one of at least 60 archaeological sites found on the Río Bravo so far and the field station has become the centre of archaeological research on the Río Bravo. The site is the subject of a long-term archaeological survey being undertaken by Dr Norman Hammond of the Boston University. In May of 1996, it received international attention with the finding of a royal Maya tomb which unearthed a male skeleton adorned with a jeweled necklace. Hiking nature trails, jungle trekking and birding are the order of the day at Las Milpas.

Guides are available at reasonable cost, and there are a number of marked trails if you want to explore on your own. You're encouraged to observe research (such as netting and tagging of migratory birds) when it's going on, as well as watching the archaeologists at work (often, contrary to our cinematic expectations, rather tedious work). Experiments are underway involving a sustainable harvest of wild allspice, chicle, and timber. Las Milpas is now believed to be the third largest Maya site in Belize (after Caracol and Lamanai). Most of it is still unexcavated or only partially excavated, and extensive looting has occurred in the past. Plans at the moment are to restore only one or two important structures, enough to give travellers a feel for the place while keeping the rest cloaked by vegetation. To line up a stay at the station, ring Programme for Belize, 1 Eyre Street, Belize City; tel: 02 75616; fax: 02 75635; email pfbel@btl.net; web: www.pfbelize.org . In addition to reserving you a room or cabana, they may be able to help arrange a lift to the site when they drive out that way (roughly 2 hours 30 minutes from Belize City).

Deeper into the conservation area is the **Hill Bank Field Station** located on the banks of the New River Lagoon. The Field Station serves as a research base for sustainable forest management and specialized tourism incorporating research activities into the forest experience. Hill Bank is an important site of Belize's colonial logging history. It served as an intensive centre for timber extraction for over 150 years, commencing in the seventeenth century. The Hill Bank experience brings to life the architecture and artefacts of colonial land use quaint, wooden buildings of logging camps, antique steam engines and railroad tracks.

Visitors are accommodated in Hill Bank's Caza Balanza which features 100% solar-powered energy, no-flush composting toilets, a rainwater collection system and grey water recycling program. Unwind each evening on your private balcony overlooking the New River Lagoon. Accommodation at Hill Bank is US$76.55 pp in the dormitory with meals.

Transportation to both sites can be organised through Programme for Belize and a cost of US$150 one way. Alternatively you can get directions from Programme for Belize and make your own way there in a rented vehicle. The journey takes about two hours from Belize City.

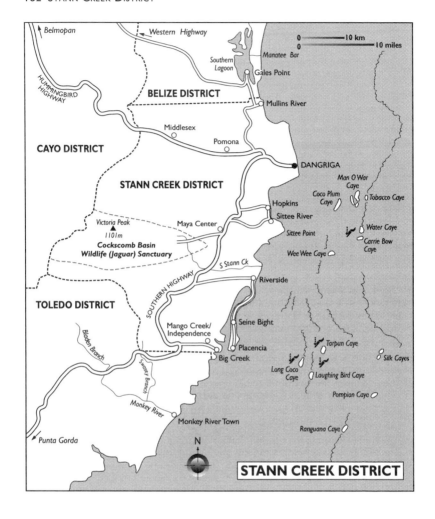

Stann Creek District

After a slow start, travellers are beginning to discover Stann Creek District, and with good reason; the district boasts scores of offshore cayes ideal for fishing, scuba diving, snorkelling, kayaking and sailing. Belize isn't noted for its mainland beaches, but the few that do exist are here in Stann Creek District.

Inland lie thousands of acres of tropical lowland forest, including the world's only jaguar sanctuary, recently expanded and open to visitors, and one of Belize's tallest mountains Victoria Peak (1,120m). Nearly half of the district's residents are Garifuna, of mixed Carib Indian and African descent (see box, page 194), lending the region their rich legacy of music, dance, art, and ritual. In fact, of Belize's standard 'tourist draws', only one is missing from Stann Creek District: Maya ruins. Some smaller Maya sites exist, including Pomona, Mayflower, Kendal, Alabama and Chucil Balam, but only serious archaeologists will be interested in a visit.

The economic lifeblood of Stann Creek District becomes apparent as your bus winds down the heavily pot-holed Hummingbird Highway: citrus. The citrus industry is Belize's second most important agricultural activity, and orange groves blanket the hills on either side of the highway. The country's two citrus processors, including Nestlé (as Belize Food Products), both have their plants in Stann Creek District. Virtually the entire harvest becomes orange juice concentrate and is shipped via Dangriga to the US. The down side to all this prosperity is also visible from the highway in places like Middlesex and Pomona: the cramped, crude housing of the pickers and factory workers, mostly Guatemalan and Salvadorean refugees.

Although citrus now dominates the local economy, sugar and bananas were once the mainstays of Stann Creek valley. Disease virtually wiped out the banana plantations early in the century, and a modest comeback in the 1970s was largely foiled by hurricanes. Rising prices in the 1980s, the introduction of a disease-resistant dwarf variety, and creation of a deep-water port at Big Creek have combined to make bananas a boom crop again, with pressure now on to carve citrus groves and banana plantations out of virgin forest. Hopefully, Stann Creek District will be able to strike a balance in the needs of its growing ecotourism and agricultural industries.

DANGRIGA

Dangriga is Belize's second largest city, a busy centre for the citrus industry. The town exudes its own brand of shabby charm, although there isn't a great deal actually to do here. Still, Dangriga is ideally situated as a jumping-off point for trips to the offshore cayes and the jungled interior, including the Cockscomb Basin

Wildlife Sanctuary (*aka* the 'jaguar sanctuary'). Perhaps most importantly, Dangriga serves as the centre of Garifuna culture and art in Belize. Of Dangriga's 9,000 residents, about 70% are Garifunas, and you'll hear their rich, Carib-based language at every street corner. The town, filled with clapboard houses raised on stilts, is divided roughly in thirds by North Stann Creek and Havana Creek. Everything of interest to the traveller lies within walking distance. Dangriga is especially pleasant on Sundays, when the Garifuna women stroll to and from church, gaily dressed in flowered dresses and bonnets.

History
English Puritans came to what is now Dangriga from the island of New Providence (now part of the Bahamas) in the early 17th century. Their trading stands ('stanns'), located at the mouths of the two creeks, gave the community its original name, Stann Creek Town. The name was changed to honour the Garifuna, whose arrival *en masse* in 1832 is commemorated every November 19 during the exuberant Settlement Day festivities. Dangriga means 'standing water' in the Garifuna tongue, although you'll still hear locals refer to their community as Stann Creek Town.

Getting there
Dangriga lies 169km by road from Belize City via the Hummingbird Highway from Belmopan. An alternative route for those with a car is via the Manatee, or New Coastal Highway. This 60km 'shortcut' is poorly maintained, unpaved washboard of a road that frequently becomes impassable during floods. Now that the Hummingbird Highway has been vastly improved, no time is saved by taking the Coastal Highway. Z-Line buses leave from the Venus Bus Station in Belize City almost every hour. James' Buses also make the run from in front of the Esso petrol station. BZ$10. The trip, which passes gorgeous forested countryside, takes 4–5 hours. There are no direct buses from San Ignacio (Cayo), so travellers headed for Dangriga from Cayo have two options: buy a ticket to Belmopan and wait there for a Z-Line bus from Belize City headed south, or continue east to Belize City and board the Z-Line to Dangriga at its origin in Belize City. The second option may seem silly, since it involves covering the same 80km of highway twice, from Belmopan to Belize City, and then back again to Belmopan. Be forewarned, however, that Z-Line buses to Dangriga are frequently jammed to overflowing by the time they reach Belmopan. Travellers boarding in Belmopan may have to stand for the entire 4-5 hour ride (virtually no one gets off until the orange-farming towns shortly before Dangriga), and sometimes there isn't even standing room. The only way to be assured a seat is to buy your ticket and board in Belize City.

Both Maya Island Air and Tropic Air have four scheduled daily flights to Dangriga, one of which leaves every day including Sundays and public holidays (BZ$55 one way from the Municipal Airport, BZ$81 from the International Airport).

Where to stay
Bluefield Lodge 6 Bluefield Road; tel: 05 22742. Clean, smart and very secure. The owner, Louise Belisle, is friendly and very knowledgeable about the town. Excellent value for money. Shared bathroom BZ$27, private bathroom BZ$38.
Chaleanor Hotel 35 Magoon Street; tel: 05 22587; fax: 05 23038. Clean rooms, with TV and fan, some with views looking out over the sea. Restaurant planned for the top floor which will have spectacular views. BZ$60 for a double. Budget rooms available at BZ$25.
Bonefish Hotel PO Box 21, 15 Mahogany Street; tel: 05 22165; fax: 05 22296; email:

bonefish@btl.net. 10 rooms, all with bath, hot water, air conditioning, cable TV. Facing the beach just west of the post office, the Bonefish is relatively new and expensive, a haunt for sport anglers bound for the reef. The restaurant, spotless but pricey, features great T-bone steak dinners. They also serve lunch (fresh grilled fish, salad, rice for BZ$15). Owner Norris Anderson can arrange inland and caye tours. Rooms from BZ$105.

Riverside Hotel 135 Commerce Street; tel: 05 22168. Almost above King Burger. 16 rooms, with shared bath, fan. Rooms facing the river theoretically cost more, but can often be had for the same price. The owner claims she doesn't provide towels, but you can usually convince her that you won't walk off with them. Clean, and conveniently located just across the bridge from the bus stop. Travellers who have endured sleepless nights here in the past will be relieved to discover that the former disco downstairs is now an appliance store. The owners can arrange boats to Tobacco Caye. US$20.

Weyohan Hotel 105 Commerce Street; tel: 05 23234. 10 rooms, some with AC others with a fan, all with HW. Newly renovated. BZ$41.

Pal's Guest House 868 Magoon Street; tel: 05 22095; fax: 05 22095; email: palbze@btl.net. Just north of the Havana Creek mouth. 18 rooms. A breezy location with a beautiful sea view in the right rooms, but a few blocks from the centre of town. BS$43 with private bath, fan; BZ$27 with shared bath.

Catalina Hotel 37 Cedar Street, tel. 05 22390. 6 rooms, with shared bath, fan. The cheapest place in town at BZ$21. Food available BZ$5.

Pelican Beach Resort PO Box 2, Dangriga; tel: 05 22044; fax: 05 22570; email: sales@pelicanbeachbelize.com; web: www.pelicanbeachbelize.com. 30 rooms, from US$75 without food; US$156 buys you the room and three meals/day. Rates are about 15% cheaper from June through October. A storybook colonial building with veranda located on the beach a ten-minute walk north of downtown (and very close to the airstrip). Food and drinks are excellent. The hotel is owned by the Bowman family, pioneers in the Stann Creek citrus industry and avid conservationists. Daughter Therese Rath and her biologist husband Tony, members of the Belize Audubon Society, act as managers. The resort offers overnight tours of the Sanctuary (see *Excursions* below), Stann Creek Valley, Dangriga town (including stops at local painters' shops), and Hopkins (see below). They offer several trips including Sittee River boat tours (with a stop at Hopkins on the way back) for US$770 pp and three-day combination birding and snorkelling trips to Man of War Caye and South Water Caye for US$572 pp, and manatee-watching trips to Gales Point (see *Excursions* below). Many of these trips can be customised and combined.

Jungle Huts Motel 4 Ecumenical Drive, PO Box 10, Dangriga; tel: 05 22142; fax: 05 23166; email: junglehut@btl.net. 8 cottages and several apartments, all with private baths with hot water. Some cottages have air conditioning. From US$25.

Where to eat

Apart from the hotels mentioned above (Pelican Beach Resort, Catalina Hotel, Chaleanor Hotel and Bonefish Hotel), there are several acceptable restaurants. Most shut down entirely except during mealtimes.

Sunrise Restaurant On the corner of Commerce Street and Rectory Road. Chinese food, including chow mein, fried rice, sweet/sour dishes, chop sueys. Dinners average BZ$10, breakfasts BZ$6. Probably the best place in town for a cheap, filling vegetarian meal. Also burgers, sandwiches, beer, soft drinks.

Ritchie's Dinette Commerce Street. Spanish and Creole food (garnaches, conch fritters, lemon pie, meat pies, burritos). Dark, dingy but a good place to hang out.

King Burger Commerce St below the Riverside Hotel. Besides the burgers (BZ$6.50), this busy cafe serves breakfasts (BZ$6), steak dinners with salad, fried potatoes, roll (BZ$4), shrimp, conch soup, ice cream, milk shakes and – almost unheard of in this, the citrus capital of Belize – real orange juice.

River Café on the south bank of North Stann Creek serves good Belizean fare at reasonable prices. Excellent source of information on travel to Tobacco Caye and the other islands.

Other recommended restaurants along Commerce Street include the **Starlight** (Chinese food) and the **Silver Garden** (Chinese). The newly opened **Xquisite** (Belizean) is on Ramos Road and popular. There are several supermarkets and grocery stores along Commerce Road heading north from North Stann Creek.

What to see

There isn't a great deal to see in Dangriga. A half-hour stroll north of town along the breezy, deserted waterfront to the Pelican Beach Resort and back via the funky charm of Commerce Street will more than satisfy most travellers.

Several Garifuna artists show their work in sidestreets south of the creek. Pen Cayetano is probably Belize's best known painter, and you can visit his studio at 5 Moho Road. Benjamin Nicholas also invites the public to see his work at 27 Howard Street. Austin Rodriguez sells traditional Garifuna drums out of his house at 32 Tubroose Street every day but Sunday. Rodriguez has been crafting drums by hand for over 30 years, using native cedar, mahogany, and mayflower for the body, and either deerskin or cowhide for the skins. His prices range from about US$25 for the smaller drums (called *primeros*) to US$150 for the large mahogany *segundo*.

Music is every bit as informal as art in Dangriga. Ask around town, keep your eyes open for hand-lettered signs, and you may be lucky enough to catch a performance by Pen Cayetano and the Turtle Shell Band (or their teenaged disciples, the Baby Turtle Shell Band). The best-known local band is Waribagabaga ('Butterfly' in Garifuna), a traditional drum and dance ensemble which has toured internationally. See *Chapter 6, Music* for more details on Garifuna musical styles. If you happen to be in town in late December, watch for performances of the John Canoe (see *Special events* below). Dangriga is full of shabby bars, including the Star Club on St Vincent Street.

The Pelican Beach Resort offers a town tour, including stops at painters' and craft shops, for US$20 pp.

Special events

Garifuna Settlement Day celebration lasts three days, November 17–19. Crowds line both side of North Stann Creek as Garifunas sail dories south from Pelican Beach and up the creek. Most hotels in Dangriga are solidly booked for Settlement Day six months or more in advance. Thomas V Ramos, a Garifuna statesman, began the observance of Settlement Day in 1943 and succeeded in having the government declare it a national holiday.

In the weeks before December 31, Garifuna dance troupes kick up the dust in Dangriga's streets doing the lively **John Canoe** (Wanaragua in the Garifuna tongue). A group of six to ten masked and costumed dancers move down the sidestreets, stopping occasionally outside a house to perform the exuberant, African-inspired dance. The dancers, usually all male and ranging in age from adolescents to men in their sixties, dress in white and festoon themselves with pink, green and yellow streamers. Elaborate straw headgear is edged with brightly-coloured pompoms and topped with three or four long feathers, either peacock, parrot or turkey. Oversized wire screen masks lend an eerie African touch to the costumes – an effect which is partly offset by the Nike high-top tennis shoes worn by the younger dancers. But the most essential portion of the costume is strapped just below the knees: strings of cowrie shells, which at every bounce and gyration

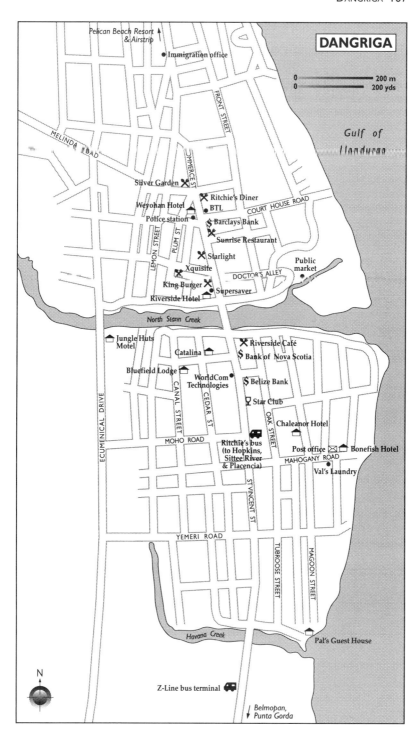

Pelican Beach Resort & Airstrip

Immigration office

DANGRIGA

FRONT STREET

0 ——— 200 m
0 ——— 200 yds

Gulf of
Honduras

MELINDA ROAD

COMMERCE ST

Silver Garden

Ritchie's Diner

Weyohan Hotel

BTL

Police station

COURT HOUSE ROAD

Barclays Bank

LEMON STREET

PLUM ST

Sunrise Restaurant

Starlight

Xquisite

Public
market

King Burger

DOCTOR'S ALLEY

Supersaver

Riverside Hotel

North Stann Creek

Jungle Huts
Motel

Riverside Café

Catalina

Bank of Nova Scotia

Bluefield Lodge

WorldCom
Technologies

Belize Bank

ECUMENICAL DRIVE

CANAL STREET

CEDAR ST

Star Club

Chaleanor Hotel

OAK STREET

MOHO ROAD

Ritchie's bus
(to Hopkins,
Sittee River
& Placencia)

Post office

Bonefish Hotel

MAHOGANY ROAD

Val's Laundry

ST VINCENT ST

YEMERI ROAD

TUBROOSE STREET

MAGOON STREET

Havana Creek

Pal's Guest House

N

Z-Line bus terminal

Belmopan,
Punta Gorda

turn the dancer into a percussion instrument. Dancers take their turns individually, performing a frenzied series of hops to the beat of Garifuna drums and chanting.

Unlike many Garifuna ceremonies, the John Canoe (variously spelled Jonkonnu and Jonkannu) serves a strictly secular purpose: in return for the entertainment, homeowners and bystanders are expected to offer money or rum to the dancers. Variations on the John Canoe are performed throughout much of the English Caribbean during Christmas, particularly in Jamaica, St. Kitts-Nevis and the Bahamas. Its origins among the Garifuna remain unclear, for the Black Caribs are not related to the Afro-Antillian groups which populate these islands (although some historians claim that slaves on St Vincent performed the dance). For that matter, who is John Canoe? Some speculate that the name derives from 'John Konny', the German nickname for an African king in league with Prussian slave traders. Others believe that John Canoe represents Noah of Old Testament fame. Still others claim that the name is a bastardisation of a West African word for sorcerer.

Information and useful addresses

The best source of general tourism advice is with Terry Valentine at Pelican Beach Resort who, at the time of writing, is the BTIA representative for the District. But Pelican Beach Resort is north of town and a bit of a hike. The Riverside Café is also up-to-date on everything happening in the area as is Louise Belisle at the Bluefield Lodge.

Cash and travellers' cheques can be changed at **Belize Bank** or the **Bank of Nova Scotia**, one block south of the creek on St Vincent Street, or Barclays Bank (on Commerce Street north of the creek).

Telephone calls can be made at the **BTL** office on Commerce Street at the corner of Courthouse Road. The post office is located at the corner of Mahogany Road and Ganey Street, a couple of blocks south of the creek. Val's Laundry is just across the street at 1 Sharp Street. Innovative and entrepreneurial, you can wait for your washing while you surf the net in what is Belize's and possibly the world's first internet laundrette. vals@btl.net. If they're closed or off-line try WorldCom Technologies at 15 Vincent Street but you have to pay for one hour at least.

The best grocery store in town is Supersaver next to King Burger. A ramshackle wooden building at the east end of Doctor's Alley along the north shore of North Stann Creek houses the public market; you'll find fish, poultry and meat, but little else except on Fridays, when fresh produce arrives on trucks from Cayo. The rest of the week, Dangriga has little to offer in the way of produce besides withered onions and potatoes.

Excursions
Near town
Melinda Food Products
Makers of the popular hot pepper sauce as well as tropical fruit jams, welcome visitors to their factory just outside town. Call 05 22360 for information.

Further afield
Hummingbird Highway
The Hummingbird Highway provides gorgeous views of forested mountainsides and as of 1999, all but a small 15km stretch in the middle has been resurfaced. It's spectacular country even viewed from a bus window, but if you're driving yourself you'll want to stop at various spots between Belmopan and Dangriga, including the

Blue Hole Cave and St Herman's Cave (see *Chapter 8*). Stann Creek District itself begins as you start your descent at Over-the-Top-Camp, 39km southeast of Belmopan. Here, the Over-the-Top Cool Spot offers food and drink. At this point you can turn north toward Five Blues Lake National Park (see *Chapter 8*) and the Indian Creek Caves. At Hummingbird Gap, another 8km, the highway begins its final descent into the Stann Creek Valley. From here on, citrus groves take over and the scenery becomes decidedly less awesome.

Tobacco Caye

The barrier reef lies 18km directly offshore Dangriga. At the southern end of two sections of this discontinuous reef, Columbus Reef and Tobacco Reef, separated by a narrow channel, lie three palm-covered specks of sand and coral: Tobacco Caye, South Water Caye and Carrie Bow Caye. All three are located directly on the reef, making it easy to snorkel right from shore. It's possible to visit all three, but Tobacco Caye remains the best bet for casual, budget travellers.

Tobacco Caye's five sandy acres are covered with palm trees and simple fishermen's shacks. Now that tourism has supplanted fishing as the economic mainstay of the island, shacks outnumber palm trees, and more are being built. Still, Tobacco Caye remains a low-key, if not exactly deserted, getaway.

The caye's first settlers came in the mid-1600s from New Providence Island, Bahamas. English Puritans, they named their new home after the first crop they planted here. Tobacco Caye later became a semi-permanent fishing camp. Devastated by a 1978 hurricane, the island quickly became grown over by vines and underbrush. Resident fishermen began rebuilding shortly afterward, but the temporary look of Tobacco Caye's wooden structures acknowledges the certainty of hurricanes yet to come. Most of the houses are simple vacation homes, but a handful of fishermen still live here, plying the nearby waters in search of lobster, snapper and deep-water sharks. Old-timers prefer hand-lines, while the younger fishermen increasingly favour spearfishing. Strolling about the island, you'll see split, salted barracuda being sun-dried like laundry on long ropes strung between palm trees.

Several lodging opportunities have developed in recent years.

Lana's on the Reef (tel: 05 22571) is basic but nice and one of the cheapest on the island. BZ$150 including meals.

Gaviota Coral Reef Resort PO Box 151, Dangriga Town; tel/fax: 05 12032, claims to be 'More beautiful than ever after "Mitch" shampooed our reef.' The backpackers' stopover and owner Bert Swasey will do a deal for people wanting to spend a few nights with him. Bert's anecdotes come highly recommended. BZ$100.

Tobacco Cay Lodge tel 05 12033; email: tclodge@btl.net. The newest place on the island, cabanas with private bath. US$150 includes three meals.

Ocean's Edge tel 05 12004; email: beltex@symet.net; web: http://ourworld.compuserve.com/homepages/beltex. Simple accommodation. Each room has a private shower/toilet with running water and electricity. BZ$75 meals included.

Reef End Lodge PO Box 10, Dangriga; tel: 05 22419. 4 rooms with private bath. US$65. They also rent out 2 cabanas.

Boatmen now meet most buses arriving from Belize City to offer rides and/or lodging. You can also arrange a boat to the caye by talking to the owners of the Riverside Cafe. Failing this, you can also wander both sides of North Stann Creek, asking local boatmen if they're headed anywhere near Tobacco Caye. If you go unannounced in this way, however, you run the risk of getting to the caye to find lodging and campsites booked up. With a tent, you can usually talk your way into camping somewhere, but be sure to bring your own food in case local supplies are limited. No matter how you go, plan on spending about BZ$30 pp each way for the boat trip. A special chartered boat could cost up to BZ$125! The boat ride itself can be quite rough; expect to get wet and protect your cameras in at least two plastic bags. And finally, keep in mind that stormy weather can occasionally prevent even the islanders' seaworthy 7m fibreglass skiffs from making the trip to or from Tobacco Caye.

Snorkelling is best from the southwestern end of the island. Enter the water near a small hut built over the water. Close by in very shallow water lies a rock spine that provided cover for a 1.5m nurse shark when we were there. Remember that although you can get quite close to these sluggish creatures, they are responsible for the majority of shark bites in the Caribbean – mostly because swimmers insist on tugging on their fins to 'wake' them. Continue out into deeper water toward the lip of the protecting reef. Here you're likely to see angelfish, filefish, grunts, squirrelfish, barracuda and an occasional spotted eagle ray. Local fishermen call these magnificent animals 'pinto ponies' because they leap high out of the water in an effort to dislodge 'sucker fish' (remoras). If the seas are calm you may be able to continue swimming around to the left. At this point you'll be on the outside of the reef, so be very conscious of surge and current that might throw you against the rocks.

A second snorkelling opportunity lies to the northwest of the island. Here, in the lee of the reef, it's fairly easy to locate moray eels. This area has recently hosted Earthwatch groups studying not only morays but also grunts and squirrelfish.

Kayakers will find the shallow, protective reef unbroken from Tobacco Caye south to South Water Caye. One tour operator, Island Expeditions Co, ferries kayakers out to Coco Plum Caye (8km west of Tobacco Caye) to avoid the open water between Dangriga and the barrier reef. From there, kayakers paddle east to Tobacco Caye and then along the reef as far as the Silk Cayes, over 50km to the south. The last leg of the trip involves a 35km paddle west to Laughing Bird Caye and Placencia. The same company will rent you a kayak in Dangriga, ferry you out to the barrier reef and turn you loose on your own. See *Placencia, Excursions* below for more information on kayak tour operators in the area.

Tobacco Caye plays host to the magnificent frigatebird, scores of which hover effortlessly on the thermals overhead. Brown pelicans provide comic relief, crashing into the sea in an ungainly but supremely effective fishing manoeuvre. Birders can also visit the brown boobies and frigate birds on Man of War Caye, a nearby sanctuary.

South Water Caye

South Water Caye lies roughly 10km south of Tobacco Caye. Largest of the three cayes along the reef in this area (440m long and 100m wide), South Water boasts the most luxurious – and expensive – accommodation.

The Blue Marlin Lodge 15 Mahogany Street, PO Box 21, Dangriga; tel: 05 22243; toll free in the US: 1 800 798 1558; fax: 05 22296; email: marlin@btl.net; web: www.bluemarlinlodge.com. Owned by Rosella Zabaneh. Charges from US$599 for three nights in a double room with fans, private bath, hot water, constant electricity and three meals included. Boat transport costs an additional US$15 pp round trip, more if you want special charter service. A special chartered round-trip costs US$125. The lodge is highly recommended and, in addition to diving, offers sailboarding, volleyball, horseshoes and billiards. The longest boat ride to dive sites takes 15min. All diving is drift diving. Dive packages run US$1,195 for a week, with two dives per day. Fishing packages run US$1,650 per week. Bring your own fishing tackle, rentals are limited. This PADI International diving resort offers scuba instruction, and runs dive trips from a fleet of boats including a 30ft Delta, a 30ft Mako and a 23ft Mako. Write PO Box 21, Dangriga (tel: 05 22243; fax: 05 22296 or toll-free in the US 1 800 798 1558) for information and reservations.

The **Pelican Beach Resort** in Dangriga rents a couple of wooden cottages on stilts sleeping 4–6 people, furnished with beds, linen, stove, cooking utensils, shower and bathroom for US$207 for a double per day plus tax. Lighting is provided by kerosene lanterns. They also rent 5 rooms at the Pelican's Pouch on the western side each with private half-baths and all the same amenities as the cottages. Each sleeps up to four, costing US$183 for a double and US$55 for each additional person per day. Transportation out to the caye costs US$30 pp or US$170 for 1–6 passengers each way. Pelican's University on South Water Caye is more suited to large groups or families. Half baths upstairs and a kitchen and recreation area downstairs. Trips can be arranged to rainforest, mangrove and marine habitats. US$65 pp includes meals.

Leslie Cottages PO Box 231, Dangriga, Stann Creek District; tel/fax: 05 37076; email: izebelize@btl.net or jall@btl.net. 5 cabanas with private baths, meals and use of kayaks and sailboat. A full service PADI dive shop and fishing charters are also available. Special rates for educational groups.

A number of good dives are located within striking distance of South Water Caye. Local fishermen discovered the most unusual of these sites, now dubbed 'The Black Hole' by Blue Marlin Lodge divemasters. Not to be confused with the Blue Hole made famous by Cousteau, the Black Hole lies about 15km north of Tobacco Caye. A sandy bottom at 9m slopes gradually to the opening at 17m. The opening itself is only 2.5m wide by 7.5m long, leading to a series of huge submarine 'rooms' and caverns. The bottom, a sand cone, lies in at least 45m of water, although divers generally explore the site at about 24m. Unlike the relatively sterile Blue Hole, the Black Hole boasts a population of sharks, including black-tips, nurses, browns and even hammerheads. Biologists from the Smithsonian Institution research station at Carrie Bow Caye are currently investigating the site. For the moment, divemasters at the Blue Marlin Lodge are keeping the spot relatively secret, and they're the only ones currently running trips there. This is no dive for beginners.

Carrie Bow Caye

This islet, 1.5km south of South Water Caye, was known until 1944 as Ellen Caye. Henry T A Bowman bought the islet in 1943, built a summer home the following year, and renamed it for his wife Carrie. At that time, the caye was roughly twice the size it is now – 120m long by 40m wide – and surrounded by mangrove. Palm trees had been planted in the early 1900s, of which a handful have survived nearly a century of storms and hurricanes. In 1972 the Smithsonian Institution established a marine biology laboratory on Carrie Bow, and research on coral reef ecology has concentrated on this portion of the Belizean barrier reef ever since. The lab welcomes visitors, but no overnight accommodations are available. Both the Blue Marlin Lodge on South Water Caye and the Bonefish Hotel in Dangriga run day trips here for snorkelling and birdwatching. The latter charges US$185 for 2-4 people, US$35 each for extra persons, travelling to Carrie Bow, Tobacco Caye, Coco Plum Caye and the bird sanctuary at Man of War Caye. The Smithsonian continues to publish scientific papers on coral reef ecology based on the research gathered at Carrie Bow.

Wee Wee Caye

About 7km outhwest of Carrie Bow Caye lies the tiny mangrove island called Wee Wee Caye. Under a lease from the Belize government, Paul and Mary Shave operate the Wee Wee Caye Marine Lab here, in conjunction with the Possum

Point Biological Station. Both field stations are available to groups for educational stays (see *Sittee River* below for details).

Gales Point and Southern Lagoon

Gales Point is a narrow finger peninsula extending 3km miles into the vast Southern Lagoon. Although it actually lies in Belize District, Gales Point has been included in this chapter because most visitor access to the area is via Dangriga.

Gales Point Village was originally founded as a logwood camp, and it's still the perfect place to experience Belize City as it must have been at the turn of the century. The village currently manages without electricity (although it's reportedly on the way), but does have a community telephone. At least two international recluses – a British woman and a former New York City lawyer – call Gales Point home and, like Placencia, the village is known throughout Belize as a hard-drinking party town. But the real draw here is the surrounding lagoon, a marshy haven for gamefish (snook and tarpon) bird life (especially ibises, herons and egrets), and manatees. Each April, May and June, manatees gather at a particular spot in the Southern Lagoon to breed, and during this time they can be readily observed at a respectful distance from a boat. Your chances of actually sighting a manatee are better here in the Southern Lagoon than anywhere else in Belize, although during the non-breeding months you may see little more than a leathery grey spatulate tail slipping beneath the surface. See *Chapter 3, Fauna* for more information on these mammals.

Driving, you can take the pot-holed Manatee (New Coastal) Highway, which heads south from the Western Highway at Mile 31, the Democracia turnoff. This 60km road often becomes impassable following heavy rains. Buses between Dangriga and Belize City taking the Coastal Highway can drop you off at the turn-off for Gales Point from where you can walk the four miles to town. If you book accommodation in advance you can arrange to be picked up. The most scenic mode of transport is by boat. Some tour companies organise trips or you can call the community telephone operator at 02 12031 to check on the latest schedule.

The Pelican Beach Resort in Dangriga offers manatee tours to the Southern Lagoon in conjunction with other local attractions. The boat portion of the trip, in a wooden dory, lasts about three hours. They also make this trip entirely by boat during good weather.

The placid inland waterway between Belize City and Dangriga via the Southern Lagoon has been used as a commerce route for years, and the view of distant mountains which unfolds as you enter the lagoon is spectacular. At the far end of Southern Lagoon, boats must pass through Main Creek before emerging into Northern Lagoon, full of shallows and submerged snares. The way now snakes through low-lying mangrove marsh to a small unnamed tributary of the Sibun River, where much of the movie *The Mosquito Coast* was filmed. After heading briefly downstream on the Sibun, the boat turns into Boom Creek, a sinuous watery path leading to Jones Lagoon. The last half hour of the journey is spent heading northeast on a straight line via Burdon Canal to Haulover Creek, and then downstream through the heart of Belize City.

Pelican Beach Resort in Dangriga offers pontoon boat trips from Belize City to Gales Point via the lagoons (or the reverse trip) for US$65 pp (3–5 people, US$225 minimum).

Just north of Gales Point the Southern Lagoon empties via a small waterway onto a beach known as Manatee Bar. Here, during the months of June and July, endangered hawksbill turtles as well as green sea turtles and loggerhead turtles lay their eggs. After an incubation time that generally lasts 60 days, the luckiest hatch and find their way into the sea. Even before hatching, the eggs are easy prey for raccoons and birds. Belizeans have recently begun patrolling the beach to prevent poaching and to help stack the deck in the young turtles' favour. This they do by screening nests from predators and helping the newly hatched young to navigate past root masses and other hazards. The programme is similar to the one started on Ambergris Caye (see *Chapter 13* and *Chapter 3, Reptiles*, and enquire at the Hol Chan Marine Reserve office in San Pedro for more information).

Manatee Lodge provides the only formal lodging in Gales Point village, and it's quite expensive, US$74 with private bath, fans. Meals add another US$30. New ownership and management since October 1999 has brought in a few changes. Although primarily a luxury sport-fishing camp, the staff will be happy to take you on wildlife cruises in the lagoon. For more information write PO Box 1242, Belize City, tel/fax: 02 12040; toll free in the US 1 800 334 7942; email: manatee@btl.net, web: www.manateelodge.com.

Cheap lodging can be had by staying with villagers with the **Home Stay Bed &Breakfast Association**. Currently, most homes are charging BZ$15 for a couple, or BZ$6 for pitching a tent. You can call ahead on 02 12031 Meals and guided trips in the area can also be arranged through the B&B Association.

Gentle's Cool Spot (tel: 02 12031) and **Manatee Shores** (tel: 02 12033) both have basic accommodation at BZ$20.

Camping is available at **Metho's Coconut Campground** (tel: 02 12031) charging BZ$5 pp.

Sittee River

The Sittee River winds its mazy way down to the Caribbean just 8km south of Hopkins. Here, Paul and Mary Shave own and operate **Possum Point Biological Station**, an educational and research site catering exclusively to groups – high school, college, general interest and natural history societies. The station, on 44 acres of pristine jungle, consists of cottage style housing for up to 30 people, a dining hall/classroom, showers and toilet facilities. The Shaves also operate **Wee Wee Caye Marine Lab** on a tiny mangrove island 14km offshore in the barrier reef chain.

Educational trips to one or both sites can be tailored to the group's particular interest. Birders have the opportunity to add over 100 species to their life lists, and the forest is home to peccaries, bats, coatimundis, paca ('gibnut'), anteaters, iguanas, boa constrictors and blue Morpho butterflies. Orchids, palms, fig trees, bamboo and native hardwoods dot the banks of Sittee River; Morelets crocodiles have occasionally been sighted. The Shaves maintain over 1.5km of trails through the forest. Snorkellers at Wee Wee Caye will find mangrove lagoons, coral patch reefs and turtle grass beds nearby, each providing a host of ecological niches for fish and invertebrates. (The Shaves don't encourage scuba diving and have no equipment, but gear can be rented at the Blue Marlin Lodge on South Water Caye.) Snorkelling here is excellent.

At both field stations, experienced guides accompany guests throughout their stay, and side trips to the Cockscomb Basin Wildlife Sanctuary, Hopkins, South Stann Creek and nearby cayes can be easily arranged.

Groups of ten or more people can spend a week at either or both field stations for US$555 pp (US$775 pp for two weeks). This price includes round trip airfare from Belize City to Dangriga, ground transport to Possum Point, boat trips, guides, a side trip to Cockscomb, lodging and three meals daily. Possum Point and Wee Wee Caye aren't resorts, nor do they aspire to be; accommodations at both sites are clean but simple, with outhouses, kerosene lamps and fresh water from cisterns.

The Shaves also operate **Bocatura Bank Campground** and cottages, 8km upstream from the mouth of the Sittee River. The campground and two cottages are open to either groups or individuals. Camping costs US$10 pp; this includes raised wooden tent platforms for 2-, 3-, or 4-person tents, drinking water cisterns, gravity showers, pit toilets and a thatched cooking and picnic area. Campers must bring their own tents, bedding and food (although a few staples can be bought in Sittee River Village). Groups (minimum 10 people) can camp for US$7 pp, or US $15 pp with food and cook provided. The two concrete cottages cost US$300–375 per week, depending on number in your party; a minimum of three nights can be booked for US$150–200. Both cottages have screened windows, tile floors, stove, refrigerator, cooking utensils, bedding and kerosene lamps; shower and outhouse are shared.

On a space available basis, guests at the campground and cottages may be able to participate in the group field trips offered at Possum Point and Wee Wee Caye biological stations. Even if this isn't possible, you can arrange natural history field trips through the Shaves. Snorkelling and natural history trips to the offshore cayes (1–4 people) cost US$100 half day or US$175 full day. Fishing trips (1–2 people) for barracuda, snook, snapper, grouper, tarpon and crevalle jack run anywhere from US$75 half day to US$175 full day depending on whether you fish the cayes or the Sittee River. An all-day guided tubing trip on South Stann Creek costs US$150 for 1–4 people (see *Cockscomb Basin Wildlife Sanctuary* below for details). Side trips to the Sanctuary itself can also be arranged.

For more information or reservations, write to Possum Point Biological Station, Sittee River, Stann Creek District (tel: 05 37021; fax 05 22038 email: possumpt@btl.net; web: www.marineecology.com). You can also try the community telephone in Sittee River Village (05 22006).

Lillpat Sittee River Resort (PO Box 10, Dangriga; tel/fax: 05 12019; email: lillpat@btl.net; web: www.lillpat.com) is a small but comfortable lodge set in 50 acres of jungle on the banks of the River Sittee. Four rooms with AC opening up to a central swimming pool. US$145 a night. Food at the international restaurant is extra. Guided canoe trips along the Sittee River, excursions to the Jaguar Sanctuary and catch and release fishing trips can be organised.

The **Pelican Beach Resort** in Dangriga also offers boat trips on the Sittee River for US$145. Customized trips that include Cockscomb Sanctuary and Hopkins can also be arranged.

In Sittee Village, you'll find overnight accommodations at **Mrs McKenzie's Guest House**. Write to PO Box 563, Belize City, or call the Sittee Village community telephone for information. **Toucan Sittee**; tel: 05 37039, has budget accommodation from BZ$14 with riverside apartments from BZ$75. They can help organise diving, fishing, and rent out canoes and bikes.

Glover's Reef Atoll Resort has budget accommodations in town, especially for guests awaiting the weekly boat out to Long Caye, Glover's Reef. Call the Lomont family at 014 8351 or write to them at PO Box 563, Belize City.

HOPKINS

Situated along a broad crescent of white sand beach eight miles south of Dangriga, Hopkins has the best natural setting of Belize's four Garifuna villages (the others being Seine Bight, Georgetown and Barranco). For the moment, Hopkins retains its peculiar ramshackle charm. There are no satellite dishes, no locked doors, no real stores or shops, no mechanized din. None of this prevents the locals from throwing a notoriously lively Settlement Day celebration, but most of the year, Hopkins feels like a forgotten tropical backwater, perfectly content to miss out on the hubbub of Belize's second largest city just 13km up the coast. Pigs roam Hopkins' single dirt road, snuffling out fallen mangoes. Fishermen use their dugout canoes to ferry goods, dragging them on tethers as they walk up the long, crescent-shaped beach. Children pause in their ball game as you pass, calling 'hello' repeatedly and in such rapid-fire succession that you suspect they may be poking sly fun; their innocent grins tell you they're not. Until the opening of the Barranco Village Guest House (see *Chapter 12, Excursions*), visiting Hopkins was the only way to experience daily life in a coastal Garifuna village.

History

Hopkins is the most recently settled of Belize's Garifuna villages, founded in 1942 after an unnamed hurricane levelled the original settlement just up the coast at New Town. The new village took its name from Frederick Charles Hopkins, a well-loved Roman Catholic bishop who drowned in 1923. Hurricane Hattie destroyed the schoolhouse along with scores of homes in 1961. The village remained inactive for a time following Hattie, but soon began rebuilding; this time around, villagers built the schoolhouse and several other structures with concrete. Hopkins was recently the site of a 'Cultural Retrieval' project, sponsored by the National Garifuna Council and the University of the West Indies, aimed at fostering pride in the Garifuna language and culture.

Getting there

The daily Ritchie's bus from Dangriga to Placencia, leaving at 11.30, passes through Hopkins. Call the community telephone operator in Hopkins (tel: 05 22033 or 05 22803) for the schedule. The ride takes about 1 hour 45 minutes. Several buses leave Placencia early in the morning but not all pass through Hopkins so check with the driver. Alternatively, try asking at the Dangriga public market before 10.00 or along North Stann Creek; fishermen from Hopkins frequently return after selling their catch at the market. The boat trip takes only about 20 minutes, but be prepared to get wet if seas are choppy. The young men hanging around the south side of the Stann Creek bridge can usually find a truck or boat headed to Hopkins, but you'll probably be asked for a 'finder's fee'. Pelican Beach Resort in Dangriga offers round-trip van transportation to Hopkins. The town's growing popularity with travellers will undoubtedly spawn more scheduled transportation, so ask around Dangriga for the latest information.

Finally, you can always hike into Hopkins. Catch the Z-Line bus from Dangriga to Punta Gorda and ask to be let off on the Southern Highway at the Hopkins turn-off. From here it's a 1 hour 20 minute walk on a perfectly straight, flat dirt road. Have mosquito repellent handy. Just west of town, the road passes through a savanna that is home to bare-throated tiger herons (*Tigrisoma mexicanum*), great blue herons (*Ardea herodias*, locally known as the 'Full Pot') and countless frogs. Hitchhiking is possible, but traffic can be erratic along this stretch. When leaving Hopkins this way, plan to hike out so that you're at the Southern Highway in time to flag down the morning Z-Line from Punta Gorda; schedules change, so ask locals. Try hitching while you wait for the bus; many of the trucks heading north will be going to Dangriga.

The road into town ends at a junction within sight of the beach; from here you can walk south along the village road which parallels the beach.

Where to stay

All lodging is simple. Regardless of where you stay, bring a flashlight, mosquito coils, and repellent; when the breeze dies, Hopkins' sandflies and mosquitoes come out to feed.

Sandy Beach Lodge A 20-minute walk south from the village junction (tel: 05 37006). Located just 50m from the beach, the Lodge was built in 1988 and consists of 2 thatched cottages divided into 6 rooms, with a communal dining hut. BZ$36. Usually reliable onshore breezes take the place of fans. The lodge is operated by the Sandy Beach Women's Cooperative Society Limited, founded by ten village women in 1986. It's one of the rare opportunities for visitors to eat genuine Garifuna food in Belize.

Jaguar Reef Lodge tel/fax: 02 12041; in the US: 1 800 289 5756; email: jaguarreef@btl.net; web: www.jaguarreef.com. A luxury lodge in Hopkins amongst beautiful landscaping that provides everything you need to relax. Double cabanas are between US$120–185 with food adding US$33. Scuba is available as are kayaks, bikes and trips to the nearby cayes.

Hopkins Inn Located just south of the centre of town away from the beach (tel: 05 37013; email: hopkinsinns@btl.net), offers budget lodging in small cabanas.

Parasol is to the north of town (tel: 05 37009) with a couple of cabins, with private bathroom, on the sea.

Swinging Armadillos is just north of town (tel: 05 37016), with a couple of rooms to rent. Near to the bar of the same name which is a must for anyone in Hopkins.

Ransom's (tel: 05 22038) is on the sea. 2-room cabanas with bikes and kayaks for rent. BZ$28.

You can also ask locals about renting houses. These can often be had for around BZ$10 a night. A secluded vacation cabin located half a mile down the beach is often available during the summer months; ask for Lisa in town, or write to the owners, Charles and Sharon Emerson, PO Box 648, Langley, WA 98260.

Where to eat
Besides the Sandy Beach Lodge, meals can be arranged with local women if you ask in advance. Most locals will point you to a house serving Garifuna food located just north of the village centre junction. Groceries are in short supply in Hopkins. Try the small shack at the junction, or the post office a short walk south of the junction on your right. These places offer eggs, warm Fanta sodas, cookies from Trinidad-Tobago and canned sardines from Japan. Cold beer can be had at the Laru Beya Club right on the beach near the junction (the name means 'seashore' in Garifuna). This is where the locals play dominoes, bantering in a lively mixture of Garifuna and occasional Creole English.

What to do
Second Nature Divers (tel: 05 37039 or 014 8012; email: divers@btl.net) is a full-service dive operation based in the Hopkins/Sittee River area. They can organise PADI courses locally as well as trips further afield to the Barrier Reef and Glover's. A good spot to use for trips. They can also organise snorkel trips, fishing, river tours and, of course, trips to the Jaguar Sanctuary.

COCKSCOMB BASIN WILDLIFE SANCTUARY
After poring over the visitor notebooks, we found that 99% of all guests leave without so much as a glimpse of jaguar tracks at what is popularly known as the 'Jaguar Sanctuary'. Your chances of seeing a jaguar remain very slim, but there does seem to have been an increase in sightings in recent years. If after a short trip you are not one of the lucky ones, don't worry, you'll be in good company. Dr Alan Rabinowitz, the founder of the Sanctuary and an expert in big cats, lived here for two months before sighting his first jaguar.

That said, you won't leave the Sanctuary disappointed. Birders are likely to fill their notebooks with scarlet-rumped tanagers, boat-billed herons and blue-crowned motmots. Budding herpetologists will find leopard frogs, anoles, basilisk lizards and fer-de-lances. Entomologists have but to stray outside their cabin at night to find the trails lit by the blue-green reflections of thousands of spiders on the hunt. Botanists can roam through kaway swamps and watch hummingbirds pollinate fire-red *Heliconias*. Climbers can tackle Belize's second highest peak. Even the most casual jungle-lover will enjoy strolling the well-kept trails through forest and swamp. And rest assured that the elusive cats are out there with you. Some have been fortunate enough to spot jaguars from their cars on day trips. Simply put, the Cockscomb Basin Wildlife Sanctuary is a must-see for any serious naturalist visiting Belize.

History

The world's only jaguar sanctuary got its start in 1983, when the New York Zoological Society sent Dr Alan Rabinowitz to Belize on a two-year study of jaguar ecology. At that time, jaguar hunting had been officially outlawed in Belize for ten years, but both poachers and local cattlemen continued to shoot *Panthera onca*, the third largest cat in the world and most powerful land predator in Central and South America. Even Maya Indians, whose ancestors had revered the jaguar, incorporating its image in their religious art, now feared and despised the big cat. Jaguars had long since been hunted out of existence in the US, and severely impacted in other parts of their former range, which extended from southern Arizona to the middle of Argentina.

After months of field work, Rabinowitz zeroed in on the moist lowland jungles of the Cockscomb Basin. The area appeared to support not only a healthy population of jaguars, but also of other endangered species including the ocelot, margay, Baird's tapir and scarlet macaw. He set up shop in a logging camp, now the site of the Sanctuary headquarters. It is incredible to roam these quiet grounds today, knowing that 20 years ago they were home to about 100 people, boasting electric street lamps, TV, video, numerous buildings and manicured lawns.

Rabinowitz's two years at Cockscomb are splendidly chronicled in his 1986 book *Jaguar*, a must-read for anyone visiting the Sanctuary (see *Appendix 2, Further Reading*). Along the way, he endured the loss of one of his Maya workers (to a fer-de-lance), the death of several of his radio-collared jaguars (to hunters), and fierce local resentment. His studies of radio-collared jaguars and carcasses convinced him that healthy jaguars rarely left the jungle to attack cattle; nearly 80% of the 'problem' cats had been shot previously. At the end of his two years, Rabinowitz argued that a sanctuary be set aside at Cockscomb, one large enough to support the jaguar's natural prey, thus minimising attacks on cattle.

The sanctuary concept immediately found enthusiastic supporters among the Belize Audubon Society and the World Wildlife Fund. Government officials, on the other hand, needed more prodding. Rabinowitz convinced them that further deforestation of the Cockscomb Basin could easily flood the ranches and citrus plantations downstream. Furthermore, siltation could smother the nation's premiere tourist attraction, the barrier reef, just 55km away. In late 1984, the government set aside 108,000 acres as a Forest Reserve. Belize went a step further in February 1986, establishing 3,640 acres within the Reserve as a Wildlife Sanctuary specifically for the study and preservation of jaguars. Maya that once lived within the forest reserve were relocated 8km away, where they formed a grass-roots conservation support group and a handicraft cooperative. The current sanctuary manager and all three wardens are villagers, as are the local guides.

Still, most of the Cockscomb Basin remained a Forest Reserve, which allowed the government the option of selling concessions for logging, agriculture and mining. Citrus growers in particular were encroaching upon the Forest Reserve boundaries. Manager Ernesto Saqui and members of the Belize Audubon Society, assisted by Conservation International and the British army, mounted a week-long expedition into the furthest reaches of the Reserve, eventually recommending that the Sanctuary be expanded. World Wildlife Fund-US stepped in at this point, offering financial support for an expansion. A bold step came in late 1990, when Minister of Natural Resources, Florencio Marin, announced that the Sanctuary would expand to include the entire 108,000 acres of former Forest Reserve. In a single courageous move, the government of Belize had increased the jaguar sanctuary thirty-fold.

Today the importance and value of Cockscomb is being appreciated more and more. In 1998, a further 12,000 acres was added to the sanctuary's boundaries to make a contiguous protected area with Bladen Nature Reserve and Chiquibul National Park.

Getting there

The reserve headquarters are located 11km off the Southern Highway on a road leading west from Maya Center. This is as close as you can get on public transportation. Many visitors take the Z-Line bus either from Dangriga or from Punta Gorda, get off at Maya Center, and walk in. You can also catch the morning bus from Placencia headed to Dangriga; the ride to Maya Center takes close to 2 hours and costs BZ$5 (see *Placencia* below for bus schedule). The walk takes most travellers about 2 hours. It's a moderately uphill grade with plenty of dips and rises, and numerous opportunities to see birds and other wildlife. There's little vehicular traffic on this road – most of the staff ride in on bicycles – but you can occasionally hitch a ride with other travellers in a rented car. We once met a couple who were picked up hitching by none other than Dr Rabinowitz himself, on a brief return visit to the Sanctuary. When walking out of the reserve, plan on leaving very early in the morning if you plan to flag down the Z-Line bus headed to Dangriga – added to that early morning is the best time to see animals along the road. Ask the sanctuary personnel about schedules, because they change frequently.

If you want to save your feet for walking the trails themselves, there are other less strenuous options: virtually every major hotel and guide service in Belize offers guided tours (generally one-day) to the Sanctuary. In Dangriga, check in at the Pelican Beach Hotel or the Bonefish Hotel. In Placencia, almost any of the hotels can arrange for a day-trip. Try Kitty's which comes highly recommended with overnight trips with a university-trained naturalist. Possum Point Biological Station and Bocatura Bank Campground, both at Sittee River, offer guided side trips to the Sanctuary for groups and individuals (see *Sittee River* above for details).

The Pelican Beach Resort in Dangriga offers transportation to the Sanctuary for about US$60 pp (minimum 4 passengers), charging extra if you want to stay overnight and be picked up the next morning.

You could also arrange for a taxi. Gregorio Chun lives in Maya Center (tel: 051 2044) and can pick you up from anywhere in Belize for a price. He is also a licensed guide BZ$40 for a day trip, BZ$65 for a night hike. A taxi to the sanctuary headquarters from Maya Center costs BZ$35.

Finally, several tour operators such as International Expeditions offer a stay at the Sanctuary as part of their package deals (see *Chapter 4, Package Tours*). These are often overnight trips and come highly recommended.

Regardless of the way you come, be sure to register first at the craft shop next to the highway in Maya Center. Here you can also support the village economy by

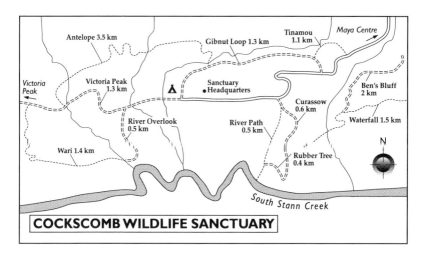

purchasing local crafts at reasonable prices. The women's cooperative offers colourful embroidery, clay beads, and slate carved with Maya glyphs. You can buy last-minute camping supplies (eggs, onions, canned goods, cold soft drinks) next door at a tiny grocery and snack stand, or there is another one on the main road.

If you arrive before the craft shop opens you can enter the park without any problems. You will be asked to pay the BZ$10 entrance fee to the park when you reach the headquarters.

Where to stay
Several lodging possibilities exist at the sanctuary.

Overnight lodging is available in basic dormitory-style cabins at the headquarters for BZ$15 pp. Cabins include simple bedding, screened doors and windows, kerosene lanterns and benches. More comfortable cabins exist which have shared compost toilets, solar-powered electricity and showers sleeping up to six people in a room at BZ$34 pp. Private cabins for four people have bathrooms, shower and toilet. BZ$90 pp.

Food is self-catering unless you come with a group that brings a cook. The kitchen has a couple of stoves and all the basic cooking and eating utensils but you will need to bring all your own food as there is none available at the headquarters. We recommend you bring towels, dish soap, dish scrubber, reliable matches (ie: not the local Toucan brand), mosquito coils, can opener, knife and an alarm clock. You can't always count on these items being in the cabin or in working order.

If you plan to stay in the cabins, and especially if you're hiking in, it's advisable to call ahead to avoid disappointment. Tour groups occasionally usurp all the cabin space. The Belize Audubon Society recommends writing to them at PO Box 1001, 12 Fort Street, Belize City, Belize or contact them at tel: 02 35004/34987/34988; fax: 02 34985; email: bas@btl.net. Unfortunately, communication between the Society and the Sanctuary can be chancy. Calling the Maya Center community telephone on 05 22666 can be helpful but they will not know of any group bookings.

Camping just west of the headquarters costs BZ$5 pp. You can sling hammocks in either of two thatched huts, or simply pitch a tent on the level grass field. Facilities include a drinking water cistern, a covered picnic table and two outhouses. Watch out for fire ants around the camping area and the cabins.

What to see

The trail system at Cockscomb includes 13 short trails totalling nearly 25km, plus a path – actually an old logging road – leading to the base of Victoria Peak. The shorter trails, ranging from 0.5km to 3.5km and each fairly distinct, can theoretically all be seen in two days of tramping, but there's no sense hurrying. All trails start close to the Sanctuary headquarters, where you'll find a map posted.

The **River Path** and **Currasow Trail** are well manicured and short (0.5km and 0.6km respectively), both leading gently downhill to South Stann Creek. These are jungle trails, despite their utterly civilised appearance. Late one afternoon we surprised a venomous tommygoff (fer-de-lance) just off the Currasow. You'll find a pleasant shaded picnic area overlooking the creek at the end of the River Path. From here you can backtrack a short distance and follow the Rubber Tree Trail as it roughly parallels the creek, intersecting the Currasow Trail after 0.4km. Both the Currasow and Rubber Tree are self-guided nature trails, with certain trees and plants numbered to correspond with an educational pamphlet available at the Sanctuary manager's office.

Fording a small, rocky tributary of South Stann Creek midway along the Currasow Trail places you at the beginning of the Sanctuary's two most popular hikes, Ben's Bluff and Water Fall. The trail remains flat for a while before ascending a short hill with a wooden bench at the top. The path then dips down the hill to a tiny creek, where the **Waterfall Trail** (0.5km) branches off to the right. Crossing the creek puts you on the most demanding of the short trails, Ben's Bluff (2km). Climbing immediately, the path becomes steep and slippery until reaching a small knoll and another wooden bench. From here the trail drops to an even smaller waterway before ascending again, passing a third bench midway up the steep slope. Just beyond the bench, the trail breaks out into sparse pine forest with fine views to the east. The path meanders up through pines and dense clusters of fern to the top of the bluff. Here you're treated to spectacular views of misty foothills and unbroken rainforest in all directions.

The Waterfall Trail (0.5km) begins a moderate climb after its junction with Ben's Bluff Trail. It levels off for a short distance, then dips abruptly, landing you on the shore of a deep and refreshingly cool pond at the base of a small waterfall. Scores of tiny fish come to nibble harmlessly on bathers.

The **Victoria Peak Trail**, broad and manicured at the start, winds through tall grasses until joining the Wari Trail Cutoff to the left at 1.3km, from where it rapidly deteriorates (see below). The **Wari Trail** (1.4km) passes through closed-canopy jungle. As the path approaches South Stann Creek, a short side trail heads off toward the river bank and a kaway swamp, a stagnant backwater studded with buttress roots and alive with blue hummingbirds with white tails. The **River Overlook Trail** (0.1km) joins the Wari near the creek bank. Don't be misled by false trails forking away from South Stann Creek; stay on the trail closest to the creek.

From the River Overlook Trail you can wade into South Stann Creek with truck inner tubes (available at the headquarters) and float down to the picnic area at the end of the River Path. One traveller we met continued down the creek for another eight hours until reaching the Southern Highway, sighting lots of birds and mammals along the way. (Possum Point Biological Station and Bocatura Campground offer this tubing trip as a guided tour for 1-4 people, US$150 full day, see *Sittee River* above).

Both the **Antelope Trail** (3.5km) and the **Gibnut Trail** (1.3km) wind through closed-canopy lowland forest. The Antelope branches off to the left from the Gibnut at a small wooden bridge, traversing high ground above the creek. At one point, the trail drops sharply to the left; ford the stream here and continue up the slope on the opposite bank. Continuing straight rather than taking this sharp left will eventually land you on the streambank, but the 'trail' dead-ends on the far side. Be aware that the Antelope Trail crosses at least three wooden bridges that aren't shown on the map at headquarters.

The **Tinamou Trail** (1.1km) is a flat, easy path that branches off from the Gibnut and eventually lands you back on the road. The road itself offers great birding, particularly in the early morning. Watch for aracaris, sleek, compact toucans, high in the trumpet trees.

Victoria Peak, at 1,130m, stood into the mist directly west of the headquarters. It's possible to spend days at the Sanctuary and never see Victoria Peak for the clouds. The summit can be reached in the dry season only – March, April or May. Once the rains begin, clouds hide the view, and the rocks near the peak become slick and dangerous. Trips as late as the end of June have been made in exceptionally dry years. You will need a permit from the Forestry Department in Belmopan if you want to climb and you have to climb with a guide costing BZ$50 per day regardless of the group size. The Sanctuary office should be able to arrange a guide for you but call in advance if you are tight for time. Seasoned backcountry hikers can make the round trip in three days, but it's far more enjoyable as a four-day trip, two in and two out. A normal trip brings you to the base of the peak itself on the second night, making the final ascent on the third day and the return to headquarters on the fourth day. You'll have to bring your own tent and food, although you may want to share some of your food with your guide; they generally bring only a small supply of tortillas for themselves. The first part of the trip follows an abandoned and overgrown logging road. Depending on how many groups have gone before you, your guide may have some extensive hacking to clear the trail. Along the way you may come across ocelots, Baird's tapirs, opposums, turtles or jaguarundis. Bird life is exceptional, and the area is loaded with orchids. The hiking is tough even during dry spells, with a number of creeks to be forded via slippery logs. The intense tropical heat makes this a new experience for even the most seasoned temperate-clime hikers, and there are ticks galore along the trail. Don't feel bad if you have to turn back; you won't be the first. At the middle or end of the second day you should be at the base, where all semblance of a trail disappears, and you'll begin hiking up and down a series of ridges slowly ascending the peak. The final scramble involves a steep rock face and some easy ropework. The peak itself is covered with low grass and rocks, affording views of the Maya Mountains in all directions (assuming the frequent mists don't obscure them).

There is talk of possibly opening up a trail to The Outlier, on most days the highest visible peak from the headquarters.

Don't miss a chance to explore the trails at night. Along the roads and open trails you're almost certain to spot the reflective amber eyes of the common pauraque (*Nyctidromus albicollis*). This nocturnal bird spends much of its time on the ground, even during the daylight hours, when it blends masterfully into the background as a 'dead leaf'. Also abundant along the trails is the tiny blue-green sparkle of spider eyes. Listen for the distinctive, woodpecker-like call of the rare spectacled owl, as well as the more commonly-heard mottled owl and ferruginous pygmy-owl.

Birding is excellent. One group that spent three days at the Reserve saw or heard an average of 90 species each day. Some of the more commonly-seen birds include: the collared trogon (*Trogon collaris*), a close relative of the quetzal; the crested guan (*Penelope purpurascens*); all three Belizean toucans, the emerald toucanet (*Aulacorhynchus prasinus*), the collared aracari (*Pteroglossus torquatus*), and the imposingly large keel-billed toucan (*Ramphastos sulfuratus*); the black hawk-eagle (*Spizaetus tyrannus*); the scarlet-rumped tanager (*Ramphocelus passerinii*) and at least a dozen different hummingbird species. Don't overlook the road during your hikes – during the early morning hours it's a great place to spot toucans and birds of prey.

Information and useful addresses

Anyone planning even a day trip to the Sanctuary should bring binoculars, a long-sleeved shirt, long pants, insect repellent, water bottles, a daypack, a complete change of clothes, swimming trunks (for tubing the creek), extra socks and reliable footwear (you'll be getting muddy at some point). Those with tender feet will need moleskin or Band-Aids. I also recommend a pair of sandals or aquasocks for fording the numerous streams in the Sanctuary. Overnight visitors should make a point of bringing a headlamp and extra batteries.

INDEPENDENCE/MANGO CREEK/BIG CREEK

The renewed importance of the banana industry in Belize – virtually eliminated by disease and hurricanes decades ago – has invigorated these three towns. They're bunched together about 75km south of Dangriga, just off the Southern Highway. Independence and Mango Creek are essentially the same town, with Big Creek located roughly 2km southeast on a good dirt road. All three are nondescript working towns, and most travellers experience them only as brief stops on the bus line or as a jumping-off point to Placencia.

Big Creek's most recent facelift – and the reason for its prosperity – is the new deepwater port which allows ocean freighters of Fyffes (United Fruit's British subsidiary) to load bananas, mangoes and other produce directly from the dock. Prior to the dredging, Belize's bananas were loaded onto barges and pulled by tug to Puerto Cortés, Honduras, or reloaded onto cargo ships in deeper water.

Getting there

All buses between Dangriga and Punta Gorda stop in Independence, the 'Banana Capital of Belize'. For information on catching a boat from here to Placencia, see Placencia, Getting there below.

Where to stay/eat

Hello Hotel 285 Fadden Avenue; tel: 06 22428, near the Independence bus stop. 18 rooms, BZ$50 with shared bath, fan; BZ$80 with private bath, air conditioning. Basic but also has a restaurant. Owners Tony and Beth Zabaneh can help arrange a boat to Placencia.
Ursella's Guest House 227 Gran Rain Street, Independence. 6 rooms, BZ$30 with shared bath.
Sherl's Restaurant Near the bus stop in Independence. Hot food, drinks, and pastries.

Information and useful addresses

The **Hokey Pokey** boat (tel: 22376) does a couple of journeys across the lagoon to Placencia at 10.00 and 16.00 charging BZ$10, useful if you don't want to travel the length of the peninsula. **Belize Bank** (tel: 06 22079) changes cash and cheques.

PLACENCIA

The Placencia peninsula begins 40km south of Dangriga and extends like a long, skinny finger for another 25km, passing palm-fringed beaches on the Caribbean side that many consider to be the finest in Belize. Along the way lies the ramshackle town of Seine Bight (one of four Garifuna villages in the country), a retirement community being developed by Canadians, and a handful of small luxury hotels in the low-key Belizean tradition. At the peninsula's southern tip lies Placencia Village, once a fishing village and now a popular resort town. Tourism has made its mark and the town gets unpleasantly crowded during holidays (especially Easter, earning Placencia the moniker 'Fort Lauderdale of Belize'). Still, Placencia manages to retain much of its fishing-village funkiness. Locals wish you good morning as you pass on the town's single sidewalk, a narrow, mile-long concrete strip through the centre of town which is underlain not with steel reinforcement bar but with hundreds of conch shells. Given the choice between Caye Caulker and Placencia as a seashore haven, I'd opt for Placencia any day.

Placencia may be one of the oldest settlements in Belize. Locals claim that the area was settled by buccaneers in the early 17th century, and a series of ancient shipwrecks now being mapped and investigated nearby adds credence to the stories. Until 1988, Placencia was accessible only by boat or airplane. With the advent of the dirt road, it's now an excellent 'base camp' from which to make jungle trips to the Cockscomb Basin Wildlife Sanctuary and the Monkey River. The offshore cayes are popular with snorkellers, divers, anglers, sailors, and kayakers, while the mangrove lagoons to the west provide a haven for birds and manatees.

Getting there

The Placencia airstrip, closed for years to discourage drug smuggling, re-opened in 1993. Maya Island Air flies five times daily to Placencia, with four of those flights operating also on Sundays and holidays (US$105 one way from the Municipal Airport, US$125 from the International Airport). Tropic Air offers four flights daily from Belize City to Placencia at the same prices. Flight time is about 25 minutes. The airstrip is located 3km north of the village, and taxis charge roughly BZ$15 into town.

By bus, there are two ways to reach Placencia. Direct buses bus leave Dangriga daily. There are two Ritchie's bus departures every day at 11.30 and 14.30 except Sunday, when only one bus runs to Placencia. The bus turns in to Hopkins and Sittee River first and then cuts west on the relatively new dirt road to Riverside, turns south and heads down the Placencia peninsula. The ride costs BZ$10 and generally takes 3 hours, but it can be as long as 4 hours when the road is muddy. A second option is to take a bus to Independence/Mango Creek (any of the daily buses going between Punta Gorda and Dangriga make a stop there), and take the Hokey Pokey ferry service that leaves at 10.00 and 16.00 daily costs BZ$10. Alternatively you can hire a dory to cross the lagoon, dropping you off in Placencia, about BZ$30.

A boat service between Placencia and Belize City, running four times a week (Mon, Fri, Sat, Sun) costing BZ$50 is to be introduced. Check the latest running times with the Placencia Tourist Information Centre (tel: 06 24045; email: placencia@btl.net) or the Marine Terminal (02 31969; email: btiajeff@btl.net) in Belize City.

To and from Honduras

There is a boat service to Puerto Cortes in Honduras that leaves Placencia on Saturday at 08.30. The service starts in Dangriga and only stops in Placencia if requested so you will have to make your booking by Friday at 17.00 at the latest. See Charles Leslie at Kingfisher Angling Adventures tel/fax: 06 23323 for details.

Where to stay

Placencia Village is loaded with small hotels, cabanas and rental rooms. Even so, it can be tough to find lodging if you show up unexpectedly at peak vacation periods such as Easter and Christmas. The best (and most expensive) hotels are located north of the village itself. You'll probably want advance reservations if you're counting on staying at the Rum Point Inn, Cove Resort or Turtle Inn. These three, as well as the simpler and cheaper Kitty's Place, are all well removed from the sights and sounds of the village, which may be good or bad depending on your mood.

The following hotels are all in Placencia village, mostly along the narrow concrete sidewalk:

Sea Spray Hotel tel/fax: 06 23163; email: seaspray@btl.net. 19 rooms with private bathrooms, hot water and fan. Beach area for relaxing in hammocks. De Tatch bar and restaurant serves good food and ice cold beers to help you get through the day without having to move more than a few metres. Owner Jodie is very helpful. Five different room rates starting at BZ$58 up to BZ$120.

Serenade Guest House tel: 06 23163; email: serenade@btl.net; web: www.placencia.com/members/serenade.html. Beautiful rooms, clean with AC, immaculate. US$65 in high season but cheaper in low season. Former restaurant owner Brenda is the cook and arranges a special menu everyday.

Cozy Corner tel/fax: 06 23280; email: cozycorner@btl.net. 6 rooms, each with two beds, fan and hot water. Close to the beach and even closer to Mr Bones. US$70 in high season.

Ranguana Lodge tel/fax: 06 23112; email: ranguana@btl.net. 5 roomy whitewashed cabanas on the beach, each one named for a local game fish, BZ$110 with private bath, air conditioning, fan. The owners also book lodging on Ranguana Caye.

Paradise Vacation Resort Next to Tentacles Dockside Bar. At time of writing the resort was being renovated. When it opens there will be 12 rooms, hot water and private bathrooms. From BZ$50.

Traveller's Inn (Lucille's) tel: 06 23190. 8 rooms, shared bath and fans. Basic but friendly place. Cheapest in town from BZ$25 for a double.

Julia's and Lawrence's Guest House tel: 06 23185. 4 rooms, hot water in shared bathrooms. Julia is one of the Placencia characters. BZ$30. New rooms coming on the beachfront from BZ$65 with a private bath.

Westwind Hotel tel/fax: 06 23255. 8 rooms with private bath, fans, hot water and kitchen. Very clean and attractive, with sun decks. From BZ$70 in the low season.

Trade Winds Cabanas tel: 06 23122; fax: 06 23201; email: trdewndpla@btl.net. 6 cabanas, with private bath, fans, refrigerator, kitchen. BZ$100 The cabanas can accommodate up to four people, making this a reasonably cheap place to stay. Also have three double rooms at BZ$50. Quiet beach front location.

Deb & Dave's Last Resort tel: 06 23207; fax: 06 23334; email: debanddave@btl.net. 4 rooms, BZ$43 with private bath, hot water, ceiling fans and a screened in balcony area. Bikes are available for rent at BZ$5 per hour or BZ$25 for the day, kayaks are BZ$80 for the day. Deb & Dave also run Toadal Adventure Belize, offering trips and excursions to local.

Barracuda and Jaguar Inn tel: 06 23330; fax: 06 23250; email: wende@btl.net; web: www.belizenet.com/barracuda. 2 thatched cabins, with hammocks and balcony area, fridge, coffee maker includes breakfast. US$45. Highly recommended trips to the jungle and reef. The secluded Pickled Parrot bar is the place to buy Placencia's most popular pizzas.

Coconut Cottage tel: 06 23234; fax: 06 23387. A pair of beautiful cabins with two rooms, private bath with hot water and deck. Right on the beach. US$30.

Lydia's Guest House tel: 06 23117; fax: 06 23354; email: lydias@btl.net. At the quieter northern end of town, 8 rooms with fans. Shared bath with hot water and fridge available. US$20. Lydia also has four houses to rent. Write for details.

Ted Berlin tel; 06 23172, is an expatriate New Yorker who runs the Acupuncture Center. He has a pair of fully furnished cabanas for BZ$195 a week or BZ$650 a month all inclusive. Acupuncture is BS$50 a session.

If you're looking to camp, **Jojo's Hotel** (tel: 06 23168) north of the Seaspray has a beach front campsite. Bathroom and showers, with a lock-up, hammock area, BBQ and cooking area. BZ$6pp. Jojo also has a basic cabana, sleeping two, at BZ$40.

North of Placencia, heading up the peninsula towards Seine Bight and Maya Beach, there are a number of more upscale, secluded hotel resorts. As a rule they are very comfortable and have beachfront accommodation. All of them have very highly recommended restaurants and bars. Also see the listings below for Seine Bight Village and Maya Beach, still a bit further north on the peninsula. Listed in order away from Placencia.

Turtle Inn tel: 06 23244; fax: 06 23245; email: turtleinn@btl.net; web: www.turtleinn.com. 7 thatched-roof cottages, but 4 have been completely renovated to include microwaves, a stove, refrigerator and coffee maker but without losing the traditional style. US$155 per night or US$1,070 for a week. A couple of the cottages are dome-styled beach houses with spacious living area and verandas. US$188 a night or US$1177 a week. A couple of cheaper cabanas are available for US$80 a night or US$525 a week. Prices do not include food, but they do include use of sea kayaks, snorkelling equipment and transfers to and from the Placencia airstrip. Bikes are available for rent and the usual array of tours can be arranged.

Kitty's Place tel: 06 23227; fax: 06 23226; email: kittys@btl.net; web: www.kittysplace.com. Rooms, apartments and weekly rentals. US$45 with shared bath, veranda overlooking beach; US$155 for renovated beach apartment with private bath, full kitchen and veranda. Meals are delicious. Located just north of the airstrip. Kitty's big draw is their bar, which features satellite TV. Excellent scuba, snorkelling, Monkey River and Jaguar Sanctuary trips, overnight stays at French Louis Caye are offered at reasonable prices. All with local experienced guides.

Rum Point Inn tel: 06 23239; fax: 06 23240; email: rupel@btl.net; web: www.rumpoint.com. 10 white concrete cabanas, US$204 with three reportedly excellent meals. About 3.2km north of the village. The igloo-like cabanas are spectacularly ugly from the outside, but tastefully plush inside. Owners George Bevier (a former World Health Organization entomologist) and his wife Corol have long been associated with the environmental movement in Belize. Their library is packed with books on Belizean natural history and the ancient Maya. The restaurant and bar consistently get raves. Fishing, scuba, snorkelling, jungle trips (including the Cockscomb Wildlife Sanctuary) and Maya ruin trips (including Lubaantun and Nim Li Punit) are available. The dive shop is well-stocked with new rental gear. Use of kayaks, Sunfish, and bicycles is free. US agent: Toucan Tur, 32 Traminer Drive, Kenner LA 70065 (tel: 1 800 747 1381 toll-free in US).

Serenity Resort tel: 06 23232; fax: 06 23231; email: serenity@btl.net; web: www.belizenet.com/serenity.html. 12 beach front cabanas and 10 rooms with AC. All with private bathrooms, hot and cold running water, fridge, coffee machines and fans. US$70 in summer, US$98 in winter, with three meals a day working out at US$38. Bikes and canoes available for use. Scuba, snorkelling and fishing can be arranged as can trips to nearby ruins and the Cockscomb Basin Jaguar Sanctuary.

Where to eat

In addition to the village hotels with restaurants, there are plenty of places to eat in Placencia. Hardly any of the town's restaurants have menus, in part because food delivery is so undependable. A few years ago during Christmas, the supply truck's weekly delivery consisted almost entirely of beer and liquor, and most restaurants had to close down for a few days. For those that do have menus, there's a fair chance that what you want may not be available. Hence, the blackboard menu out

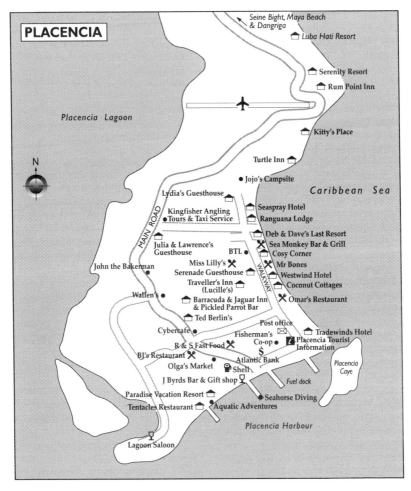

front has become a popular marketing device. Service seems to be universally slow – some would say glacial – in Placencia.

BJ's Restaurant On the dirt road leading out of town. Excellent food with coleslaw or salad, rice and beans. Also serves breakfast.

Tentacles Bar and Restaurant On the beach at the far southern end of town. A big place on stilts, with a pair of noisy parrots which perch underneath the restaurant. Lobster dinner (US$12.50), most other dinners US$3.50–4.50. Fried chicken, tasty fried rice, shrimp, conch, steaks, drinks.

Omar's Restaurant is a tiny little place on the walkway, but always packed. Cosy atmosphere with excellent food, usually a three-course set menu. A good place to eat… if you can get in.

Mr Bone's is right on the beach front close to the Cozy Corner. Good food in a comfortable, chilled atmosphere.

Sea Monkey Bar & Grill is next to Julia's and Lawrence's Guest House. The menu is not extensive and the surroundings are simple, but the impact is unforgettable. A smile, good service and very tasty food. Possibly the best-kept secret in Placencia.

Lagoon Saloon out on the western side of the peninsula has 'cheap drinks, bad jokes, great sandwiches and beautiful sunsets.'

Miss Lilly's is the place to go for a real Belizean dining experience. Located somewhere just passed the BTL and back from the walkway, Miss Lilly serves simple Belizean food at cheap prices.

R&S Fast Food near the gas station, serves freshly made *garnaches, panades* and *salbutes*.

Information and useful addresses

The BTL office is just off the walkway. There are a few public phoneboxes dotted round the peninsula.

The new **tourism office** is on the dockside at the southeastern tip of the peninsula. Opening hours are 8.30–11.00 and 14.00–17.00 Mon–Fri and Saturday morning. Email: placencia@btl.net. The local tourism industry is very well organised and most people will be able to help you if you're looking for answers.

The Placencia branch of the **Belize Tourism Industry Association** has set up a website with general information on the peninsula and specifically about services provided by its members: www.placencia.com.

Cybercafé on the main road next to the Big Thatch is currently the only dedicated internet café but many hotels have terminals that you can use.

Wallen's Super Market, on the main road, is open Mon, Tue, Wed, Fri and Sat from 08.00–12.00 and 16.00–19.00; on Thursdays and Sundays, hours are 08.00–12.00. Besides the usual mix of canned and dry goods, they stock beer, liquor, sunglasses, sandals and other sundries. They also cash travellers' cheques. Fresh fruits and vegetables come by truck on Saturday night; on Sundays there's always a big wait for produce. During the rest of the week, the fruit and vegetable situation is dismal.

Olga's Store, close to the petrol station, also stocks a range of fresh and dry goods.

The **Fishermen's Cooperative** at the beginning of the sidewalk sells fresh fish and shrimp (BS$5 per kg) as well as ice. They close at 17.00.

Placencia's bakery, **John the Bakerman**, is an unassuming brown wooden house that's easy to miss. Walking out of town on the dirt road, look for the first clearing on your right; the bakery is tucked in among the trees. You can also get to it from the walkway, cutting through just after the BTL office.

Cash and travellers' cheques can be changed at the **Atlantic Bank** which keeps to the general opening times of mornings and afternoons. Many, but not all, of the hotels in town will cash travellers' cheques, especially if you're staying there.

Drinking water is mostly rain water from cisterns. Ice is available from the Fishermen's Cooperative, but you probably shouldn't use it in drinks.

Excursions
Near town
Snorkel trips

The cayes and barrier reef, roughly 21km offshore at this point, provide fine snorkelling and scuba diving. Again, marine life here is no match for the atolls (Lighthouse, Turneffe and Glover's), but Placencia's attractions are more easily and cheaply accessed. And while you may see fewer fish on Placencia's cayes and reefs than in the San Pedro/Caye Caulker area, you're also guaranteed to see far fewer people.

Laughing Bird Caye National Park, an elbow-shaped sliver of white sand studded with palm trees about 21km offshore, is probably the single most popular day trip. Laughing Bird is the quintessential island paradise, blessedly free of sandflies, and surrounded by shallow coral reef that's fine for snorkelling. Unfortunately, it's been discovered recently by a cruise ship – the same one which puts in at Placencia – but environmentalists in Placencia are trying to get the area taken off the itinerary. Kitty's Place runs highly-recommended snorkel trips to Laughing Bird and other cayes for roughly the same price, as do all the dive shops on the dockside and several of the smaller hotels.

If you'd like to camp on the cayes, Kitty's Place and a number of boat operators will be glad to run you out to the beautiful Silk Cayes, drop you off, and pick you up on the appointed day (but bring extra food and water in case of stormy weather delays). On the way back in, they'll bring you to other snorkelling spots such as the Pompion Cayes. Prices are negotiable, and local guides know the kayak tour schedules so you won't have to share your caye with a group.

Scuba diving trips

Diving in the area has grown in popularity dramatically recently and there are now some dedicated dive shops. **SeaHorse Dive Shop** tel/fax: 06 23166; home: 06 23356; email: seahorse@btl.net; web: www.belizescuba.com is run by Brian Young. Former divemaster for Rum Point Inn, Brian is very active in balancing the desire to look for new sites with the need for conservation awareness. **Aquatic Adventures** tel/fax: 06 23182; email: glenmar@btl.net is run by Glenford Eiley. Aquatic, like SeaHorse, provide certification resort courses, dive trips, night dives, refresher courses, open water certification and can organise a range of other trips in the area. These operators will also rent out gear or you can bring your own.

Out of town **Rum Point Inn** (see details above) has their own dive operation with certification courses, underwater cameras for rental and the 42ft jet boat *Auriga II*. The other larger hotels refer guests to the dive operations.

Scuba trips, regardless of the operator, generally come in two options: 'outer reef' trips, offering the best diving but subject to weather, and 'inner reef' trips, cheaper and easier in the winds that frequently buffet the Placencia area. 'Outer reef' refers to the ocean side of the barrier reef itself. Due to surge and steep walls, these dives are best suited to intermediate and advanced divers. 'Inner reef' refers to the fringing and patch reefs within the protection of the barrier reef, and much closer to land. 'Inner reef' dives are suited to all diver skill levels. An 'outer reef' trip frequently includes Rock Head, about a 45-minute boat ride from Placencia. This can be a brutal ride in bad weather, but the rewards include gorgeous coral formations in 7–18m of water. Surge can be a problem. Rock Head is a good spot to see spawning cubera snapper (April-June), as well as sharks and eagle rays. Another good 'outer reef' dive is Little Water Caye (often referred to simply as Water Caye). Barracuda and needlefish are plentiful here, and it's an ideal snorkelling and picnicking spot. Water Caye, like Laughing Bird, is an elbow of white sand studded with palms, often a day camp for Creole fishermen. Other 'outer reef' dives include Northern Reef Wall, featuring a sheer vertical wall covered with barrel sponges and frequented by jacks, groupers, and an occasional hammerhead shark. Pompion Cayes also offer good 'outer reef' diving.

Prices and service levels are pretty standard so it's a question of finding someone you like to dive with. A two-dive day trip costs BZ$130, snorkelling is BZ$70. Prices usually include lunch which is generally a seafood beach BBQ on one of the nearby cayes. Lunch is usually so enjoyable and the scenery so idyllic that leaving to go diving can seem like a waste.

Be aware that if you sign up for an 'outer reef' trip, weather may force you back to the inner reef for your second dive. Decide with the operator before setting out how you'll be charged if this happens.

'Inner reef' dives usually include Long Coco Caye and Laughing Bird. Long Coco, about 25 minutes by boat from Placencia, isn't anything spectacular. The diving at Laughing Bird, on a sloping coral face, is much prettier; but there are not too many fish. Groupers, horse-eye jacks, and barracuda frequent the dive sites near Laughing Bird. Other 'inner reef' sites include Moho Caye and Tarpun Caye. The latter is a mangrove island, and while there are no coral formations, you are likely to see the namesake tarpon as well as millions of juvenile fish among the mangroves. Ask your guide to point out the black coral.

If you are in the area between April and June you may get a chance to see whale sharks feeding on snapper spawn. The arrival of these 45ft-long, plankton feeders to dine on the fish eggs makes Placencia, according to Brian Young, the only place in the world where this migration can be predicted. It is hoped that the area will become a multi-use marine reserve in the near future.

New and interesting dives like **Shark Hole** – a big sink hole that attracts sharks – are being found in the area as bigger and faster boats have more of the cayes accessible from Placencia. Trips to Glover's Atoll are US$100 pp with a minimum of six people.

Be sure to bring sunscreen, a shirt, wide-brimmed hat, sunglasses and drinking water. Bring a warm top for the journey back which may be cold if the clouds come in. Remember that you and everything aboard might get wet on the ride out.

Fishing trips

Fishing for bonefish, tarpon and permit is excellent in Placencia's nearshore flats, estuaries and bays. Outside the barrier reef, anglers have a chance at king mackerel, billfish, wahoo and dorado. **Kevin Modera** (tel: 06 23243; fax: 06 24018; email: info@kevinmodera.com; web: www.kevinmodera.com) offers a complete guiding service with fly fishing, spincasting, trolling, bottom fishing. US$225 will provide one boat for two people for a full day's fishing He can also arrange trips to Monkey River incorporating fishing and/or manatee watching.

Charles Leslie at **Kingfisher Angler Adventures** (tel: 06 23323; email: kingfisher@btl.net) also comes highly recommended. He can tailor a day-trip to your needs, supplying all the gear if necessary. The north-of-town hotels – Rum Point Inn, Turtle Inn and Kitty's Place – all offer fishing trips at a wide range of prices.

For further information on fishing, see *Chapter 6, Fishing*.

Sailing

Kevin Modera is planning to offer sail and power boat excursions. See *Fishing trips*, above, for details.

Bicycling

Some of the hotels have bikes you can rent for a half day or more. In town, Deb & Dave's has bikes for rent at BZ$25 a day. Out of town, Kitty's and Rum Point Inn rent bicycles at reasonable prices for trips around the peninsula.

Placencia Lagoon

The calm, mangrove-lined waters of Placencia Lagoon go virtually unnoticed by most travellers. Yet the lagoon harbours abundant bird and fish life, as well as a healthy population of manatees. SeaSpray and Miss Lydia's have a couple of kayaks that can be rented for lagoon trips and manatee-watching. Go at sunrise for the best wildlife.

Offshore cayes
A couple of cayes have been developed as private resorts. The quality and standards vary dramatically from the Robinson Crusoe desert island to the luxury

Whipray or Wippari Caye is 14km east of Placencia. Originally a fishing camp, the location is ideal for fishing or kayakers wanting to camp out in the wilds. The caye offers a beautiful, unspoilt environment but is not suited to the visitor looking for a modern resort, but rather to the adventurous traveller looking for a unique experience. There is a furnished cabin that sleeps four at US$50 pp and three rooms at US$40 pp. Camping is US$7 pp. Food can be provided but is extra. Transportation to Whipray and accommodation booking through Julian Cabral; tel: 06 23130; fax: 06 23130.

Little Water Caye (tel/fax: 06 12019; web: www.belizecaye.com), an idyllic treasure island, secluded yet with the comforts of hot water, is for comfort seekers. The restaurant serves fresh meals daily and there is a bar for watching the sunset. Three days and two nights, including all meals and transfers from Placencia, is US$450 for two.

Seine Bight Village
Just 8km north of Placencia village on the dirt road, Seine Bight is one of four Garifuna villages in Belize (the others being Barranco, Hopkins and Georgetown). To reach Seine Bight, walk from Placencia Village via the road or beach, take the morning bus, or hitchhike. Privateers of the Earl of Warwick first settled the area in 1629, and the site was later inhabited and given its present name by French Acadian fishermen deported from Nova Scotia, New Brunswick, and Newfoundland in 1755. The present inhabitants are descendants of Garifunas who began landing in the area in 1869, led by Emmanuel 'Walpy' Moreira, John Martinez and Mateo Augustine. Hurricane Hattie levelled the village in 1961. No lives were lost, however, and the town was quickly rebuilt, wooden houses on stilts replacing the thatch-walled homes of former times.

Today, Seine Bight Village is a funky, ramshackle village of some 500 Garifuna who depend mostly on fishing for a living. The Placencia peninsula is scarcely 300m wide here, so that Seine Bight is sandwiched between the mangrove lagoon to the west and a fine sandy beach to the east. Food and drink can also be had at Dave's Grocery, Verns, and KulchaShak; the latter sometimes has live entertainment. Ask around town for Nick, who sells beautiful handmade baskets. In the weeks prior to December 31, it's possible to see an authentic John Canoe dance (see *Dangriga, Special events* above) here. Garifunas here as elsewhere don't take kindly to cameras, so if you must take pictures, ask first.

Lola Delgado (tel: 014 7447) has a studio displaying naïve art in beautiful bright colours. Leave the main road alongside the football pitch and work your way through the swamp.

Where to stay
Formal lodging in Seine Bight used to be non-existent, but several new spots have opened up within the village and along the beach to the north:

Auntie Chigi's tel: 06 22015. 4 rooms, BZ$80 with shared bath. A simple but clean cheapie right in the village. Contact Edna Martinez in Seine Bight Village.

Nautical Inn tel: 06 23595; fax: 06 23594; email: nautical@btl.net; web: www.nauticalinnbelize.com. 12 beach front AC rooms with telephones, private bath, mahogany and wicker furniture with a nautical theme. The 'Oar House' restaurant overlooks the Caribbean. The dive shop can take snorkellers and divers to the reef. Tours to Monkey River and Jaguar Reserve leave are available. There is a sandy beach and a fresh water swimming pool. Rates US$125 high season and $85 low season.

Blue Crab Resort tel: 06 23544; fax: 06 23543; email: kerry@btl.net; web: www.BlueCrabBeach.com. 2 thatched cabanas, with private bath, hot water, fan and porch. US$85 and livefront AC rooms US$95. Meals are US$35 extra per person.

Bahia Laguna Beach Resort tel: 06 24081; fax: 06 27043; email: bahialaguna@btl.net; web: www.bahialaguna.com. Formerly Hotel Seine Bight. 7 thatched cabanas facing the sea, in a simple yet natural setting. Family-owned and operated and if you're not careful, you'll get treated just like one of the family as well. The restaurant serves Garifuna and international fare. Prices range from US$80–100 plus taxes.

Luba Hati tel: 06 23402; fax: 06 23403; email: lubahati@btl.net; web: www.lubahati.com. 8 rooms tastefully decorated with art from African and Garifuna culture. Each room has a semi-private terrace opening out onto the beach. US$150 plus taxes. 4 beach front casitas, with AC, have recently been added. US$180 plus taxes. The price includes continental breakfast served in your room, use of bicycles and kayaks and airport transfers. Francos's Restaurant, serving Mediteranean cuisine, comes highly recommended and is widely believed to be the best on the peninsula.

Maya Beach

Roughly 4km north of Seine Bight Village and 30km from the road to the Southern Highway, Maya Beach is a rapidly growing vacation condo complex along a pleasant stretch of beach. This far north on the peninsula, you're too far for easy walking access to Placencia village, but if you hanker for quiet and a bit more luxury, there are three fairly new resorts in the area:

Green Parrot Beach House tel/fax: 06 22488; email: greenparrot@btl.net; web: www.greenparrot-belize.com. 6 mahogany houses sleeping up to five people, right on the beach front – a beautiful spot. Each has kitchenette and bath on ground floor. The restaurant menu, with seafood, Belizean and International dishes changes daily. US$125 exclusive of taxes. Price includes breakfast and airport transfers. Bikes, canoes and windsurfers available for rent.

Singing Sands Inn tel/fax: 06 22243 or in the US: 1 800 649 3007; email: ssi@btl.net; web: www.singingsands.com. 6 thatched cabanas, all on the beach, US$108 (winter) US$85 (summer) with private bath, ceiling fan, hot water and fridge in room. Full service restaurant and bar, serving fresh seafood, vegetarian and local cuisine. Specialising in snorkelling trips with a 25-foot skiff going as far north as the Silk Cayes and as far south as Ranguana Caye for both inner and outer reef snorkelling trips. Mountain bikes, canoes, are also available. Swedish massage and Reiki treatment on the premises.

X-Cape General Delivery, Placencia; tel: 06 37002; email: scape@btl.net; web: www.gotobelize.com/xcape/ is in the heart of Maya Beach, 5 miles north of the airstrip. The rooms are large, basic and clean with private baths and ceiling fans. US$50.00. The restaurant serves Belizean food with a south Texas flair. Not catering for the luxury market, the emphasis is more on fun and relaxation. All the usual tours in the area can be arranged.

Further afield
Kayak trips

The protective barrier reef and palm-studded cayes near Placencia provide ideal conditions for kayakers of all abilities. Three tour operators run trips which concentrate in the Placencia area.

The best-known outfit running kayak trips in the area is **Slickrock Adventures, Inc**, an American firm with many years of experience in Belize. Their week-long itinerary generally includes Bugle Caye (a mangrove islet within sight of Placencia), Laughing Bird, Little Water Caye, the Queen Cayes (also known as the Silk Cayes), Pompion Caye and Ranguana Caye. No paddling experience is necessary – you'll get several hours of instruction, including water exits, before you set out – but you should be in decent shape; six hours of paddling per day isn't uncommon. In case of wind – more common in February and March than later in the season – powerboats stand by to ferry kayaks and people out to the cayes and protected paddling water. Even so, there are days when high winds can keep guests pinned down on an island. Guests can join in the guides' afternoon search for dinner, fresh seafood either speared or hand-lined.

Slickrock runs trips ranging from four to nine days (seven days actually spent on the water and cayes) for between US$595–1,950. Price includes all travel within Belize, round trip air between Belize City and Placencia, final night in a hotel, all meals, kayaks (hard shell singles and doubles, Aguaterra Chinnok/Sea Lion and NW Kayak Seascape), kayaking accessories including camera and gear bags, hammocks, sling spears, fishing handline and two guides per trip. Slickrock uses both Americans and Belizean guides. You supply camping gear (except kitchen things), tent, sleeping bag and snorkelling gear. Groups are limited to a maximum of twelve kayakers, not including guides. They schedule about 13 such trips a year during the dry season, early February through mid-May. Extension trips following kayaking are offered in conjunction with Chaa Creek Inland Expeditions to the Cockscomb Wildlife Sanctuary, Wee Wee Caye, Belize Zoo, Guanacaste Park, Xunantunich and Tikal. They are now concentrating on trips to Glover's Reef, the most remote of Belize's three atolls (see *Chapter 14*). For information and reservations contact Slickrock Adventures, Inc, PO Box 1400, Moab, UT 84532, USA (tel: 801 259 6996; fax: 801 259 8698; email: slickrock@slickrock.com; web: www.slickrock.com).

Island Expeditions Co of Vancouver, Canada, runs eight and 12-day kayak trips based out of Dangriga, following the barrier reef cayes south from Tobacco Caye (see above). The eight-day trip finishes up in Big Creek, while the 12-day trip continues down to Monkey River Town and then up the Monkey and Bladen Rivers (see below) to a takeout on the Southern Highway. It's a unique way to see both the cayes and rainforest all from a kayak in a single trip. They've just added an eight-day kayaking and optional scuba diving trip on distant Glover's Reef, with an inland trip that includes Garifuna villages (US$1,040). Island Expeditions uses both Belizean and North American guides, and donates profits towards local conservation and education initiatives in Belize. The eight-day trip costs US$930, including air transportation to Dangriga, airport taxes, accommodations in Belize City for the night prior to departure, kayaks, tents, guides, all meals (including those in Belize City). They also offer the option of adding rainforest and Maya ruin tours. And as far as I know, they are still the only outfit renting kayaks to experienced paddlers in Belize; double and single kayaks can be rented in Dangriga for US$60–30 per day, and they can provide motor boat transport out to the barrier reef. Write to 368–916 W Broadway Avenue, Vancouver, BC V5Z 1K7, Canada (tel: 604 452 3212 or toll-free: 1 800 667 1630; fax: 604 452 3433; email: info@islandexpeditions.com; web:www.islandexpeditions.com).

In terms of sheer distance, the most ambitious kayak trip was offered by **Ecosummer Expeditions**, another Canadian outfit. They used to run a 25-day Belize Explorer trip which includes kayaking from Belize City all the way to the remote Sapodilla Cayes (see *Chapter 12*) and then to Punta Gorda, a distance of some

160km. The tour then headed inland to visit Maya villages, camp on the Monkey River, ride horses in the Mountain Pine Ridge, visit Tikal and float river caves. They now offer a number of week-long trips that can be taken individually or joined together for the more ambitious kayaker. Write to 5640 Hollybridge Way, Unit # 130, Richmond, BC V7C 4N3, Canada; tel: 604 214 7484l or toll-free 1 800 465 8884; fax: 604 214 7485; email: trips@ecosummer.com; web: www.ecosummer.com

Ranguana Caye

This isl t is located about 28km south east of Placencia and is excellent for snorkelling, diving and fishing. Lodging can be had at **Ranguana Reef Resort** (tel/fax: 06 23112, email: ranguana@btl.net; web: www.ranguanabelize.com) 3 rustic self-catering cabins equipped with full kitchen, private porch and shared bathrooms with hot and cold water. US$48 for two people but the cabins will sleep three. Camping is also possible for US$10 pp. Kayaks can be rented out from the resort but bring all other equipment that you want. Round trip transport to the island is US$170 for up to four people.

Monkey River

The Monkey River makes its serpentine way through the jungle of Toledo District rather than Stann Creek District. It is included in this chapter because all guides and services for the trip downriver originate in Stann Creek District, mostly in the Placencia area.

The Monkey River is fed by two major tributaries: the Swasey Branch, originating in the Cockscomb Basin (home to the Jaguar Sanctuary); and the Bladen Branch, flowing southwest from the Maya Mountains. Both of these branches flow under bridges on the Southern Highway west of Independence/Mango Creek, so that canoes or kayaks can easily be dragged down from the highway and launched downriver. Narrow, twisting, and rimmed on both sides by jungle, both the Swasey and Bladen branches are ideal for sighting wildlife in a pristine setting.

By the time the branches join to form the Monkey River itself, the channel has widened, and the claustrophobic exhilaration of a watery jungle maze is largely lost. For this reason alone I recommend against taking the day trips offered by many tour operators. These trips usually involve motoring in a large launch from Placencia, entering the river mouth at Monkey River Town and running upstream. One problem is that motorboats can only penetrate a short distance upriver before the water becomes too shallow, particularly during the low-water period of April- May. This means that you'll see only the most uninspiring section of the river closest to civilisation. Secondly, you'll be besieged by the noise and exhaust fumes of an outboard engine for at least the upriver portion of the trip. Thirdly, much of the wildlife along the river bank will flee the boat's mechanised din long before you've uncapped your binoculars. My prejudices aren't shared by all travellers. I've spoken to several people who highly recommended the trips run by Kitty's (US$40 pp with lunch) and saw lots of wildlife, including the namesake howlers.

The best way to experience the Monkey River, then, is the slow way: a two-day trip by canoe or kayak down either the Swasey or Bladen Branch, camping overnight on one of hundreds of sandbars.

The most popular option, is a guided overnight canoe trip. A number of local tour guides out of Placencia now make these trips, and virtually every hotel in the village can set you up on an overnight canoe or kayak trip down the Monkey River. Costs usually run about US$70 pp. **Monkey River Expeditions**, 1731 44th Ave SW,

GARIFUNA

Few ethnic groups in the Caribbean can claim a more complicated history than the Garifuna (guh-RIHF-uhnuh). A people of mixed African and Carib Indian ancestry, the Garifuna remain unclear about many details of their origins. Even the word 'Garifuna' has only been widely accepted by non-Garifuna for two decades, and remains an imperfect term. Garifuna generally refer to themselves as Garinagu; Garifuna is the language they speak. Prior to the 1970s they were known as 'Black Caribs' or simply 'Caribs', words which today carry a somewhat pejorative meaning.

The Garifuna trace their origins to St Vincent in the Windward Islands. For centuries, the island was home to the peaceful Arawak Indians, until raiding parties of Carib Indians from South America overran them, killing the Arawak men and taking the women for wives. Their offspring, known as Island Carib, adopted the ancestor worship practised by the Arawaks. But unlike the Arawaks, the Island Carib revelled in warfare. They were also an egalitarian people, without hereditary chiefs, who sneered at the Europeans' obedience to crowned heads of state. Jealously guarding their liberties, they fought both Europeans and other Indians with equal ferocity.

St Vincent was under Carib rule when two Spanish ships carrying West African slaves went aground in 1635. Given the Caribs' brutal reputation, it is unclear how the slaves managed to survive on St Vincent. But they did, and the African population of St Vincent grew with the arrival of fugitive slaves from Barbados. Africans began intermarrying with Island Carib women, and their offspring became known as 'Black Caribs'. From their Amerindian mothers, the Black Caribs inherited most of their language as well as the Carib cult of ancestor worship. From their fathers, they inherited physical characteristics which were decidedly African. Visitors to Belize often mistakenly assume that the Garifuna are of pure African descent.

By 1700, the Black Caribs had become geographically and politically distinct from the Island or 'Red' Caribs. Their population expanded rapidly throughout the 18th century. The French and English, who for years had battled for control of the Lesser Antilles, reached an accord in 1763 which awarded St Vincent to the English. But the Black Caribs refused to surrender their land. The English won the ensuing war, but their victory was short- lived. Black Caribs formed an alliance with the French and began a full-scale revolt, briefly retaking the island. Bloody conflict raged for 17 years. Following the death of their leader Chief Joseph Chatoyer, the Black Caribs and the French surrendered to the British in 1796. The British wasted little time in deporting the war's few survivors. In spring of 1797, some 1,700 Black Caribs were taken from St Vincent and Baliceaux and sent to Roatan, off northern Honduras. Their new 'home' proved dry and infertile and almost all the Black Caribs quickly left. Most threw in with the Spanish in Trujillo, Honduras.

From Honduras the Garifuna quickly fanned out along the Caribbean coast. Since most Garifuna at this time had French surnames and spoke French, their arrival in Belize was not greeted with much enthusiasm by the British. They found work with the Baymen as mahogany loggers and labourers. Garifuna coastal traders also became adept at smuggling British goods into Honduras. Early 19th century Garifuna settlements in Belize included Stann Creek (now Dangriga), Red Cliff (now Barranco) and Punta Gorda (presumably named after the Garifuna town on Roatan).

The Honduran Garifuna sided with the Royalists against the new Republican government there. When the Royalists were defeated in 1832, thousands of Garifuna fled north to Belize. Most Garifuna – some 200,000 – still live in 43 towns along the Honduran coast. Belize is home to about 15,000 Garifuna, mostly living in two towns (Dangriga and Punta Gorda) and four villages (Barranco, Hopkins, Seine Bight and Georgetown). Guatemala has two Garifuna settlements, as does Nicaragua. There are Garifuna enclaves in the US as well as in England and Canada. The Garifuna live largely among themselves, preserving their unique culture. Those who leave the villages become schoolteachers, and they are especially noted for their ability to pick up languages. Garifuna teachers in the Maya villages of Toledo, for instance, frequently speak English, Kekchi Maya, Mopan Maya and Spanish. Three traditions serve to link the Garifuna people worldwide: language, ancestor worship and dancing/drumming.

Most Garifuna are nominal Catholics, but their deepest allegiance is to the *gubida*, or ancestral spirits. Following death, the spirit of a Garifuna begins a long journey to the afterworld. At some point, usually within six months, most *gubida* feel the need for a bath, clean clothes and refreshment. Appearing to a relative in a dream, the *gubida* requests an *amuldahani*, or ritual bathing. Amuidahanis are simple ceremonies, performed by family members in the back yard of the dead person. Relatives place offerings of bread, coffee and liquor. They hang clean clothes nearby, and fill a hole with bath water, so that the *gubida* can journey on refreshed. Eventually – rarely sooner than ten years after death – *gubida* begin to hunger for something more substantial. The *gubida* may appear, requesting either a *chugu* feast or the elaborate *dugu* ceremony. During a *chugu*, relatives gather at the deceased person's house to offer food to the *gubida*. A shaman (*buyei*) must be present, and many of the most famous *buyei* in Belize are women. Except for ritual singing, the *chugu* involves no music, drums or dancing.

The *dugu*, or feast of the dead, is the apotheosis of Garifuna ancestor rites. A *buyei* must preside over the ceremony, which takes place in an earthen-floored Garifuna temple (*dabuyaba*), and includes spirit possession and small animal sacrifice. Often the *dugu* is required to appease a *gubida* who has afflicted living kin with an illness. If this sounds sinister, you should know that the *dugu* involves three days and nights of feasting, rum drinking and dancing. Preparations may take a year, and relatives often come from Honduras, Canada or the United States. Two days prior to the ceremony, fishermen go out to the cayes. When they return at dawn of the third day, laden with fresh fish, the merriment begins. Guests are often welcome at these rites. But you would be very lucky indeed to participate in one. Far easier to witness is the traditional dance known as John Canoe (*Wanaragua* in Garifuna). Each year at Christmas, elaborately costumed dancers roam the streets of Dangriga and other Garifuna towns, performing for money and rum. The John Canoe carries no spiritual connotation; it's sheer, exhilarating entertainment (see *Special events* below).

Perhaps the best way to experience Garifuna culture is to visit Hopkins (see page 174) or Barranco. The latter is a small coastal village in Toledo District. The town is now participating in the Village Guest House Programme as the only non-Maya village. You can spend the night in a local guesthouse, eat traditional foods with Garifuna families, hear Garifuna music, and visit the nearby Temash River the next day. Best of all, the money you pay for this benefits the entire community. See *Chapter 12, Excursions* for details on the Guest House Programme and Barranco.

Suite 100, Seattle, WA 98116 (tel: 206 660 7777) runs six-day trips involving four days kayaking down the river, two on Lime Caye offshore, and one of the inland days is spent jungle trekking. The cost is US$1,295 pp, including all transport within Belize, all meals, camping gear, kayaks, and two nights lodging in Placencia.

A second option involves kayaking up the Monkey River and its Bladen Branch as part of a guided tour which includes the cayes offshore of Placencia and Dangriga. Two kayak trip operators make this trip (for details, see *Kayak trips* above).

Canoe trips down the Monkey River can't usually be made in September due to high water. The January through May period is best. The river runs lowest in April and May, when sections of the Swasey Branch shrink to 1.2m in width. Trips are often possible during this time if you're willing to portage a good deal of the sand and gravel bars. Birdwatching is best in February, during the mating season.

Our canoe trip one December began with a dory ride from Placencia to Big Creek, where we loaded our canoe into a pickup. Placencia puts most travellers in a state of beach-blanket torpor; gripping a rum drink in one hand and a paperback in the other, they're often hard to rouse for a trip into the bug-infested interior. We had been lucky enough to find a young British couple, Susan and Phillip, willing to share expenses for the Monkey River trip. Half an hour later, after a bumpy, dusty ride on the Southern Highway, we hauled the canoe and our provisions down a grassy slope beneath the Swasey Branch bridge. David Muschamp, our Belizean guide, manned the bow.

After less than a dozen strokes of our wooden paddles, we spotted the first iguana high in a tree limb above us. During the next two days, we saw literally hundreds of iguanas, most of them 0.5m long, ranging in colour from lime green to bright orange to a charcoal black. Some blinked lazily from their perches. Others – David assured us that the female iguanas were more skittish than the males – scrambled to the narrow branches overhanging the river, and plunged in with a resounding bellyflop. Belizeans use this habit to their advantage when hunting iguanas, known locally as 'bamboo chickens'. One hunter climbs the tree, while a second treads water directly beneath the lizard, grabbing it when it hits the water.

Wood storks (*Mycteria americana*), locally nicknamed 'boobie birds', waded the shallows in search of fish, snakes and frogs. Great white egrets (*Casmerodius albus*) flew gracefully downriver as we approached, waiting invariably for us around the next bend. Their close relative, the pinnated bittern (*Botaurus pinnatus*), stood its ground boldly, allowing us to drift within a few feet. Even powerboats rarely scare this species into flight. We also spotted two of Belize's three species of toucans, scores of parrots, oropendolas, vireos, cormorants and a brilliant scarlet and black bird which we never identified (David referred to it as a 'banana bird').

The current made paddling optional, but there is no white water as such on the Swasey Branch. The neighbouring Bladen Branch contains a few short sections of white water. Now and then we found ourselves fouled on fallen snags, and on two or three occasions shallow water forced us to portage short distances. My inept steering veered us at times into overhanging tree branches and vines. There is one particular hanging vine, furry as a cat's tail but packing a nettle-like sting, which cured me of this habit after a few river kilometres.

Sandbars had been scarce during the first two hours of paddling, but now we found them at nearly every bend in the river. Towards dusk we settled on one as a campsite. David first inspected the area carefully for tapir tracks. Belizeans claim that these 'mountain cows', although harmless, will blunder recklessly through tents during their nocturnal forages. We gathered firewood, set up tents and helped David prepare a gibnut (paca) stew, flavoured with achiote paste.

Next morning we broke camp after a breakfast of coffee, fry jacks and canned meat. We found sandbars downstream crisscrossed with tapir tracks, lending some credence to David's warning the night before. David pointed out ceiba trees ('cotton tree' to Belizeans) towering over the forest canopy, as well as two banana farms along the left bank. Except for a tiny Indian village, these farms were the only signs of human habitation in two days following the Swasey. Finally, we paddled past the confluence of the Bladen Branch, its darker waters joining the Swasey to form the Monkey River proper. As if on cue, black howler monkeys filled the forest with calls like rolling thunder. Why the Monkey River should have howlers, but not its tributaries the Swasey and Bladen, is something that no one could explain.

The river widened, slowed, and for the first time in two days we saw other boats: a group of wild pig hunters, a local couple going snook fishing. It was mid-afternoon when we rounded the final bend and paddled into Monkey River Town (see below).

The entire trip requires about eight to ten hours of actual paddling, with six of those hours spent on the Swasey Branch. David brought five gallons of rainwater, although he himself drank directly from the river, which he guaranteed was safe. Bring binoculars, sunglasses, long sleeved shirts, flashlights and insect repellent. You may also want to bring gloves (paddles are rough wood rather than fibreglass) and some sort of cushion for the canoe seats.

Monkey River Town

Monkey River Town inexplicably shows up on many world maps, atlases, and even globes, implying that it is something more than a tiny fishing village of some 100 souls. You'll find a shack which serves as both grocery and bar, a police station facing the sea, a community telephone (tel: 06 22014) and at least one house for rent to the few travellers who spend the night here. **Enna's Hotel** (BZ$40) provides basic accommodation but asking around should put you in contact with someone who can put you up. Lobster fishermen clean their catch on the river's sandy banks, kids play on the beach with iguanas and American shark-fishing boats anchor off the mouth, bound for the reef and markets in Honduras and Guatemala.

The town is located at the mouth of the Monkey River, mostly on the right bank, about 24km south of Mango Creek. There is a dirt road into Monkey River Town on the river's left bank, but it becomes impassable during rainy weather. The only reliable way to reach the town is by motorised dory from Placencia, Big Creek, or Mango Creek, or else via the Monkey River (see above). Between Monkey River Town and Big Creek lies a fascinating maze of mangrove islets, including Little Monkey Caye, Great Monkey Caye, Palmetto Caye and Harvest Caye. Passing between these in a small boat, you'll find the mangroves at times forming a virtual canopy over the waterway.

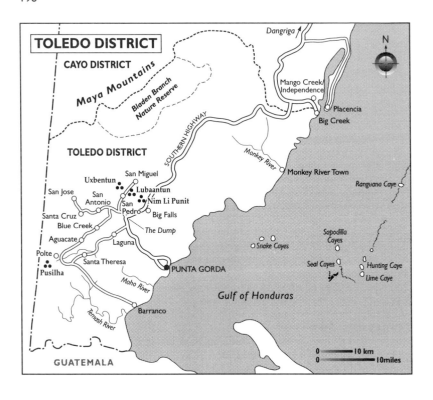

TOLEDO DISTRICT

CAYO DISTRICT

Maya Mountains

Bladen Branch
Nature Reserve

TOLEDO DISTRICT

Dangriga

Mango Creek/
Independence

Placencia

Big Creek

SOUTHERN HIGHWAY

Monkey River

Monkey River Town

Ranguana Caye

San Miguel

Uxbentun

Lubaanfun

San Jose

San
Antonio

Nim Li Punit

San
Pedro

Big Falls

Santa Cruz

Blue Creek

The Dump

Aguacate

Laguna

Sapodilla
Cayes

Polte

Snake Cayes

Seal Cayes

Hunting Caye

Santa Theresa

Pusilha

Moho River

PUNTA GORDA

Lime Caye

Gulf of Honduras

Ternash River

Barranco

GUATEMALA

0 ▬▬▬ 10 km
0 ▬▬▬ 10 miles

N

Toledo District

Belize's southernmost district is also its least visited. Travellers who make it to Punta Gorda, the district capital, often treat it strictly as a convenient gateway to Guatemala. The region's low tourist profile may be compounded by two other factors: rainfall averages a staggering 4,445mm per year which falls mostly at night, making Toledo the nation's wettest district; and it is here that the barrier reef lies furthest offshore, some 32 miles from Punta Gorda.

Nevertheless, the region boasts a number of impressive attractions – not the least of which is the scarcity of travellers. Belize's ethnic gumbo is at its most varied in Toledo, where Mopan and Kekchi Maya mingle on market days with East Indian, Lebanese, Guatemalan and Chinese shopkeepers, as well as with the Garifuna majority, descendants of africans intermarrying with Amerindians (see *Chapter 11, Garifuna*). Several lesser-known but splendidly serene Maya sites are concentrated in the forests of Toledo district. Thatch villages to the west of Punta Gorda provide an unusual chance to visit modern Maya in a distinctly ancient setting. And finally, adventurous travellers may find the distance from shore to barrier reef an advantage rather than a hindrance; seldom visited by fishermen, the Sapodilla Cayes provide an undisturbed haven for marine life of all kinds.

As of mid-1998, Toledo District had the lowest population density in Belize, with only three people per square kilometre (eight per square mile). Maya Indians make up 62% of the district's population; nowhere else in Belize exists such a sizeable Amerindian population which still retains its language and culture.

Toledo District has long been the principal rice-growing region in Belize, supplying 80% of the nation's total harvest. Other agricultural products include corn, red kidney beans, cacao, citrus, honey, cattle and swine. Some marijuana grows in the area, although the Toledo pot harvest is estimated to be minuscule compared with the northern districts. The Toledo Agricultural Marketing Project, funded by USAID, is promoting crop diversification among the milperos, with mixed success.

PUNTA GORDA
History
Punta Gorda – 'PG' to Belizeans – was little more than a hamlet at the beginning of this century. In the early 1800s, Garifunas began moving from Honduras to the southern coast of Belize, taking up work in the mahogany camps or running British contraband back to Honduras. A new wave of Garifunas arrived in 1832, when they were forced to flee Honduras after throwing in with the Royalists in an unsuccessful bid to oust the republican government there.

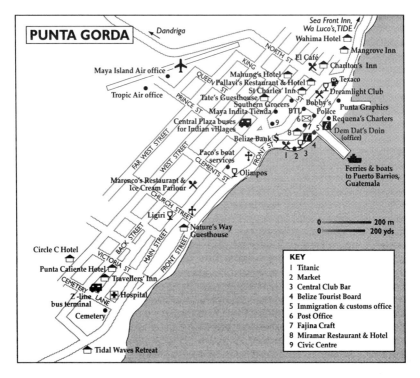

The Garifuna were not the only civil war refugees who found a safe haven in Punta Gorda; following the defeat of the Confederacy in the United States, several hundred southerners emigrated to Belize and began planting sugar cane. They also introduced bananas to southern Belize. The remnants of their Toledo Settlement, abandoned a few years later, lie a few miles south of Punta Gorda. Strong ties between Belize and the southern US – particularly Louisiana – exist to this day as a result.

Chinese immigrants came in 1866 from northern Belize, less than a year after their arrival from Kwangtung Province. Originally imported as labourers and farm workers, they met with hostility in the north and were hastily transferred to Toledo District. Punta Gorda also boasts a large East Indian population. Many are descendants of Sepoy rebels exiled to British Honduras in the mid-1800s. Today, East Indians make up the bulk of the populace just northwest of Punta Gorda.

The American Mayanist John L Stephens visited Punta Gorda at about this time and found it a cornucopia of local produce: 'Besides cotton and rice, the cahoon, banana, coconut, pineapple, orange, lemon, and plantain, with many other fruits which we do not know even by name, were growing with such luxuriance that at first their very fragrance was oppressive'. Stephens stayed just long enough to witness a handful of the local Garifuna being baptised Catholics. Then, like many modern-day travellers, he continued south to Guatemala's Río Dulce. The irrepressible archaeologist Thomas Gann arrived in Punta Gorda in 1903, the first of many visits. During a later trip in 1927, Gann described a festival in which the local Garifuna dressed in Maya garb. He used the town as a base from which to explore – some would say plunder – the nearby ruins of Lubaantun.

Getting there and away

MayaIsland Air runs scheduled 8-seaters to Punta Gorda four times daily from Belize City (US$135 one way), with only two flights daily on Sundays and public holidays. Flights leave the Municipal Airport, but can stop at the International Airport to pick up passengers, as well as at Dangriga and Big Creek along the way. Tropic Air also flies to Punta Gorda four times a day for US$138 one way. Flight time is about 50 minutes if no stops are made. Maya and Tropic sell tickets at the Punta Gorda airstrip.

James and Z Line buses have several buses a day leaving from 05.00 throughout the day until 19.00. The fare is BZ$22 and the journey takes around 10–12 hours. If you're an old hand on Latin American bus journeys this is nothing special, but if you're new to the game you might want to consider flying back. James buses leave from opposite the gas station on Cemetery Road in Belize City. Z-line leave from the Venus Bus Terminal.

The buses go to Belmopan, Dangriga and then stop at Independence picking up passengers along the way before finally making it to Punta Gorda.

When leaving Punta Gorda, buy a ticket the day before at the bus station to be sure of a seat. The bus picks up passengers along the way as it heads north out of town, but unless you are sure of the stop, it's probably best to get aboard at the station.

To reach San Antonio (as well as a number of other Maya villages including San José, Santa Cruz, San Miguel, Blue Creek and San Pedro Columbia) via public transportation, catch the buses run by Chun's Bus Company from Punta Gorda. Your best bets are Wednesday and Saturday, both local market days for the Indians. Fares are ridiculously cheap. Alternatively, you can take any bus from Punta Gorda to 'the Dump' then hike west about 2 hours to either San Antonio or San Pedro Columbia.

Boats to and from Guatemala

A couple of private ferries ply the route daily between Punta Gorda and Puerto Barrios in Guatemala. The journey costs BZ$25. **Pacos** (3 Clement Street; tel: 07 22246) leaves at 08.30. **Requena's Charter Service** (12 Front Street; tel: 0722070; email: watertaxi@btl.net) usually has a boat in the afternoon at 16.00.

The ride, which can be quite rough, takes about 1 hour and costs US$6.50. The ticket agent will want to see your passport and perhaps demand a visa for Guatemala. A visitor's permit will be issued in Puerto Barrios for US$6, good for 30 days. Before leaving Belize on the ferry, get an exit stamp at Immigration where you will have to pay the exit fee of US$7.50.

Plan on arriving a day early and spending the night in Punta Gorda if you intend to take the ferry; the morning bus from Belize City won't get you to Punta Gorda in time to catch the ferry.

If there are sufficient numbers of people, the ferry will call in at Livingston, if not, once in Puerto Barrios, most travellers wanting to continue on to the Garifuna town of Livingston, Guatemala and the Río Dulce will require a second ferry trip from Puerto Barrios to Livingston as there is no road. Maddeningly, this ferry must head back towards Belize in a northwesterly direction for almost an hour to reach Livingston. In addition to the ferry, there are plenty of launches that make the trip for about US$1.50 pp and take about 45 minutes to 1 hour.

For a price, travellers frustrated with the wait for tickets and the circuitous path to Livingston can charter a direct boat from Punta Gorda which can be organised through Paco's or Requena's.

In the opposite direction (Guatemala to Belize), the ferries leave Puerto Barrios in the afternoon. You must get an exit stamp prior to buying your ticket, and Immigration won't give you a stamp until the day before departure. Meanwhile, Guatemalans are buying advance tickets without this stipulation, so that the ferry is sometimes full before you've had a chance to queue up at the ticket office. Once again, the only alternatives are to wait a few days or hire a private boat – and Puerto Barrios is a somewhat dismal place to wait. Kill time visiting the Hotel del Norte, once the headquarters of the United Fruit Company, now a showpiece of faded grandeur.

If your final destination is Puerto Cortes in Honduras, Requena's will make the journey for BZ$1500.

Where to stay

Nature's Way Guesthouse 65 Front Street, Box 75; tel: 07 22119. An American-Belizean, William ('Chet') Schmidt, who has lived in Belize for over 30 years, runs the hotel and Belize Adventure Travel. 12 rooms, plus 4 new ones on the second floor, BZ$26 with fan, shared bath. Very friendly, clean, quiet, and highly recommended. Reservations are a good idea during the high season. Good dinners run about BZ$8 (usually beans, rice, plantains, and either fresh fish or chicken; fry jacks for breakfast, lunch also available). Health food and vegetarian meals are available. Order meals in advance and bring your own beer, liquor, soft drinks and mixers. Cheap trips to neighbouring Maya villages, ruins and caves can be arranged here, as well as canoe rentals, trips to the nearshore cayes and barrier reef (see *Excursions* below), even to Livingston and the Río Dulce in Guatemala (see *Trips to and from Guatemala* above). The single best source of adventure travel information in Toledo District.

Traveller's Inn 106 Jose Maria Nunez Street; tel: 07 22568. 7 rooms, BZ$134 with private bath, air conditioning, cable TV. There's a restaurant and bar.

Circle C Hotel 117 West Street; tel: 07 22726. 7 rooms, BZ$13 with shared bath, US$25 with private bath.

Punta Caliente Hotel 108 Jose Maria Nunez Street; tel: 07 22561. 8 rooms, BZ$50 with private bath, fans.

Tate's Guest House 34 Jose Maria Nunez Street; tel: 07 22196. 2 rooms, BZ$30–70 with private baths, fan.

St Charles Inn 23 King Street; tel: 07 22149; fax: 07 22199. 15 rooms, with shared bath. From BZ$40. Very friendly, recommended.

Mahung's Hotel 11 Main Street, PO Box 92; tel: 07 22044/22874. 12 rooms, BZ$17.50, with one bathroom out back for the whole hotel. The manager can be rather taciturn. Bobby's Restaurant and Bar is across the street.

Miramar Hotel 95 Front Street, PO Box 2; tel: 07 22033. 11 rooms, with private bath, fan. US$70 with AC, TV, refrigerator. Clean, and undeniably the most modern hotel in town, but overpriced and with a noisy soldiers' bar down below. Foreigners off the night bus are frequently steered here, and sometimes it's the only place with rooms left. Mediocre Chinese food, hamburgers, sandwiches, liquor, local beer, Guinness and Tooth's Stout in the restaurant/bar below. Upstairs the rooms are BZ$107 for a double, downstairs BZ$42.

Pallavi's Hotel 19 Main Street; tel: 07 22414. 5 rooms upstairs, BZ$32 with shared bath. Formerly Foster's Hotel. Basic and clean, good restaurant downstairs.

Charlton's Inn 9 Main Street; tel: 07 22197. 16 rooms, with private bath and fan. Basic but clean. BZ$32.

Wahima Hotel 11 Front Street; tel: 07 22542. 6 rooms with private baths. Very basic. At time of writing being renovated, but early signs are promising. BS$25 for the room with rates by the month available.

Tidal Waves Retreat is through the cemetery at the end of Main Street; tel: 07 22111; email: bills_tidalwaves@yahoo.com. A beautiful spot in 15 acres of rainforest for relaxing with several accommodation options. Cabinas (BZ$100), rooms (BZ$38), camping (BZ$28) and a treehouse that should be finished by the time you read this. Price includes breakfast and connections to bus terminal and airport.

Sea Front Inn PO Box 20; tel: 07 39917; fax: 07 22684; email: seafront@btl.net. A very comfortable hotel with many fine touches. Each of the 14 themed rooms have private baths with hot water, AC and cable television. International menu in the Rose Wood Restaurant. Observatory to view the Caribbean skies. BZ$95. Price includes breakfast and pick-up from the airport in a genuine London black cab.

Camping is possible at **Arvin's Landing** outside of town on Joe Taylor Creek, (tel: 07 22015). The Arvins also have three budget rooms with shared bath.

Where to eat
Besides the hotels listed above (Nature's Way and Miramar), you'll find several other spots to eat.

Mangrove Inn 3 Front Street. A great restaurant with a lively atmosphere serving a mixture of international and Belizean food.

Paradise Café is an open-air restaurant above the market area is good for breakfast, basic Belizean fare and anything with fry jacks. Excellent view.

Titanic Great view looking out over the bay from this first-floor café, with excellent breakfasts in a relaxed setting.

El Café is just round across the road from Mahung's on Main Street. Good breakfasts.

Bobby's 12 Main Street serves excellent seafood and creole dishes. Dinner only. If you want a beer with your meal you'll have to bring your own. Bobby is also an excellent fishing guide. Start him talking and he won't stop!

Carmelo Palma Tortilla Factory at the intersection of Queen Street and Main Street. Snacks such as garnaches, soft drinks.

Marcenco's Ice Cream Parlour & Restaurant serves serves excellent *burittos* and other dishes. Good value for money.

If you want to do something in the evening, Wa Luco's over Joe Taylor Creek occasionally has live music. In the centre of town the Dreamlight Disco on Main Street across from Mahung's Hotel operates on Fridays and Saturdays only. Things don't really start to roll until about 23.00. Ligiri ('The Point' in Garifuna, but with a double meaning) is a shack of a bar near Main and Church Streets, with recorded reggae and punta rock, dominoes and more than a few drunks bumming drinks. The Central Bar on Front Street is a simple, airy place for a beer close to the water. Olimpos Bar down the street is simpler, airier, and has two pool tables.

What to see
Like most Belizean towns, Punta Gorda itself has no specific tourist sights. There is no real beach, and if you venture out for a dip ask locals first; stingrays and jelly fish abound in certain areas and certain times of the year. The waterfront makes for a nice stroll, however, and there are spots where you can see the lights of Guatemala and even Honduras on clear nights. Light but constant breezes off the Gulf of Honduras rustle the palms and mango trees on Front Street. It's a sleepy, pleasant town of 5,010 which provides a base camp for more interesting trips nearby. At the local market in the centre of town, you'll see plenty of Maya from villages to the west. Some sell fabric bracelets and small woven baskets, but most of the goods are manufactured and quite tacky. Certainly nothing sold here rivals

the handicrafts available in nearby Guatemala or Mexico, but the Saturday food market is worth visiting if you're in town.

You can walk easily anywhere in town, including to the air strip.

Information and useful addresses

The **Belize Tourist Board** is on Front Street opposite the Miramar Hotel. It's a useful place for information as well as catching up on the latest issues in this hotbed of Belizean development. **Dem Dat's Doin** have an information booth by the dock where the ferries from Guatemala arrive.

Chet at **Nature's Way Guest House** is a wealth of information on the area, in addition to his role as contact for the Toledo District Guest House programme.

TIDE (Toledo Institute for Development and Economy) is a tourism group that works to develop sustainable development in Toledo. Research is one aspect of their work including fish tagging programmes. They are also involved in guide training programmes to facilitate tourism development in the region. Visit them on the road north out of Punta Gorda near Joe Taylor Creek or contact them at tidetours@btl.net or www.belizeecotours.org.

Belize Bank at the intersection of Main and Queen Streets changes cash, travellers' cheques and can arrange cash advances. If the Bank is closed try **Pallavi's** who may be able to help. **Vernon's Grocery** (downtown on Front Street, across from the Miramar Hotel, open Mon-Fri until 17.00, Sat until 13.00) also changes cash and cheques. Hotels will usually change US dollars, particularly if you're a guest. Get rid of your Belizean dollars if you're headed on to Guatemala; if you wait until Guatemala, you'll receive only about one quetzal per Belize dollar. Vernon's Grocery or the Southern Grocer's Supply on King Street may be able to supply you with quetzales. There is normally a moneychanger meeting the boats who will change money for you. Make sure you have an idea of the exchange rate before parting with your cash. If all this fails, try to meet travellers off the ferry.

BTL is on Main Street and King Street, open 08.00–16.00 Mon-Fri, 08.00–12.00 Sat.

Punta Graphics, 2A Front Street, PO Box 99; tel: 07 22852; email: acapps@btl.net is currently the only place to link up to the net and surf in Punta Gorda. If you want to receive email, have your name put in the subject area.

Local tour operators include: **Nature's Way Guest House** (see *Where to stay* above); Bobby Polonio at **Bobby's Bar** (tel: 07 22135), who runs fishing trips and boat trips to the cayes; and **Dem Dat's Doin'** (see *Excursions* and *Further afield* below). **Sea Front Inn** can also arrange trips in the area.

The **hospital** is located on Main Street at the southern edge of town (ominously, right next to the cemetery). The doctor is reported to be very competent.

Several grocery stores on Front Street are fairly well stocked with canned and dry goods, beer and liquor. **Southern Grocer's Supply** on King Street carries much the same items.

Maya Indita Tienda on Middle Street sells souvenirs from Guatemala, El Salvador, and Belize. **Black Thunder Record Shop** sells tapes of Jamaican, American and Belizean music. **Fajina Craft Centre** is a women's weaving cooperative located near the dock area.

Excursions
Near town
Joe Taylor Creek
You can paddle up this narrow, mangrove-lined creek for some way, occasionally startling white egrets. Rent a dugout canoe at Nature's Way Guest House (about

US$7.50 for the day) and paddle north about 20 minutes up the coastline until you reach the creek mouth. If you must jump out along the way, shuffle your feet along the bottom to scare off stingrays, which are common here. Once in the creek, you'll come to Arvin's Landing, owned by Jack and Barbara and a pleasant place to stop for a break. They have lodging and will let you camp on their property. Call 07 22015 for details. Two or three more bends up the river and you'll leave the mangrove ecosystem and enter rainforest. Remember, you're too close to civilisation to see many animals, but it's a pleasant day's outing. Nature's Way Guest House provides a guided 3 hour paddle trip up the river for US$38 (2-3 people), with BZ$10 being donated to a protection fund for the creek.

Punta Gorda Nature Trail

This programme, when completed, will involve a 6.5km nature trail through protected forest, mangrove, and guided visits to sustainable-farming plots, Maya homes and East Indian farms. Conceived several years ago, the Nature Trail has had lots of teething problems but is receiving more support as eco-tourism grows in Toledo District and may be operational when you visit. Local guides will lead the trail.

Cerro Hill

Guided hikes to the top of Cerro Hill cost BZ$30 pp and last two hours. The view on clear days is magnificent, and you can see the coastline of both Honduras and Guatemala, as well as the Sapodilla Cayes. The hike, up a 50° incline at times, is strenuous. Contact Nature's Way Guest House for details.

Mr. Enriquez' Farm Tour

Mr Enriquez, an affable Garifuna man, delights in showing visitors his edible and medicinal plants. His farm is located about 1.5km outside town, and he charges BZ$20 for a two-hour tour. Nature's Way Guest House can put you in touch with Mr. Enriquez.

Boden's Cave

A guided tour of this two-chambered, bat-filled cave costs BZ$15 pp for 2–3 people, includes a botanical tour along the way, and lasts about two hours. Some climbing and crawling is involved. The cave is a 10-minute drive outside of town. Nature's Way Guest House has details.

Home Visits

One of the simplest and most popular 'trips' in Punta Gorda consists of dinner with a local family. You'll accompany family members to the market to shop for food, visit with them in their home, and learn how to prepare a traditional Belizean meal. See Chet at Nature's Way Guest House for details.

Fishing

If you hit it off with a local fisherman you may be able to spend the day in a motorised dugout canoe, helping him fish with throw nets and hand lines off the coast of Punta Gorda. This isn't big-game fishing, mind you – the largest fish you're likely to catch will be a 'barra' (barracuda), and most of the fish will be smallish grunts. It is, however, a lot cheaper than a guided fishing trip (you'll probably pay the fisherman around BZ$30, with the option of keeping a few fish to have cooked at a local restaurant). You'll also have the opportunity to observe and take part in the daily life of rural Belize, accompanying the fisherman as he catches baitfish with a throw net in the morning and helping him sell the day's catch to the eager crowds which meet you ashore. These aren't 'tours' as yet – arrange things informally through Nature's Way Guest House, which will put you in touch with local Garifuna fishermen.

If you want a more conventional fishing experience, find Bobby at his restaurant at 12 Main Street.

Further afield

It's possible, but not easy, to see most of the inland sights in Toledo District via a combination of public transport, hitching and walking. See *San Antonio* for information on local buses. For all of the destinations listed below, you can arrange reasonably-priced transportation with either Nature's Way Guest House (see *Where to stay* above), Dem Dat's Doin' (see listing below), or Dionísio Bol (see *San Antonio* below). It saves money to get a group of travellers together, since most tours charge by the carload rather than per person.

Southern Highway and vicinity

Two roads lead out of Punta Gorda. The southernmost, Saddleback New Road, passes the former Camp of the British Defence Force base, where a sign warns 'Caution Live Firing'. Driving north on Front Street past the Texaco petrol station, you'll cross Joe Taylor Creek and come to the area called Cattle Landing ('Catlanding' to locals). An extensive shallow shelf extends offshore here, and cattle were once herded through the saltwater and onto waiting barges for shipment to Belize City. The road then veers west through Forest Home Village an area largely populated by East Indians.

Both roads out of Punta Gorda join some 8km northwest of town, continuing west through agricultural land, passing the Machaca Southern District Forestry Station. Here, private vehicles and buses are sometimes stopped by inspectors attempting to prevent agricultural pests from being transported around Belize. Twenty-three kilometres from Punta Gorda lies the junction with the Southern Highway. This area is commonly referred to as 'the Dump', owing to the tons of dirt dumped here to fill low-lying swamp just west of the junction. You'll find the Shell petrol station here which is generally open all week. The road west leads to San Antonio, the ruins of Lubaantun, Uxbenka, Pusilha, the Blue Creek Caves, Dem Dat's Doin' 'eco-farm', and a score of Maya villages (see below).

Dem Dat's Doin'

Heading west, the right fork leads to this self-sufficient farm and 'resource centre for microenterprises'. It's open to visitors (US$5 pp) and definitely worth a look if self-sufficiency is of interest to you. Alfredo Villoria quit his aerospace engineering job in California in 1980 and turned his dreams and talents loose on a small patch of Belizean farmland. He and his wife Yvonne now tend 55 varieties of fruit trees, vegetable gardens, orchids, a cottage industry making native perfumes, an insect dryer and a methane biogas digester that utilizes pig waste, they also export seeds and iguana farming is on the cards. They'll be more than happy to show you around and discuss their vision of a self-sufficient and ecologically sane future, but it's best to arrange your visit beforehand. Write to the Villorias at Dem Dat's Doin', PO Box 73, Punta Gorda (tel: 07 22470), or ask for them in town at their information stand by the pier near customs. Allow a couple of hours for the tour. Their farm is located about 6.8km west of the junction with the Southern Highway. Head west at 'the Dump' toward San Antonio, take a right turn in 4km (as if going toward San Pedro Columbia), and after 2km (just on the other side of a small bridge) veer off to the right on a smaller dirt road. Buses headed to San

Miguel will drop you off at the signpost, or Chun's buses from Punta Gorda to San Antonio (see the section on San Antonio below) will drop you off within 3.2km of the place. To return to Punta Gorda, walk back to 'the Dump' and wait for the daily bus from Belize City at the Shell Station or hitch.

Big Falls

A right turn at the junction puts you on the Southern Highway, northbound for Mango Creek, Independence, and Dangriga. Just 0.8km north of the junction stands a Texaco petrol station (also open daily) and King's Cool Spot refreshment stand. Continuing another 7.25km you'll come to Big Falls bridge over the Río Grande. This low-head waterfall and riverside beach is a popular spot with locals, possibly worth a stop if you're in the mood to picnic. Beyond the falls another 6.5km lies Big Falls Village, where you'll find a grocery store selling cold soft drinks, beer and stout. Belize's only hot springs, muddy and unimpressive, lie on a nearby farm; ask for directions at the store if you're interested.

Nim Li Punit

North of Big Falls, the Southern Highway covers another 52km in Toledo District. You'll pass Whitney's lumber mill and general store on the east side of the highway, followed on the west by the small Maya site at Nim Li Punit.

Oil company workers stumbled across this Maya site in 1976, barely 0.8km from the Southern Highway. Small in scale, Nim Li Punit can boast an impressive collection of carved monuments, which are curiously absent at nearby Lubaantun. Twenty-five stelae have been uncovered at the site, eight of which are carved. Included among these is one 9.4m in length, making it the longest stela ever found in Belize. It was never erected, possibly due to an error in the inscription carving, and one can only wonder at the fate of the unlucky stonemason! Time and weather have not been kind to this particular stela, nor most of the others which are lain out under small thatched shelters. Yet next to the long stela on the east side of the site you'll find a single well-preserved monument, Stela 14. This stela includes a carved figure who sports a huge headdress, lending the site its Maya name ('Big Hat').

Nim Li Punit commands a scenic ridge in the foothills of the Maya Mountains. Nearby is the Kekchi village of Indian Creek, and a *milpa* creeps up the ridge almost to the very southeastern boundary of the site. The ceremonial centre includes two main plazas encircled by four structures, the tallest rising 11m above plaza level. A low-lying structure across the plaza on the east side measures an impressive 65m in length.

Norman Hammond, responsible for the excellent work at Lubaantun in the early 1970s, first examined Nim Li Punit shortly after its discovery. Richard Leventhal began excavations in 1983, and three years later unearthed a royal burial site. This pit, which you'll find on the west side of the site, contained numerous ceramic treasures and is still being excavated.

Researchers have noted the architectural similarities with Lubaantun, postulating a strong link between the two settlements. Both flourished during the Late Classic, and the original hypothesis that Nim Li Punit served merely as a funeral site for Lubaantun has been abandoned; recent work suggests that upwards of 5,000 Maya might have lived nearby.

These days, the only person you're likely to encounter at Nim Li Punit is the caretaker. Kekchi girls may wander up and try to sell you fabric wrist bands, baskets, and 'Maya calendars'. At dusk, even the caretaker heads down the hill, and pacas ('gibnuts' in Belizean argot) emerge from hiding and scamper about the plaza. A gargantuan ceiba tree towers over the eastern entrance to the site, its trunk encircled with lianas.

Nim Li Punit is located just off the Southern Highway, a few kilometres north of Big Falls Village. Coming from the south, be prepared to turn when you come upon Whitney's Lumber Mill and general store on the east side of the highway. Just north of here, an unmarked dirt road on the west side will take you to the site. (Incidentally, several maps – including the usually reliable 1:250,000 scale published by the Lands and Surveys Department – erroneously put Nim Li Punit on the east side of the highway!) It used to take 15 minutes to reach the ruins up a jungle path. In 1990, the government unwisely decided to carve a road directly to the site. Not only is the new road hideous, it appears as if the bulldozers ran roughshod over some chiselled Maya building stones along the way. Adding to this insult is the fact that the new road is really too steep and unstable for most vehicle traffic except 4WD.

It's easy to reach Nim Li Punit by public bus from Punta Gorda. The 05.00 Z-Line will drop you off at around 06.30. Most visitors, however – avid Mayanists excluded – will be satisfied with an hour or two of ruin browsing. Then you'll either have to hitch a ride or wait for one of the southbound buses. With its shady trees and view of the valley below, Nim Li Punit makes an ideal picnic spot.

North of Nim Li Punit there are no specific 'tourist sights' in Toledo District. The district does undergo a fascinating change of scenery, however, in the final 40km of Southern Highway before entering Stann Creek District to the north. With lush tropical forest both to the north and south, the Southern Pine Ridge located between Deep River and the Swasey Branch comes as something of a shock. Here you'll find pine barrens not unlike those of the southern United States, wispy grasses the only ground cover beneath the trees.

Bladen Branch Nature Reserve
Third largest of Belize's protected areas (after Río Bravo and Cockscomb), this 97,000-acre wilderness area remains off limits to all but bona fide biologists, archaeologists, and other scientists and educators. Nevertheless, it deserves a brief mention here because it may be the largest chunk of totally undisturbed rainforest in all of Belize. This rugged wilderness takes in a portion of the southeastern slope of the Maya Mountains and the fringing limestone karst foothills at lower elevations. The reserve takes its name from the Bladen Branch of the Monkey River, which runs northeasterly through the area. Caves and sinkholes pockmark the region, and at least one Maya ruin site, Quebra del Oro has been discovered. Minister of Natural Resources Florencio Marin signed the reserve into being in 1990, after much groundwork by the Belize Audubon Society and Lighthawk, among others. At some point in the future, limited tourism may be permitted. Contact the Belize Audubon Society for details.

Maya villages
At least 20 Maya villages are accessible via unpaved roads from Punta Gorda, offering a cultural experience that in Belize, at least, can be found only in Toledo District. Many of these villages – including San Antonio, San Pedro Columbia, San Miguel, Santa Cruz, Blue Creek village and San José – can be reached by public bus (see the section below on San Antonio for details on buses). Others must be reached by hitching, hiring private vehicles, driving yourself, bicycling, or hiking. Of these, hitching is the least reliable, since few vehicles ply these roads. Most of the villages lie no more than 25km from San Antonio, although roads are rough in the dry season and become impassable later in the rainy season. Four Maya ruins are nestled near the villages: Lubaantun and Uxbentun near San Pedro Columbia,

Uxbenka close by Santa Cruz, and Pusilha near San Benito Poite. These ruin sites and several of the more interesting villages are discussed in detail below.

Accommodation in the area has been developed with the idea of providing services to visitors without denigrating the Maya culture. Consequently beyond traditional hostel accommodation, which you will find dotted throughout most of the villages, there is the Guest House and Homestay Programmes which provide the visitor with the opportunity to stay with villagers either as guests or as a participating family member.

Village Guest House Ecotrail Programme

This programme, formed in 1990, has attracted international attention and in 1996 won the 'To Do!' Prize for the most socially responsible community-based ecotourism programme and should be on every traveller's Toledo District agenda. The programme allows travellers to spend a few days in a living Maya or Garifuna village, taking part in its daily life, and exploring the countryside nearby – all the while contributing directly to the cause of sustainable agriculture, conservation and a cultural renaissance among the local Maya and Garifuna.

Overnight stays in Maya villages have been possible all along, of course, even if it meant pitching a tent on the roadside or renting hammock space. But such laissez-faire tourism threatens both the Maya way of life and, eventually, its appeal to visitors. Most travellers have witnessed once-rustic hamlets transform themselves into little more than quaint tourist traps, the streets filled with tawdry souvenir stands, hordes of gringos toting backpacks and children charging for photos.

With careful planning and grass-roots community involvement, the Toledo Ecotourism Association (TEA) has been able to avoid such a dismal scenario. TEA's members, including local community activists and Maya villagers themselves, have drawn up an ambitious list of objectives for the Village Guest House Programme: to preserve and enhance the cultural integrity of the villages; to generate money with which villagers can improve health care and education; to encourage a return to sustainable organic Maya farming methods rather than a sole reliance on nomadic slash-and-burn; and to develop nature reserves surrounding the villages, eventually linking them with an extensive green belt corridor.

If all this sounds lofty but a bit naive, you need to stop in for a chat with William 'Chet' Schmidt, one of the programme's early proponents (and owner of Nature's Way Guest House in Punta Gorda). Schmidt's 30 years as an environmental activist in Belize have tempered his ideals with a dose of political reality, but not tarnished them. According to Schmidt, the Village Guest House Programme works like this: Villages deciding to join the programme hold regular meetings and elect a local representative. Implicit in this first step is the agreement to develop their ecotourism potential as a group rather than as individual entrepreneurs competing with each other and with other villages. Villagers conduct a zoning study of the area, setting aside some land as a Community Conservation Area (CCA) to be protected from hunting, farming or other disturbance. 'Eco trails' are established within and between these CCAs, and local guides are familiar with their trails' secrets – where a particular bird nests, where a certain medicinal herb grows. The programme's philosophy includes participation of as many villagers as possible, spreading the benefits as widely as possible, and a commitment to ecotourism which dignifies rather than demeans the Maya and Garifuna.

Next, each village pitches in to build a simple thatched guest house. A maximum of only eight guests may visit the village at any one time, ensuring that both the working and cultural lives of the villages – most of which are home to

LIVING WITH THE MAYA

As 'guinea pigs', we were among the first visitors to Laguna, the pilot village in the programme. Following a brief bus ride some 25km northwest of Punta Gorda, we hiked the remaining 5km down a dirt road to Laguna, accompanied by Kekchi Maya villagers returning from market. Santos Coc, Laguna's representative, showed us to the thatched visitors' hut. He explained that 10-20 men could build such a house in two days, spending the first day lashing poles and the second day thatching the roof with cohune leaves. The only concession to Western building was the concrete floor (most Maya homes have earthen floors). We slept in hammocks, but the villagers have now added bunk beds; mosquito netting, hammocks, bedding and towels are provided. Outside the guest house are bathing areas and pit toilets.

Corn forms the basis of every Maya meal, and at Santos' home we lunched on a stack of homemade tortillas, thick, soft, and steaming. Kekchi homes are quiet, and long periods of silence don't bother these people as it does us hyperkinetic urbanites. After weeks in Belize among the boisterous Creoles and Garifuna, we came to appreciate the hushed quality of Kekchi life.

That evening, Santos' youngest daughter shyly requested some English lessons. We in turn learned a phrase or two in Kekchi Maya, a soft language that is easy on the ears. Kekchi and the other Maya tongues sound to most Westerners like little more than a series of tongue clicks. That belies the important differences between Maya languages. Kekchi and Mopan Mayan, for instance, are mutually unintelligible; even the word for the ubiquitous corn tortilla is different in each tongue.

The next day we hiked for several hours to a cave overlooking an unbroken vista of rainforest. Nearby caves contain Maya paintings and, during the dry season, visitors can visit Laguna's namesake lagoon, a nesting site for hundreds of birds. During the hike, Santos pointed out various medicinal plants, offered us bites of the edible species, and identified birds we spotted along the way. As always in the rainforest, wildlife surrounded us constantly but was maddeningly difficult to spot through the foliage. Our most thrilling sight came as we hiked home: a jaguarundi, the charcoal black relative of the jaguar that is maybe a fifth of the bigger cat's size.

Surviving within earshot of civilisation, the jaguarundi seemed to us like a metaphor for the enduring Kekchi themselves. But we also wondered: will this sort of ecotourism, well-intentioned and controlled as it is, end up diluting Kekchi culture just as surely as busloads of camera-toting love boaters? Perhaps, but as the *Belize Review* reasoned in a recent issue, 'Since the tourists are coming anyway, it is certainly worth a try'.

250–400 Maya – remain relatively undisturbed. Guests pay a set daily fee for lodging (BZ$18 pp) and food (BZ$6 pp per meal). Granted, this amounts to somewhat more than you'd pay wandering into a village on your own and bargaining for a spot to hang your hammock. On the other hand, it's still a pittance by First World standards and, more importantly, the money is shared by the community rather than hoarded by individuals which avoids jealousy.

Guests eat each meal with a different family, and villagers rotate duties as guides on the 'ecotrails'. A half-day walk costs BZ$28 pp. An hour of traditional music with four local musicians playing handmade instruments costs BZ$50. Villagers can also tell Maya stories in English. These costs can be shared by groups of up to eight, but many guests are finding that it's well worth it to be alone with the villagers or in very small groups. Small, village-run craft shops and natural history museums will soon be a part of the programme.

The following villages have guest houses at the time of this writing: Laguna, San José, San Pedro Columbia, San Antonio, Medina Bank, Blue Creek, Barranco (Garifuna), Pueblo Viejo, Santa Elena, and San Miguel. All the villages have their special attractions; Laguna its caves, San José its old growth rainforest, San Miguel its Tiger Cave. Five day trips taking in several villages and local sights are being planned as part of the Maya Eco-Park. The park, if successful, will encompass what is left of national lands in Toledo, including Toledo Ridge and a wetland. The theme is sustainable living, and the tours will include visits to commercial cash crop farms, local craftspeople, permaculture farms, even an iguana breeding centre. Bikes, kayaks, and horses will provide transportation from village to village, and local caves, lagoons, and other sights are to be visited along the way. The final leg of the trip is a day of kayaking downriver to Barranco, one of Belize's most secluded Garifuna villages.

Information on the Village Guest House Programme is available at Nature's Way Guest House in Punta Gorda. If you're on a tight schedule, plan to arrive in Punta Gorda on a Tuesday or Friday night; this allows you to catch the local public buses which operate most frequently during the Wednesday and Saturday markets. Bring day packs, water bottles, hiking shoes or boots, insect repellent and binoculars. Evenings can be chilly. Women in particular should dress conservatively. And if you must take pictures of the Maya, please ask first.

Homestay Programme

This programme has the visitor actually staying with the family as opposed to the Guest House scheme which provides a degree of privacy and separation. With the Homestay Programme you live as the locals live, getting involved with the daily routine of making tortillas, working on the land, finding out what the kids are up to. It's rough and ready, and the families on the Homestay Programme are not tour guides, but it might be appealing to you.

There are currently seven villages involved in the programme; San Pedro Columbia, Silver Creek, San Antonio, Na Luum Ka, San José, Santa Cruz and Santa Elena.

The scheme has been devised to make sure the financial benefits of visitors are shared throughout the village and positions of authority within the scheme are rotated to make sure the benefits do not accrue to one individual or family.

Once the programme has been explained to you in all its realistic details, you travel out to the village of your choice. There is a registration fee of BZ$10 and then BZ$10 for each night's accommodation plus BZ$4 for meals.

The Toledo Visitor's Information Centre or Dem Dat's Doin in Punta Gorda can provide information and send you on your way.

San Antonio

This is the largest of the villages (population 1,087 in 1981), serving as a sort of informal hub for the area. Consequently, it's not as picturesque as some of the smaller villages such as Santa Elena. At present it is the only village with a hotel: **Bol's Hilltop Hotel**; tel: 07 22124, seven rooms, BZ$30 pp, with shared bath, clean and with good views of the surrounding countryside, meals available if requested. Manager Dionísio Bol is a wealth of information on the area and can set you up with local guides. The village now has a guest house (see *Village Guest House Programme* above).

San Antonio was the original settlement site of Mopan Maya in Belize, and remains today the largest Amerindian village in southern Belize, dominating the economic and cultural life of the neighbouring villages. The inhabitants are virtually all Mopan Maya.

The original inhabitants fled across the Guatemalan border in 1883 from San Luís, Petén Department, in order to avoid military service. Crops failed in the new location, and the villagers soon suspected the reason: in their hasty desertion of San Luís, they had left behind their *santo*, the statue of their patron saint San Luís Rey. Armed with a keg of gunpowder, a small group of village men made their way at night back across the border to San Luís, a distance of 65km. The gunpowder proved unnecessary – the church door had been left unlocked. The raiding party made off with not only three statues, but three 18th century church bells, returning triumphantly to San Antonio. The villagers realised that a reprisal from the men of San Luís wouldn't be long in coming, however. Leaving out a few petty details, they petitioned the Governor in Punta Gorda for arms to defend themselves against what they described as an unprovoked attack on their peaceful new community. The governor granted the request.

When the retaliatory attack came, the men of San Antonio were away from the village, and the women managed to hold off the attackers for a time. The men returned to the battle but were subsequently captured and returned to Guatemala. A deal was eventually struck. The villagers were released on the condition that they would never return to San Luís.

Unfortunately, you won't see either the original statue of San Luís Rey or the church built to house it in San Antonio. Mysterious fires destroyed both the original thatch church and then a wooden one, causing some villagers to suspect that their larcenous ways were being punished by the Almighty. These days, a third version of the church graces San Antonio – this one made of stone – and the statue of San Luís inside is a reconstruction cast in Guatemala. American nuns currently run the church and mission house, which stands across from Bol's Hilltop Hotel. A set of eight stained-glass windows bear both German and English inscriptions. These originally were part of a church in St Louis, Missouri, and parishioners there donated the windows when their church was being demolished. San Antonio's church is still a focal point for worship, and Indians will travel from distant villages to light devotional candles before their santo.

In recent years, San Antonio residents have revived traditional feast day celebrations honouring San Luís. These happen sporadically beginning on August 15, and culminate with a deer dance and parades on September 25.

To reach San Antonio (as well as a number of other Maya villages including San José, Santa Cruz, San Miguel, Blue Creek and San Pedro Columbia) via public transportation, catch the buses run by Chun's Bus Company from Punta Gorda. Depending on the village, these arrive in Punta Gorda early in the morning on Monday, Wednesday, Friday and Saturday and return the same day, leaving from the main plaza at 13.00 (but none too punctually). Your best bets are Wednesday and Saturday, both local market days for the Indians. Fares are ridiculously cheap, and Americans will have a nostalgic trip of it – Chun's buses are all yellow school buses from public schools in the US. Alternatively, you can take the 05.00 Z-Line bus from Punta Gorda to 'the Dump' (the intersection of the road to Punta Gorda with the Southern Highway; a Shell petrol station stands there), then hike west about 2 hours to either San Antonio or San Pedro Columbia. Jeeps or other private vehicles can sometimes be hired in both these villages for further travels. A jeep trip from San Pedro to the Blue Creek Caves and back to the Highway, for example, costs about BZ$30.

San José

Not quite 1km east of San Antonio, a road branches off to the north toward the tiny Mopan village of Crique Jute (3km from the main road), on to Salamanca, where a British Army camp maintains watch on nearby Guatemala, Na Luumka (a new Mopan settlement), and finally to San José, at 10km from the main road. This village of about 600 Mopan Maya is now a participant in the Village Guest House Programme (see above). Trips to a nearby cave and sinkhole can be arranged as part of a guest house stay. The most unique attraction is the nearby old growth rainforest, with some of the tallest trees in Toledo District.To reach San José via public transportation (Chun's buses), see the section above on San Antonio.

San Pedro Columbia

This village of both Kekchi and Mopan Maya stands 10.5km northeast of San Antonio on unpaved roads. The 'Columbia' refers to the Columbia Branch of the Río Grande running just north of the village, and is usually appended to distinguish the village from San Pedro, Ambergris Caye. The village is now part of the Village Guest House Programme. Maragarita Lara serves cold beer and soft drinks, and stocks a modest assortment of dried beans, flour and canned goods. The town is little more than 1.5km from the Lubaantun ruins.

With over 800 residents, San Pedro ranks as the largest of some thirty Kekchi villages in Belize. Its sleepy nature belies that standing; women still grind corn for tortillas, still wash their clothing in local streams, still plant seedlings with a sharp stick, cook over fires and wear traditional dress. On muddy trails you'll be greeted shyly by villagers hauling cohune palm fronds on their backs; they'll use these as thatch coverings for the traditional huts that dominate San Pedro. A single road sign in town wryly underscores San Pedro's disregard for the 20th century: along the deeply rutted and potholed dirt track, it reads 'Speed Limit 50 mph'.

To reach San Pedro via public transportation (Chun's buses), see the section above on San Antonio.

Lodging is available at the **Fallen Stones Butterfly Ranch**, PO Box 23 in Punta Gorda, tel/fax: 07 22167. Six cabins, US$165 including three meals, US$120 without meals. Add US$50 one-way transport from PG for 1-3 people. Blue morphos and other butterfly pupae are being raised. The ranch has spectacular views. Another lodging possibility is **OH's Traveller's Farm**, Chano Creek, San Pedro Columbia Village, with five rooms with shared bath.

Lubaantun

At some of the better-known Central American ruins – Chichén Itz· and Uxmal come to mind – one can easily conjure up a mental picture of the Mayan heyday. Bustling with tourists and vendors as they once did with priests and labourers, these ceremonial centres look much like they must have in ancient times: orderly and well-groomed, surrounded by open spaces and agricultural clearings.

Lubaantun evokes a far different image. Cresting the jungle ridge where Lubaantun stands, the visitor is transported not to the 8th century but to the late 19th century. Here are Maya ruins as Stephens and Catherwood must have stumbled upon them: tumbledown, surrounded by rainforest, choked with vines and underbrush, eerie reminders of a once-mighty civilisation mysteriously fallen silent.

It helps that few travellers get to Lubaantun. During a recent peak holiday season, the register book showed thirty visitors in as many days; your chances of finding the place deserted for the entire day are excellent. It also helps that the site hasn't been meticulously restored. It was Thomas Gann who in 1924 dubbed the place Lubaantun (Mayan for 'Fallen Stones'), a name which aptly describes the ruins even to this day.

Given a different setting, Lubaantun would be rather unremarkable. None of the 11 major structures are carved or decorated; archaeologists presume that such decorations would have perished along with the wooden structures which sat atop the existing stone platforms. There are no stelae, and the few carved stone monuments found at the site are either badly weathered or removed to museums. Yet Lubaantun's air of serenity and decay amid lush jungle surroundings nicely complements the more heavily-trafficked Maya sites. And when you've seen the ruins themselves, you can explore the maze of footpaths in the forest nearby.

Confederate refugees from the United States who had settled in Toledo following the Civil War first reported a ruin site here in 1875. The Governor of the Colony invited Thomas Gann to make a preliminary exploration of the site in 1903, the first of Gann's several trips to the area. Twelve years later, Harvard's Peabody Museum Central American Expedition reached Lubaantun (known then simply as the 'Río Grande Ruins'). Expedition leader RE Merwin found and removed three ball court markers near the southern end of the site, significant in that this was the first evidence of ball courts in the Maya lowlands. These stones probably marked the centre line of the court, and each bore carvings of two players facing one another with the ball in between them. Later expeditions uncovered numerous figurines dressed for the famous ball game known as pok-ta-pok; the sport was apparently of great importance at Lubaantun.

Thomas Gann returned to Lubaantun in 1924, this time on a privately financed expedition with the adventurer FA Mitchell-Hedges and his travelling companion, Lady Richmond Brown. A year later they were joined by members of the British Museum Expedition led by TA Joyce. Mitchell-Hedges had brought along his seventeen year-old adopted daughter Anna-Marie, and one day in 1927 she stumbled upon the single most famous – and controversial – artefact unearthed in southern Belize: the Crystal Skull (see page 216).

That same year, Joyce returned to Lubaantun with the 2nd British Museum Expedition. This time he was accompanied by J Cooper-Clark and the man who was soon to become the most celebrated Mayanist of all, J Eric Thompson. But the discovery of nearby Pusilha (see below) cut short the excavations at Lubaantun; Pusilha was given priority because, unlike Lubaantun, it contained sculptured stelae with hieroglyphic inscriptions. For the next 42 years, Lubaantun remained untouched by scholars.

Dr Norman Hammond began excavating in 1970 under the joint banner of Cambridge and Harvard Universities. His exhaustive work revealed Lubaantun as the hub of an extensive trading network. Almost forty percent of the animal remains unearthed at the site were marine fish, implicating the Río Grande as a major canoe route to the coast and open sea. The bones of parrot fish, mackerel, and shark suggest that the Maya sailed not only to the cayes for fishing, but to the deep water beyond. Pyrites and slate mirror backs found their way to Lubaantun via the steep southeastern slopes of the Maya Mountains.

Corn probably served as the medium of exchange for such local trade, but Hammond found evidence of even longer-range commerce: lava, obsidian and jade, which must have come from the volcanic Guatemalan highlands. These exotic articles demanded some other medium of exchange, and Hammond suggested that Lubaantun's soil and micro-climate perfectly suited it to the farming of such Maya 'money': cacao beans. To this day, local Maya continue trade with

RIVER TRANSPORT
Informal and sometimes infuriating, boats still play an important part in the country's transport system
Above: *Fishing boats on Belize River* (JN)
Below: *The ferry to Sarteneja* (JB)

CONSERVATION
A third of the country is set aside as wildlife preserves
Above: *Cockscomb Jaguar Preserve* (AG)
Below: *Sign at the Belize Zoo* (AG)

THROUGHOUT THE WORLD, TROPICAL FORESTS ARE BEING DESTROYED. AND ANIMALS, DEPENDENT ON THESE FORESTS, ARE DISAPPEARING. MUCH OF BELIZE REMAINS FORESTED, AND HEALTHY POPULATIONS OF ITS WILDLIFE LIVE ON. BELIZE STAND PROUD—AS A NATION, THE RICHNESS OF YOUR FLORA & FAUNA WILL BE AN EVERLASTING ENHANCEMENT TO YOUR NATURAL HERITAGE

THE MAYA
The hilltop citadel of Xunantunich, one of over a dozen Maya sites in Belize
Above: *Xunantunich from afar (AG)*
Below: *Maya frieze* (JB)

Cooling off at the foot of the waterfall in Cockscomb Jaguar Preserve (JB)

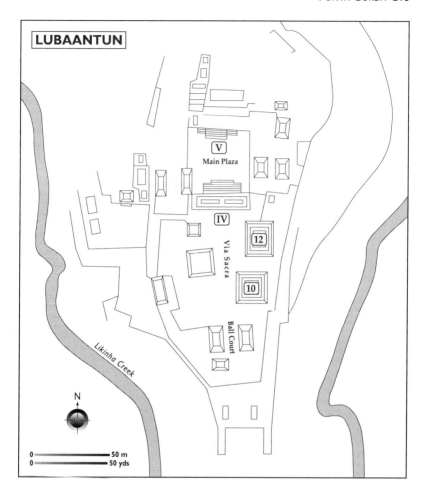

the Guatemalan highlands, although cacao has been replaced by the more prosaic quetzal and Belize dollar.

Hammond's *Lubaantun: A Classic Maya Realm* remains a model of brilliant archaeological analysis (see *Appendix 2, Further Reading*). It's a massive tome including maps and appendices that comprise over half of its 428 pages. A quick glance will convince you that archaeology has come a long way from the days of reckless swashbucklers like Thomas Gann and Mitchell-Hedges.

The site consists of 11 major structures and five large plazas. Hammond suggested that the innermost buildings served religious functions. These were surrounded by a zone of ceremonial structures (including the ball court), encircled in turn by a zone of residential housing. Lubaantun's buildings are remarkable in that the builders used no mortar; each stone was meticulously measured, cut, and fit snugly against its counterpart. All of this perches on a ridge which the Maya levelled, terraced, and faced with stone. The terracing served a practical rather than aesthetic purpose: terraces kept the soil from washing downhill after the *milpa* was cleared.

The most impressive structure is Pyramid 12 (12.4m high) just east of Plaza IV where the caretaker has his thatched hut. From the top you can look east across

THE CRYSTAL SKULL

By the time he was 32, Frederick A Mitchell-Hedges could already lay claim to an exotic and chequered past: English by birth, he had joined an Arctic expedition at age 16, worked as a stockbroker in London, a gambler and realter in Canada, a ranch hand in Central America and had thrown in with the Villistas in Mexico. He returned to Canada in 1917 and adopted a ten-year old orphan named Anna-Marie Le Guillon. Despite his lack of formal schooling, Mitchell-Hedges was fascinated by Maya culture, and became obsessed with the notion that the lost continent of Atlantis lay somewhere near the Bay Islands of Honduras. After an exploratory trip to Central America, Mitchell-Hedges grew convinced that the remains of a lost city linked to Atlantis waited for him in the jungles of British Honduras.

Mitchell-Hedges, his travelling companion Lady Richmond Brown, Thomas Gann and an army of Belizeans eventually hacked their way into Lubaantun (which Gann had first investigated 21 years earlier) in 1924. Two years later, 16-year old Anna-Marie joined them and excavation began. Early in 1927 – reportedly on Anna-Marie's 17th birthday – she unearthed a quartz crystal skull beneath a collapsed altar.

Despite the continuing controversy over the Crystal Skull's origin and authenticity, it is undeniably a magnificent piece of artwork. Carved from a single chunk of quartz, it weighs 5.2kg, measuring 12.7cm high, 17.8cm long and 12.7cm wide. The movable jawbone was apparently cut from the original skull at some later date.

Microscopic examination suggests that no mechanical or even metal tools were used in the carving. Its smooth surface was probably hand-rubbed with a sand-water poultice, a process that may have taken hundreds of years of constant work. Both hand-ground and natural lenses within the crystal direct light rays focused at the base of the skull and transmit them into the eye sockets. For this reason, some have suggested that the skull might have been suspended above a hollow altar and illuminated from below by a candle. Anatomically correct in many respects, the skull was almost certainly based on a real female skull due to peculiarities in the glabellar region between the 'eyebrows'.

rainforest, *milpas*, and the coastal plain some 25km away. Break a leaf from the smooth, white-trunked tree which perches atop the pyramid; the familiar fragrance is allspice.

Cross the great stairway northeast of Pyramid 12 and you'll find yourself in the largest court at Lubaantun, Plaza V. This massive 'amphitheatre' was the site of important social, political and religious ceremonies, accompanied by music, song and dance. The mounds to the west may have delineated another ball court. At the northern edge of this attractive, grassy plaza you'll find stairways leading to an ancient grandstand. These days the crowds have been supplanted by an occasional hummingbird licking nectar from brilliant *Heliconia* blossoms.

Directly south of Pyramid 12 stands another terraced structure, Pyramid 10 (also

Beyond these readily-measurable qualities, however, the Crystal Skull remains a bone of contention among archaeologists, art experts, historians and mystics. Quartz cannot be aged by carbon dating, and no similar work has been found at Maya sites. Speculation on its origins ranges from Mixtec Mexico, Babylon, Egypt, southern Africa, Tibet, even Atlantis.

How did the Crystal Skull reach Lubaantun? Sceptics suggest that Mitchell-Hedges himself brought the piece there and encouraged Anna-Marie to find it, either to cheer her up on her birthday or possibly to bolster his claims of a city linked with Atlantis. Academic archaeologists continue to ignore the skull; there is not a single mention of it in Hammond's massive treatise on Lubaantun. Perhaps the truth will never be known. Mitchell-Hedges, who reportedly kept the Skull at his bedside in Farley Castle near London, died in June 1959.

The Skull has been loaned to various museums and was once even used as collateral for a loan. Beginning in 1964, the Crystal Skull was entrusted to American art restorer Frank Dorland, who meticulously examined it for the next six years.

Anna-Marie reclaimed the Skull in late 1970, returning with it to her home in Kitchener, Ontario, Canada. Since then, she briefly loaned it to New York's Museum of the American Indian, but later reclaimed it. It was offered for sale in 1979, with an asking price of US$500,000, but didn't sell. Belize's Archaeological Commissioner at the time, Dr Elizabeth Graham, saw the Skull in 1986. Both Belize and Mexico (which believes it to be of Mixtec origin) lay claim to the controversial piece.

In the meantime – and not surprisingly, considering the popularity of New Age mysticism – the Crystal Skull has fuelled all sorts of supernatural speculation. Various witnesses claim to have seen images of temples, faces, mountains, even other skulls within the Crystal Skull. Strange sounds, halos and hypnotic trances have been attributed to it. Anna-Marie herself contributed to this aura of mysticism by suggesting that, in the wrong hands, the Skull could be used as an instrument of death. Many of these reports are chronicled in Richard Garvin's 1973 book, *The Crystal Skull* (see *Appendix 2, Further Reading*).

A remarkably similar crystal skull, retrieved from Mexico in 1889 by a Spanish military officer, is now housed in the British Museum. The Royal Anthropological Institute of Great Britain and Ireland theorised in 1936 that the two skulls were too alike to have separate origins; indeed, the crude British Museum piece might have been an artist's study for the Crystal Skull. A much smaller and more dissimilar skull, presumed to be of Aztec origin, resides in the Musee de l'Homme in Paris.

12.4m high). Beyond this lies the ball court, faced on the east and west by mounds, where Merwin discovered the three carved markers. Two more plazas continue down the slope of the ridge to an area known as Flora's Milpa, where researchers discovered a number of burial sites filled with jade pendants, pyrite mirrors, conch trumpets, figurines, plaques and animal bones. Most of these were apparently broken and scattered around the tomb. This suggests that the Maya were deliberately thwarting grave robbers, rendering the funerary goods worthless except to the gods.

Excavations unearthed a number of ceramic whistle figurines throughout Lubaantun. Archaeologists consider these remarkable, since figurines from the Classic Period are extremely rare except from Mexico's Campeche coast, the island of Jaina in the Gulf of Mexico, and Lubaantun itself.

Lubaantun appears to have been founded near the end of the Late Classic, around AD730, reaching its architectural and influential peak around AD790. The city and surrounding realm probably supported upward of 50,000 people during this time. Scholars disagree on why the site was settled at such a late date. Hammond believes that political pressure provoked a shift of power from Pusilha to Lubaantun; others hypothesize that Pusilha's expanding population migrated east in search of farming land. In any case, Lubaantun remained a major centre for only about 160 years.

The forest surrounding Lubaantun – some would say devouring it – is almost as enchanting as the site itself. Besides the majestic ceibas and cohune palms, you'll find the area studded with gumbo-limbo trees, their red, peeling bark earning them the moniker 'tourist tree'. Look also for small fan-like palms called jippy-jappa, whose small single shoots can be pulled up and eaten as hearts of palm. The Kekchis use this same plant to make baskets. Amongst the groundcover grow clumps of calantro (cilantro or Chinese parsley), a favourite herb in both Belizean and Mexican cooking.

Walk down the slope to the west and you'll quickly run into Likinha Creek, which enters the Columbia Branch downstream near San Pedro. A maze of trails crisscross the forest here, with the main trail running back to San Pedro village. Kekchi Indians use this trail system daily, lugging cohune palm fronds or goods from nearby villages.

To reach Lubaantun either by car or on your own, you must first get to San Pedro village. Lacking a car, catch the 05.00 Z-Line bus leaving Punta Gorda daily. Ask to be let off at 'the Dump' (Vernon's Shell Station), then hike west on the road for about 2 hours (6.4km) to San Pedro. You may be able to hitchhike in with a carload of tourists or locals, but there's generally little traffic on this road. Pass through the village and take the first right after passing the church on your left, to cross the concrete bridge spanning the Columbia Branch. Continue about 0.3km past the bridge until the dirt road on the left – there used to be a sign but it is old and battered now. From here, it used to be a pleasant 20-minute hike to the ruins. Cars can now drive all the way in (0.8km).

A recently finished Museum has some interesting displays and information boards putting Lubaantun in context with other Maya sites.

Uxbenka

This relatively small ceremonial centre wasn't discovered until 1984, when the Maya caretaker at Nim Li Punit investigated a report of looting near Santa Cruz village. Dr Richard Leventhal subsequently surveyed the site and made some minor excavations.

Uxbenka ('The Ancient Place') consists of a central plaza surrounded by six structures, the tallest of which stands 8m. Twenty-one stelae, six of them carved, have been discovered in and near the central plaza. Some of these have been protected from further deterioration beneath thatch shelters. While its structures are not nearly as impressive as those at other local sites such as Lubaantun, Uxbenka exhibits well the Maya custom in southern Belize of sculpting and terracing natural hillsides so that they complement and blend with the ceremonial sites themselves. Uxbenka occupies a barren hilltop just east of Santa Cruz village, some 6.5km along the road running west from San Antonio. There is no regularly-scheduled public transport along this stretch, but you may be able to arrange a ride in San Antonio by talking to Dionísio Bol at the Hilltop Hotel. If you visit Santa Cruz a trip to Uxbenka and the Río Blanco Falls will undoubtedly be a part of your stay. A caretaker from Santa Cruz watches over the site.

Blue Creek Village and Hokeb Ha Cave

At a turnoff 3.5km east of San Antonio stands the small Kekchi and Mopan village of Mafredi. There's a Mennonite church here as well as a small store/bar, Roy's Cool Spot. Continuing southwest for 4.5km, you'll reach Blue Creek Village. This Kekchi village spans both sides of the creek, its picturesque thatch huts dwarfed on the north side by a luxuriant jungle ridge. Indian children frolic on the cement bridge with the simplest of toys, propellers made of reeds and sticks. Meanwhile their mothers, naked to the waist, beat laundry on stones upstream.

A 20-minute walk upstream from the cement bridge at Blue Creek Village will bring you to the **Blue Creek Caves** (also known by the Maya name Hokeb Ha). The trip would be worthwhile even if the caves didn't exist at all. Along the way you'll wander through virgin rainforest, the trees rising to dizzying heights, draped with vines and festooned with bromeliads. The dirt path begins just north of the cement bridge and is easy to follow as it skirts the left bank of Blue Creek. A 10-minute stroll will land you in a jungle clearing of magnificent tall trees, their canopies blocking all but a few shafts of sunlight. You'll probably have this idyllic spot to yourself, however. The creek slows here to form a massive blue-green pool which beckons swimmers (although the cave entrance farther upstream is equally fine for a dip). For those who want to plunge in with a splash, try the rope swing, or you can try out the canopy walk.

To reach the caves without a guide, continue on the path which parallels the creek. After a few minutes, the trail veers away from the main stem of the creek and seems to peter out near a smaller creek bed which is often dry. Cross this creek bed, heading to the left back toward Blue Creek. At this point there isn't much of a trail, but you can't really get lost; just clamber over rocks along Blue Creek, heading upstream at the base of increasingly steep limestone cliffs. You can steady yourself with vines and other vegetation, but watch out for spines. In a few minutes you'll reach the main cave entrance at the head of an imposing box canyon. Watch your step on the slick, mossy rocks.

The cave entrance fairly begs for a place in the next Indiana Jones movie – a gaping limestone maw some 25m high, from whose gloomy depths the creek gently spills before plunging down a rocky chute. Vines hang from the sheer rock wall above the cave mouth, framing this eerie scene. It is not at all surprising that the ancient Maya held the cave sacred. Over the years, a number of their artefacts have been found inside.

The calm water at the main cave entrance is perfect for swimming during most of the year. The light dims quickly once you've swum around the first corner, and a fairly water-resistant headlight would be a help if you plan further exploring. After a short swim you can begin your exploration on foot. Dedicated spelunkers who want to penetrate still further can hire a guide through the Village Guest House Programme to lead them out the other end, about 4 hours. The smaller cave on the far side of the creek is also accessible in the drier months, when water isn't gushing from its mouth. No one should attempt entering any of these caves during the rainy season due to the possibility of a sudden rise in water depth.

To reach Blue Creek via Chun's buses, see the section above on San Antonio. From San Antonio, you can also arrange a driver with Bol's Hilltop Hotel. Nature's Way Guest House in Punta Gorda can put together a van trip for a reasonable price. Blue Creek Village is now part of the Village Guest House Programme.

Pusilha

Less than 3km from the Guatemalan border, this is one of the most remote of Belize's Maya ruins, and consequently one of the most difficult to reach. Indeed, several local Maya told us they believed Pusilha was in Guatemala, underscoring the fact that political boundaries still don't carry much weight with the one-time rulers of this entire region.

Rumours of a site in the area circulated throughout the 1920s, but Pusilha wasn't discovered until 1927, when loggers led by James Mason drove a tractor through the site to move timber. Soon thereafter, J Eric Thompson visited Pusilha and noted the unique feature which distinguishes it from all other known Maya sites: stone abutments which once supported a bridge spanning the Pusilha Branch of the Moho River. Only a few other Maya bridges are known (including Palenque and Aguacate), and only Pusilha's was made of stone. Archaeologists decided to suspend work at Lubaantun and devote their time to Pusilha, potentially a more important site, and Thomas Gann began excavating the following year. Among other finds, Gann unearthed a grotesque human mask carved in limestone, pottery shards decorated with plant and animal motifs, and a stela which was shipped to the British Museum.

Pusilha was apparently an important Late Classic ceremonial centre, occupied between AD530 and AD790, and possibly under the control of Quiriguá in Guatemala. Marine artefacts and jade attest to trade with the coast and the Guatemalan highlands. It is, however, a relatively small site spanning both sides of the Pusilha Branch, which flows through the ceremonial centre year round. Virtually all of the plazas and pottery caves lie within less than a kilometre of the ancient bridge. Forested hills surround the site on all sides. The main plaza, consisting of six mounds, sits on a natural rise where most of the site's monuments were discovered. The site is overgrown, and the tallest structures are only 5m high.

Pusilha is difficult to reach, requiring that you first hike to the small Kekchi village of San Benito Poite. There are two paths to San Benito Poite, one from Santa Teresa village and one from Aguacate, both accessible by dirt road from Punta Gorda. You can either hire a truck in Punta Gorda or get as close as possible on public buses (see the section above on San Antonio) and walk the remainder. One cheap way to reach Aguacate is to get a ride with Keith Mullet of Toledo Farmer's Supply in Punta Gorda, who sometimes goes to Blue Creek Village twice a week to deliver supplies; he'll charge BZ$2 pp to Blue Creek and roughly BZ$12 extra to Aguacate, which lies 8km southwest of Blue Creek. Once in Aguacate, ask for Santiago Tush, who can help with more information, lodging for the night, and a guide.

From either Santa Teresa or Aguacate, it's then roughly a 20km hike along a rainforest path to San Benito Poite. The path from Santa Teresa is the more beautiful route, but it's made difficult by the rise of the Moho River, which may be impassable depending on weather conditions. The path from Aguacate requires only a single river crossing quite close to San Benito Poite, and you can have a dory take you across. Once in San Benito Poite, ask for Pedro Ical, who can find a place for you to spend the night and arrange a guide to take you the remaining 1km south to the site. Peace Corps volunteers in the villages can also help with information. Bring all your own food for this trip; nothing but tortillas is available in Poite, a poor community which can scarcely afford to feed affluent travellers.

Barranco and the Temash River

This, the southernmost coastal village in Belize, lies 19km south of Punta Gorda and just 14km north of the Sarstoon River which demarcates the Guatemalan border. Settled over 100 years ago by a Garifuna turtle fisherman named Santiago Avilez, Barranco once prospered courtesy of the banana trade. It's also well known for pineapple and as the hometown of Belizean *punta* rock superstar Andy Palacio. Many of the younger Garifuna have left Barranco in recent years, however, and it is becoming something of a ghost town, albeit a very pleasant one. A number of gingerbread houses remain, all perched atop the town's namesake red clay cliffs (Barranco Colorado, the original but seldom-used name, means 'red cliff'). There are no formal overnight accommodations at Barranco, although by the time you read this, the town should be a participant in the Village Guest House Programme (see above). The general idea and prices will be the same, except that the food, stories, music, and ambience will of course be Garifuna rather than Maya.

The Temash River empties into the Gulf of Honduras roughly 3km south of Barranco. The Temash boasts one of the tallest stands of black mangrove – some over 30m high – in all of Central America. This is a thickly jungled, serpentine river right out of Conrad. The tallest mangroves grow in the vicinity of Temash Lagoon, about 13km from the mouth, where Sunday Wood, Vieras and Conejo Creeks join the Temash. The area is also a haven for wildlife.

Nature's Way Guest House in Punta Gorda will run you by boat to Barranco and up the Temash River area for around BZ$150. As part of the Village Guest House Programme, however, you can stay overnight in Barranco, enjoying Garifuna music, food and stories, with an optional trip up the Temash (if you're a real mangrove fan) for a very reasonable price which will benefit the local Garifuna community.

Sarstoon-Temash National Park, created in 1994, is one of Belize's newest protected areas covering 16,956 hectares. The park was established to protect large tracts of tropical rainforest and the largest area of red mangrove swamp in Belize. The largely unpopulated area is also home to the rare-bellied heron.

Nearshore cayes

A number of tiny cayes dot the Gulf of Honduras just north of Punta Gorda. Moho and Frenchman's Cayes lie about 20km from PG (about 1 hour 15 minutes by boat), providing decent but not outstanding snorkelling. Moho Caye is an unofficial marine bird sanctuary. Wild Cane Caye served as a Maya cemetery during the Late Postclassic, yielding artefacts that suggested Spanish influence. The Snake Cayes sit another 5km to the northeast (2 hours by boat). Larger than Frenchman's or Moho, the Snake Cayes provide more opportunities for snorkelling, although you'll see the same types of corals and fish. Nature's Way Guest House will run a snorkelling trip to Moho Caye for BZ$150 a boatload (up to 10 people), to Frenchman's Caye for BZ$150, and to the Snake Cayes for BZ$175. Ask about snorkelling among the mangroves if you're interested in seeing this rich ecosystem close up.

Sapodilla Cayes

The Sapodilla Cayes are the southernmost extension of the barrier reef, some 55km from Punta Gorda and therefore seldom visited by travellers. Both Hunting Caye and nearby Lime Caye provide excellent snorkelling, although growing crowds of Guatemalan tourists threaten the area in the future if the government doesn't give it some sort of protective status. Increased enforcement is also needed to prevent illegal fishing by Guatemalan and Honduranean boats. On Hunting Caye you'll find a small campground, a picnic area, cabins, a police station and a three-man Belize Defense Forces Maritime Squad.

Because of the distance from the mainland, it's neither easy nor cheap to reach the Sapodilla Cayes. Diving the Seal Cayes, including Seal Caye Wall, was pioneered by Rum Point Divers out of Placencia. Their divemaster has now explored much of the area and will take you there on the inn's 42-foot jet-drive boat. The wall dives here are unspoiled, and you'll see huge vase and tube sponges as well as black coral. See the listing for Rum Point Inn in *Chapter 11*, *Placencia*, for details. Nature's Way Guest House in Punta Gorda will take a boatload out to Hunting Caye for US$300, camping overnight or for several days if you wish. You can also check with Bobby Polonio at Bobby's Bar on Main Street, and at Paco's at 3 Clement Street in Punta Gorda. The trip takes about 4 hours and can be quite rough. Indeed, bad weather can either postpone a visit to Hunting Caye or keep you there far longer than expected! Bring extra food just in case. Also, avoid holidays and weekends, when hordes of Guatemalan tourists visit the area, especially Lime Caye.

Seahunt Adventures (One Mile PG San Antonio Road, PO Box 107, Punta Gorda; tel: 07 22845) offers dive trips to the Sapodilla Cayes in their new 25ft boat. Seahunt also runs fishing trips for tuna, wahoo, permit and tarpon.

Easily the most ambitious way to reach the Sapodilla Cayes involves kayaking there. See *Chapter 6*, *Sea kayaking*, page 75, for details on a kayak trip from Belize City to the Sapodilla Cayes.

AMBERGRIS CAYE

Ambergris Caye extends like a 40km-long finger from the southernmost tip of Mexico's Yucatan Peninsula. Only a narrow channel separates Belize from Mexico at Ambergris' northern extremity, a channel that the ancient Maya apparently dredged to make navigation easier. Although the largest and most-visited of the Belizean cayes, much of Ambergris remains undisturbed mangrove swamp, sourgrass savanna, freshwater lagoon and broadleaf forest. Virtually all of Ambergris Caye's residents live in San Pedro, near the southern end of the island.

History

The early Maya favoured Ambergris as a strategically located coastal trading centre. Recent evidence from Marco Gonzalez, Ambergris' best-studied ruin site, suggests strong trade and cultural links with the great inland city of Lamanai. Later, English and French pirates capitalised on the caye's strategic location, making it a coastal stopover. But the basis of today's population arrived in 1848 as refugees from the bloody Caste War in the Mexican Yucatan.

The caye traces its name to early whaling days, when ambergris, a waxy musk-like substance, was extracted from the intestines of sperm whales for use as a fixative in the perfume trade. Whalers occasionally found lumps of the stuff weighing almost 450kg, and one such lump sold in 1910 for US$30,000. Other fisheries, particularly for spiny lobster, soon replaced whaling and Ambergris Caye still remains dependent to some degree on its rich fishing grounds.

In late October 1990, the Belize government bought from private interests most of the northern two-thirds of Ambergris Caye. Known formerly as the Pinkerton Estate, this 22,000-acre chunk of land does not include most of the eastern shoreline, which is in private hands. Still, the purchase gives the government the opportunity to swap lagoon frontage on the western side of the caye for beach frontage. The buy-out does not mean that the entire area will remain greenbelt, however, and the former owners are now suing for repossession of the land.

At the northern end of the island, Belizeans have been participating in a voluntary sea turtle conservation project for the last several years. Biology teachers from throughout the country bring their classes to a beach near Basil Jones, about 19km north of San Pedro, where loggerhead turtles (and a few green turtles) lay their eggs. They patrol the beach mainly to prevent egg poaching, which has decreased almost 40-fold since the programme began. They also tag the nests to estimate hatching date, and return to help the young turtles make their way safely from beach to water. These week-long forays have been jointly financed by the Hol Chan Marine Reserve and the US Fish and Wildlife Service. For more

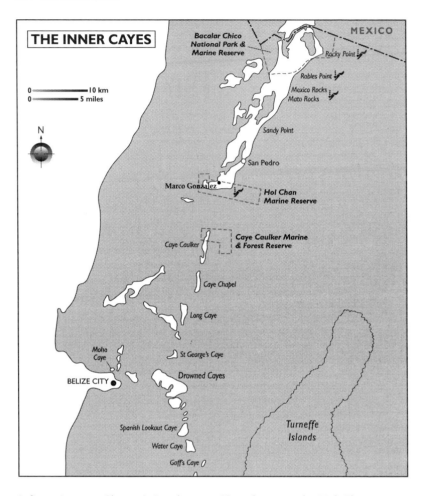

information, see *Chapter 3, Reptiles*, page 28, and contact the Hol Chan Marine Reserve office in San Pedro.

For an excellent overview of Ambergris history, shipwrecks, Maya ruins, botany, biology and beachcomber tips, try to find a copy of *The Field Guide to Ambergris Caye* by Richard L Woods, S T Reid, and A M Reid, available in San Pedro (see *Appendix 2, Further Reading*).

SAN PEDRO

For the time being, San Pedro remains the single most popular destination for travellers to Belize. Scuba divers began flocking to San Pedro in the mid-1960s, and although they deserve credit as the pioneers of Belize tourism, few of them ever saw anything else of the country. Then as now, the attraction was the barrier reef, clearly visible from town as a broken line of frothy white breakers about 1.2km east. Divers still make up the lion's share of San Pedro visitors, but windsurfers, snorkellers and sport anglers are increasingly showing up.

As a result of this influx, San Pedro is no longer the sleepy one-hotel paradise that it was only a couple of decades ago. But neither has it become a Cancún or even Cozumel. The tallest building stands three storeys. The streets are unpaved, with lengths of ship mooring line laid down as speed bumps or 'sleeping policemen'. Perhaps most importantly, San Pedranos themselves mirror the town's informality and friendliness. Most are descendants of Mexico's Caste War exodus, and you'll hear Spanish spoken at every street corner.

Everything is easy to reach in San Pedro. There are only ten streets in town (all recently renamed – Front Street, for example, has become Barrier Reef Drive), and you can walk from the ocean side to the lagoon side in less than a minute. Golf carts are a favourite local vehicle. You may wonder, in fact, how anyone could make a living driving cab in San Pedro (a few of the pricier hotels outside town provide the passengers, it turns out). The barrier reef is visible offshore, a mere 10min ride in a slow boat. But despite its location, San Pedro doesn't have much of a beach; it's more a thin strip of sand between buildings and docks.

Hurricane Mitch in late 1998 damaged or destroyed many of the piers and dockside businesses in San Pedro, but virtually all have been rebuilt since then. Dive shops near the water are all back in operation. There has even been an unforeseen benefit: Wave action resulting from the hurricane cleaned many of the local beaches and left others with a great deal more sand than they had pre-Mitch.

Getting there
Flying is the easiest way to reach San Pedro, and the 20-minute flight usually gives you a good look at the barrier reef. Maya Island Air runs eleven scheduled flights daily (BZ$47 one way from Belize City Municipal Airport, BZ$77 from the International Airport). Tropic Air has 11 flights daily, between 07.40 and 17.30 for the same fare.

By boat, you can reach San Pedro on the Triple J which leaves the Bellevue Hotel dock in Belize City at 09.00 Mon-Sat (BZ$25 one-way, 1 hour 15 minutes); they make the return trip at 15.00. The Andrea I leaves from the same dock at 15.00 Mon-Sat returning at 07.00. The Thunderbolt departs from the riverside behind the gas station at daily at 13.00 returning the following day at 07.00. A number of other boats make the trip on an irregular basis; you can ask around the docks near the Swing Bridge. Boats leave daily from Caye Caulker, inquire at the hotels or on the piers.

Where to stay
San Pedro is not a great town for budget accommodations. Belize's most expensive hotels, after all, are located here. Still, finding a cheapie isn't impossible owing to the demographics of tourism in San Pedro. The diving crowd, which still forms the bulk of San Pedro's trade, mostly books reservations with the middle- and upper-range hotels outside town, while budget travellers still prefer the slightly funkier digs on nearby Caye Caulker. This means that the handful of budget hotels in San Pedro often have vacancies in the summer, although even these can be filled in the winter high season.

All of the cheaper hotels – and many pricier alternatives – are located within the town. At the northern edge of town, beyond the San Pedro River, lie a group of pricier hotels including Journey's End, Capricorn and Captain Morgan's. Even further north are newer hotels including Mata Chica, Caye Villas and Casa Caribe. Pricier hotels also lie to the south of town.

All told, there are at least 50 hotels, apartments and condominiums in San Pedro. The listing below includes most of the budget joints (less than BZ$60) and a smattering of the more expensive places that have been recommended. For a complete list, write to the Belize Tourist Board, PO Box 325, Belize City, Belize; tel: 02 31913; fax: 02 31943; toll free in the US and Canada: 1 800 624 0686; email:

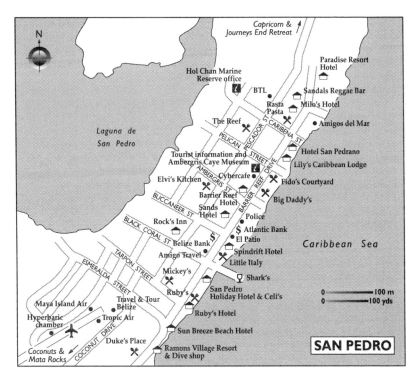

Capricorn &
Journeys End Retreat

N

Paradise Resort
Hotel

Hol Chan Marine
Reserve office

BTL

Sandals Reggae Bar

Rasta
Pasta

Milo's Hotel

The Reef

Amigos del Mar

Laguna de
San Pedro

Tourist information and
Ambergris Caye Museum

Hotel San Pedrano
Lily's Caribbean Lodge

Elvi's Kitchen

Cybercafe

Fido's Courtyard

Barrier Reef
Hotel
Sands
Hotel

Big Daddy's

Rock's Inn

Police

Atlantic Bank

Belize Bank

El Patio

Caribbean Sea

Amigo Travel

Spindrift Hotel
Little Italy

Mickey's

Shark's

Ruby's

San Pedro
Holiday Hotel & Celi's

0 ━━━━ 100 m
0 ━━━━ 100 yds

Maya Island Air

Travel & Tour
Belize

Hyperbaric
chamber

Tropic Air

Ruby's Hotel

Sun Breeze Beach Hotel

Duke's Place

Coconuts &
Mata Rocks

Ramons Village Resort
& Dive shop

SAN PEDRO

info@travelbelize.org; web: www.travelbelize.org, for their pamphlet *Belize Visitor's Guide*.

Rubie's Hotel PO Box 56; tel: 026 2063; fax: 026 2719; email: HYPERLINK mailto:rubys@btl.net rubys@btl.net. 17 rooms, BZ$30 with shared bath and fan or BZ$60 with private bath and AC (older rooms) or BZ$90 (newer rooms). Probably the best known of San Pedro's cheapies. Some rooms face the water. Rubie's now has an excellent café and bakery for breakfast. Rubie and her parents are friendly and accommodating.

Paradise Resort Hotel PO Box 25, San Pedro Town, Ambergris Caye; tel: 026 2083; fax: 026 2232; email: paradise@btl.net; web: www.ambergriscaye.com/paradiseresort. 25 rooms, US$35 with private bath and various options including fan, AC, kitchenette. Prices between US$80 and US$130. Thatched buildings in a pleasant beach surrounding. This is one of the few hotels in town with more than a few metres of sand to relax on. The restaurant serves tasty food and snacks. For some odd reason, the bar tries for a 'safari' ambience, with a rather distasteful display of zebra heads and skins. American Express, MasterCard and VISA accepted.

Milo's Hotel tel: 026 2033; fax: 026 2198. 9 rooms, from BZ$50 with shared bath, fan. San Pedro's cheapest hotel, somewhat dilapidated inside and out, but still very popular with budget travellers. There is a store-cum-guide shop below.

Lily's Caribbean Lodge tel: 026 2059. 10 rooms, BZ$120 (winter) or BZ$100 (summer), with private bath, fan. Some rooms have a veranda and water views. The newly-remodelled restaurant downstairs is one of San Pedro's best and most reasonably priced.

San Pedrano Hotel tel: 026 2054. 7 rooms, BZ$50–80 with private bath and partial air conditioning. Some rooms overlook the water, as does the hotel veranda. In the heart of town, with very clean rooms.

Sun Breeze Beach Hotel tel: 026 2191; fax: 026 2346; email: sunbreeze@btl.net. 39-nine rooms, US$150 with private bath, AC, fan. Very large, clean rooms, a new swimming pool, and bicycle rentals. The restaurant and bar, BC's, are highly recommended. A two-storey hotel facing the water at the very southern end of town. The hotel dive shop rents and sells scuba gear. They accept MasterCard, VISA and American Express.

San Pedro Holiday Hotel PO Box 1140, Belize City; tel: 026 2014; fax: 026 2295; email: holiday@btl.net; web: www.ambergriscaye.com/holiday. 18 rooms, from US$100 with private bath, AC and fan. Rooms have verandas facing the water. Restaurant, bar, gift shop and scuba shop on the dock.

Spindrift Hotel tel: 026 2586; fax: 026 6225; email: spinhotel@btl.net. 24 rooms. All rooms with hot water and private bath. Economy rooms start at US$55. Beachfront rooms are US$76 with fully equipped beachfront apartments at US$127.

Barrier Reef Hotel tel: 026 2075; fax: 026 2192; email: barrierreef@btl.net. 11 rooms, BZ$170 with private bath, AC, fan. There's a restaurant and bar.

Sands Hotel tel: 026 2510. 7 rooms, BZ$150 with private bath, AC, fan.

Caribbean Villas tel: 026 2715. BZ$250 with private bath, AC, and kitchenette. South of town about 10 minutes. Complimentary bicycles, and home to the Lalas Bird Sanctuary and 'people perch'.

Capricorn Resort tel: 026 2809; fax: 026 2091; email: capricorn@btl.net; web: www.ambergriscaye.com/capricorn. A small place to escape, just three miles north of San Pedro, ideal for relaxing in the beach bar or enjoying the excellent food in the restaurant. Capricorn has 3 cabanas with views out to the beach US$90. Suites with AC US$115.

Captain Morgan's Retreat tel: 026 2567 or toll-free in the US on 1 888 653 9090; fax: 026 2616; email: captmorgan@btl.net; web: www.captainmorgans.com. 21 thatched-roof casitas, US$120 (May–December) or US$170 (December–April), with private bath, fan, porch with water view. Breakfast, lunch, and dinner cost US$35 pp per day. Located 4.8km north of town. There's a fresh water pool, poolside bar, restaurant, dock and a 12m-high observation tower. Reef fishing, fly fishing and deep sea fishing trips are offered at additional cost, as well as local scuba diving, snorkelling, and day sailing trips. Dive trips to the offshore atolls and Blue Hole are offered in conjunction with the Reef Roamer fleet.

Ramon's Village Resort tel: 026 2071; fax: 026 2214; email: ramons@btl.net; web: www.ramons.com. 61 rooms in thatched cabanas, from US$140 or from US$550 for a seven-night stay, with private bath, AC, fan. Located south of town facing the beach. There is a new swimming pool. The restaurant is highly recommended as is the dive shop and tours.

Journey's End Caribbean Club PO Box 13; tel: 026 2173 or toll-free in the US on 1 800 460 5665; fax: 026 2397; email: information@journeysendresort.com; web: www.journeysendresort.com. Beachside (US$198) and poolside (US$160) cottages in an idyllic setting. US$1,029 for a seven-night stay, including breakfast, dinner, transfer from Belize City and activities on four days. Located north of town, a 10m ride by free water taxi. The diving operation is highly recommended, with two 26ft boats and accommodating knowledgeable guides. They have several diving and fishing packages to choose from.

Banana Beach tel: 026 3500. South of town. BZ$150 for ocean front room, with kitchen, AC, cable TV. There is a pool.

Rock's Inn tel: 026 2326. US$90 with private bath, AC, kitchenette. Large, clean rooms. In town, on the water, and highly recommended.

Coconuts tel: 026 3500; fax: 026 3501; email. US$75–100 with private bath, AC, fan. About ½ mile south of town. Small and personal. Large rooms with a sea view from all. Restaurant with a good breakfast, and Sunday barbecue dinner. Bar on the beach.

Mata Rocks Resort tel: 026 2336 or toll-free in the US 1 800 288 8646; fax: 026 2349; email: matarocks@btl.net. 9 rooms, BZ$220–300 with private bath, AC, fan, kitchenette. One mile south of town, just south of Banana's. There's a pool and bar on the beach.

There is no place to camp in San Pedro, nor does the thin strip of developed beach offer any opportunity.

Where to eat

Restaurants in San Pedro, like hotels, tend toward the pricey, but at least you've got a wider selection of foods than the usual fried chicken, rice and beans. The quality of most restaurant meals in San Pedro is also generally higher than in the rest of Belize, making the bill somewhat easier to accept. Seafood, not surprisingly, is the mainstay of San Pedro restaurants, and just about the only item that doesn't have to be flown or boated into town from the mainland. A fish dinner will generally cost BZ$18–28. Lobster dinners are almost twice the price here compared to Caye Caulker. Even beer is slightly more expensive in San Pedro.

Most of the larger and pricier hotels out of town have their own restaurants. Ramon's and the SunBreeze are especially recommended.

The lobster season runs June 15 – February 15. Insist that your lobster be of legal size, and don't fall for the line that it is legal to eat frozen lobster out of season. Please don't eat sea turtle or turtle eggs, both of which are sometimes offered by unscrupulous locals.

Elvi's Kitchen The roof is thatched, the floor is beach sand, and a huge tree grows in the middle of what is probably San Pedro's most popular restaurant. Trendiness aside, the food and service are quite good, portions are large, and prices far more reasonable than you might assume, given the surroundings. Lobster, chicken, Maya chicken in banana leaves. Closed Sundays. Live music. Full dinner with drinks will run US$20. The Yucatecan Maya-style dishes (chicken in banana leaves), lobster, and key lime pie are also good.
El Patio South of town, across the street from Caribbean Villas, near Rock's II grocery store. Lunch and dinner run BZ$30–50.
Estel's On the water, just north of the Spindrift Hotel. Highly recommended.
Fido's Courtyard Breakfast, lunch and dinner. Steak, chicken, lobster, key lime pie, and margaritas. Dinners run about BZ$20 with drinks. After 21.00 it's a live music bar. The Reality Café is also housed in Fido's Courtyard.
Duke's Place Across from Ramon's. Great breakfasts and lunches. One of the few restaurants in Belize which serves gibnut (paca) now and then.
Little Italy Located in the Spindrift Hotel, this is consistently one of San Pedro's most recommended eating spots. Italian dinners start at about BZ$20 and there's a good lunch buffet for BZ$16. The Lobster Alfredo is recommended. The Pier Lounge has a veranda which overlooks the water.
Rasta Pasta Excellent breakfast, lunch and dinners. The owners, Maralyn and Robert Gill, offer a huge and scrumptious menu, including everything from shrimp pizzas, fresh grilled fish, curries, conch fritters, Jamaican jerk chicken, and burritos to home-baked macaroons. One of the few restaurants in Belize serving Garifuna dishes like *hudut* and cassava bread. Dinners run BZ$10–20. Robert's band plays reggae at night.
Sandals Reggae Bar offers great BBQ chicken, pork, and fish, US$5-6. The *ceviche* is also good.
Big Daddy's Tasty barbecued shrimp, grouper and chicken. Nightly BBQ chicken at reasonable prices.
Lily's Newly remodelled and still one of San Pedro's best seafood restaurants. If you've been out fishing, they'll cook your catch at a reasonable price.
The Reef A casual lunch and dinner spot on Pescador Drive frequented by locals. Fish, and conch dinners, with rice and beans. BZ$10 for lunch, BZ$20 dinners with drinks.
Mickey's on Tarpon Street. The atmosphere is nothing special, but BZ$12 buys a huge, tasty dinner. Burritos are a specialty.

Celi's on the water at the San Pedro Holiday Hotel. The deli is open for breakfast, the restaurant only for lunch and dinner. Cheap take-out lunch specials. Excellent banana bread and cinnamon rolls. Dinners run BZ$30, and specialities include snapper, stuffed grouper, lobster, and key lime pie. Closed Wednesdays.

Capricorn About 3 miles north of town, this scenic restaurant is reached by water taxi or golf cart. Italian, French, and East Indian gourmet dinners in a romantic setting. Lobster, fish and stone crab claws are featured, BZ$30–40. They also serve lunch.

Ruby's Cheap take-out breakfast and lunches. Great cinnamon rolls, fruit juices, and real fresh-brewed coffee.

Special events

Garifuna Settlement Day (November 19) is celebrated in San Pedro with fireworks and food stalls set up on the main drag. All this is fun but rather inexplicable in this 'Spanish' town with only recent Garifuna presence. The Costa Maya Festival in August has sailboarding, kite-flying, tug-of-war, fishing contests and volleyball.

Information and useful addresses

Ambergris Caye has an excellent website at www.goambergriscaye.com.

Changing money is easier in San Pedro than anywhere else in Belize, with two banks and a number of travel agencies, gift shops and hotels ready to change both cheques and cash. It's not even necessary in many cases, since US dollars and travellers' cheques are so widely accepted in San Pedro. **Belize Bank** on Barrier Reef Drive is open 08.00–15.00, Mon–Thu, 08.00–13.00 and 15.00–18.00, Fri, and 08.30–12.00, Sat. Across the street, **Atlantic Bank** runs on more or less the same schedule, except that it closes during lunch (from 12.00–13.00) on weekdays.

Telephone calls can be made from the **BTL** office at the north end of town on Pescador Street, open 08.00–12.00 and 13.00–16.00, Mon–Fri, and 08.00–12.00, Saturday. You'll find a **cybercafé** on Barrier Reef Drive near Big Daddy's.

Several travel agencies offer easy booking of inland, caye and diving tours throughout Belize: **Amigo Travel** (tel: 026 2180) and **Travel & Tour Belize Ltd** (tel: 026 2137).

Shopping in San Pedro is pretty much limited to the T-shirt/postcard/sun visor variety, although some of the numerous gift shops like **Eva's**, the **Salty Dog**, **D&G** and **Frainie's** stock zericote carvings and other Belizean handicrafts. Prices are much cheaper in Belize City or elsewhere in Belize.

Amigo Travel rents mopeds, bikes, and horses. Bicycles rent for BZ$20 per day.

Belize's only **hyperbaric chamber** is located next to the San Pedro airstrip. The chamber is supported by contributions from divers. When you sign up for a dive trip, tour operators will ask that you contribute US$1 per tank. Although voluntary, this contribution entitles you to free chamber treatment in case of a diving accident requiring recompression. (Members of DAN, the Divers Alert Network, are automatically covered; see *Chapter 6, Scuba diving,* page 71, for details about joining DAN). The phone number for the chamber in case of emergency is 026 2851/2852.

The town does its washing with de-salinated seawater. Rainwater from cisterns is reportedly safe, but even most of the locals drink the bottled water, which you'll find in all the stores.

Supermarkets and dry goods stores in San Pedro stock mostly canned and bottled goods, including cold bottled drinking water. As with the local restaurants, everything is expensive since all of it has to be flown or boated in. **Rock's Shopping Centre** at the corner of Black Coral and Pescador Streets has a fairly typical selection, as do the markets below Martha's Hotel and Milo's Hotel. **San Pedro Distributors** south of the airstrip probably has the largest selection. There are one or two fruit and vegetable stands on the outskirts of town where you can buy mangoes or have a pineapple cut into pieces and bagged, but these, too, are imported from the mainland and therefore pricey.

Divers slake their thirsts at one of several San Pedro bars, although much of the action remains at the hotel bars just outside of town. **Big Daddy's** and **Rasta Pasta** offer reggae, soca and sometimes Belize's own punta rock on weekends. **Sandal's** and **Fido's Courtyard** are both lively and informal watering holes which have music, pool, and sand floors. The old Tackle Box was destroyed by Hurricane Mitch, but has risen Phoenix-like in the form of **Shark's Bar**. The **Palace Casino** offers slot machines, cards, and a big screen TV. And for more off-beat gambling, there's the **Pier Lounge Bar**, hosting their popular 'chicken drop game'.

Excursions
Near town
Diving and snorkel trips near San Pedro

For scuba divers and snorkellers, San Pedro serves both as debarkation point for boats headed to the atolls far offshore, and as a base for exploring the nearby barrier reef. The section below describes only the diving and snorkelling possibilities near San Pedro itself.

One of the most popular local dive spots is **Mexico Rocks**, roughly 10km north of San Pedro. The 'rocks' are actually scattered coral formations, havens for small fish and invertebrate life including elkhorn coral, brain coral, and a variety of sponges. Mata Rocks, 3km south of Mexico Rocks, has similar attractions.

Socorrito is noted for schools of horse-eye jacks (*Caranx latus*) and, at times, spotted eagle rays. **Palmetto Reef**, **Sandy Point** and nearby **Punta Arena**, also north of town, provide about the closest thing to wall diving in the San Pedro area, the hard coral shelf bedecked with vase sponges and long yellow pencil coral. The walls are pockmarked with caves which lead to the top of the reef in about 17m of water and sand-filled surge channels. Divers can swim through a series of short coral 'caves' at the Caverns.

Other popular dive sites include **M&M Caverns**, which features tunnels and coral caverns at 90 feet; **Amigos Wreck**, a shallow wreck sunk specifically for divers in 30ft of water; **Eagle Ray Canyon**, famous for large schools of the namesake rays; **Cypress Canyons**, where hand-fed snappers mob divers; and **Pescador Cave**, a 100-foot cavern loaded with large lobsters and snappers.

Most of these dives listed above lie on the windward side of the reef in 15–24m of water, so snorkelling is not an option. Mexico Rocks, however, offers good shallow snorkelling opportunities. Dive sites on the outside of the reef are often subject to very rough weather, and beginning divers may find entries and exits a bit unnerving on windy days. Most local dive trips spend the first dive outside the reef, then move inside for de-gassing and the second dive. Rocky and Robles Points are among the good dive sites inside the reef, both about half and hour north of town. At dive sites like Renegades, it is possible to see mating groupers in November and December.

If you're interested in seeing the offshore atolls (Turneffe Islands, Lighthouse Reef and Glover's Reef), which offer the very best diving in Belize, see *Chapter 14, The Atolls*.

The coral of the barrier reef close to San Pedro grows at such shallow depths that boats can only reach the seaward side via seven narrow openings, or 'cuts'. And it is here, on the outside of the reef near the cuts, where you'll find the best diving in the San Pedro area. Most experienced divers, however, probably won't want to spend more than a few days here. This is because the underwater topography is fairly uniform from dive site to dive site: spur and groove channels, canyons formed by massive stone and coral fingers pointing seaward with sand between them. And except for the protected Hol Chan Reserve (see below), the entire area is easily accessible to fishermen, so that fish – especially large fish – aren't abundant. Be aware that some dive charters are reluctant to spend the gas getting to the dive sites north of town, where the local diving is best.

As in Cozumel, there is no scarcity of dive guides. Besides the major hotels, there are at least 50 independent dive tour operators in town, plus a number of gear rental shops. Local day-trips, either one- or two-tank dives on the reef, usually take place from 8m open skiffs. Most guides make two trips each day, with a morning dive leaving around 09.00 and an afternoon dive leaving around 13.00 or 14.00. It's best to book a day ahead, although with as many tour operators as there are in San Pedro, no one gets left behind on the beach. The best way to find an acceptable guide is simply to ask other divers, talk with the guides themselves, and take a look at their boats. Dive guides which are consistently recommended include the Blue Hole Dive Center, Ramon's Dive Shop, Hustler Tours, Aquarius, Gaz Cooper's Dive Belize, Aqua Dive, and Amigos del Mar. Amigos del Mar is the oldest of the bunch, and is run by Changa Paz, a contributor to local conservation causes and consistently one of Belize's most-recommended dive masters. Amigos is located on the beach just north of Lily's in town. A recent arrival is Tortuga Divers, operated out of the Belize Yacht Club, with San Pedro's largest boat (49ft). Most of the above-mentioned dive shops offer complete NAUI or PADI certification, and some (including Ramon's) offer instructor and specialty certifications (Nitrox, for example).

Not surprisingly, prices for local dives are quite competitive, with most two-tank dives costing US$50 (price includes tanks, weight belt, boat and guide, soft drinks and sometimes lunch). Well-maintained rental equipment is available at all the above-mentioned dive shops.

Hol Chan Marine Reserve

By far the most popular snorkelling site near San Pedro – in all of Belize, for that matter – is the Hol Chan Marine Reserve, located 6.4km southeast of town. Scuba divers also flock to the Hol Chan 'cut', generally diving just outside of the reef. A number of conservation groups and government agencies worked to establish this diverse marine ecosystem as a reserve, among them the World Wildlife Fund, USAID, Wildlife Conservation International (a global field research division of the New York Zoological Society), the Belize Department of Fisheries (Ministry of Agriculture, Forestry, and Fisheries) and the Belize Audubon Society.

On May 2 1987, the government of Belize established the Reserve, which has four main goals: to maintain a coral reef ecosystem in its natural state, to provide recreation services and preserve the fishery value of the area, to provide an opportunity for education and research and to conserve genetic resources.

Hol Chan – Mayan for 'little channel' – covers about 3,200 acres and is divided into three distinct ecological zones. Most casual snorkellers only visit Zone A, the inside of the coral barrier reef or 'cut'. Here, in 3–12m of water, you'll find a colourful profusion of leaf, brain, scroll, finger and elkhorn coral, and schools of smaller reef fish such as blue tangs, fairy basslets, queen and French angelfish, stoplight parrotfish and trunkfish. This area also offers an opportunity to see some larger fish as well, including nurse sharks, groupers and green moray eels. The strong tidal current in the area amounts to a nutrient 'conveyor belt', encouraging a dense population of filter-feeding sponges and other invertebrates. This is an excellent spot for a night dive offered by a number of other local tour operators.

Don't expect to have the reef to yourself. The area always teems with snorkellers and divers of varying degrees of experience. And unfortunately, you don't have to swim far to witness the destruction that inept, unthinking and uneducated snorkellers can inflict on this fragile ecosystem: bleached coral 'skeletons', the remnants of once-living reef that have been broken by a careless touch or fin-kick. (Please read *Chapter 3, Coral reef etiquette*, page 35, before snorkelling or diving.)

The current along the inside of the reef and 'cut' reverses most days, and is strongest during outgoing tides and near the cut itself. Although I don't normally advocate the use of fins during reef snorkelling trips – they knock down more living coral than your average Caribbean hurricane – all but the strongest swimmers will probably want to wear fins here due to the currents. And take a good look at your boat after slipping over the side, this will save you the embarrassment later of wondering which of the scores of similar-looking boats is yours when it's time to swim back.

Zone B makes up the central and largest portion of the Reserve, a vast saltwater lagoon composed of sand and seagrass beds. Although not as showy as the coral reef itself, this peaceful marine 'meadow' has its own charms: juvenile fish of many species use the seagrass beds as a staging ground and feeding area. Scattered here and there among the seagrasses, you'll find naturally isolated patches of coral. Keep your eyes open for conch and lobster, but don't forget to scan the area for boats on a regular basis; since this portion of the Reserve isn't as popular with snorkellers, boaters don't always keep a sharp watch while speeding through the area. Within this zone lies the **Boca Ciega** ('Blind Mouth') cave. This 'blue hole' is a collapsed sinkhole on a much smaller scale than the famed Blue Hole at Lighthouse Reef. Only cave-certified scuba divers may enter Boca Ciega, and only after contacting the Reserve Manager at the office in San Pedro. The cave is considered dangerous even by some experienced cave divers, and visibility in the area is generally poor.

Zone C at the southwestern tip of Ambergris Caye consists of seven mangrove islets. Seldom visited by snorkellers or divers, this area nevertheless represents one of the richest tropical marine habitats. Within the submerged roots of red, black and white mangrove, huge numbers of juvenile fish – including angelfish, grunts and snapper – find shelter and food. Sea horses, crabs and other, smaller crustaceans also prefer the tangled mangrove forest. There is little current here, and a fine layer of silt covers many of the mangrove roots and the bottom itself; be careful not to kick up clouds of the stuff as you swim by.

From San Pedro, scores of boats leave the beaches and docks each day for snorkelling trips to Hol Chan. Trips generally last half a day (2–3 hours of actual snorkelling time), with a trip to Shark Ray Alley (see below). Most boats charge BZ$30 pp, not including gear. Mask, snorkel, and fins rent for about BZ$15 a day. Ask at your hotel, stroll down Front Street, or check at the many tour shops located at docks along the beach to decide on a boat. Prices, time on the reef and quality of the boat itself are all quite comparable, so you might as well make your decision based on personality of the guide. Most boats leave the dock at around 09.00 and make an afternoon trip at around 14.00.

From Caye Caulker, roughly a dozen boats make snorkelling trips daily to Hol Chan. These generally cost BZ$30 pp, the trip lasting from 10.00 to 16.30, with a 2-hour layover in San Pedro for lunch, shopping and banking (San Pedro banks, unlike those in most of Belize, remain open during lunchtime). For those based on Caye Caulker, these trips are a great way to get a glimpse of San Pedro without actually staying there. Actual snorkelling time amounts to about 2–3 hours, half before lunch and half after. Guides will allow you to spend more time in the water if you wish, but most snorkellers find that they are beginning to shiver after an hour on the reef. Boats accommodate about nine snorkellers, and the ride from Caye Caulker to Hol Chan can be rough when it's windy. During the ride, watch for flying fish skimming the water surface on wing-like pectoral fins as your boat cruises past. If you miss the morning boats, there are one or two boats that do an early afternoon trip from Caye Caulker to Hol Chan. If you don't have mask, snorkel or fins, boat operators will stop en route at one of the Caulker rental shops so that you can rent them.

Whether you're visiting Hol Chan from San Pedro or Caye Caulker, you may be asked to pay a BZ$3 entrance fee, payable to the Reserve Patrol boat upon arrival although this often depends if anyone is in attendance. You'll get a receipt good for the whole day. The fee helps pay to police the area and to keep the Reserve office open. Bring a long-sleeved shirt and T-shirt to protect against sunburn, a wide-brimmed hat, sun screen, a towel and something to drink. Many boats supply divers and snorkellers with soft drinks as part of the price.

Before you go, drop in at the Hol Chan Marine Reserve office (tel: 026 2247) on Caribena Street. This is the home base for the friendly and helpful Reserve staff. You'll find maps, brochures, underwater photographs, displays explaining the Reserve, and posters for sale. If you're of a more scholarly bent, you'll appreciate the small research library with scientific papers and fish identification keys. The staff can also fill you in on marine turtle conservation efforts both locally (near Basil Jones at the northern end of Ambergris Caye) and nationwide. The office is open 08.00–12.00 and 13.00–17.00 Mon–Fri.

Shark Ray Alley

The sharks are nurse sharks, the rays are southern sting rays. The 'alley' is a shallow cut in the barrier reef just south of Hol Chan Marine Reserve, to which it was officially annexed in August 1999. The site became a gathering point for sharks and rays when local fishermen began regularly feeding them. Recently, local guides realised the tourist potential for an underwater petting zoo. The idea isn't new. A decade ago, guides at Grand Cayman Island discovered that a sandy offshore area used by fishermen to clean their catch attracted docile southern sting rays by the hundreds; tourists with snorkel gear have been flocking to the Caymans' 'Sting Ray City' ever since. It's hard to call Shark Ray Alley a 'natural' or 'ecotouristic' attraction. Indeed, the atmosphere is more that of an underwater circus, with sharks, rays and snorkellers armed with cameras jostling each other for food and photos. On the other hand, it's great fun for snorkellers, and doesn't appear to have any real environmental drawbacks. There are even educational advantages: sharks and sting rays lose much of their unwarranted bad reputation once you've frolicked with them unharmed at close quarters. The recent annexation also places Shark Ray Alley under the same monitoring and environmental protection programme as the Hol Chan Reserve.

Skin Diver Magazine named Shark Ray Alley among the 'seven best animal dives in the Caribbean'. Snorkellers have the chance to literally rub elbows (and fins) with sharks and rays, feeling the light sandpaper texture characteristic of both species. The nurse sharks average four to six feet in length, while the rays have 'wing' spans of about three feet. The Alley itself lies entirely in water that is 8–10ft deep, so it is ideal for snorkellers. Upon arrival of the tour boats, sharks and rays begin congregating, attracted in a Pavlovian manner by the sound of boat engines. Divemasters carry sealed containers of chopped fish, and are immediately mobbed by swarms of both species.

Snorkelling trips to Shark Ray Alley are now a standard part of Hol Chan snorkel trips. Most visitors bring disposable underwater cameras for close-ups of the docile rays and sharks. For scuba divers wanting to explore the area at depth, there is a wreck nearby in about 80ft of water, home to moray eels, turtles, and – not surprisingly – more nurse sharks.

Fishing trips

San Pedro offers good fishing on the reef or sand flats for bonefish, permit, tarpon, red and yellow snapper, cubera snapper, barracuda, jacks, grouper, Spanish mackerel, blackfin tuna and wahoo. Well outside the barrier reef, deep-sea anglers go for wahoo, blue and white marlin, sailfish and tuna. See Chapter 6, Fishing for more information on tackle and guides. San Pedro is loaded with fishing guides, and the best way to find one is to talk to other visitors who've already been out. For most fishing trips, you'll want to get a boatload together to keep costs down. Some of the more established guides are: Luz Guerrero and Romel Gomez, (tel: 026 2034); Melanie Paz (tel: 026 2990); Billy Leslie (tel: 026 2128); and Roberto Bradley (tel: 026 2116). The Coral Beach Club (tel: 026 2013) and Captain Morgan's Retreat (see *Where to stay* above) have also been recommended. Nearly all the big expensive hotels offer fishing trips for guests and drop-ins. Expect to pay in the neighbourhood of BZ$240–300 (price is per boat, most of which will take two to four anglers) for a day of reef or flat fishing. The price escalates to over BZ$600 for deep-sea fishing.

Windsurfing (Sailboarding)

San Pedro is the best place to windsurf in Belize. From November to April, the winds are good for beginners and intermediate boarders, with winds ranging from Force 2 to Force 4. In June and July, the winds increase to Force 5. **SailSports Belize**, located at Fido's dock at the San Pedro Holiday Hotel, rents Hifly and Mistral boards, with Tushingham, RAF, and Cam sails. They provide lessons for all skill levels, both on the water and with a land-based simulator.

Marco Gonzalez Maya site

This small Maya ruin lies on 16 acres of mangrove swamp at the southwestern tip of Ambergris Caye. Named for the island boy who first led archaeologists to the site in 1984, Marco Gonzalez was excavated beginning in 1986 by Elizabeth Graham and David Pendergast of the Royal Ontario Museum. They concluded that the site was founded as early as 300BC (probably a temporary fishing camp at first) and was still occupied when the Spanish arrived in AD1544. The locale was apparently used for salt-manufacturing during the Late Classic.

Forty-nine structures have been identified, all low platforms made of coral blocks, ground coral and seashells. Graham and Pendergast also uncovered traces of 11 human burials, some interred with the stingray spines reserved for Maya elite. The ancient Maya apparently used Marco Gonzalez as a link in the coastal trade route, as evidenced by finds of grey obsidian (from the Guatemalan highlands), green obsidian (from central Mexico), slate ware (from the northern Yucatan) and jade, granite and mainland limestone, none of which are found on Ambergris Caye.

But the most striking finds at Marco Gonzalez, however, were pottery remains which suggest a trade and cultural link with Lamanai, the largest ancient Maya city in present-day Orange Walk District (see *Chapter 10, Excursions*, page 154). Lamanai prospered long after the collapse of lowland Maya civilisation, and Marco Gonzalez may have been its primary trading port.

As with many smaller Maya sites, there isn't a great deal here to interest the non-archaeologist. Although accessible via a trail through the mangroves from San

Pedro, the site is difficult to find without a guide, and boat access is actually the preferred way to visit Marco Gonzalez. See the folks at Travel & Tour Belize, Ltd., located in the **Spindrift Hotel** (tel: 026 2137), to arrange a day trip.

Bacalar Chico Marine and Wildlife Reserve

Bacalar Chico, established as a reserve in June 1996, lies at the northern end of Ambergris Caye on the Bay of Chetumal bordering Mexico. A 'surf and turf' reserve similar to Lighthouse Reef, the marine portion of Bacalar Chico boasts loggerhead and green sea turtle nesting sites between Rocky Point and Robles Point, a dense population of queen conch, and spawning habitat for yellowfin and Nassau groupers near Rocky Point. Manatees, saltwater crocodiles, and the jewfish are other threatened marine life found in the reserve. The lagoon is a mosaic of patch reefs of coral and sandy sea grass beds. The terrestrial portion includes mangrove forests, savannah, and semideciduous forest. The channel separating Belize and Mexico is flanked with stands of red, white, and black mangrove. Birding opportunities abound, especially in the channels. At one inlet along the channel are a series of seven pools providing snorkellers with an opportunity to see sting rays and snapper. Within the reserve are seven Maya ruin sites, two of which – Chac Balam and San Juan – can be reached by trail and are partially excavated. Another Maya site, Santa Cruz, may be added to the reserve by extending the boundaries

Bacalar Chico is accessible only by boat, and has only recently attracted the attention of guides and travellers. Facilities now include a ranger station and visitor centre near the Chac Balam Maya site. Reserve staff are in the process of developing an eco-tour, the cost of which will help fund the reserve. Overnight camping is available and palapas and barbecue grills are under construction near the ranger station. Staff are planning on renting kayaks and snorkel gear. Tours can be arranged with most of San Pedro's guide services. Phone the Hol Chan Reserve office (tel: 026 2247) for information on guides and the current state of the facilities or call the reserve staff on 014 7308. The reserve is also accessible by boat from Sarteneja Village, Corozal District. Check with tour guide Fernando Alamilla in Sarteneja on tel: 04 32085.

Lalas Bird Sanctuary

This small privately owned sanctuary just south of San Pedro at the Caribbean Villas, is named for local birder Susan Lala. Its distinctive feature is a 'people perch', a multi-level wooden tower which provides views over the sanctuary and an ideal vantage point for birding. Contact Caribbean Villas for information.

CAYE CAULKER

Caye Caulker is a sand and mangrove island lying one mile inside the barrier reef, 34km northeast of Belize City, and 18km south of Ambergris Caye. The caye is 6.4km long, divided roughly in half by a narrow channel called the Cut or Split. The northern half is uninhabited mangrove swamp, as is much of the southern half. The village takes up only about a 1.5km-long stretch of land just south of the Cut.

Caye Caulker Forest Reserve, the northernmost 100 acres of the island, was created in May 1998 as a Forest Reserve. The area was used as a coconut plantation before Hurricane Hattie in 1961, but has not been in active use since, so the native littoral forest has had nearly 40 years to regenerate.

Caye Caulker Marine Reserve runs adjacent to the Forest Reserve, and includes 11.1 linear kilometres of reef. It includes the turtle grass lagoon adjacent to the

Caye Caulker Forest Reserve and the Belize Barrier Reef that runs parallel to the entire Caye, extending approximately one mile beyond the reef. This area has been used for snorkelling, scuba diving and sport fishing for some time and it is hoped that the protected status will ensure these areas are carefully managed to avoid damage in the future.

Like Mexico's Isla Mujeres and Guatemala's Panajachel, Caulker has long served as Belize's magnet for the young, hip and laid back. Much of Caulker's charm lay in the fact that, despite the influx of travellers, it remained primarily a lobstering community where tourism took the economic back seat. You arranged meals with housewives, rented a cottage, slung a hammock or stayed at Edith's low-budget 'hotel'. Locals were friendly but independent; they saw no advantage installing air conditioning, gift shops or other such frippery. Unfortunately, Caulker's charms have tarnished somewhat in the last ten years or so. The lobster population has declined even as the tourist population skyrocketed. Hotels and restaurants are springing up like sandflies at dusk. Prices are on the rise. Pseudo-Rastas offer 'smoke' and coke along the island's sandy streets. There have even been a few armed robberies on the village's sandy pathways. A distinct air of terminal hipness pervades the caye and locals, while still friendly, are noticeably chafing at the hordes of visitors which flood their island all year long and the economic necessity of pandering to them. Still, Caulker is the highlight of a Belizean vacation for many travellers.

History

Caye Caulker's first visitors were undoubtedly lured by the fishing. The Maya fished from camps at nearby Caye Chapel and Ambergris Caye, and may have stayed occasionally on Caulker, although they established no permanent base there. Largely mangrove swamp, Caye Caulker – you'll sometimes see it spelled Corker – remained uninhabited until the 1840s, when thousands of Mexicans fled the Caste War in the Yucatan. A handful settled Caulker, and many of today's residents can trace their ancestry to these original Mexican refugees. Wealthy landowners planted coconut trees in the late 1800s, and the *cocals* (coconut plantations) vied for years with fishing as the island's economic base. It wasn't until the 1920s that Caulker fishermen turned to the spiny lobster – formerly considered a 'trash fish' because of its abundance – as a means of livelihood (see box on page 244).

In 1961, Hurricane Hattie destroyed nearly every house on the eastern side of the island within a space of fifteen minutes. The islanders rebuilt, moving their main street further inland. By the late 1960s, adventurous travellers had discovered Caulker, and its mystique continued to grow with the backpacking crowd throughout the 1970s, when the first hotels appeared. By 1983, a dozen hotels were operating, and today there are at least 36.

Getting there

Islanders for years discouraged the periodic attempts to establish an airstrip, but it finally happened in 1991. Maya Island Air run eight scheduled flights to Caye Caulker at a cost of BZ$47 from the Municipal Airport, BZ$77 from the International Airport. Tropic Air do not have scheduled flights but any of the eleven daily flights to San Pedro from Belize City (BZ$47 one way from the Municipal Airport, BZ$84 from the International Airport) will stop at Caye Caulker on request. From Corozal flights connect to San Pedro three times a day from where you can catch one of the taxi boats to Caye Caulker.

Most travellers still come to Caulker by boat. Large outboard skiffs leave throughout the morning and early afternoon seven days a week from the Belize

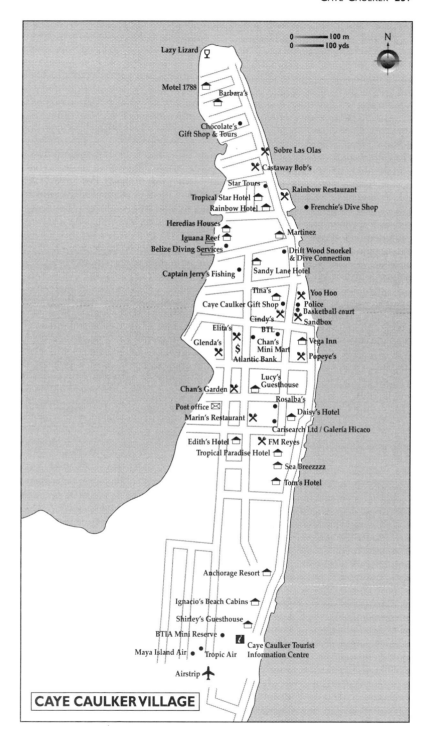

0 ▬▬ 100 m
0 ▬▬ 100 yds

N

Lazy Lizard

Motel 1788

Barbara's

Chocolate's
Gift Shop & Tours

Sobre Las Olas

Castaway Bob's

Star Tours

Tropical Star Hotel
Rainbow Hotel

Rainbow Restaurant

Frenchie's Dive Shop

Heredias Houses

Iguana Reef
Belize Diving Services

Martinez

Drift Wood Snorkel
& Dive Connection

Captain Jerry's Fishing

Sandy Lane Hotel

Tina's

Caye Caulker Gift Shop

Cindy's

Yoo Hoo
Police
Basketball court
Sandbox

Elita's

BTL
Chan's
Mini Mart

Glenda's

$
Atlantic Bank

Vega Inn

Popeye's

Lucy's
Guesthouse

Chan's Garden

Rosalba's

Post office

Marin's Restaurant

Daisy's Hotel

Carisearch Ltd / Galería Hicaco

Edith's Hotel

Tropical Paradise Hotel

FM Reyes

Sea Breezzzz

Tom's Hotel

Anchorage Resort

Ignacio's Beach Cabins

Shirley's Guesthouse

BTIA Mini Reserve

Maya Island Air

Tropic Air

Caye Caulker Tourist
Information Centre

Airstrip

CAYE CAULKER VILLAGE

Marine Terminal (tel: 02 31969; fax: 02 78710; email: btiajeff@btl.net) next to the swing bridge. If you need to leave your bag, there is secure storage at the Marine Terminal.

Six departures a day make the 45-minute journey, the first leaving at 06.30, the last at 15.00. The cost is BZ$15 and tickets can be bought from the office at the Maritime Terminal. A reduced service of just one boat operates on Sundays and bank holidays.

Be prepared on choppy days to take a pounding, and on rainy ones to become thoroughly drenched (even huddling under the plastic tarps).

Leaving Caye Caulker, its best to book your ticket from the water taxi office the day before to be certain of getting a seat.

From San Pedro, Ambergris Caye, there are any number of boats which run passengers to Caulker. Boats leave every three hours or so from the main pier on the western side of the island.

Where to stay

There are now plenty of places to stay on Caulker at reasonable prices. This, combined with the high turnover rate of travellers on the island make reservations unnecessary except perhaps during the winter holidays. Hotels at the south end of the village tend to be quieter, but their proximity to the mangroves also means more sandflies.

Edith's Hotel (tel: 022 2161). 10 rooms, with private bath, fan. BZ$45 .The very first formal accommodations on Caulker. Small area for groups. The rooms are rather dismal, and some travellers have found the owners unpleasant.

Barbara's Basic Clean rooms at BZ$20. Shared bathroom. There is also a secure bunk room for BZ$10pp. Barbara is also proprietor of the Drift Wood Snorkelling Connection.

Tom's Hotel (tel: 022 2102). 30 rooms that have recently been refitted, with shared bath, fan. BZ$27. 3 bungalows available for BZ$50. Managers Tom and Zeda run a popular, friendly and cheap hotel that's consistently recommended by travellers.

Sea Breezzzz (tel: 022 2176; fax: 022 2276). 6 rooms with private bath, fan. BZ$80. A clean place with a lovely garden yard and good but pricey restaurant/bar. Chuck Balfour, originally from Montauk, New York, looks the part of the quintessential tropical expatriate and mixes a mean drink in the bargain. His wife Bonnie is Belizean.

Shirley's Guest House (tel: 022 2145; fax: 022 2264). 5 rooms, with shared bath, fan. US$27.50–67. A quiet, pleasant place with hammocks to really chill out.

Ignacio's Beach Cabins PO Box 1169, Belize City (tel: 022 2212). 9 cabins on stilts, with private bath, fan. BZ$20 At the south end of the village, surrounded by palms and featuring a swimming dock. Has faded from its former glory and you have to stay for a minimum of two nights.

Anchorage Resort (tel: 02 2391; fax: 02 2304; email: anchorage@btl.net) 12 double rooms, with private bath and fans. BZ$90. Quiet beach area with private pier.

Tropical Paradise Hotel (tel: 022 2124; fax: 022 2225). 25 rooms, with private bath, hot water showers. BZ$50. Cabanas cost BZ$80–100. Suites cost BZ$140 and are definitely overpriced. The restaurant cashes travellers' cheques for hotel guests at the going rate.

Daisy's Hotel (tel: 022 2150). 11 rooms with fan and shared bath. BZ$20. With private bath BZ$25.

Heredia's Houses (tel: 022 2132). Fully equipped houses for rent from BZ$60 a night.

Lena's Hotel (tel: 022 2106). 16 rooms, BZ$30 with private bath. Upgraded and no longer the real cheapie it used to be.

Lucy's Guest House (tel: 022 2110). 15 rooms. BZ$25 with shared bath, fan, BZ$50 with private bath. Clean and friendly, Lucy takes a lot of care to make sure the little things are right. Recommended.

Tropical Star Hotel (tel: 022 2374). 21 rooms, with private bath and fan. BZ$30. A big two-storey building to the north of the village, with verandas for looking east across the ocean. Sometimes a bit noisy, but a good place to meet other travellers.

Rainbow Hotel (tel: 022 2123; fax: 022 2172). 8 rooms, with private bath, fan. BZ$58–85. Also overlooking the sea, the hotel is near the Rainbow Bar.

Martinez' Hotel One of the many unspectacular places in the BZ$25 bracket.

Tina's The cheapest in town with shared dormitories for BZ$10. Includes hot water, kitchen and shared lounge with TV and stereo.

Motel 1788 tel: 022 2388; fax: 022 2153. Up near the Cut, rooms have hot water, AC (BZ$70) or fans (BZ$50.) There is also a six-person apartment available for BZ$130 a day. The owner meets most boats coming in on a pink golf cart and gives a free lift to the motel.

Sandy Lane (tel: 022 2217). 13 rooms. BZ$20 with shared bath, fan. BZ$30 with a private bath.

Iguana Reef PO Box 31; tel: 022 2213; fax: 022 2000; email: iguanareef@btl.net; web: www.iguanareefinn.com. Smart new place up near the football pitch. 6 immaculate rooms, beautifully decorated with stylish touches. Full AC, HW, fridge. US$75 (summer), US$100 (winter)

Vega Inn PO Box 701, Belize City (tel: 0222142; fax: 022 2269). 10 rooms, US$65 with private bath, fan. A two-storey wooden building with Caulker's only camping area out front (US$8pp). Some find owner Tony Vega a colourful local character and like this place; we found him quite unpleasant. Not recommended.

Where to eat

Until a few years ago, Caulker boasted not a single restaurant per se. A handful of homes on the island served simple food in simple surroundings. While some of these may still exist, the trend is toward restaurants. One or two now sport naugahyde and chrome furniture and professionally printed menus. Lobster (in season, BZ$16–25) is the staple on Caulker, served boiled, broiled, curried, in pies, even scrambled with eggs for breakfast. A variety of other seafoods is available, along with standard Belizean fare. Caulker has more than its share of shops and homes selling sweet cakes, pastries and fresh fruit juices.

Martinez Caribbean Inn Lobster and fries BZ$14, breakfast BZ$6. Also burgers, garnaches, panuchos, tacos (BZ$1), shrimp (BZ$16), fry chicken (BZ$8) and arguably the best breakfast burritoes on the island.

Sobre Las Olas Belizean food, BZ$10–20 for a meal, with a dock, bar, and tables near the water and indoor dining across the street.

Sand Box A trendy spot and the place to be seen. Good seafood dishes with regular specials, but a bit pricey.

Chan's Garden Better than average Belizean-Chinese food with a few local dishes (lobster burgers) to add to the variety. Very popular.

Popeye's Down on the beach, with a gentle dockside atmosphere. Breakfast of lobster with eggs (BZ$7). Was half buried in sand by Hurricane Mitch but you wouldn't know. The owner Ronald is a registered guide.

Cindy's Balconied café with home-baked buns, book-swap and small gift shop.

Yoo Hoo Excellent coffee and real food, real fast… well that's what they say. Subs, excellent Cuban sandwiches and you can email them (!) caulker@btl.net.

Rainbow Restaurant Great spot looking out over the bay serves food and drink all day.

Castaway Bob's tel: 022 2294. Exclusive little restaurant run by Bob from London. Breakfast is spectacular and usually includes the option of fresh lobster. Evening meal is by reservation only. Intimate 3-course meal with the menu set by the first to place reservations. BZ$35. You will not be disappointed.

Tropical Paradise Restaurant Lobster (curried, fried, stewed) dinners range from BZ$16–25. Breakfast (including fry jacks, or scrambled eggs and lobster BZ$10). They also have a well-stocked bar serving a few cocktails and ice cream. The decor is garishly out of place for Caulker and service can be painfully slow, but they can be counted on to have what's on the menu.

Marin's Restaurant Excellent dinners, including lobster (BZ$16). The modern, citified decor doesn't sit well in Caulker but the place is very popular.

Glenda's Good breakfast (cinnamon rolls BZ$0.50), lunches (garnaches BZ$1 for three) and juices (fresh-squeezed orange BZ$3 per bottle).

Sea Breezzzz Dinners are expensive by Caulker standards (lobster BZ$30), but do come with salad and homemade biscuits. Real brewed coffee (a rarity in Belize) for breakfast.

Elita's Fast Food Central Street. Good, simple food with quick service. Open for breakfast and throughout the day and the cheapest on the island.

Syd's Central Street. Good food, quick and tasty. One of the cheapest.

FMReyes next to Tropical Paradise Hotel. Will provide you with a good-sized pack lunch if you want to go off on a day trip somewhere.

What to see

Sandy thoroughfares, appropriately named Front, Central and Back Street, run the length of the village, with a handful of cross streets. You can easily walk the entire inhabited length of the caye in half an hour. There are two public piers (locals refer to them as 'bridges'). Front Bridge faces the reef, and Back Bridge faces the mainland. Numerous other piers dot the reef side of Caulker, but they are all private, and you should ask permission before using them. Those owned by the local hotels are ostensibly for their guests only, but life is still informal enough on Caulker for this to be ignored in all but high season. Since Caulker has no real beaches, the piers become the focal point for sun worshippers, bathers, and board sailors.

Information and useful addresses

A comprehensive map of the island costing BZ$10 is available from Caye Caulker BTIA (PO Box 43, Caye Caulker; tel: 022 2251) close to the airstrip. The office is located in a mini-reserve of marine trees with a good selection of books on the island. Caye Caulker has it's own BTIA internet site (www.gocayecaulker.com). While this is an excellent example of how the internet can be used, it is in no way a comprehensive guide to accommodations and services on Caye Caulker.

Changing money is easy at the **Atlantic Bank** on Central Street. A few of the more upmarket hotels will also change travellers' cheques.

Telephone calls can be made at the **BTL** office on Front Street. There are several are a few public telephones dotted round the island. Internet access is popping up in any shop or restaurant with a spare corner so just keep your eyes open.

Transport on the island is by foot unless you feel like renting one of the golf buggies for a short drive round the island.

Most of the many local gift shops offer pretty much the standard assortment of beach resort wares. **Chocolate's Gifts** on Front Street south of the Cut offers good quality hammocks, T-shirts, jewellery and Guatemalan crafts, as does the **Toucan Gift Shop** at the Public Front Dock. The best – and least touristy – are **Sea-Ing is Belizing** (tel: 021 2079) and **Galería Hicaco** (tel: 022 2178; email:

sbf@btl.net). The latter is located across from the cemetery and features Maya and Garifuna crafts, clothing, and drawings by local artist Philip Charles Lewis.

Sea-Ing is Belizing (tel: 021 2079; email: tourism@cayecaulker.org.bz; web: www.gocayecaulker.com) offers a guided Nature/Bird Walk of Caye Caulker's littoral forest, mangrove forests, and seashore. US$15 pp. Environmental slide shows, one on the reef, the other covering the rainforest, are also available at US$3 pp. Owner James Beveridge is a licensed tour guide with the Belize Tourism Board and is a long-time member of the Belize Audubon Society. He and his wife are excellent sources of information on the Belize Audubon Society and Belize's protected areas in general. He learned to scuba dive in 1957 in Scotland, later becoming an instructor there. He bought his first underwater camera in 1968 and he's been doing serious UW photography on Belize's reefs for eleven years; his rainforest wildlife photos are equally impressive. He's lived in Belize since 1972, is now a Belizean national.

Sea-Ing is Belizing has a large selection of stock photography and sells images as prints and duplicate slides. Jim also does photography work on assignment.

CariSearch Ltd (CSL) offers scientifically oriented marine tours and seminars based on reed ecology, caye ecology and bird rookeries organised by local environmentalist Ellen McRae (tel: 022 2178; email: sbf@btl.net) Ellen worked to set-up the Caye Caulker Marine Reserve and is now involved with ensuring it is properly maintained and regulated.

Drift Wood Snorkelling and **Dive Connection** provide good general information. **Star Tours** is up by the Tropical Star Hotel.

Rent bicycles at **Caye Caulker Gift Shop** opposite the police station. BZ$5/hr or BZ$25 for the day. Sailboards can be rented at Galería Hicaco for BZ$15–20 per hour. **Vega Inn** rents Sunfish sailboats (BZ$25 per hour).

Caulker has several small grocery stores (**J&L's Supply** and **Chan's Mini Mar** to name a couple). For liquor, try **Shaley's Liquor Store** behind Driftwood Snorkel Shop.

Rosalba next to CSL does laundry.

Caulker's sandflies ('no-see-ums') are notorious, as are the mosquitoes. One can only marvel at the stamina of those who lived here before the islanders began spraying Malathion periodically. Still, a good breeze is the best protection from these pests. Be especially prepared while walking through the mangroves at the south end of the island, anywhere at dusk, and whenever the wind dies. See *Chapter 5, Insects and insect-borne diseases*, page 48, for more advice.

A number of pseudo-Rastas have moved to the island recently from Belize City, bringing drugs (including crack) and crime to what was once a truly bucolic place.

Excursions
Near town
Snorkel trips
Not too many years ago, arranging a snorkel trip on Caulker involved rounding up a group of fellow travellers, locating a lobster fisherman willing to bring you out to the reef, and haggling over the price. Nowadays, at least ten full-time reef guides line up customers on a daily basis for a price that is fixed pretty much island-wide. Admittedly, it's a lot more crowded out on the reef these days, but you're also assured – barring weather, of course – that a boat will be available when you're ready to go.

Snorkel trips from Caulker are generally of two sorts. Trips to the barrier reef directly east of the island last about 6 hours. This may not sound like much time, but even the most avid snorkellers are usually sated by this time, and there are plenty of goosebumps evident on the way back to the island. Boats accept around 12 passengers, charging BZ$30 pp. You'll snorkel at two or three sites on the inside of the reef, the whole group slipping over the side while the guide stays in the boat at anchor in about 4–6m of water. The normal trip visits Shark Ray Alley where nurse sharks and stingrays come to feed on food provided by guides. While seeing these animals close up is enjoyable, it is nothing compared to a genuine sighting. Not all guides contribute to the creation of this open zoo, but apart from asking operators before leaving on the trip and complaining to guides there is little that can be done. A second dive involves snorkelling at the Hol Chan Marine Reserve followed by a lunch stop in San Pedro, Ambergris Caye, and then back to the reef for more snorkelling. These trips last from about 10.00 to 16.00, with a couple of hours in San Pedro. For more information on Hol Chan Reserve, see *San Pedro, Excursions* above.

There are plenty of guides to choose from and while many companies compete for business, most clients are pooled together in one trip when demand is insufficient. Most companies include gear rental in the price but rent any gear you need beforehand. Bring sunscreen, two T-shirts (one to wear snorkelling), snacks and something to drink. The boat ride to Hol Chan and San Pedro can be rough and wet on windy days.

There are several snorkelling operations on Caye Caulker. **Drift Wood Snorkelling and Dive Connection** (tel: 022 2011; fax: 022 2328) is very helpful when organising trips and asking for information in general. For a more scientifically oriented trip, contact marine biologist Ellen MacRae at the Galería Hicaco across from the cemetery. Her guided nature trips to the reef cost BZ$39 pp.

Scuba diving trips

Most day scuba trips from Caulker involve diving at depths from 12–24m on the outside of the barrier reef. On windy days, however, dive trip operators are sometimes tempted to drop you on the inside of the reef – which offers less-than-spectacular diving – rather than simply call the trip off. To avoid disappointment, arrange beforehand to cancel or postpone the dives in case of bad weather.

Two-dive trips to the Blue Hole cost BZ$285, three-dive trips to Half Moon cost BZ$315.

If you are looking to learn, the dive operations on Caye Caulker offer NAUI and PADI open water certification. The 4-day PADI course costs US$500.

Two dive shops operate out of Caulker. The oldest and best known is Belize Diving Services (mailing address PO Box 20, Caye Caulker, tel: 02 2143; fax: 022 2217; email: bzdiveserv@btl.net), located just west of the soccer field. Owners Dawn Williams and Kathy Dalton offer scuba instruction (PADI certification, four-day class US$250, includes all equipment), gear rentals and dive packages. Their gear is all top quality and amazingly well cared-for. Dive options include a two-tank dive on the nearby barrier reef for US$50 (includes boat, guide, tanks, backpacks and weights). One-tank night dive costs US$35. Four-day packages are also available (includes night dive, US$300).Belize Diving Services prides itself on the focus given to customer service and their patience and flexibility makes your diving as stress free as possible. Belize Diving Services accepts MasterCard and VISA. Shop hours Mon–Sat 08.00–18.00, Sun 08.00–16.00.

Frenchie's Dive Shop (tel: 022 2234; fax: 022 2074; email: frenchies@btl.net; www.belizenet.com/frenchies.html), located on a pier towards the north of the island also offers dive trips. The equipment appears well cared for. Two-tank dive on the outside of the barrier reef costs BZ$110. A single-tank dive costs BZ$65 (these packages include boat, guide, tanks, backpack, and weights). This same two-tank package with all gear included (BC, regulator, mask, fins, snorkel) is BZ$75. PADI open-water certification can also be arranged.

Sailing trips

CSL rents out kayaks. BZ$25 for a half-day, BZ$40 for a full day. **Sea-Ing is Belizing** owner James Beveridge occasionally runs extended sailboat trips which include photography, snorkelling and scuba.

Birdwatching

Birders should contact biologist Ellen MacRae at the **Galería Hicaco** (see above). She offers instructive and well-informed nature walks (BZ$24 pp) among the mangroves at the south end, pointing out rails, herons, ibises and other local avifauna. Bring binoculars, insect repellent, long sleeves and long pants. Look for the black catbird (*Melanoptila glabrirostris*, 'siwa-ban' in Yucatec Maya), found in numbers only on Caye Caulker. A second population in southern Ambergris Caye is rapidly disappearing as development encroaches on its forest habitat. A nature preserve has been proposed for this shy relative of the mockingbird on the south end of Caulker. For more information, write to the **Siwa-Ban Foundation**, 143 Anderson, San Francisco, California, USA. You won't need a guide or binoculars to enjoy the scores of brown pelicans (*Pelecanus occidentalis*) which rest on Caulker's piers between feeding forays along the shore.

CAYE CHAPEL

This privately owned, palm-dotted island sits just 2km south of Caye Caulker. Although only 4.8km by 1.6km, Caye Chapel boasts a marina, a golf course and driving range, two tennis courts, basketball courts, Belize's second-longest airstrip and a single luxury hotel. The Caye has undergone considerable changes recently. The reasonably priced Pyramid Island Resort has been demolished and the deluxe **Caye Chapel Golf Resort & Marina**, still under construction at time of writing, will take its place.

Accommodation will be limited to 12 deluxe villas. Everything is first-class as you would expect for a price that will be in the region of US$1,000 a night, food not included. Outside the range of most travellers, the market for the island will be corporate meetings and retreats. At times when there are no corporate meetings, the island will be open to the public, with the goal of attracting high-end travellers who want a luxury Caribbean setting with golf, tennis and other activities close at hand. For more information, contact Caye Chapel Golf Course & Marina, PO Box 192, Belize City; tel: 02 28250; fax: 02 28201; email: golf@btl.net.

As interesting as the island itself is the controversy surrounding construction of the resort. Environmentalists are concerned about the damage that will be caused by dredging on the northern end of the island and the potential damage caused by rainwater run-off from intensive pesticide and fertiliser use. Locals in Caye Caulker can update you on the latest developments, but it makes a good case study of who normally wins when it's the environment against big business.

Caye Chapel can be reached on virtually any of the boats headed from Belize City to Caye Caulker (see *Caye Caulker, Getting there*, above). Simply tell the skipper and he'll stop on his way to Caulker. You can also fly to the island on Maya Island Air (five flights daily from Belize City) or Tropic Air (11 flights daily). The eight-minute flight costs BZ$47 from the Municipal Airport or BZ$77 from the International Airport.

LONG CAYE

Long Caye (not to be confused with the coral island of the same name on Lighthouse Reef) is a low-lying, mostly mangrove island roughly 5km south of Caye Chapel. There are currently no visitor facilities at the caye. If you want to stay

LOBSTERS AND LOBSTERING

Lobster is fished in other locales along the Belizean coast – San Pedro and Placencia, for example – but Caye Caulker reigns as the country's undisputed lobster capital. Lobster traps are stacked ten high beneath coconut palms (the island's former economic base), and restaurants offer the crustacean in everything from pies to scrambled eggs.

The spiny or Caribbean lobster (*Panulirus argus*) depends on a prickly exterior for protection, unlike its North American relative (*Homarus americanus*) which is outfitted with two oversized claws. Gourmets may debate their relative merits, but both lobsters command a high price on international seafood markets. It was a Canadian exporter, Captain R E Foote, who first saw the money-making possibilities of Belizean lobster during a visit there in 1921. He experimented with various versions of the wooden lobster trap used in the Canadian maritime provinces, fishing them at Water Caye, just 38km south of Caye Caulker.

For the next 14 years, Foote trained local fishermen and set up a cannery near Caye Caulker's rich lobster beds. The depression in the US put a temporary damper on the lobster market, but the fishery recovered and grew throughout the 1940s. For many years, however, a single US buyer monopolised the market, forcing Belizean fishermen to accept ridiculously low prices for their luxury product. Resentment grew, and with it grew efforts at forming a local fishing co-operative. After years of political turmoil, Belize's first fishing co-operative came into being. The idea was later picked up by fishermen in San Pedro and Placencia. With the co-operative in place to assure a fair market price, Caulker's lobstermen became quite prosperous by Caribbean standards. Yet nothing in Caulker's sleepy outward appearance changed with this new affluence.

Caye Caulker lobstermen fish primarily with traps. These are slatted wooden boxes with a funnel-shaped opening at one end which makes it easy for

the best bet is to get the very latest information from the Belize Tourist Board (see *Belize City* for details). To reach Long Caye, you'll have to negotiate with one of the boats near the Marine Terminal in Belize City.

ST GEORGE'S CAYE

Just 14km from Belize City, St George's Caye was the site of Spain's last attempt to wrest control of Belize from the British. The decisive sea battle took place on September 10 1798, as the Spanish fleet attacked British settlers and a single English warship at St George's Caye. Many of the Spanish casualties were buried on Caye Chapel (see above), while a small British graveyard is located here on the southern tip of St George's. Besides the pretty little cemetery, there isn't much to see, and unless you're staying at one of the two lodges, you can't visit the caye. The British army used to train soldiers here, and the island is dotted with a few weekend cabanas. There are only two options for lodging: **Cottage Colony**, PO Box 428, Belize City (tel: 02 77051; fax: 02 73253; email: fins@btl.net), with 15 luxury cottages built in old Caribbean colonial style, (US$120) plus US$40 for three meals a day. Diving and fishing is available, contact the Cottage Colony for details.

The longest-established place to stay is **St George's Lodge**, PO Box 625, Belize City, tel/fax: 02 12121; email: sgl.belize@btl.net; web: www.gooddiving.com

a lobster to enter but almost impossible to exit. Traps are weighted with chunks of coral or rocks, and checked every three to seven days. Caye Caulker lobstermen haul their traps by hand, snagging them with an 8m-long hooked pole.

For years now, islanders have staked informal claims to particular lobster beds surrounding the caye; to enter the fishery, a young man must inherit a territory from a relative. These territories are well known to the locals, and many of the tall sticks you'll pass in shallow water on the way snorkelling mark fishing boundaries. Within these territories, however, the actual placement of traps remains a well-kept secret. Trap theft is common enough to preclude the use of marker buoys, so an individual fisherman will set his traps in a pattern known only to him – a zig-zag perhaps, or any number of more complicated schemes. Most lobstermen set between 150 and 500 traps, and they must know the location of every one.

Those who can't afford traps or haven't managed to inherit a fishing territory often dive for lobster. So far, all the lobster diving has been done without scuba or surface-supplied air. Divers simply fill their lungs, head for the bottom, and start looking for the telltale lobster antennae extending from dark crevices in the coral. Most divers use a short metal hook to dislodge the lobster from its den.

Lobster season opens throughout Belize on June 15, closing on February 15. The minimum size limit of 113g presumably saves pre-reproductive lobster, although you'll see and hear of undersized lobsters being sold. Opinions are still divided on whether or not the fishery is headed for collapse. There's no doubt that the last few seasons have been poor ones. Then again, crustacean populations often undergo huge swings that are perfectly natural. And the 1995 season saw record catches on opening day. You can do your part by refusing to eat lobster out of season and demanding that you be served only legal-sized lobsters.

(in the US tel: 1 800 678 6871 toll-free; fax: 941 488 3953; email: Aw2trav2bz@aol.com).

The main lodge, with ten rooms and a restaurant/bar, sits on 10 acres near the southern end of the island. It was built with beamed cathedral ceilings made from local rosewood and Santa Maria wood. There are also six raised, thatch-roofed cottages overlooking the mangrove lagoon behind the main lodge. The lodge was spared any real damage by Hurricane Mitch in 1998. Meals, including fresh seafood, fruit, and homemade desserts, bread, and soup, are excellent. There's a hot tub and sun deck. Bring your own bottle. Ex-Californian Fred Good caters almost exclusively to scuba divers. After some 25 years in business, the lodge continues to get high marks from both beginner and veteran divers. Ex-Californian Fred Good and partner Fran Chang cater almost exclusively to scuba divers; there's no real beach to speak of. Good is arguably the best diving instructor in Belize, and has added Nitrox certification classes to his year-round schedule of classes, which includes everything from beginning to Instructor levels. Good has three compressors, and three dive boats ranging from 22ft to 33ft. Oxygen is available, and unsupervised buddy diving is permitted. The diving is mostly along the barrier reef, within 15min of the lodge, in 12–30m. For an extra fee, Good will take divers out to the nearest of the offshore atolls, Turneffe Islands (see *Chapter 14*), for spectacular wall diving. All the resort's dive packages are highly recommended and

Good is consistently regarded as one of Belize's top scuba divemasters. Enquiries in the US through Alice Wilhoit, 1604 Maple Street, Nokomis, Florida 34275-2429; tel: 1 800 678 6871; tel: 941 488 3788; fax: 941 488 3953; email: Aw2trav2bz@aol.com .

GALLOWS POINT CAYE

This peaceful caye within sight of Belize City is where convicted murderers once swung from the gibbet. The only lodging is at **The Wave** (formerly Gallows Point Resort), which offers six rooms US$140 for two people, including three meals per day and boat transport from Belize City. The rooms have private baths and fans. Simpler shared-bath rooms go for US$15 pp.

SPANISH LOOKOUT CAYE

South of Gallows Point Caye, and a half-hour boat ride from Belize City, Spanish Lookout Caye is a mangrove island covering over 200 acres. The only lodging is at the **Spanish Bay Resort**, PO Box 35, 71 North Front Street, Belize City (tel: 02 31960; fax: 02 72797 or toll-free in the US 1 800 359 0747). The resort has five cabanas on stilts facing the beach, each cabana with two separate rooms, with private baths and fans. The restaurant/bar is perched over the water, and the food is recommended. Dive packages are available.

MIDDLE LONG CAYE

This extensive mangrove island sits 26km southeast of Belize City, and a 45-minute boat ride away. This is no sandy, palm-fringed desert isle, but it does provide habitat for saltwater crocodiles, numerous birds and manatees. The only lodging on the island is **Moonlight Shadows Lodge** (tel: 08 22587 in Belmopan). With two thatched cabins, it's fairly cheap by caye standards, US$50 with private bath. Owner Rudolf Avila will provide meals at an extra charge as well as snorkel, fishing, and nature tours. No dive equipment is available. You can cook your own food.

BLUEFIELD RANGE

The Bluefield Range, consisting of three small cayes, lies about 3km south of Middle Long Caye and 35km southeast of Belize City. Here you'll find one of the most secluded lodging opportunities in the cayes: **Ricardo's Beach Huts**, PO Box 55, Belize City (tel: 02 44970 or VHF Channel 68 to talk directly to Ricardo Avila, the owner). Five rustic huts on the water, US$75 with shared bath, transfers from Belize City, and all meals. The minimum stay is two nights. Additional nights are US$30. The meals consist of fresh seafood and are highly regarded. You can also camp on your own for US$3 pp. Sr Avila provides highly recommended snorkel, fishing and nature tours to nearby cayes. These could include Alligator Caye, just 4km to the south, which owes its name to the saltwater crocodiles which still inhabit the area.

OTHER CAYES IN THE BELIZE CITY AREA

English Caye, Goff Caye and Rendezvous Caye all lie within about 30km of Belize City, and consequently draw locals for weekend picnics and fishing trips. None of them offer overnight lodging – indeed, they're so tiny you can run around them in a couple of minutes – but they're perfect for day trips, snorkelling and sunbathing. Don't expect to be alone; these sandy, palm-studded islets draw locals and travellers alike, especially on weekends. Unless you can convince a local fisherman in Belize City to ferry you out, the only way to reach these cayes is via a local travel agency or hotel, which can line up a boat.

The Atolls

Atolls are coral islands in which the living reef surrounds a lagoon. Although the Pacific Ocean boasts over 300, atolls in the Caribbean are extremely rare. Most geologists recognise only ten Caribbean atolls, and three of them are off the coast of Belize: Lighthouse, Turneffe, and Glover's reefs. For more information on the natural history of atolls, see *Chapter 3*.

All three lie well outside Belize's barrier reef. Turneffe, the closest to the mainland, is some 30km from Belize City even at its nearest point. Lighthouse lies about 75km east of the coast and nearly 50km east of the barrier reef. Despite their great size – Turneffe spans about 60km from north to south – most of the atolls' enclosed lagoons consist of submerged coral or marshy mangrove islets. Lighthouse Reef, for example, contains only four small sand and coral islands (cayes) within a total area of 50,560 acres.

But the atolls' real attractions lie underwater anyway. Here, divers will find spectacular walls and virtually undisturbed coral reefs abounding with fish and invertebrate life. Among the world-class dives is the Blue Hole of Lighthouse Reef, made famous by Jacques Cousteau's 1970 exploration. Simply put, the atolls offer the best diving in the country, the diving that Belize is famous for. Sport fishing draws raves as well. The world record bonefish (7.6kg) was landed at Turneffe Flats in 1991. Permit and tarpon fishing is also excellent. And terrestrial pursuits aren't entirely lacking; Half Moon Caye, Belize's first nature reserve, teems with thousands of nesting seabirds. Isolated and wild, the cayes here are among the most beautiful in the Caribbean.

HISTORY

Because of their distance from the mainland, the paucity of inhabitable dry land, and the lack of fresh water, Belize's atolls have never attracted many settlers. On Turneffe's Calabash Caye and Blackbird Caye (also known as Northern Bogue Caye), archaeologists have uncovered prehistoric shell mounds and Maya pottery from the Late Classic and Early Postclassic, but there is no evidence of permanent settlement. The ancient Maya apparently also used Glover's Reef, probably as a fishing camp. Lighthouse Reef, on the other hand, hasn't yet offered up any evidence for early Maya presence. In the 1530s, Spanish ships surveyed the atolls in their search for New World treasure. 18th century pirates occasionally hid themselves in these remote islands, and German submarines are reported to have used Half Moon Caye as a clandestine refuelling station during World War II.

Even today, the atolls remain sparsely populated. Now and then you'll happen upon a rustic fishing camp, its salted barracuda catch hung like laundry to sun dry.

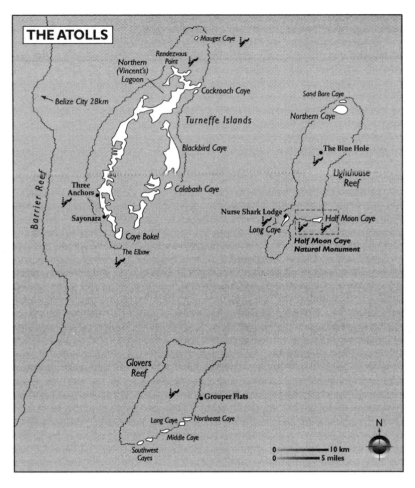

A handful of resorts catering to divers and anglers have opened in the past decade, but many overnight visits are still made in live-aboard boats.

GETTING THERE

You have several options for visiting the atolls. You could book a stay at one of the diving/fishing resorts located directly on the atolls. As an alternative, you could make reservations on one of the luxury live-aboard dive boats that ply the outer islands. Both these options can run into quite a bit of money – sometimes you're required to stay a minimum of a week – but they are probably the most relaxing and comfortable ways to go. There are also a handful of cheaper, smaller live-aboards based out of San Pedro or Caye Caulker. These often make 2–3 day trips, and you'll probably end up tent camping or sleeping on deck (generally quite pleasant, often superior to a stuffy stateroom). You could take any number of one-day trips on small, fast boats based out of San Pedro, Caye Caulker or Belize City. Also, you can now fly to Lighthouse Reef, Glover's Reef and Blackbird Caye on Turneffe, arranging beforehand to meet a boat for diving, fishing or sight-seeing. Live-aboards and land-based resorts are listed in this chapter; for day-trip boats, see

Chapter 13. Finally, you can opt for a kayak tour of Glover's Reef, or sign on as part of a study tour involved in coral reef and bottlenose dolphin research at Lighthouse or Turneffe (see below).

Visits to the atolls aren't cheap. Whether you're booked into a resort or just a one-day dive trip out of San Pedro, you'll be paying the considerable expense of simply getting out there. In fact, this is often the most expensive portion of any atoll trip, so that a two- or three-day stay on a live-aboard dive boat, for example, often costs little more than a day trip. My advice – unless you are incredibly strapped for time – is to spend at least two days in the atolls if you're going to go at all. At this writing, probably the very cheapest accommodations on the atolls are those at Glover's Atoll Resort (see *Glover's Reef* below), which runs at about BZ$24 pp for camping, or BZ$40 pp for a cabin.

Boat rides out to the atolls can get quite rough, even bone-crunching. It's a long ride over some big water. The catch-22 here is that the larger, more stable boats are usually the slowest, while the fast little boats are going to pitch and roll a good deal more. Once out on the atolls, the water is generally flat as a millpond owing to the protective coral reef. But seasickness on the trip out – which in some of the slower boats headed to Lighthouse can last as long as five hours – is quite common. There used to be no real option for those prone to motion sickness, but the airstrips mentioned above have changed that. (Incidentally, the traditional taboo against flying after diving isn't violated by these low-altitude flights.)

Diving and snorkelling are excellent throughout the year, with visibility often 60m and rarely less than 30m. But if you have the choice, book your trip for spring and summer, when generally benign winds blow from the east. In the winter, northern storms blow straight down the open-water channels between the barrier reef and atolls, making boat trips uncomfortable and eliminating some dive sites from consideration.

Live-aboard dive boats

The following live-aboards take divers to the atolls for trips ranging from two days to a week. Prices quoted include all meals, snacks, tanks, weights and guides. Beverages are extra in most cases and it's customary to tip the divemaster and crew.

Belize Aggressor Aggressor Fleet Ltd P.O. Drawer K, Morgan City, LA 70381, USA (tel: 1 800 348 2628 toll-free in US or 504 385 2416). A 30m luxury boat which concentrates on Lighthouse Reef (including the Blue Hole) and Turneffe (including The Elbow). 5 double staterooms and 2 triple staterooms for a total capacity of 16 divers, US$1,295 pp for one week of diving. Virtually unlimited fresh water, air conditioning, 24hr electricity, on-board compressors, private dive gear lockers, chase boat, three heads, four showers, TV, VCR and E-6 film processing. Pricey, and more luxury than many of us need, but highly recommended by every diver I've met. Based out of Moho Caye near Belize City.

Wave Dancer Peter Hughes Diving Inc, 1390 S. Dixie Highway, Suite 1109, Coral Gables, FL 33146, USA (tel: 305 669 9391; fax; 305 669 9475; email: dancer@peterhughes.com; web: www.peterhughes.com). The newest and largest addition to Belize's live-aboard fleet, a 36m luxury boat with ten cabins with private heads and showers, video and still camera rental, E-6 film processing. Seven-day, seven-night packages US$1,595–1,895.

LIGHTHOUSE REEF

Lighthouse Reef covers an area of 50,560 acres, a vast coral plain punctuated by only four specks of dry land: Sandbore Caye, Northern Caye, Half Moon Caye, and Long Caye. Indeed, the 16th century Spaniards referred to Lighthouse Reef as Cuatro Cayos ('Four Cayes'). Sandbore and Half Moon are so tiny that you can literally see from one side to the other. They're also home to the two lighthouses that have given the atoll its modern name. The reef's treacherous coral outcroppings have claimed scores of ships over the centuries, and even the lighthouses didn't entirely eliminate the danger. Two years after the first lighthouse was built (1820), the Spanish galleon Juan Baptista struck the coral reef and sank carrying the equivalent of US$800,000 in gold and silver bullion. Divers have never located the wreck and its treasure.

Where to stay/eat
Lighthouse Reef Resort Northern Two Caye, PO Box 1435, Dundee, Florida 33838 (tel: 941 439 6600 in Florida or 1 800 423 3114 toll-free in US; email: LARC1@worldnet.att.net; web: www.scuba-dive-belize.com/home.htm). This is the only option for formal lodging on Lighthouse Reef. Opened in 1989, the resort has long since worked most of the bugs out of their operation (they still needed more reliable boats at last check, but this may have changed by the time you read this). Tropic Air meets incoming flights at Belize International Airport to deliver guests to the resort. Mahogany cabanas with view of the lagoon, private bath, oversized beds, fans and air conditioning, are standard; guests can upgrade to Victorian suites at additional cost. All rates are based on week-long packages, running from Saturday to Saturday, including three meals a day, snacks, and round trip air from Belize International. The dive package (three boat dives per day, plus night dives) costs US$1,460–1,645 pp, depending on the type of room; a resort package for lodging and meals alone costs US$1,140–1,335 pp. The excellent bar and restaurant, a few steps from the caye's single dock, offer a commanding view of the lagoon and nearby Sand Bore Caye. Absolutely quiet at night, and not for partygoers. No TV or phones, but there's a radio telephone for emergencies. The lagoon offers decent snorkelling for non-divers. They have a resident bottlenose dolphin in the waters nearby. The resort suffered some sea wall damage during Hurricane Mitch in 1998, but no other problems. Overall, highly recommended. The resort owns 36ft and 26ft dive boats, and they carry oxygen. Unsupervised buddy diving is allowed.

What to see
Half Moon Caye Natural Monument
Half Moon Caye, widely regarded as one of the most beautiful islands in Belize, lies on a prominent elbow along the southeastern edge of Lighthouse Reef. Within a mere 45 acres, Half Moon Caye can boast all the ingredients of the quintessential island paradise: coconut palms, a strip of white sand beach, a lush forest of native hardwood, a nesting colony of seabirds, a fringing coral reef, a shipwreck visible to the north, even the lighthouse for which the entire atoll was named.

Owing to its special features, Half Moon Caye and 10,000 acres of the surrounding reef was made a Natural Monument in March 1982, making it the country's first nature reserve.

The caye's most famous asset – and a prime reason for the Natural Monument status – is its nesting colony of red-footed boobies (*Sula sula*). Red-footed boobies are probably the most common of the booby species; they're found worldwide surrounding the equator, but only on tiny, isolated islands with low-lying trees in which to build nests. About 4,000 boobies nest here year-round. It is the only such colony in Belize and one of only a few in the Caribbean (the nearest being Little

Swan Island off Honduras and St Giles Island off Tobago, where a colony about a third the size of Half Moon's nests). The caye's boobies are also unusual in that 98% of them sport white plumage. Most red-footed booby populations are made up primarily of the pale brown colour phase. At St Giles, for instance, brown boobies outnumber whites by twenty to one.

An elevated viewing platform puts visitors at eye level with not only the nesting boobies, but hundreds of their chief rival, the magnificent frigatebird. Due to the low oil content of their feathers, frigatebirds risk drowning if they attempt to enter the water to catch fish. As a result, they must either use their beak to skim the water surface for fish, or else rob other birds of their fish in mid-flight. Boobies are prime targets for the thieving frigatebirds, which pester them until they drop their catch. The sight of these two vast and colourful bird colonies is an amazing one that captivates even non-birders. Nearly a hundred other bird species have been recorded on the caye, of which three-quarters are migrants. The tiny caye is also home to iguanas, wish willys (*Ctenosaura similis*, a somewhat smaller iguana) and a species of anole lizard (*Anolis allisoni*) that inhabits only islands. Endangered hawksbill and loggerhead turtles lay their eggs on the caye's sandy beaches.

The island is divided into two distinct ecosystems. The western half is densely vegetated, with stands of zericote trees (the hardwood favoured by Belizean woodcarvers), fig trees and gumbo limbo trees, all fertilized by guano from the seabird colony. The eastern portion – site of the lighthouse, picnic/camping area and boat dock – contains coconut palms and a few patches of vegetation on the otherwise sandy surface. This division owes little to nature, however. Beginning in the late 1920s, the dozen or so fishermen who lived on the caye cleared the eastern portion and planted the palms as a sustenance crop.

The original lighthouse was built in 1820 at the same spot where the present one stands. It was replaced in 1848, and the existing steel superstructure was attached to the brick base in 1931. The lighthouse now runs on solar power. Since becoming a nature reserve, the caye's only residents are the lighthouse keeper and his family, who help to watch over the fragile environment. In 1961, while Hurricane Hattie obliterated many of Belize's small cayes, Half Moon Caye survived, no doubt due in part to its heavy ground cover.

Despite the lighthouse's presence, the reef's treacherous shallows continue to claim ships. You'll see one such grounded wreck about 1,500m directly north of the lighthouse. Several dive boat operators claim that the rusted hulk still swarms with an army of ravenous rats. They've apparently survived thus far by cannibalizing each other and picking off the occasional bird that is unfortunate enough to touch down on its decks. If you hear the tale late at night, over a campfire on Half Moon Caye, it's sometimes embellished with grisly hints of what might have befallen human visitors to the wreck.

The **Half Moon Caye Natural Monument** is sponsored by the government of Belize, the Macarthur Foundation, and the Belize Audubon Society. Contact the Audubon office in Belize City for more information. Visitor facilities include informational signs and a map, a couple of trails, the bird viewing platform, and picnic tables. A wooden dock can accommodate boats which draw less than about 1.5m of water. Some dive boats ask their guests and crew to stand on the bow when leaving the dock to keep the propeller clear of sand. The big live-aboard dive boats are now required to anchor in designated areas to prevent further damage to living corals.

Keep in mind several other rules. Stay on the trails to avoid disturbing either the plants or nesting birds. Bring all your own water – there's none on the tiny island. Do not fish, spearfish, or collect anything on the island, including rocks, coral, shells, and plants.

There are two small trails to the bird observation deck. Bring binoculars and cameras. Apply insect repellent before entering the densely-vegetated eastern half of the island; it's swarming with mosquitoes. On the caye's north side (the side with the boat dock), walk west along the beach until you see the sign. Then enter the zericote forest, following the trail and signs. On the caye's south side, walk west along the beach until you see a stick with a flag on it, then enter the forest and follow the signs. Within the zericote forest, keep your eyes open for iguanas and wish-willys basking on tree limbs or scampering through the underbrush.

You'll know you're close to the observation deck when the leaves overhead appear heavily spattered with guano. You'll also be greeted with a cacophony of squawks and screeches. The wooden observation deck, directly at tree level, supposedly supports only eight people. Atop the deck, you'll probably find yourself within a few metres of nesting boobies and frigatebirds.

The north side of the caye offers a thin strip of sandy beach. The south side has rocky tidepools and thousands of coral skeletons in bizarre shapes. Don't pocket any for souvenirs; if you'd like to take something off the beach, let it be the abundant plastic flotsam that washes up on this, the windward side of the caye. The snorkelling here on the south side is superb, a classic shallow-water coral patch reef with an abundant supply of fish owing to its protected status. For some reason, very few divers or snorkellers know about this spot, and you're likely to have the reef all to yourself. Unfortunately, winds often make it impossible to snorkel comfortably this side of the island.

The Blue Hole

The Blue Hole of Lighthouse Reef is Belize's most famous dive, and arguably its most exciting. *Outside* magazine included the Blue Hole among the four 'World's Great Dives', and one local tour operator bills it as 'the most awesome ten minutes of diving you'll ever experience'. English writer and diver Ned Middleton called it 'one of the most astounding dive sites to be found anywhere on earth'. During my first trip there, a fellow diver pretty much summed it up by saying, 'It's like diving on the moon!'

First explored by Jacques Cousteau in 1970, the Blue Hole lies near the centre of Lighthouse Reef, amid 50,000 acres of treacherously shallow coral reef. It's an almost perfect circle of cobalt-blue water plunging to 124m, ringed at the surface by coral except for two narrow openings. Viewed from the air, both its symmetry and the contrasting colours of deep and shallow water make it one of Belize's most popular postcard photos. Even from the top deck of a boat, the Blue Hole draws appreciative gasps from first-time visitors.

Just below the surface, and all along the Blue Hole's 313m inside diameter, lies a gorgeous coral reef extending to a depth of about 6m. Perfect for snorkelling and shallow diving, it offers plenty of fish – including squirrelfish, stoplight parrotfish, puffers, trunkfish and even tarpon – as well as elkhorn, finger, fan and brain corals that remain completely undamaged. Beyond this, the bottom turns to sand, gently sloping to about 15m, where the bottom drops out of sight down a sheer vertical wall of limestone.

The dive itself begins with a short surface swim toward the centre of the Hole. This puts you out in deeper water, some 15m above the subsurface rim where the sandy plain drops off precipitously. Dropping down directly over the wall rather than swimming down the sand slope saves precious bottom time on this deep dive. At about 39m, the sheer vertical wall suddenly gives way to a massive cavern punctuated with equally massive limestone stalactites. Many of these stalactites measure more than 1m in diameter and 6m in length. Cousteau reported a few that hung 12m long and were 1.8m wide. His book *Three Adventures* (see *Appendix 2,*

Further Reading) contains a lengthy description of the 1970 exploration by divers and minisub. Since stalactites can form only in the open air, Cousteau and geologist Dr Robert F Dill reasoned that the Blue Hole was at one time a true cave, above the water's surface.

The original cave was probably cut from limestone by freshwater streams some 15,000 years ago. As Ice Age glaciers melted, the sea level gradually rose, and the weight of this water eventually caused the cavern roof to collapse. Similar processes have created 'blue holes' in the Yucatan and the Bahamas, but these come nowhere close to the dimensions of Belize's Blue Hole. Cousteau and Dill also noted that some of the stalactites leaned slightly to the side rather than hanging straight down. Geologists believe that these canted stalactites provide further evidence for continental drift.

You'll spend the rest of your short bottom time weaving through these eerie limestone formations, penetrating further under the overhang to a depth of about 42m. The combination of the dim light, filtering down from the Blue Hole's surface, and the gargantuan dimensions have even inspired religious metaphors: divers often compare the cavern to a cathedral, and Cousteau refers to the site as a 'Gothic cloister', the side vaults as 'chapels'.

Aside from the awesome physical majesty of the place – and the thrill of a dive that, for many, will be the deepest of their life – there isn't a great deal to get excited about. The absence of life below the sand plain is striking, and the reason fairly obvious: the Blue Hole discourages sunlight penetration necessary for photosynthesis and blocks the ocean currents that carry food to more vibrant habitats. If you're lucky you may spot the occasional barracuda, shark, ray, turtle or even hammerhead shark. Mostly what you'll see is a pallid assortment of filamentous algae, encrusting sponges, and tube worms. Fortunately, most dive groups make an informal safety stop (this is a no-decompression dive) during ascent so that you'll have a few minutes to enjoy the abundant life in the shallow coral reef. Tarpon occasionally frolic here, their silvery scales so bright that strobe-lit underwater photos of them look washed out.

If I had only one dive to make in Belize, I'd go elsewhere to see more corals and fish. But luckily, even the one-day Lighthouse trips include a second dive, so you won't have to make that kind of tough decision. That being the case, I highly recommend the Blue Hole to all experienced divers. Eerie, alien, grandiose in its dimensions, there is nothing else quite like it in Belize, or anywhere else in the Caribbean for that matter.

Because of the depth involved, this is the ultimate 'hen-and-chicks' dive. Divemasters will insist that everyone in the group stay close at all times, descending and surfacing together. Larger groups often have a divemaster leading and a second following the dive group. Virtually all tour operators make the Blue Hole a no-decompression dive, meaning a total bottom time of only 10min. Divers who are having difficulty clearing on descent may be sent back to the boat rather than cutting short the bottom time for the rest of the group. Descents at the Blue Hole can be disorienting, and most divemasters recommend that you stay close to the wall and face it as a reference point. If you drop a camera, strobe, or light, it's gone for good; the bottom of the Blue Hole at 124m is by now one of the world's great Nikon graveyards.

The Blue Hole isn't for everyone, but neither is it a particularly dangerous dive when made with a responsible dive tour operator. My wife tackled it after logging only five dives outside her basic scuba class, and thoroughly enjoyed it. (I cannot recommend this to others, however!) If you feel uneasy about the dive for any reason, go snorkelling instead in the shallow coral rim; it's one of the few great snorkelling spots visited by the dive tour boats. Some operators will even let you dive the shallow rim while the rest of the group is in the Hole. Discuss this in advance, however, to avoid disappointment. And be aware that some boats or resorts may require an advanced open-water C-card before allowing you to make this dive – once again, ask in advance.

Single-day trips to the Blue Hole (including a second wall dive later in the day and a picnic lunch ashore) leave San Pedro daily. Cost is around US$130. Unless you are really strapped for time, your best buy is one of the overnight trips of two or three days. One of the big costs of reaching the atolls is petrol, so as long as you're paying the petrol bill, why not spend some time once you've paid to get all the way out there?

Other dive sites at Lighthouse Reef

Half Moon Wall is one of the Caribbean's most spectacular wall dives, and virtually every tour boat makes it a point to drop in here. Located directly east of the caye, and within the Natural Monument boundaries, this extensive site offers big fish (including schools of spotted eagle rays), massive yellow tube sponges, gorgonians, living coral spurs, narrow sandy grooves and a sheer wall plunging well beyond the usual 45m visibility. Long Caye Wall, depending on who's talking, might refer to any of a half-dozen sites due west of the caye. The confusion isn't particularly troublesome – these are all superb wall dives beginning in about 10.5m of water. This is a good place to come eye to eye with gargantuan Nassau groupers. Just north of here lies Nurse Shark Lodge, a series of coral tunnels and alcoves in 15m of water that provide rest and shelter for not only sharks, but large grouper as well.

The East Side Wall is one of a handful of known Nassau grouper spawning sites in Belize. Here, just before the first full moon each January, hundreds of groupers converge to spawn in deep water near the lip of the wall. Within a few days – generally on the third night following the full moon – females and males release their eggs and sperm in a frenzied cloud. Biologists haven't decided precisely what evolutionary advantage is conferred by spawning in tandem with the full moon. Since this lunar cycle corresponds with higher tides, some scientists have suggested that eggs fertilized during this time are more likely to be swept off the reef, where they can develop far from the hordes of predatory reef fish. On the other hand, the full moon may serve as a simple cue for groupers – solitary, territorial fish for most of the year – to come together and spawn.

Study tours at Lighthouse Reef

The non-profit Oceanic Society is involved in long-term coral reef and bottlenose dolphin research at Lighthouse Reef. Using scuba, researchers and paying volunteers are mapping the area subtidally and collecting data on key indicators of reef health such as coral bleaching, coral black-band disease, algal cover and species diversity. Participants also monitor sediments (which may smother coral) and fish and invertebrates on the reef, especially parrot fish, surgeon fish and sea urchins. Dolphin research is aimed at documenting human-dolphin interactions, information which will prove useful in the protection and management of dolphin populations. The work itself involves underwater line transects, still and video photography. Participants (who must be comfortable with their scuba skills) pay around US$1,800 for the week-long trips; the cost includes accommodations at Lighthouse Reef Resort, all meals, excursions (including dives at the Blue Hole) and charter flights within Belize. Contact **Oceanic Society Expeditions**, Fort Mason Center, Building E, San Francisco, CA 94123, USA; tel: 415 441 1106; tel: 1 800 326 7491; fax: 415 474 3398; web: www.oceanic-society.org.

Sand Bore Caye

The northernmost of the four cayes on Lighthouse Reef, Sand Bore serves as a funky fishing camp and base for the reef's second lighthouse. It's within sight of Northern Caye, and a few of the live-aboards dock here for the evening. Sand Bore can't compete with Half Moon Caye for idyllic charm, but it's a good place to meet lobster fishermen, buy fresh fish or climb the lighthouse (watch for rusting rungs on the ladder!).

TURNEFFE ISLANDS

The largest of Belize's three atolls, Turneffe spans an area of over 128,000 acres. It's also the closest to the mainland, some 30km from Belize City at its nearest point. Within the 130km-long fringing ring of coral and mangrove islands lie three 'lagoons' of protected water: Northern Lagoon (also known as Vincent's Lagoon), the vast Central Lagoon and Southern Lagoon. The narrow passages between these lagoons and the open sea are known locally as 'bogues'. The Southern Lagoon was home to a thriving natural sponge fishery at the turn of the century. Fishermen cultured the sponges on concrete blocks, allowing them to grow in the lagoon until they were big enough to harvest. These blocks can still be seen in the Caye Bokel area, but they are just about all that remains of the industry; disease and competition from synthetic sponges put a virtual end to the fishery in the late 1930s. Turneffe's coconut farms have met a similar fate. The atoll's few permanent residents mostly fish for a living, landing conch, lobster and a variety of finfish. Turneffe's sportfishing – for tarpon, permit and bonefish – is legendary. Anglers can also hook grouper, Spanish mackerel, tuna, kingfish, sailfish, marlin, wahoo and dolphin (meaning dorado, not the marine mammal!). Tarpon run in the spring. Permit and bonefishing is good year round. Blackbirds, pelicans, frigatebirds and cormorants are plentiful.

Where to stay/eat

Turneffe Island Lodge Caye Bokel, Turneffe Islands, PO Box 480, Belize City; tel: 02 30236 or 11904 Hidden Hills Drive, Jacksonville, FL 32225, USA; tel: 800 874 0118; fax: 770 534 8290; email: info@turneffelodge.com; web: www.turneffelodge.com. Owned by Americans Dave and Jill Bennett and managed by Hugh and Theresa Parkey, the lodge has 8 rooms (6 doubles and 2 quads), all with private baths, hot water and electricity 24hrs a day. Rates are based on seven-night, six-day packages, running from Saturday to Saturday. The diving package costs US$1,195 pp; the fishing package costs US$1,1,595 pp; non-diver/fisher packages cost US$900 pp. Options exist for combined diving/fishing packages. The regular diving package includes three dives per day at Turneffe sites most of which are only three minutes away by boat; dives at other atolls, including the Blue Hole, involve special charters (an advanced open water C-card may be required for diving the Blue Hole). During the off-season (July 11-October 31), the above rates are reduced. Included in these packages are all airport transfers, boat transportation from Belize City to the lodge and all food and lodging (double occupancy). The Bennetts boast three high-speed dive boats: a 25ft Privateer, 30ft Offshore, a 38ft Grand Slam and a 43ft Lafayette. A typical morning includes a wall dive followed by a shallower reef dive, with another wall dive in the afternoon. There are no snorkelling or beach diving nearby. They have four instructors on staff who teach advanced open water scuba courses. They don't teach basic certification classes, but can accommodate open water referrals. They also offer 'resort courses' for guests who want a taste of scuba. Bring your own diving gear, since the lodge has only six full sets of gear as back up. The resort also has a bar, dining room and sun deck. The food at Tuneffe Island Lodge is a plentiful, multi-course affair each day, and highly recommended. Rooms are cooled by breezes and fans only. Once fishing-oriented, the lodge has become more diver-oriented since the Bennetts took over. To prevent overfishing, the owners limit the number of anglers to six per week.

Turneffe Flats PO Box 1676, Belize City (tel: 02 30116; fax: 02 78808 in Belize City, or toll-free in the US 1 800 815 1304; email: flats@blackhills.com; web: www.tflats.com). Located at the northeast tip of Blackbird Caye, this small resort has six cabanas with private bath, fans. A seven-day, six-night diving package costs US$1,295, including three dives daily, one night dive, unlimited shore diving, all meals, and transportation in Belize. You must have a computer to dive here. They also offer similar package fishing trips, with a guide and skiff per two fishers, costing US$1,800 pp. Good snorkelling both from shore and from boats. The resort owns three 31-foot boats, and they carry oxygen. The US booking agent is at PO Box 36, Deadwood, SD 57732.

Blackbird Caye Resort Blackbird Caye, tel. 02 73129, fax: 02 73092 in Belize or in the US 305 969 7945 or toll free 1 888 271 3483; email: dive@blackbirdresort.com; web: www.blackbirdresort.com. In addition to the usual diving and fishing options, this 8-cabana resort boasts a series of nature trails on the island. Lodging for a week (Saturday to Friday) in thatched cabanas with private bath costs US$1,100 pp, including transport from Belize City airport, all meals. A week-long fishing package (catch and release) costs US$1,550, while a week's diving package cost US$1,350, including 12 dives, with one day at Lighthouse Reef to dive the Blue Hole and Half Moon Caye Wall. Snorkelling, birding, and dolphin watching trips can also be arranged.

What to see

Turneffe's long-established dive sites have in the past been focused on the southern end of the atoll, mostly because of their proximity to the Turneffe Island Lodge on Caye Bokel. While the southern sites are excellent, there is a lot more to Turneffe, and lots of new dives up north are being discovered every day by the live-aboards and day-trip boats. We can expect more in the Blackbird Caye area as the relatively new resorts there continue to draw divers.

Turneffe's most highly touted dive is probably **The Elbow**, at the extreme southern tip of the atoll. This is a current-swept drift dive in deep water, often well away from the wall, and thus for advanced divers only. The Elbow may well be the single most reliable dive site anywhere in the Caribbean for spotted eagle rays. They are virtually always present gliding along the wall, and some lucky divers have reported schools of several dozen on occasion. Besides eagle rays, the Elbow hosts other large fish, including great numbers of horse-eye jacks and snapper, with blacktip sharks, sea turtles and even dolphins making cameo appearances at times. Unfortunately, windy weather frequently precludes diving this site for days at a time.

Of the numerous wrecks scattered around Turneffe, the most popular is the *Sayonara*, a wooden passenger boat intentionally sunk in 1985 by the owners of the Turneffe Island Lodge, and now resting in about 15m of water. It's neither big enough nor safe enough, however, to crawl around inside, and acts mainly as a fish attractor and holdfast for colourful invertebrate life. Other popular southern sites include: The **Black Forest**, one of the few spots where black coral still exists in relatively shallow water; **Gorgonian Bluff**, a drop-off thickly encrusted with the namesake colonial invertebrates; **Cabbage Patch**, known for its huge elkhorn coral and swarms of grunts and **Three Anchors**, named for the only lasting remnants of an 18th century shipwreck.

At Turneffe's northerly tip, both Rendezvous Point and Mauger Caye boast some spectacular wall diving at spots such as **The Abyss**. Divers may also find spotted eagle rays on the sandy shelf above the wall. The area is probably best known as the former site of the Manta IV's shark dives; the crew chummed the shallow flats with offal early in the day, returning late in the afternoon after some nearby wall diving. Protected by the sort of steel shark cage well-known to TV viewers, divers and more offal were lowered into the midst of a feeding frenzy. After a change in ownership temporarily ended these trips, the Manta IV now plans to resume them near Cockroach Caye, a short distance south of Mauger. There, the flat sandy bottom will be set with a chum line to attract blacktip, whitetip, gray reef and nurse sharks.

The non-profit Oceanic Society offers study tours on Turneffe where participants help researchers study free-ranging bottlenose dolphins. During daily boat excursions to the lagoons and reef, group members help with every aspect of the study, including observing and photographing the dolphins underwater and recording data aboard the boat. The underwater work involves snorkelling (no scuba), with plenty of photo opportunities. The study aims to provide new information on the behaviour, ecology, and social organisation of bottlenose dolphins in a pristine habitat. Study results will help current efforts to declare Turneffe a Marine Sanctuary. Participants pay US$1,340 (eight days) or US$1,540 (ten days), this cost including accommodations at Blackbird Caye Village, all meals, boat transfers, and excursions. Contact **Oceanic Society Expeditions**, Fort Mason Center, Building E, San Francisco, CA 94123, USA; (tel: 415 441 1106).

GLOVER'S REEF

Named for the English pirate John Glover, who used the area as a base of operations, Glover's Reef is the least-visited of Belize's atolls. Although the diving and fishing rival those of the other two atolls, Glover's location – 50km southeast of Dangriga – puts it well beyond easy reach of most dive charters, which are based further north at Ambergris Caye or Belize City. Even the live-aboards stick mostly with Lighthouse and Turneffe because of their relative proximity to the northerly ports. Virtually the only way to visit Glover's, then, is as a guest at one of the two resorts operating on the southeast corner of the atoll. One is a luxury dive resort, while the older one offers the cheapest accommodations on any of the three atolls. Glover's Reef was designated a Marine Reserve in May 1993.

Glover's is the most symmetrical of the atolls, a nearly perfect oval of coral reef with only four major 'cuts' giving access to the interior lagoon. The lagoon's shallow, protected waters are dotted with some 700 coral patch reefs that allow for superb snorkelling. Just outside the lagoon, the reef drops off beginning in depths as shallow as 9m, plunging to 600m, and wall diving is predictably excellent. Five English merchant ships sank here during the 1700s and reportedly can be dived.

Dive sites exist all around Glover's fringing reef, with the East Wall, North Point, Hot Fish Hollow, Hole in the Wall, Grouper Flats, Spaghetti Western and Barrel Head being the favourites. Virtually all the dives are wall drift dives, most of them within 10-20min of the island by boat. Eagle rays, turtles, dolphins and moray eels are common sights. Whale sharks and manta rays are sometimes seen, and of the three atolls, Glover's probably has the edge on large pelagics. The coral is superb, perhaps on a par with the best of Little Cayman's famous Bloody Bay.

Fishing for bonefish is great all year, and it's often possible to catch them right from the beach. Permit, barracuda, snapper, wahoo, jacks and tuna are also caught year around. Billfish run best from March through May, while tarpon fishing is best from March through June and in November. Grouper are most available during December and January.

On the down side, Glover's Reef may have the worst sandflies ('no- see-ums') in the entire country, and they seem to be a problem at all times of the year. Even if you've braved these pesky insects on other cayes, prepare yourself for Glover's with lots of DEET, long sleeves, long pants and hats.

Kayak tours of Glover's Reef are offered by two companies. **Slickrock Adventures**, PO Box 1400, Moab, UT 84532, USA; tel: toll-free 1 800 390 5715; fax: 801 259 6996; email: slickrock@slickrock.com; web: www.slickrock.com, offers a ten-day trip (six of it kayaking) based out of Northeast Caye for US$1,350 including all transport within Belize, meals, lodging, and sailboards on Glover's. They now also offer various scuba options, both for certified divers and those who want either a resort course or open water training course (NAUI or PADI certification). These options are based out of Long Caye in conjunction with Becky Cabral, the local divemaster. Slickrock is one of the best-known kayak tour outfits and has the longest history in Belize. They use both American and Belizean guides. **Island Expeditions Co**, 368–916 W Broadway Avenue, Vancouver, BC V5Z 1K7, Canada; tel: 604 452 3212 or toll free on 1 800 667 1630 or in Belize City on 05 23328 (November–May); web: www.islandexpeditions.com. They offer a seven-day tour for US$1,129, including lodging, all transport in Belize, and meals.

Where to stay/eat

Manta Reef Resort PO Box 215, 3 Eyre Street, Belize City; tel: 02 31895; fax: 02 32764 in Belize City or 1 800 326 1724 toll-free in the US; email: info@mantaresort.com; web: www.mantaresort.com. Located on the most southerly of the two Southwest Cayes, the resort offers 10 thatched-roof, mahogany panelled cabanas, all with private bath, fans, wicker furniture, and hot water. The restaurant/bar extends out over the water. The resort sustained enough damage from Hurricane Mitch in 1998 that it temporarily closed, but things are back to normal now. Eight-day, seven-night dive packages cost US$1,150 during the off-season and US$1,350 in winter. These week-long packages include three dives per day, airport and boat transfers from Belize City, and all meals (which are very tasty). Shorter four-night packages cost US$875 regardless of the season. Snorkelers pay US$1,050–1,150 for a week-long package. Fishing packages run at US$1,750–1,850 for a week (but bring your own gear or plan to rent it there). The resort owns two 25ft dive boats accommodating 10 divers each, and they carry oxygen. Unsupervised buddy diving is allowed. You can catch bonefish in the sand flats directly off the beach. The boat trip from Belize City, which used to take 4–5hrs, now takes only 2–3hrs in the resort's new boat, but it still is a rough, bumpy ride. Their US address is 151 Cypress Way E., Unit A-105, Naples, FL 33942, USA.

Glover's Atoll Resort Long Caye, Glover's Reef, or PO Box 563, Belize City; tel: 05 12016; radio telephone to the resort 014 8351; email: glovers@btl.net; web: www.belizemall.com/gloversatoll. Located on Long Caye amidst palms and white sand beaches, this is the most rustic of the atoll resorts and by far the cheapest. The Lomont family charges US$99 pp plus 7% tax for a week's stay in their dormitory, including boat transport from Sittee River on the mainland. Two weeks costs US$150, also including boat transport. There are 8 cabanas on stilts, each with two double beds, and private outhouses (one cabana has an attached bath and toilet). There is no running water or electricity, but constant breezes make fans unnecessary. Candles provide the light, and although linen is provided, you must bring your own towels. Do your own cooking on the kerosene stove (kitchens have all the basic utensils, pots and pans) or if you arrange in advance, the Lomonts can provide meals. They charge US$149 for a week's stay in a cabin, or US$199 for a cabin on the 'best beach'. Fresh drinking water comes from the mainland and must be purchased at around US$1 per gallon. Although the Lomonts may have some food to sell you in a pinch, plan on bringing your week's food from the mainland. Camping is even cheaper, at US$80 pp for a week (again, bring all your own camping equipment and food). The 'resort', formerly closed from September through November, is now open year around. The Lomonts also own nearby Northeast Caye, which they lease for part of the year to kayak tour groups. The family's motor boat picks up guests at Sittee Village on

Sunday at 08.00, and the boat returns on the following Saturday, arriving in Sittee around 14.00–15.00. Boat schedules depend on weather and sea conditions, which can be rough. The trip takes up to 6hrs, and you'll want to keep everything you own covered against salt spray and waves. The family has a gues bunkhouse in Sitte River Village for in-transit guests (BZ$10–16 pp). Becky Cabral is the resident divemaster and, having been raised on Glover's, she knows every subtidal nook and cranny. She offers NAUI or PADI certification courses, both open water and resort course. Although reservations are always a good idea, the Lomonts promise that they'll always find space for travellers who show up on their sandy door step.

Red-footed booby

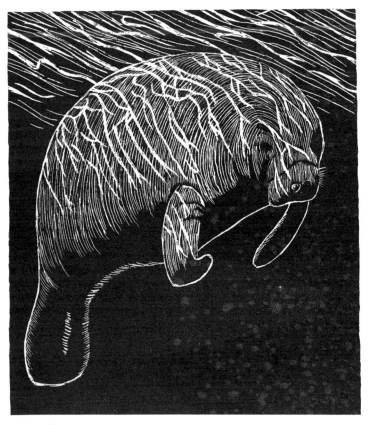

Manatee

Appendix 1

GLOSSARY AND ABBREVIATIONS

4WD Four-wheel drive.

AC Air-conditioning.

ahauob Maya kings.

alcalde in Maya villages, the equivalent of a mayor.

Baymen Early English settlers in Belize, mostly involved in logging and piracy.

bromeliad A plant that usually grows on other plants and trees, getting its moisture and nutrients from the air and rain.

BTL Belize Telecommunications Limited, the country's telephone company.

C-card Scuba certification card.

cabanas Cabin-style tourist accommodation, generally, but not always, made using local materials.

casita A small house or home.

Caste War Bloody rebellion by the Maya in Mexico's Yucatan beginning in 1848.

caye An island, universally pronounced 'key' in Belize.

ceiba One of the largest of forest trees, *Ceiba pentandra*, considered sacred by the Maya. Called 'cotton tree' by Creoles.

chiclero Forest worker who taps chicle trees for the sap, used in making chewing gum (Spanish).

ciguatera A form of food poisoning contracted by eating fish that have ingested natural toxins.

cohune The palm tree *Orbygnya cohune*, whose fronds are used as thatch and whose seed produces oil.

comedor [plural *comedores*] Basic restaurant.

dugu Garifuna feast of the dead.

duende Mythic, dwarf-like forest creature with four fingers on each hand (Spanish).

epigrapher Scholar who deciphers glyphic texts.

fry jacks Deep-fried triangles of dough, usually eaten for breakfast.

Garifuna People of mixed black and Carib Indian ancestry (more properly, the language they speak).

gibnut Belizean slang for the paca (*Agouti paca*), a large wild rodent frequently eaten as game meat.

glyph Symbolic figure or character inscribed in stone.

Gubida Ancestral sprits of the Garifuna

hierbatero Herbalist (Spanish).

h'men Maya doctor-priest.

John Canoe A Garifuna dance performed near Christmas.

karst A region of limestone with sinkholes, caves and underground streams.

mauger A dry, intensely hot period in August when winds and rains subside for a week or two.

Maya Adjective and noun (singular and plural) used in conjunction with the dominant indigenous people of Belize.

Mayan The language(s) of the Maya people.

Mayanist A scholar who studies the Maya people and culture.

milpa A farm plot cleared by slash-and-burn (Spanish).

milpero A farmer who tends a milpa (Spanish).

NAUI National Association of Underwater Instructors, a major scuba certification agency.

PADI Professional Association of Diving Instructors, a major scuba certification agency.

palpa(s) Palm-roofed circular wooden hut, often without walls.

PG Common slang for Punta Gorda, the capital of Toledo District.

piñata Brightly-coloured, papier mâché figure which smashes open when hit by a stick, spraying the contents, usually sweets, all over the floor. Used at children's parties.

pp Per person.

punta rock Popular Belizean dance music based on traditional Garifuna rhythms.

quetzal Monetary unit of Guatemala; also the Guatemalan national bird.

sisemito Ferocious mythical forest monster.

stela An inscribed stone slab used for commemorative purposes (plural stelae).

tommygoff Belizean term for any of four venomous pit vipers, but especially Bothrops asper.

USAID US Agency for International Development, an agency which funnels foreign aid money into Belize.

zericote A dark, lustrous hardwood used for carvings.

Appendix 2

FURTHER READING
Books
General – history, the country, the people

Barry, T *Belize: A Country Guide* Inter-Hemispheric Education Resource Center, Albuquerque, NM, USA., 1989. Detailed insights into Belizean politics and economy.

Foster, B *The Baymen's Legacy* Cubola Productions, Belize City, 1987. A lively history of Belize City from the very beginning to Hurricane Hattie. Available in Belize City bookstores and gift shops.

Gonzalez, N L *Sojourners of the Caribbean: Ethnogenesis and Ethnohistory of the Garifuna* University of Illinois Press, Chicago, 1988. The author has carefully researched Garifuna history and culture. She concentrates on Livingston, Guatemala, but visited all the Belizean Garifuna villages.

Sawatzky, H L *They Sought A Country: Mennonite Colonization in Mexico* with an Appendix on Mennonite Colonization in British Honduras, University of California Press, Berkeley, USA. 1971

Setzekorn, W D *Formerly British Honduras: A Profile of the New Nation of Belize* Ohio University Press, Chicago, 1981. A good general overview of Belizean history, culture, people, and natural history.

Stochl, J J *A Dictionary of Central American Carib* Belize Institute of Social Research and Action, 1975. Here's your chance to learn a few phrases in the Garifuna language. Three volumes.

Woods, R L, Reid, S T and Reid, A M *The Field Guide to Ambergris Caye, Belize, C.A., including Other Areas* Richard L Woods, Belize. History, shipwrecks, Maya ruins, botany, biology, geology, blue holes, beachcomber tips. Look for this one in San Pedro.

The Maya world

Coe, M *The Maya* Thames and Hudson, New York and London, 1987. Arguably the best single introduction to Maya archaeology.

Foster, B (ed) *Warlords and Maize Men: A Guide to the Maya Sites of Belize* Cubola Productions, Belize City, 1989. A valuable overview of all of the important ruins, including site maps. Available at most gift shops and bookstores in Belize.

Gann, T *Discoveries and Adventures in Central America* Charles Scribner's Sons, 1929. Enjoyable accounts of the amateur archaeologist's travels in Belize.

Garvin, R M *The Crystal Skull: The Story of the Mystery, Myth, and Magic of the Mitchell-Hedges Crystal Skull Discovered in a Lost Mayan City During a Search for*

Atlantis Doubleday & Co., New York, 1973. A rather fanciful but interesting account of the Crystal Skull. Lots of nonsense here, including the suggestion that Mitchell-Hedges 'discovered' Lubaantun.

Hammond, N *Lubaantun: a Classic Maya Realm* Peabody Museum of Archaeology and Ethnology, Harvard University, Cambridge, MA, USA, 1975. Extensive archaeological report on the field work done by Hammond in 1970–71. Much of this is far too scholarly for the casual traveller, but the summaries are rewarding.

Roys, R L *The Ethno-Botany of the Maya* Tulane University, New Orleans, USA, 1931. A remarkable survey and translation of Maya medicinal recipes, arranged by ailment.

Schele, L and Friedel, D *A Forest of Kings: The Untold Story of the Ancient Maya* William Morrow and Company, New York, 1990. Co-author Friedel, who studied the Cerros ruins, says it best: 'I am changed by this book. I cannot look at a Maya ruin now and think of the people who built it … as abstractions'.

Stephens, J L *Incidents of Travel in Central America, Chiapas, and Yucatan* Rutgers University Press, NJ, USA, 1949. Best-sellers in the mid-1800s, these two volumes started the rush to understand the ancient Maya. Frederick Catherwood's drawings of ruins amidst the jungle are masterful. The two explorers really just passed through Belize, but Stephens' account is still enjoyable.

Wright, R *Time Among the Maya* Weidenfeld & Nicolson, New York, 1989. The single best introduction to the Maya world, past and present, ever written. Deftly combines history, politics, and travelogue. The very first chapter or two concerns Belize, but the whole book is terrific.

Natural history

Cousteau, J-Y and Diol, P translated from the French by J F Bernard *Three Adventures: Galápagos, Titicaca, The Blue Holes* Doubleday & Co., New York, 1973. An interesting account of the first scientific exploration of the Blue Hole of Lighthouse Reef. A must-read for divers.

Forsyth, A and Miyata, K *Tropical Nature* Charles Scribner's Sons, New York, 1984. A highly readable introduction for the lay reader on rainforest ecology in Central America.

Halcrow, M and Halcrow, M L *Orchids of Belize* Government Printer, Belize City, 1967. Descriptions and sketches of 75 species.

Horwich, R H and Lyon, J *A Belizean Rainforest: The Community Baboon Sanctuary* Orang-utan Press, Gays Mills, WI, USA, 1990. Excellent descriptions of all Belizean flora and fauna.

Humann, P (ed DeLoach, N) *Reef Fish Identification: Florida, Caribbean, Bahamas* New World Publications, USA 1991. The most comprehensive and useful fish identification book for Caribbean species. More than 330 colour photos.

Miller, C M and Miller, B W *Exploring the Rainforest: Chan Chich Lodge, Belize* Wildlife Conservation International 1991. Describes not only nature trails near Chan Chich but Belizean flora and fauna in general, with detailed appendices of species sighted. The best layperson's guide to local flora.

Peterson, R T and Chalif, E L *A Field Guide to Mexican Birds: Mexico, Guatemala, Belize, El Salvador* 1999. Arguably the best field guide for this part of the world.

Rabinowitz, A *Jaguar: Struggle and Triumph in the Jungles of Belize* Arbor House, New York, 1986. Fascinating account of the early days of the Cockscomb Basin Wildlife Sanctuary by its biologist founder. A must for visitors to Cockscomb, and highly recommended for any traveller in Belize.

Smithe, F B *Birds of Tika*. Natural History Press, New York. 1966. Contains good pictures and information on most of the inland birds found in Belize.

Stevens, K *Jungle Walk: Birds and Beasts of Belize, Central America* Angelus Press, Belize City, 1989. Brief, non-technical descriptions (with drawings) of all the common fauna. Available at most gift shops.

Wood, D S, Leberman, R C and Weyer, D *Checklist of the Birds of Belize* Carnegie Museum of Natural History, Pittsburgh, PA, USA, 1986. A small booklet showing where you're most likely to see all of Belize's birds, and how common they are. No pictures or descriptions of the birds themselves, so you'll want a field guide to accompany this.

Guidebooks

Box, B (ed) (published yearly) *Mexico & Central American Handbook* Footprint Handbooks, Bath, England; Passport Press, Lincolnwood, USA. The ever-reliable 'Bible' of Latin American travel, with 60 pages on Belize.

Glassman, P *Belize Guide* Passport Press, Champlain, NY, USA, 1989.

King, E (published yearly) *Emory King's Driver's Guide to Belize* Tropical Books, Belize City. Road maps, service stations, driving tips. Very useful if you've rented a car. Updated yearly. Available in Belize City bookstores, but also from Quator Travel Publications, 280 Beaverdam Road, Candler, NC 28715, USA, for US$12.

Mahler, R and Wotkyns, S *Belize: A Natural Destination* John Muir Publications, Santa Fe, NM, USA, 1991.

Mallan, C *Belize Handbook* Moon Publications, Chico, CA, USA, 1991.

Meyer, F .O *Diving and Snorkelling Guide to Belize* Pisces Books, Houston, TX, USA, 1990. Actually, this guide deals exclusively with scuba dives on the offshore atolls (Lighthouse, Turneffe, Glover's).

Rauscher, F (ed J. Wilensky) *Cruising Guide to Belize and Mexico's Caribbean, including Guatemala's Río Dulce* Wescott Cove Publishing, Stamford CT, USA, 1991. Meticulously detailed charts and narratives on anchorages, weather, all points of interest in the cayes. Indispensable for sailors.

Health and general travel advice

Dawood, R *Traveller's Health* OUP, Oxford 1989. Helpful, concise information on all aspects of staying healthy abroad.

Hatt, J *The Tropical Traveller* Penguin, 1993. Delightfully idiosyncratic but useful advice for anyone travelling in the Third World.

Robin, M and Dessery B *The Medical Guide for Third World Travelers* K-W Publications, San Diego CA, USA, 1991. A detailed field reference actually written by medical professionals who've spent years tramping through Latin America. In fact, I met co-author Brad Dessery on a dive trip in Belize.

Seah, S S K *Don't Drink the Water: The Complete Traveler's Guide to Staying Healthy in Warm Climates* Canadian Public Health Association, 1983.

Wilson Howarth, Jane, and Ellis, Dr Matthew *Your Child's Health Abroad: a Manual for Travelling Parents* (Bradt, UK, 1998).

Fiction

Edgell, Z *Beka Lamb* Heinemann, London, 1982. Perhaps the best-known of the books about life in Belize. A girl's account of growing up Belizean.

Edgell, Z *In Times Like These* Heinemann, London, 1991. A Belizean student's political and moral coming-of-age in London during the late 1960s, and her return to Belize during the troubled early 1980s.

Ellis, Z *On Heroes, Lizards, and Passion* Cubola Books, Benque Viejo del Carmen, Belize, 1989. Short stories that really touch on the Belizean character. Insights into race relations, emigration, and daily life.

Godfrey, G D *The Sinners' Bossanova* Cubola Books, Benque Viejo del Carmen, Belize, 1987. An amusing romp with spies, smugglers, and expats in Belize City during World War II. Written by a former Minister of Tourism and the Environment.

King, E *Hey Dad, This is Belize* Tropical Books, Belize City, 1984. A whimsical look at life in Belize by one of the country's best-known authors.

Westlake, D E *High Adventure* Mysterious Press, New York, 1985. The master of the modern crime caper turns his talents to Belize, with a cast that includes Maya Indians, American bush pilots and nefarious artefact looters. Great fun, and American author Westlake manages to evoke perfectly Belize's 'No big t'ing, mon' national mood.

Websites

The Belize tourism industry has grabbed the internet with both hands and the online experience is just a few clicks away. It's difficult to imagine what other information about Belize could actually be put onto the internet. Virtually every establishment with a spare cent seems to be on the web: if the vacation experience is ever available online you can be certain Belize will be ready.

In the meantime here are a few pointers that will get you surfing in the right direction. Listing all the websites for Belize here would create another book, not just an appendix.

General

www.belize.gov.bz/ The official government site providing the very latest information.

News and views

www.turq.com/belizefirst/ Online comparison of all things Belizean with reports on accommodation and tour operators.

www.belizereport.com General coverage of news, conservation and national issues.

Nature and conservation

www.belizeaudubon.org The original conservation organisation in Belize, the Belize Audubon Society has links with most organisations involved in conservation in the country.

www.pfbelize.org Programme for Belize is the main contact for visiting the Río Brave Conservation Management Area.

Country and regional guides

www.belizenet.com A well-rounded site giving insight into all things Belizean as well as links to many of the hotels.

www.belizeit.com General information site for visitors

travel-belize.com/ general travel site

Regional sites

www.belizex.com/index.html Website for Cayo District

www.placencia.com/ Website for Placencia

ambergriscaye.com Website for Ambergris Caye

www.gocayecaulker.com Website for Caye Caulker

Search engine

www.belize.net A search engine with a load of good links thrown in to make you revisit!

NOTES

NOTES

NOTES

NOTES

Index